P9-AFC-548

Development's Displacements

Edited by Peter Vandergeest,
Pablo Idahosa, and Pablo S. Bose

Development's Displacements: Ecologies, Economies, and Cultures at Risk

15 14 13 12 11 10 09 08 07   5 4 3 2 1

Printed in Canada on ancient-forest-free paper (100% post-consumer recycled) that is processed chlorine- and acid-free, with vegetable-based inks.

Library and Archives Canada Cataloguing in Publication

Development's displacements : ecologies, economies, and cultures at risk / edited by Peter Vandergeest, Pablo Idahosa, and Pablo S. Bose.

Includes bibliographical references and index.
ISBN-13: 978-0-7748-1205-4
ISBN-10: 0-7748-1205-2

1. Economic development projects – Social aspects – Case studies. 2. Economic development projects – Environmental aspects – Case studies. 3. Internally displaced persons – Case studies. I. Vandergeest, Peter, 1955- II. Bose, Pablo, 1972- III. Idahosa, Pablo, 1954-

HD75.8.D49 2006   306.3   C2006-905203-4

Canadä

UBC Press gratefully acknowledges the financial support for our publishing program of the Government of Canada through the Book Publishing Industry Development Program (BPIDP), and of the Canada Council for the Arts, and the British Columbia Arts Council.

This book has been published with the help of a grant from the Canadian Federation for the Humanities and Social Sciences, through the Aid to Scholarly Publications Programme, using funds provided by the Social Sciences and Humanities Research Council of Canada.

UBC Press
The University of British Columbia
2029 West Mall
Vancouver, BC V6T 1Z2
604-822-5959 / Fax: 604-822-6083
www.ubcpress.ca

Contents

Acknowledgments

This volume and the research project from which it emerges have been the result of many conversations, collaborations, and encounters over the past years. In particular, our learning from friends, colleagues, and students in different locations has been an unceasing encouragement through the process of putting this book together. We would like to begin by thanking Peter Penz, principal investigator of the Ethics of Development-Induced Displacement (EDID) Project, who brought all of us together in this collaborative research effort. Jay Drydyk also deserves particular mention for his work on development ethics and his new framework for understanding and limiting displacement, which has been particularly useful and helpful for our work here. Other colleagues we wish to thank include Michael Cernea, Darryl Reed, Wesley Cragg, Craig Southey, Shubhra Gururani, Robert Shenton, Denis Goulet, Anthony Oliver-Smith, Charles Geisler, Shelly Feldman, Johnathan Barker, Ato Sekyi-Otu, Dickson Eyoh, Carmen Schifellite, Linzi Manicom, Union Edebiri, Allison Sauer, Adriel Weaver, Alejandra Roncallo, and Joseph Abudufour.

We are especially grateful to the Social Sciences and Humanities Research Council of Canada for its ongoing support of both the EDID research project and this volume in particular. The editors are similarly appreciative of the support given by the Shastri Indo-Canadian Institute for the EDID project and the input and feedback we have received on our work from several of our colleagues in India. As well, we wish to thank Dr. David Dewitt and the Office of the Vice President Research and Innovation at York University for their support of this publication. We would also like to acknowledge several research networks, projects, and conferences for the opportunity to present and refine the work that appears in this book: in particular, the International Development Ethics Association, the Canadian Association for the Study of International Development, the International Network on Displacement and Resettlement, the York Centre for Asian Research (York University), and the Queen's University Seminar in Studies in National and

International Development. Considerable logistical help has been provided by the Centre for Refugee Studies at York University and in particular by Colleen Burke, Myron McShane, Michele Millard, and Susan McGrath. As well, we would like to acknowledge Cathy Guirguis and Stephanie Hobbs, research assistants with the EDID project, whose assistance has been greatly appreciated.

We would also of course like to thank the contributors to this volume for their cooperation, patience, and meticulous revisions. We also appreciate the hard work and encouragement given to us by our editor, Randy Schmidt, as well as others at UBC Press including Andrea Kwan, Emily Andrew, and Darcy Cullen. Finally, we wish to thank our families and friends, in particular Luin Goldring, Dr. Pamela Barnett Idahosa, and Leah Burns, for their patience, support, and good humour.

Introduction

Peter Vandergeest, Pablo Idahosa, and Pablo S. Bose

This book is a contribution to the current debates regarding the costs associated with international development and is concerned in particular with the phenomenon of development-induced displacement (DID). The increasing attention given to the plight of millions of people in developing countries who have been compelled or persuaded to move from their residences and their environments, as well as uprooted from their livelihoods, has become a central feature of a critique that has put the "Global Faith" (Rist 1999: 4) of the world of development on the defensive. Much of this attention has focused on the relocations and disruptions that resulted from the tremendous growth of infrastructural projects that characterized development planning in the 1960s and 1970s, projects that have continued into a less state-regulated development environment from the mid-1980s until the present day.

The considerable impact of development projects on people's lives in terms of displacement from homes, jobs, and cultures has meant an increasing level of scrutiny over the past two decades from social movements and NGOs, if not from national governments and multilateral institutions. Since the mid-1980s, there has been in particular a proliferation of NGOs who define their missions in terms of monitoring and contesting large development projects (groups such as Mining Watch, Oil Watch, and the International Rivers Network, for example). The outcome has been a growing number of battles around the world centred on specific projects, including conflicts over dam building, mining, oil development, forest plantations, and nature conservation. A broader critique has also emerged – less focused, perhaps, than the intense critical scrutiny accorded to large projects – of the indirect displacement effects of development policies in general, including land reform initiatives, economic liberalization, and privatization. A key element in both of these indictments of development practice is the fate of those many millions whose displacement can be attributed to development. It is this fate – its causes, its effects, its justifications – with which this book is concerned.

The following chapters present the results of ethnographic fieldwork conducted in Africa, Asia, and Latin America on specific and diverse cases of development-induced displacement. The research was organized under a broader project titled the Ethics of Development-Induced Displacement (EDID), and in each instance aimed to collect data to reveal the process by which DID occurred, its impacts on those displaced, and the various ways in which DID was justified and contested through debates around the meanings of development. This empirical, case-based examination is in each chapter compared to the current standards and development orthodoxies found in the literature and policy on DID. In most instances, the chapter authors suggest that a considerable gap between practice and orthodoxy persists in the face of seemingly rigorous policies among development institutions and proponents aimed at minimizing and ameliorating DID.

By combining economic, political, and cultural analyses with extensive ethnographic field research, the collected essays present a picture of displacement that illustrates the depth as well as the breadth of the issue. The range of state, civil society, and non-governmental actors and sectors under consideration, the diversity of geographic locations examined, and the varying nature of the examples of displacement encountered all demonstrate the complexity of the situation. With cases that range from mining to logging, from dams to water privatization, from biodiversity conservation to land tenure reform, the scope of examples in this volume asks the reader to reconsider the meaning of displacement itself. By highlighting indirect and often invisible displacement effects of both projects and policies, the essays collected here suggest that a thorough analysis of DID must extend beyond specific project types, such as dams – often seen as the archetypal DID example – to a consideration of the broader developmental policies and programs through which projects are actually planned and implemented.

Our goal as scholars is to bring together two literatures. The first is that on development, which, although aware of the obviousness – even the violence – of displacement in the development process, rarely foregrounds its nexus, especially when appraising how it manifests itself indirectly. The second is the literature on DID, which is often oblivious to the wider debates in development, except in the narrower sense of policies that cause displacement. The studies in this book weave together strands from both traditions to focus on relationships previously left unexamined: examples include the intersection of conflict and development, the relationship between the peculiarities of neoliberalism and displacement, and the particularly gendered nature of much of DID. The case studies thus reveal a consistent pattern, both thematically and individually, that points to the ways in which displacements are recurrent in development.

Background: Development's Pains and DID

The increased critical attention[1] given to DID is the outcome of several coincidental features of the contemporary development world. First, as mentioned above, has been the emergence of a critique of development that aims not to repair development but rather to reject the entire project as fatally flawed. If, for some, DID has been a crucial lens through which to perceive development's malaise, the debates around both its impoverishing effects and its solution are hardly new, within neither development studies nor the wider discussions of modernity and progress (Cowen and Shenton 1996). A good part of development thinking has long been about addressing circumstances where large parts of the human population are deemed to suffer from inequities in the distribution of resources and power. Much of the recent pessimism about development, however, has assumed that these inequities are inherent to the project of development itself. They are an outcome of a history in which development emerged as a form of authoritarian or paternalist trusteeship that betrayed and displaced – often violently – those in whose name modernist progress had been invoked but who had little say in the planning or implementation of the development that affected them (Ki-Zerbo 1997: 88). Whether or not we agree with these critiques of development, or believe that they have run their theoretical course (Hart 2001: 656), they nonetheless remain influential for people seeking to draft into practice values for alternative forms of development, and they continue to inform many of the normative dispositions of those practical and activist networks that critique development in action. Even trend-setting organizations such as the World Bank have had to take cognizance of these critical post-development assessments and incorporate or, at a minimum, pay lip service to them in their emphasis on the values of participation and the importance of recognizing culture in development.

The second is the accompanying pessimism concerning the fate of those forced to move. Over the past several decades, evidence has accumulated about both the massive scale of development-induced displacement and the painfulness of many settlement experiences. A final crucial concurrence has been the ascendancy of neoliberalism and the so-called Washington Consensus.[2] The fact that the World Bank's support of many DID projects often ran parallel to the policies of neoliberalism, with their perceived limitations and failures, also served to make these projects focal points of widespread and reproachful assessments of development in general and of DID in particular. That is to say, the recent attention given to DID can be attributed partly to the fact that most multilateral, regional, and bilateral agencies simultaneously encouraged market-driven, deregulatory growth and development strategies, and were (and continue to be) among the foremost supporters and funders of development projects that have brought widespread displacement. As is evident in many of the following chapters, these agencies are not only behind much of the funding for development projects accompanying displacement but are also at the intellectual and legal hub of conceptualizing both the practice of DID and the theoretical and operational models for mitigating its consequences. Yet, as we shall also see, the attempts to moderate development's ills have been contradictory; and in some instances they have done less to diminish the criticism and more to focus the optics of disenchantment so that the entire project becomes a nightmarish dream in which promises of a better life for all are betrayed by multiple and often massive forms of impoverishment.

Is development by its very nature an inherently violent process that inevitably destroys the livelihoods of the poor? Is population displacement an unfortunately disruptive side effect of development that can be minimized and ameliorated through improved accountability, transparency, and civil society participation in project planning? In what ways can the benefits of development justify or be used to compensate for any displacement that may be necessary? These are hardly academic questions, as they clearly enter into the everyday sites of people's livelihoods, posing problems and highlighting disputes manifest in the conflicts around thousands of specific projects and policies supported and/or funded by major development agencies, private corporations, and national and regional governments. Opposition to specific development projects has often coalesced around contending claims with respect to the actual effects brought on by displacement.

It is difficult to deny that displacement is an acutely symptomatic phenomenon, reflecting a larger global, and often unrecognized, crisis. Millions of people around the world have been displaced by development projects and policies. Many have effectively become refugees, not simply across borders but, in a majority of cases, within their own countries. These are the so-called internally displaced persons, individuals and communities made refugees not only by wars and ethnic or religious violence but primarily by development policies, programs, and projects. Involuntary or forced migration due to political conflicts and upheaval is such a pressing problem that one conservative estimate claims upwards of twenty million people have been displaced worldwide by both cross-border and internal strife (Hampton 1998). Yet some critics estimate that five times as many people, in fact over a hundred million, have been dislocated as a result of processes of economic development (McDowell 1996). A further ten million people continue to be dislocated on an annual basis by large dam projects alone (Cernea and McDowell 1996: 18).

The effects of development-induced displacement are felt especially strongly among socially and economically vulnerable (and often politically marginalized) groups and indigenous communities worldwide. Although it would be a mistake to identify DID with the impact of neoliberalism alone, as DID predates the most recent development orthodoxies, the ascendancy of neoliberal policies during the last fifteen years or so has arguably served to intensify DID. Economic liberalization policies, structural adjustment, and stabilization programs have facilitated investment in displacement-inducing activities and undermined livelihoods vulnerable to global market competition and rich-country dumping of subsidized agricultural products (Oxfam 2002).

Faced with these figures and stung by the critiques of increasingly mobilized social movements and popular protests, development institutions such as the World Bank, as well as numerous regional and bilateral agencies, have been pushed into creating new policies and guidelines to address the potential displacement effects of development policies and projects. To date, the most detailed set of guidelines is Michael Cernea's (1997) Risks and Reconstruction Model for Resettling Displaced Populations (RRMRDP). In sum, this model advocates that the risks of impoverishment should be explicitly and systematically tackled through resettlement planning. DID experts such as Cernea implicitly agree with the post-development critics that displacement is recurrent in development, but, unlike the critics, they argue that the benefits of development justify a certain amount of displacement, provided that the displaced are able to capture some of these benefits and reconstruct their lives and livelihoods. But the formulation and adoption of explicit DID guidelines have simply prompted a new round of criticisms regarding their perceived limitations and inadequacies, many of them contained within the chapters of this book (cf. Dwivedi 2002; Fox and Brown 1998; Drydyk 1999).

The essays collected together in this volume explore these issues through a series of case-illustrative studies drawn from around the globe. Cases were selected with a view to representing as much as possible some of the enormous diversity in development-induced displacement across different world regions. Contributors focus on examples of development-induced displacement in Latin America, Asia, and Africa, telling stories about why and how displacement occurred and outlining its effects on communities, ecosystems, and economies. Through these stories, the authors explore the complex relationship between development and displacement, as well as the normative or ethical positions held by key actors involved in each of the cases. They examine a range of rationales used to justify specific development projects and policies, rationales that have often changed and evolved over time, as have the means and methods proposed to deal with displacement impacts.

The questions raised within this book do not confine themselves to a narrow definition of the issue of DID. Instead, other important critiques and considerations tie into greater issues concerning the subject. For example, as manifest in the Washington Consensus that has guided development practices for the past two decades, neoliberal policies are of great interest in the majority of the cases we present. A critical assessment of what the recent and prevailing development orthodoxies of "participation," "good governance," and "development from below" mean in practice also runs through these studies; in our view, these orthodoxies are intimately linked to neoliberalism. Our case studies also highlight and explore the tensions between human rights, on one hand, and, on the other, a sometimes vaguely articulated but nonetheless strongly held belief in the right to develop even at the cost of displacement.

Finally, our contributing authors examine the often violent and coercive nature of both development and displacement. We argue that violence and destruction have long been recognized as inherent to development, even if they are not always described in these terms. For the purposes of this book, we have adopted a definition of displacement that foregrounds the fact that it is coerced. But the studies in this volume demonstrate that the violence is not just about definitions. In some cases, it is open and intense; in others it lurks beneath the surface as a threat that is not necessarily acted upon but that frames the displacement process. To the degree that displacement can be causally linked to neoliberal policies, this volume also reveals the coercive and violent side of neoliberalism.

Another important theme woven through the case studies concerns natural resource extraction and environmental protection, which appear in many of the chapters as causes of displacement. Although these studies are not intended to be comprehensive, we note that they find little evidence of widespread displacement due to resource scarcity caused by population increase or livelihood uses, contrary to the popular literature on "environmental refugees," those displaced as a result of environmental degradation (Suhrke 1994; Fields 1985; Hugo 1996; Black 2001; Wilkerson 2002). They do, however, reveal displacement due to resource degradation produced by the activities of mining, plantations, and other large private actors. And they provide examples of displacement due both to policies that supposedly protect the environment and to high or increasing resource value. Neither of these driving factors is necessarily linked to increasing resource scarcity, as is consistent with Nancy Peluso and Michael Watts' (2001) critique of the environmental refugee literature.

Finally, this volume raises important questions regarding North-South interactions as they relate to displacement. In particular, by examining cases pertaining to the public, private, and non-governmental sectors, our authors interrogate the role and responsibilities of Canada, among others, within global development processes and institutions. How, for example, does Canada as a significant donor country ensure that its development assistance is applied in an ethical manner? What types of moral and ethical codes govern the behaviour of businesses that function in developing nations? How do non-governmental organizations interact with the various regional, national, and international layers of civil society in developing nations? Through chapters organized within three thematic sections, the present volume seeks to examine such pressing questions.

Structure and Organization of Chapters

Part 1, "Displacement, Multinationals, and the State," examines the role of resource corporations in producing DID. Chapter 1, David Szablowski's exploration of the World Bank's involuntary resettlement policy in a large mining project, discusses current regulatory and legal policies and practices concerning displacement by focusing on the relations between a Canadian-owned transnational mining enterprise and local communities in a rural district of Andean Peru. In Chapter 2, Amani El Jack scrutinizes the effects of development and displacement in the Sudanese oil and energy sectors, with a particular emphasis on the impacts felt by marginalized women, especially within the context of the long-running civil war between the north and the south. In Chapter 3, Keith Barney links development-induced displacement in rural Thailand and Malaysia to expansions in pulp and paper plantation forestry. He argues that, in both locations, two underlying processes act to facilitate this displacement: a bureaucratic reworking of legal and informal land tenure arrangements and an intensification of the commercialization of land.

Part 2, "Displacement and Neoliberalism," examines in greater detail the relationship between neoliberal economic policies – which are increasingly driving international development programs – and displacement-inducing policies and projects. In Chapter 4, Michelle Kooy looks at water policy in Thailand to show how the regulation and management of displacement effects by multilateral banks are connected to their belief in and promotion of a neoliberal economic program. In Chapter 5, Peter Vandergeest focuses on the displacement effects of "the new land tenure reform agenda," as illustrated by land tenure reform in Laos and Thailand. Sheila Gruner's Chapter 6 description of displacement in the Naya and Yurumanguí river communities of the Colombian Pacific is particularly important because it shows how neoliberal development can be based in openly violent appropriation of resources – a contrast to the seemingly less violent but still coercive processes described in Part 1. In Chapter 7, Pablo Bose focuses on a dam-building project in India's Narmada Valley and argues that dams offer an excellent lens through which to view displacement in both its local (project-specific) and global (policy-oriented) effects. More specifically, he draws our attention to the contest between decentralized, "people-centred" models of Gandhian political and economic principles and industrialization/modernization programs aimed originally at state building, but more recently adapted towards integration into a neoliberal globalization agenda.

Part 3, "Conservation and Displacement," examines the politics of nature's protection and exploitation as related to displacement. In Chapter 8, Colette Murray considers the differential situation of two communities of African descent living in Costa Rica's Limon Province over a thirty-year period. She focuses in particular on the racialized displacement that followed the establishment of two national parks in the early 1970s and the resulting conflicts over access to resources and changing definitions of territory, ownership, and local identity. In Chapter 9, Sharlene Mollett concentrates on the inter-ethnic tensions and animosities that have arisen over recent decades with respect to land tenure development policy in Honduras. In particular, she shows how state agrarian and conservation policies have combined to reproduce resource tenure insecurities for peasant and indigenous populations.

Although they are grouped within the three broad categories listed above, the essays in this volume intersect at many other points of connection and debate. For example, Chapters 1 and 3 both examine legal frameworks with regard to displacement. Chapters 6 and 7 pay particular attention to indigenous communities and their mobilization against displacement. Chapters 5 and 9 focus on the issue of land reform as an important facet of understanding the complex relationship between development and displacement. In Chapters 1, 2, and 3, the authors also ask important questions about the role that private capital, rather than the state, plays in the dynamics of DID. What obligations and responsibilities do corporations bear for displacement? How do different states interact with both local and transnational corporations? As the Chapter 1 case study on mining in the Andes indicates, the relationships between Canadian mining companies and the Canadian and Peruvian states are complex ones. Focusing on resource extraction in the oil and logging sectors, El Jack and Barney raise similar questions regarding the roles and regulation of private interests that engage in displacing practices.

Many other themes and issues link the following chapters. One of the most common threads is the opacity with which displacement-inducing projects and policies have been carried out in the absence of local participation and influence in decision making. Many of the chapters point to a lack of consultation with – and, in some instances, outright deception of – the displacement-affected communities. Indeed, many of the development projects described here exhibited the traditional top-down model of planning and implementation, and were driven by a paternalistic notion that experts, whether state bureaucrats, agency-based development practitioners, or representatives of private capital, were best suited to understand and evaluate both general conditions and local impacts. This paternalism belied the new rhetoric of participation and transparency that much of the development world has now claimed as its own.

The lack of involvement of the displaced in the project planning that affected them was so pronounced that in many instances they were unaware of its potential impacts or indeed that plans existed at all. For example, in the case of the Narmada development, the first sign that villagers had of plans to create an interlocking system of 30 large dams, 135 medium dams, 3,000 minor dams, and over 30,000 micro water-harvesting schemes was when strangers appeared, took measurements, and wrote numbers on stones. Only later did the villagers learn that these were surveyors and that the numbers indicated how many metres of water would submerge the land on which they lived. Therefore, the struggle for participation in Narmada, and in other areas as well, began with a demand for access to basic knowledge of DID plans – planned project benefits, a list of costs, and a description of measures designed to mitigate impacts. Vandergeest's Chapter 5 discussion of land tenure reforms and land use zoning shows that these programs work from current development orthodoxies to mobilize the participation of villagers – but only in zoning their villages, not in the overall design of the program. It is Chapter 1, however, that is perhaps most telling in its account of how detailed formal guidelines for community participation can be circumscribed by the need to meet project objectives and timelines, and how participation often remains based in the paternalism or notion of trusteeship that has run through development since its emergence in Europe.

Several of the chapters also problematize the notion that negotiation between stakeholders is an alternative to top-down development, bureaucratic inefficiency and corruption, or outright (and often violent) conflict. Such negotiating mechanisms are often constructed with the state's intervening as a supposedly neutral arbiter between competing interests. But, as many of our contributing authors indicate, such a dynamic is deeply problematic for a variety of reasons, not least of which is the fact that the conflicts are not between private capital, on one hand, and peasants, migrant workers, or indigenous peoples, on the other, but rather between the displaced and the state itself. Moreover, "stakeholder" rhetoric often posits a flattened notion of negotiation, one that fails to acknowledge the vast power differentials that exist between different actors. In Chapter 8, for example, Murray describes how, in the creation of two national parks in Costa Rica, "differential power is central to understanding the nature of participation," particularly with regard to the access that various interest groups have to resources and the legal and administrative apparatus of both the state and civil society organizations.

Even when processes of negotiation are created with such power differentials in mind, their genuine adoption and enforcement remains in question. In Chapter 2, El Jack, describing gendered violence and displacement during oil development in Sudan, suggests that a lack of both proper monitoring and the political will to enforce protective negotiating mechanisms has led to human rights violations and massive impoverishment. Similarly, in his Chapter 3 discussion of commercial logging in Malaysia and Thailand,

Barney argues that local communities have to some extent protected themselves against state-driven displacement through a negotiated appeal to both customary rights and colonially developed regulation, but that such protection is contingent upon the ability of the judiciary to actually uphold the laws. Power and position, once again, are central to our understanding of these dynamics.

We have left it to the individual authors to assign specific meanings to the key terms of DID through the presentation of their cases. However, in the remainder of this Introduction, we will explore some of these terms and concepts in more depth, focusing in particular on the ways in which displacement connects with development, neoliberalism, transnationalism, and ethics.

Development and Displacement

A volume with a set of case studies devoted to "development-induced displacement" must grapple with some obvious questions: What do we mean by both "development" and "displacement"? That is, what kinds of processes are encompassed by the term *displacement,* and under what circumstances can we causally link displacement to something called development?

Any brief review of current texts on development reveals widely divergent definitions or understandings of the subject. Perhaps the most common approach is that taken by authors such as Philip McMichael (2000: xli, 7), who, in his widely used critical introductory text, refers to development as "nationally organized economic growth" and to the "development project" as the adoption of a European model of economic growth or modernity. McMichael effectively identifies development with modernity and, as Gilbert Rist (1997) says, its naturalization within the nation-state. This view is consistent with those of more optimistic early development economists such as Arthur Lewis (1955: 9-10), for whom maximizing per capita GNP was the basis of development strategy. As Lewis wrote in *The Theory of Economic Growth,* the growth of output per capita "gives man greater control over his environment and thereby increases his freedom," a basic idea that one finds in many other early texts on development (cf. Peet 1999: 17).[3] It further implies that there are some historical processes through which many countries have passed (though not all authors might agree on which of these processes are necessary) in order to get to this state of greater income and freedom, involving social and economic changes such as commercialization, industrialization, urbanization, secularization, individualization, and globalization. Many of these changes imply at some level the displacement, voluntary or otherwise, of people, and more recent critical texts such as McMichael's tend to highlight these negative impacts. McMichael's account of development, replicated in many other development texts, finds that development as a project was initiated during the 1940s and gathered strength through the 1970s with the proliferation of multilateral, bilateral, and private development organizations and the decolonization of Africa and Asia. According to McMichael, globalization is now remaking or displacing development as economic growth becomes globally rather than nationally organized.

For Arturo Escobar (1995) and the many scholars who have been influenced by a particular interpretation of Foucauldian social science, development is primarily a set of discourses and practices that has produced and sustained the "third world" as an object to be developed. Despite some differences in relative emphases accorded to political economy and discourse, Escobar, like McMichael, indicates that the end of the Second World War marked the initiation of a coherent development project, a project that encompassed the total restructuring of the underdeveloped world in the pursuit of material prosperity and economic progress. Authors working from this perspective emphasize development as a form of power essential to the increasing influence of the state and development organizations in the everyday lives of people in Africa, Asia, and Latin America. This strand of scholarship, sometimes labelled "post-development," often asserts that this power is fundamentally destructive of traditional ways of living, for which it fails to offer viable or sustainable alternatives.

Although some of the insights opened up by post-structuralist approaches inform this Introduction and many of the chapters in the volume, we think that these frameworks need to be both qualified and supplemented in important ways. In relation to the historical accounts of development, alternative views that date development back to the nineteenth century (Cowen and Shenton 1996; Cooper and Packard 1997; Rist 1997) not only offer a more grounded conception of development but also consider ideas that are particularly useful to the diverse approaches represented in this volume. Michael Cowen and Robert Shenton's (1996) landmark analysis is particularly important because it offers a way in which to understand contemporary debates about DID. The authors distinguish between two analytically distinct but often conflated uses of the term: as immanent process and as an intentional action on the part of development agents. The former is a premodern, cyclical use that enters into the modern notion of development – where, in a cycle resembling that of plant life, decay and destruction are an essential part of the development process. With the advent of capitalism, development was refashioned as the "potential and possibility for a linear movement of human improvement" (Cowen and Shenton 1996: 7). The latter – in many ways the more familiar conception of development – now points to *planned* interventions by the state and other associated agencies to shape and direct socio-economic change. The key is that these interventions are meant to bring order to the sometimes chaotic changes that result from the radical alterations of social structures and relationships effected by the emergence and workings of capitalism. Cowen and Shenton argue that these two forms of development co-emerged and were in fact counterpoised to one another during the nineteenth century as a way of bringing order to progress. They suggest that much intentional development by colonial administrations, despite its lack of success, was designed to limit the destructive effects of immanent capitalist development, or progress. In this sense, then, intentional development (as opposed to the cyclical process of development and decay) was meant "to ameliorate the disordered faults of progress" (Cowen and Shenton 1996: 7).

Anthropologists (Li 1999a, 1999b; Moore 1999; Gupta 1998) and other social scientists who draw on Gramscian analyses have identified various contestations, negotiations, compromises, and even "cooperation" in the practice of development. They argue that relationships between colonial states, indigenous societies, and the various actors within communities, local and national states, and, more recently, global institutions, shape the character of the increasingly complex interactions between and among development subjects, agents, and institutions. These authors tacitly or explicitly question the somewhat simplified understanding of power in some post-structuralist and Foucauldian-influenced views of development. That is, they assert that power is not entirely encompassed by a monolithic, one-dimensionally imposed "hegemony" exercised by overbearing development states and multilateral development agencies, or even a somewhat more subtle but still coherent governmentality enacted through a development "industry" that creates its development objects through its discourses. Through careful, often site-specific research, they have demonstrated the multiple ways through which the historical constitution of communities, environments, and territories is constantly in the process of reconstructing meaning and identity.

In this volume, we are particularly interested in how these shifting meanings in the language of development pivot around the complex claims on resources expropriated and used by post-colonial states, global capital, and multilateral agencies. Like Tania Li (1996, 1999a, 1999b), Donald Moore (1997, 1999), and Akhil Gupta (1998), we see development as a site within and through which multiple contestations over power and identity take place. In this view, development both creates and confronts symbolic aspects of community claims and struggles that materially transform communities, or as Moore (1996: 127) puts it, "cultural meanings are constitutive forces, that is, shapers of history, and not simply reflections of a material base." Also highlighted in these specific, nuanced, and thick depictions of development as contested meanings and compromised practices are the different ways in which local, regional, national, and global scales intersect – where the meanings and claims regarding territories and resources that are the material path of development are spatially regulated and fought over, especially, as we shall see, by development-displaced population, or those who would claim to speak for them.

In general, many of the approaches cited above contribute to our understanding of development; each has its limits, but each has its uses. However, given the historically informed character and contested and complex ways in which development is deployed, we have avoided imposing a single definition of development here. Instead, as mentioned above, the authors were encouraged to define for themselves what they meant by development, as related to the displacements they described. Still, because the project as a whole sought to provide causal accounts and to find the agents responsible for displacement, the studies here tend to focus largely on *intended* development; that is, they examine development that is about purposeful intervention and that seeks (or claims) to bring human improvement to its subjects. This focus does not imply that development actors are not accountable for unintended consequences. On the contrary, it is the tacit contestation in this volume, to be made more explicit in a companion volume, that "development" in its various meanings raises fundamental ethical questions. Indeed, it is the very tension and ambivalence between the intentional and the immanent in development that those who would justify displacement often seek to exploit. It should be clear from the chapters herein that there are many processes and events that ought to be anticipated by development planners, making the analysis of DID that much richer, more complex, and, indeed, both poignant and normative. We will briefly touch on this below in the section on development ethics.

Although we have refrained from a categorical definition of development, there are, nonetheless, certain central ideas as to how the concept of development emerged and has been contested that are crucial to the study of development-induced displacement. Most important is the idea that development processes can achieve improvement only through destruction and that development as intentional practice has long been organized, at least in part, around finding ways of limiting the destructive effects of capitalism. The current attention to minimizing DID and reconstituting lives and livelihoods after displacement occurs can be understood as the latest phase in a movement that has had different manifestations over two centuries. This tension between the processes of destruction, displacement, and renewal has been evocatively described by Marshall Berman in his *All That Is Solid Melts into Air.* Berman directs our attention to the fact that authors including Goethe, Baudelaire, and Marx organized their narratives of modernization around the dialectic between destruction, displacement, and renewal, and traces what this has meant for the modernization of cities through city planning. Today, this same tension continues to frame the debates over development and whether it should be jettisoned or renewed in the face of its recent failures. In other words, the idea that development is inherently destructive does not originate with contemporary critics but can instead be traced to the beginning of development thinking. It has always been a prominent feature of Marxist-influenced development theory, which draws on Marx's account of the development of capitalism as a double process of a violent separation of workers from the means of production to create a proletariat, and an equally violent appropriation of surplus through primitive accumulation to create capital. Some Marxists go so far as to argue that the destruction inherent in capitalism, though necessarily violent, is justified in the end because it develops the productive means that make socialism possible.[4]

Outside of Marxist critiques, coercion and violence in development have often been played down but have nonetheless been central to much liberal economic thought since Adam Smith. At the very least, there has been ambivalence or an agnosticism about the character of states and what they could or would do to achieve development aims. Some strands of early political modernization thinking, and the more recent modernization and neoliberal development doctrines from the 1950s to the present, have implicitly argued their way around the need for coercion through the idea that the benefits brought by development can induce people to voluntarily change their ways -- thus, in effect, rendering the destruction of livelihoods non-coercive. Despite this, we must keep in mind that various forms of modernization theory always stressed that traditional ways of life had to be destroyed or disciplined in order to make way for modern man (Inkeles and Smith 1974; Cooper and Packard 1997). Indeed, in economic thought at least, these were transitions that had to be borne if growth were to be achieved; the passing of "traditional society" was not to be lamented.

If development as a discourse, an ideology, and a practice carries within it seeds of such a necessarily destructive nature, how then does one conceptualize displacement? In the most literal definition, development-induced displacement is the forcing of communities and individuals out of their homes, and often also their homelands, for the purposes of economic development. Such geographic displacement can be within a city or district, or from one village or neighbourhood to another; it can also involve displacement across long distances and borders, sometimes to economically, socially, and culturally quite different settings. However, a wider conception of displacement is also possible. We have chosen to define displacement very broadly to include the loss of access to the means of livelihood, economic activities, and cultural practices without the necessity of geographic movement. In other words, people do not have to physically move in order to be displaced.[5] They are displaced, for example, when they lose access to some local resources important to livelihoods and identities – water, forests, fisheries, grazing land, and so on. People can also be considered displaced when their occupations are undermined, as occurs, for example, through the adoption of neoliberal pricing policies for agricultural products. In Chapter 4, Kooy extends the idea of displacement to include a situation in which people become marginalized from participation in decisions affecting resource access and management – this marginalization will arguably contribute to growing reliance on migratory labour as a way of supplementing inadequate incomes in Northeast Thailand. This broad definition is consistent with our emphasis on indirect as well as direct forms of displacement. Such a definition helps us to encompass the diverse destructive processes of development described previously.

It is important, in this sense, to recognize that development-induced displacement is not an inherently negative process, though the term conjures a sense of loss and unwilling removal. Changing the status quo, redressing inequalities in social relations, and creating more equitable and sustainable modes of living also require the destruction of at least some existing structures. Indeed, within the development donor community, the growing realization of the negative impacts of DID has led not to a rethinking of development itself but rather to attempts to better anticipate and manage those consequences. But, underlying proposals for improving resettlement programs, such as those advanced by Michael Cernea (1997), a former World Bank senior advisor for sociology and social policy, is the idea that the destruction can be justified if the benefits of a project can be distributed so as to restore and improve the lives of people whose livelihoods are lost, to the point where they become willing participants. The issue then becomes, if affected populations are willing participants, can they be listed among the displaced?

This question takes us back to the thorny problem of coercion and displacement – whether the destruction inherent in development can be justified if it is not coerced, and whether the loss of livelihood and identity can in these cases be considered a form of displacement. In this volume, we have adopted the broad position that displacement is by definition coerced. To put it another way, we hold that when, on a completely voluntary basis, a person leaves one place or activity for another, this process would not be considered displacement. It is precisely the production of such voluntariness – through a series of incentives and the promised restoration of livelihoods – that Cernea proposes as an ideal mechanism for dealing with displacement. Such a logic seems circular: the problem of displacement is abated by making participants willingly and happily endorse a development project or program – and thereby negating its displacement effects. In such a scheme, one could argue that displacement no longer occurs, since coercion no longer exists.

In the real world of development projects and policies, however, such an idealized situation rarely, if ever, exists. In some instances, certain participants have been able to profit from a particular project – as in the example of local landowners who sell their lands at prices that have risen in anticipation of a proposed large-scale venture such as a dam, airport, or highway. But these situations tend in any case to consolidate existing power inequities, enriching those who already have access to property and resources. There is often little redistributive benefit to these processes. The vast majority of individuals and communities affected by DID are land-poor and otherwise marginalized groups such as indigenous populations who often have little or no formal property rights to exploit. In the cases described in this volume, moreover, those who were displaced almost never obtained a significant share of the project benefits, and in no example were livelihoods and ways of life completely restored. In actuality, the failure to produce voluntariness through distribution of benefits or restoration of ways of life not surprisingly ended in coercion, a pattern that figures prominently in all the case studies in this volume.

Significantly, those who argue that displacement can be addressed by voluntariness typically pay little attention to the sometimes difficult-to-see processes through which consent is manufactured within the context of unequal power and the structuring of choices. Although this theme is not strongly elaborated here, post-structuralist accounts of the production of subjectivity might have much to say regarding it. In most of the case studies, power worked less through open coercion than through subtle processes of unequal negotiation and compromise.

Neoliberalism and Displacement

When this project was launched, we did not intend it to become an examination of the displacement effects of neoliberal development policies.[6] This theme emerged because the broader project enabled the authors to conduct fieldwork in contemporary instances of development-induced displacement. Although the case studies are grounded in the historical past, because they focus on contemporary situations it was inevitable that various faces of neoliberalism would emerge as manifest and decisive backdrops and contexts for understanding the displacement process. But contrary to what one might expect, given the critical orientation of many of the authors, this book is *not* just another clear-cut demonstration of the singularly impoverishing effects of neoliberalism. Instead, rather than asserting that neoliberal development has unprecedented displacement effects – a historical claim that would be difficult to substantiate – the authors more usefully highlight the fact that displacement has become more visible and contested because of certain contradictory features of neoliberalism.

On one hand, the studies show how neoliberal development policies (such as the facilitating of resource extraction, the need to clarify property rights,[7] and the promotion of market-based allocation, export-based growth, and a deregulatory political economic environment) do in fact produce widespread indirect and direct displacements. On the other hand, they also reveal how the promotion of "good governance" and the mobilization of civil society groups around greater accountability, transparency, and participation in the development process have contributed to the increased visibility of displacement and have given considerable leverage to groups that oppose displacement-inducing policies and projects. These latter processes are arguably not outside of neoliberalism, but directly linked and increasingly inherent to neoliberalism. In other words, neoliberal development norms have spilled over into mobilizations around demands for liberal democratic procedures that become weapons against DID. This requires further elaboration, not least because, although one increasingly hears that the Washington Consensus is no longer in play, its legacy lives on in reconfigured forms, as, for example, through the conditionalities and programs forcing the decentralization of power and property.

Certain strands of liberal development thinking are shifting *from* the idea that the subjects of developments are in effect "wards" of the trustees of development agents (the state, experts, etc.) to a notion that they should be rights-bearing agents able to make informed choices. As Szablowski writes in Chapter 1, "Liberal legal systems derive their legitimacy from a conceptualization of the individual as an active rights-bearing agent who is protected from arbitrary government action by the rule of law and by the principles of procedural fairness. A person is entitled to know the rules she or he faces and is also entitled not to be dispossessed without the opportunity to present a case that contests the facts and legal interpretations asserted by another party. Within the liberal legal framework, abuse of these rights delegitimizes the result."

Although liberal legal principles have been criticized on many counts – for example, because their protection of individual rights translates into the protection of private wealth and power over collective goods – they are nevertheless what gives Szablowski's critique of the World Bank's involuntary resettlement policy its traction. It also opens up a broader debate about how development subjects *should* be able to participate in making decisions about development processes. Examples can be found in many chapters in the volume: in Chapter 4, for instance, Kooy shows not only how neoliberal restructuring transforms water from a "gift" to a commodity but also that the transformation is tied to a change in how subjects and their entitlements are constituted through attempts to make water-delivery organizations accountable to service "users." Thus, we would argue that tensions exist within neoliberalism that structure conflicts around displacement with unintended consequences.

It is also important to stress that these case studies demonstrate the uneven evolution of neoliberalism's purposes from its earlier incarnations, which principally emphasized economic adjustment and stabilization reforms.

These studies variously reflect the irregular way in which the specificities of the tensions within neoliberalism have been applied and executed in their global, national, regional, and local contexts, the working milieus of neoliberalism, as it were. Here, we are dealing with a number of cases in which, at least until the early 1990s, neoliberalism operated under the guise of political non-interference, and in which multilateral, regional agencies and some "donor" governments frequently appeared indifferent to liberal democratic and more participatory forms of governance in certain parts of the world.

Especially, but not only in Africa, however, early agnosticism about liberal democratic governance withered, in part due to the mounting criticism of the failure of these policies in and of themselves. Additional criticism focused on the inappropriateness of appearing to collude with authoritarian partners to effect economic reform during a time of increasing demands for democratization from below, within civil society, and from local and international non-governmental organizations (see Haggard and Webb 1994: 1-36; and Mkandawire 1994: 155-73). The realization that politically liberalizing governments could add legitimacy to economic reforms sealed the pragmatic consideration of coupling them with political and administrative reform. Particularly in Africa, there was the posing of conditionalities in terms of practices and structures for "good governance," understood in terms of liberal democratic reforms that opened up political processes to limited participation by certain sectors of civil society, promoted accountability and the rule of law, and so on. This package of liberalization set out a relationship between the creation of a minimally procedural democracy, which was consonant with the regulatory, administrative, technical, extractive, and proprietary aims of adjustment, and a new contractual relationship between different development constituencies (see Abrahamsen 2001; Doornbos 2001).

Especially in an environment of conditionality and debt, neoliberalism became, then, not just an economic program to free up market processes, but also a reconstitution of citizenship as a contractual, market-type relationship between state agencies, development organizations, certain NGOs as service providers, and citizens as clients (see Callaghy et al. 2001; and Chapter 4 in this volume). Rather than being just a set of deregulatory adjustment and stabilization procedures, neoliberalism can now be viewed as a package of policy prescriptions that both links up with and reconfigures a variety of actors, agencies, and institutions. This remains true even though it is by no means uniform in its application or effect across the case studies presented here and, in some instances (Chapter 2), it appears to be absent.[8] In short, this history, as all the case studies demonstrate, is more or less bounded by both the conceptual ambiguities and the practical exigencies of these changing maps of development practice, and the need to seek new vistas for development practices and their unforeseen outcomes.

This reconstitution of the relationship between development proponents and clients appears to have undermined, or at the very least confused, the ideological basis of the inherently paternalistic idea that developers are in effect "trustees" (Cowen and Shenton 1996: x-xi) of less developed societies, trustees whose status as development agents empowers them to make decisions on behalf of the world's poor until such time as they develop their own capacities. Whether these new dispensations decentralize paternalism and empowerment from above remains to be seen.[9] What many of the case studies in this volume show, however, is that development and state agencies work with only partial success to incorporate and tame forces unleashed by the neoliberal reconstitution of citizenship. The result has been an intensified contestation over policies and projects that cause displacement, the transnationalization or even globalization of opposition movements, and repeated efforts to contain opposition to neoliberal development institutions.

Transnationalism and Displacements

Although a full elaboration upon the phenomenon of transnationalism lies beyond the scope of this book, it is useful to note that diverse transnationalisms – or transborder, transboundary, or transterritorial processes and flows – have important implications for development in general and DID in particular. Here, we use transnationalism as a basic shorthand for two things, both of which involve (and sometimes converge around) dialectical relationships between globalizing processes and local practices, or between local initiatives and the mechanisms and workings of globalism.

The first is linked to social movement analysis, which (among other things) examines the organization of the transnational identities and practices of national or local social movements (Kriesberg 1997: 3-19; Keck and Sikkink 1998: Introduction, passim). Here, local leaders have organized international or global openings for local actors to shape movements' goals and strategies through international networking, seeking to gain support for causes and issues beyond the locale, region, or state within which they reside. Conversely, international organizations have also sought to give support for the aims and practices of such local movements. It should be evident that many questions concerning displacement have been mobilized by agents in this way, whether in the language of human rights and/or of development (see Schmidt 2001; and Chapters 7 and 8 in this volume). For example, the increasingly transnational and networked character of anti-dam movements has facilitated the systematic collection of information about the scale of dam-induced displacement, assisted many particular movements through the enlisting of allies around the world, and provoked a thorough assessment by development proponents of the value of dams, given their widespread displacement effects (World Commission on Dams 2000).

Second, transnationalism has been used by authors such as Alejandro Portes, Luis E. Guarnizo, and Patricia Landolt (1999) to describe economic and other forms of displacement that have taken place in parts of Latin America and that have resulted in immense international migration and "new diasporas," primarily (but not only) to urban centres. This is a migratory system that is itself tied to the global neoliberal reorganization of production, which, due to the economic crisis of the 1980s and the resultant move from import substitution to export-oriented development, was reshaped in part by neoliberal policies and by conflicts around various parts of the world (Portes, Guarnizo, and Landolt 1999; Van Hear 1998: 4-7).

Two further pertinent elements of transnationalism are the ways in which the migrants' identities are shaped in being incorporated into their new countries, and the ways in which they also remain active in the places they left (see Levitt 2001). If development implies that people move or ought to move, not just from their immediate locales to places beyond their communities, but also in ways that produce transborder and transnational communities or networks, what are the implications for themselves and those whom they leave behind? Does transnationalism now enter into a normative discussion of the benefits and costs of displacement in a world that includes both a dramatically changing global economy and changing migratory and immigration policies? These are questions that cannot be answered in a volume focusing largely on locality-specific case studies but that nonetheless warrant further thought in future work on development and displacement.

Ethics and Displacement

In drawing out these causal links between development and displacement, the essays in this volume also explore the normative-ethical positions held by key actors in the cases. Until recently, development practitioners and agencies rarely displayed the patience to consider the ethics and morality of their decisions. Development ethics emerged as a sub-field of development inquiry in the mid-1970s, to evaluate change that presumed to improve people's lives. Authors in this field assert the need to seek out, explore, reveal, and test the moral values, stated or unstated, explicit or implicit, in the prescriptive goals of development theory and practice (see Gasper 1994; Goulet 1995: 5-7). We cannot explore here the various ethical approaches, though many of them will be taken up in a companion volume; nonetheless, at a very basic level, all the chapters in this book seek to integrate the meanings of development into debates around essential ethical questions: What are the costs of change and who bears them? How can we decide when costs are outranked by gains? Who has the right to intervene, by what procedures, and to promote what ends? What is social improvement? What fundamental changes are desirable or undesirable? What are appropriate goals in planned interventions, and what actions are acceptable as the means by which they are achieved? Specifically, in relation to displacement, how is displacement justified? How have such justifications evolved over time and what might some future trends be? Our intention here was not to adopt a judgmental or morally prescriptive attitude with regard to the cases we examined. That is, our contributing authors did not look to identify "villains" and unethical behaviour by individuals and organizations in various contexts, even though for DID there are a surfeit of cases of social injustice. Rather, we chose to focus on the normative or ethical frameworks underpinning both the projects and policies that displace as well as the attempts to challenge and address these problems.

The dominant normative-ethical position used to rationalize projects that displace has historically been utilitarianism, with its simple theory and results that seem easy to apply. It appears to allow for degrees of right and wrong and provides an unambiguous choice among alternative actions applicable for every circumstance: always choose that which has the greatest utility. In concrete, project-related terms, this choice is usually expressed as "the public interest" or as "public goods." An assumption running through many projects holds that often vaguely defined benefits that accrue at larger scales (national, global) trump concrete losses experienced at smaller scales. Projects have often explicitly served the purpose of nation (or state) building, and project proponents have often made direct appeals to nationalist rhetoric or paramount utility of "national interests" to further their objectives. One of the best examples of this appears in the justification of dam building in the post-colonial world. In India during the 1960s, the country's first prime minister, promoting the Narmada Valley Development Projects, exhorted villagers to sacrifice their lands and livelihoods for the benefit of "Mother India." Nehru himself had once famously referred to dams as the "temples" of a modern and secular India, and he laid the foundation stone for the Sardar Sarovar Project, the planned linchpin for the Narmada projects. Such language is still echoed loudly in the justifications given for major projects that displace, whether they are dams, highways, railroads, planned cities, or other similar initiatives.

But, as the other cases in our volume indicate, such language continues to resonate with other situations as well. A broadly utilitarian framework underpins the explicit rationalization of many projects and policies. Today, the villagers in Narmada are told to abandon their homes not only to build a stronger India but, more explicitly, to save impoverished farmers and townspeople in drought-stricken regions of the country. The very concept of "the public" on whose behalf a "good" is being created has been greatly expanded.

In Chapter 8, Murray describes parks creation in Costa Rica as an ethical imperative spurred in large part by the efforts of Northern environmental groups concerned with preserving nature as a "global" good, but with little discussion of local effects or social justice concerns. In many of the other cases, economic benefits for a vaguely defined "majority" – derived primarily from resource extraction – are seen to trump the rights of minorities. In Sudan, oil development, with its devastating effects on ecology and people alike, is justified in order to "better" the population as a whole. In Andean Peru, mining is promoted as a way of "improving" the lives of local people, through more jobs and affluence.

If utilitarianism has been the primary ethical lens through which development that displaces has been both seen and justified, it has also been the chief underlying normative framework in efforts to address or ameliorate the situation. Cost-benefit analysis (CBA), for example, has emerged as the main evaluative tool used by development agencies and national governments to decide whether projects should be undertaken. Examples include operational directives for the World Bank and various regional development agencies, directives that are predicated on the use of CBA. This is particularly true in more open political situations where it is difficult (though as our cases demonstrate, certainly not impossible) to plan DID projects and policies from on high and with little oversight or local participation.

But cost-benefit analysis has itself been critiqued as being on its own an inadequate determinant of just or equitable development policy and practice. Those who have challenged processes of DID, including the authors in this volume, claim that cost-benefit analysis is altogether too limited and constrained by utilitarian frameworks, which demand winners and losers, and that it is fundamentally a tool that enshrines existing power inequities. Therefore, it is insufficient for any truly equitable, let alone transformational, development discourse. These critics have asked how one decides what is in the larger good, as well as who gets to act as arbiter in such determinations. By default, the role of arbiter is usually filled by the state, which is hardly neutral in these decisions.

We can identify at least two rather different attempts to find alternative bases for a development ethics and development practice. The first, drawing in effect from post-development argumentation that alternatives need to be found outside a dominant Western model of development, seeks to recover displaced and marginalized non-Western ethics.[10] There are many examples, including the recovery of *adat* law in Indonesia, customary forms of property, or culturally diverse forms of trusteeship. In Chapter 6, Sheila Gruner's interest in outlining the moral basis of local autonomous economic models among indigenous and Afro-descendent peoples illustrates this approach; she is careful to maintain a distinction between these alternative economic models and development. To the degree to which these alternatives are framed as existing outside of development and modernity, however, this approach sits uneasily with an understanding of development and modernity that not only allows for multiple modernities but also is skeptical of attempts to distinguish between the West and the Rest, non-colonized and colonized. Adat, for example, far from being a non-Western customary legal and ethical code, was produced by Dutch colonizers as a way of formalizing and recognizing customary practices; though not invented by the Dutch, adat was a codification of research conducted by Dutch proponents of recognizing the traditional laws (Peluso and Vandergeest 2001; Zerner 1994). This is not to dismiss the exploration of marginalized alternatives, but to suggest that they might be more important as a basis for collective action opposing displacement (as described in Chapter 6) than as distinct non-Western ethical systems.

A second alternative is a rights-based approach to DID. Rights-based approaches are used increasingly to assess development (see Maxwell 1999) and are deemed a fairer and more just evaluative tool for managing (or, better, avoiding) displacement. Indeed, several recent initiatives for addressing DID have adopted an explicitly rights-based approach, including the guidelines on internal displacement produced by the Brookings Institution and the UN Refugee Agency. Although not without its problems, this approach at least provides for a matrix of evaluation that sees decisions less in terms of a calculus of costs and benefits and more in ways that are inclusive of fundamental benchmarks in terms of rights criteria: a rights-based approach sets the achievement of human rights as an objective of development and uses thinking about human rights as the scaffolding of development policy. It invokes the international apparatus of human rights accountability in support of development action and is not solely concerned with civil and political rights (Maxwell 1999: 2). Some of the rights that figure into this approach include the right to a sustainable livelihood, to services including health and education, to life and security, to be heard, to maintain or create distinct identities, and so on. These themes appear frequently in this book as well. We cannot judge claims for the best evaluative framework; rather, we simply point to the need to remain vigilant regarding the way in which these projects are appraised.

Conclusion

What this volume makes clear is that the ills of development are not likely to be fixed by increasingly elaborated models for accomplishing good resettlement. At the same time, the case studies fail to support the post-development view that the only ethical response is to reject development altogether. Rather, we find hope in those movements that see within the contradictions of development a challenge to the paternalism or trusteeship that has characterized development for two centuries. Such challenges, voiced by those who typically do not reject development, offer the best chance of bringing people who bear the consequences of DID into the development process as subjects, to work through the unavoidable dialectic of improvement/destruction in ways not organized by development's experts. These case studies are worth reading if for no other reason than to explore the various and repeated challenges directed at displacement's justifications by both the authors themselves and the displaced people whose participation in the research process contributed to the narratives produced here.

Notes

1 For overviews of the DID literature, see Dwivedi (2002), who provides an excellent review of current models and methods in DID; Sanchez-Garzoli's (2001) lengthy bibliography on internal displacement; and the special issue of the *International Social Science Journal* edited by Feldman, Geisler, and Silberling (2003) on DID, which presents a useful set of case studies and a critical analytical framework for understanding DID.

2 Neoliberalism emphasizes trade liberalization and export-led growth, as well as financial market liberalization and financial capital mobility, fiscal and monetary austerity, privatization, and labour market flexibility. The package is sometimes labelled "the Washington Consensus" in reference to the institutions based in Washington, DC, that promoted these policies (World Bank, IMF, US government).

3 Peet (1999: 17), for example, outlines five main *approaches* to development – economic, sociological, neo-Marxist, post-structural, and feminist – all of which begin within the economic and the notion of growth.

4 Lenin, for example, held this view, though it is not at all clear that Marx did, despite his description in Chapter 31 of *Capital* and his searing evocations in *The Communist Manifesto.*

5 The notion of displacement in the absence of *de-location* might strike some as an oxymoron, in that displacement implies removal. However, as we show here, and as is clear from many of the chapters in this volume, people who are not physically relocated can still be displaced from their livelihoods. Displacement thus also points to the sense of loss that accompanies the deprivation of the means and resources through which to continue those livelihoods. For many people, the issue of "improvement" is neither here nor there: the real issue lies in their ability to choose the shape that their lives will take.

6 Although most of our case studies have obviously not assessed the longitudinal effects of displacement, Chapters 2 and 6 describe long patterns of displacement that have recently boiled to the surface in Sudan and Colombia. In these instances, displacements have come out, revealingly, in moments of violent, deeply structured historical conflict. However, it is no accident that they have occurred within the context not only of civil war but also of wars linked to resource extraction. In these chapters, El Jack and Gruner argue that these resource wars are not only coincidental to liberalization but also consonant with it. Although neither we nor the authors claim a direct correlation between displacement, conflict, and neoliberalization, we are all of a mind that neoliberalism matters deeply.

7 Until recently, it was habitually assumed that changes in property rights were linked to a complex growth process that ultimately ought to tend towards, if not end in, Western types of tenure security. As is made clear throughout this volume, however, and as the World Bank now realizes, there are many circumstances in which the historical and cultural patterns of geographic mobility of actors are crucial to the safeguarding of livelihoods. Such mobility is not only made viable through customary land tenure systems; it is also the foundation of their *flexibility* and permits both the assimilation and variability of rights within and between communities where migration is an essential part of people's livelihood cycles (see Platteau 1996).

8 Even here, the Islamist government in Sudan embarked upon home-grown adjustment programs in a climate of conflict and civil war in the early 1990s.

9 For a recent, and devastating, critique of the pretensions of the World Bank and similar agencies that claim to ameliorate poverty, see Paul Cammack (2002). He shows that under the guise of pro-poor development, the "new development orthodoxy" of neoliberalism has been purposely expanded, overturning the development state orthodoxies of the 1960s and introducing pro-capitalist policies that are now, deceptively, linked to socially beneficial outcomes. Using successive World Bank reports, he demonstrates that the "Bank and other institutions, far from disseminating recipes for development that will benefit all sectors of society, are constructing a legitimising ideology that conceals the contradictions of capitalism as a global system, and re-presents it as a remedy for the very human ills it generates" (160).

10 We thank one of the anonymous reviewers of this chapter for reminding us of this option.

References

Abrahamsen, Rita. 2001. *Disciplining Democracy: Development Discourse and Good Governance in Africa*. London: Zed Books.

Berman, Marshall. 1982. *All That Is Solid Melts into Air: The Experience of Modernity*. New York: Penguin Books.

Black, Richard. 2001. "Environmental Refugees: Myth or Reality? New Issues in Refugee Research." Working Paper No. 34. http://www.unhcr.ch/refworld/pubs/pubon.htm.

Callaghy, Thomas, Ronald Kassimir, and Robert Latham, eds. 2001. *Intervention and Transnationalism in Africa: Global-Local Networks of Power*. Cambridge: Cambridge University Press.

Cammack, Paul. 2002. "Neo-Liberalism, the World Bank and the New Politics of Development." In Uma Kothari and Martin Minogue, eds., *Development Theory and Practice: Critical Perspectives*, 157-78. London: Palgrave.

Cernea, Michael. 1997. "Risks and Reconstruction Model for Resettling Displaced Populations." *World Development* 25 (10): 1569-87.

Cernea, Michael, and Christopher McDowell, eds. 1996. *Risks and Reconstruction: Experiences of Resettlers and Refugees*. Washington, DC: World Bank.

Cooper, Frederick, and Randall Packard. 1997. *International Development and the Social Sciences: Essays on the History and Politics of Knowledge*. Berkeley: University of California Press.

Cowen, Michael, and Robert Shenton. 1996. *Doctrines of Development*. London and New York: Routledge.

Doornbos, Martin. 2001. "Good Governance: The Rise and Decline of a Policy Metaphor?" *Journal of Developing Studies* 37 (6): 93-104.

Downing, Ted. 1996. "Mitigating Social Impoverishment When People Are Involuntarily Displaced." In Christopher McDowell, ed., *Understanding Impoverishment: The Consequences of Development-Induced Displacement*, 34-48. Providence, RI: Berghahn Books.

Drydyk, Jay. 2003. "Guidelines Pertaining to Displacement and Resettlement in Development: A Critical Review." Project Report for Population Mobility in Development: An Indo-Canadian Exploration in Development Ethics. Shastri Indo-Canadian Institute, CIDA-SICI Partnership Programme.

Dwivedi, Ranjit. 2002. "Models and Methods in Development-Induced Displacement." *Development and Change* 33 (4): 709-32.

Escobar, Arturo. 1995. *Encountering Development: The Making and Unmaking of the Third World*. Princeton, NJ: Princeton University Press.

Feldman, Shelley, Charles Geisler, and Louise Silberling, eds. 2003. Special Issue, *International Social Science Journal* 55 (175).

Fields, Rona M. 1985. "Refugees from Environmental Degradation ... the Truth behind African Migration." *Migration Today* 13 (4): 18-25.

Fox, Jonathan, and D. Brown, eds. 1998. *The Struggle for Accountability: The World Bank, NGOs, and Grassroots Movements*. Cambridge, MA, and London: MIT Press.

Gasper, D. 1994. "Development Ethics – An Emergent Field? A Look at Scope and Structure with Special Reference to the Ethics of Aid." In R. Prendergast and F. Stewart, eds., *Market Forces and World Development*, 160-85. London: Macmillan.

Goulet, Denis. 1995. *Development Ethics: A Guide to Theory and Practice*. New York: Apex Press.

Gupta, Akhil. 1998. *Postcolonial Developments: Agriculture in the Making of Modern India.* Durham, NC: Duke University Press.
Haggard, Stephan, and Steven B. Webb. 1994. "Introduction." In Stephan Haggard and Steven B. Webb, eds., *Voting for Reform: Democracy, Political Liberalization, and Economic Adjustment,* 1-36. Washington, DC: World Bank.
Hampton, Janie. 1998. *Internally Displaced People: A Global Survey.* London: Earthscan.
Hart, Gillian. 2001. "Development Critiques in the 1990s: Culs de Sac and Promising Paths." *Progress in Human Geography* 25 (4): 649-58.
Hugo, Graeme. 1996. "Environmental Concerns and International Migration." *International Migration Review* 30 (1): 105-32.
Inkeles, Alex, and David Horton Smith. 1974. *Becoming Modern: Individual Change in Six Developing Countries.* Cambridge, MA: Harvard University Press.
Keck, Margaret E., and Kathryn Sikkink. 1998. *Activists beyond Borders: Advocacy Networks in International Politics.* Ithaca: Cornell University Press.
Ki-Zerbo, Joseph. 1997. "Education as an Instrument of Cultural Defoliation: A Multi-Voice Report." In Majid Rahnema and Victoria Bawtree, eds., *The Post-Development Reader,* 152-60. London: Zed Books.
Kriesberg, Louis. 1997. "Social Movements and Global Transformation." In Jackie Smith, Charles Chatfield, and Ron Pagnucco, eds., *Transnational Social Movements and Global Politics: Solidarity beyond the State,* 3-19. Syracuse, NY: Syracuse University Press.
Levitt, Peggy. 2001. *The Transnational Villagers.* Berkeley: University of California Press.
Lewis, Arthur. 1955. *The Theory of Economic Growth.* Irwin: Homewood.
Li, Tania. 1996. "Images of Community: Discourse and Strategy in Property Relations." *Development and Change* 27: 501-27.
–. 1999a. "Compromising Power." *Cultural Anthropology* 14 (3): 295-322.
–. 1999b. "Marginality, Power and Production: Analyzing Upland Transformation." In Tania Li, ed., *Agrarian Transformations in Upland Indonesia,* 1-44. London: Harwood Academic Publishers.
McDowell, Christopher, ed. 1996. *Understanding Impoverishment: The Consequences of Development-Induced Displacement.* Providence, RI: Berghahn Books.
McMichael, Philip. 2000. *Development and Social Change: A Global Perspective.* 2nd ed. Thousand Oaks, CA: Pine Forge Press.
Maxwell, Simon. 1999. "What Can We Do with a Rights-Based Approach to Development?" Overseas Development Institute Briefing Paper 3. London. http://www.odi.org.uk/publications/briefings/3_99.
Mkandawire, P. Thandika. 1994. "Adjustment, Political Conditionality and Democratisation in Africa." In Giovanni A. Cornea and Gerald K. Helleiner, eds., *From Adjustment to Development in Africa: Conflict, Controversy, Convergence, Consensus?* 155-73. London: Macmillan.
Moore, Donald. 1996. "Marxism, Culture and Political Ecology: Environmental Struggles in Zimbabwe's Eastern Highlands." In R. Peet and M. Watts, eds., *Liberation Ecologies,* 125-47. New York: Routledge.
–. 1997. "Remapping Resistance: 'Grounds for Struggle' and the Politics of Place." In Steve Pile and Michael Keith, eds., *Geographies of Resistance,* 87-106. New York: Routledge.
–. 1999. "The Crucible of Cultural Politics: Reworking 'Development' in Zimbabwe's Eastern Highlands." *American Ethnologist* 26 (3): 654-89.
Oxfam. 2002. "Rigged Rules and Double Standards: Trade, Globalization, and the Fight against Poverty." http://www.maketradefair.com (accessed 15 April 2004).
Peet, Richard. 1999. *Theories of Development.* With Elaine Hartwick. New York, NY: Guilford Press.
Peluso, Nancy Lee, and Peter Vandergeest. 2001. "Genealogies of the Political Forest and Customary Rights in Indonesia, Malaysia, and Thailand." *Journal of Asian Studies* 60 (3): 761-812.
Peluso, Nancy Lee, and Michael Watts, eds. 2001. *Violent Environments.* Ithaca: Cornell University Press.
Platteau, J.-P. 1996. "The Evolutionary Theory of Land Rights as Applied to Sub-Saharan Africa: A Critical Assessment." *Development and Change* 27: 29-86.

Portes, Alejandro, Luis E. Guarnizo, and Patricia Landolt. 1999. "The Study of Transnationalism: Pitfalls and Promise of an Emergent Research Field." *Ethnic and Racial Studies* 22: 217-37.

Rist, Gilbert. 1997. *The History of Development: From Western Origins to Global Faith*. London: Zed Press.

Sanchez-Garzoli, Gimena. 2001. *Selected Bibliography on the Global Crisis of Internal Displacement*. Washington, DC: Brookings-CUNY Project on Internal Displacement.

Schmidt, Hans Peter. 2001. "When Networks Blind: Human Rights and Politics in Kenya." In Thomas Callaghy, Ronald Kassimir, and Robert Latham, eds., *Intervention and Transnationalism in Africa: Global-Local Networks of Power*, 149-72. Cambridge: Cambridge University Press.

Suhrke, Astri. 1994. "Environmental Degradation and Population Flows." *Journal of International Affairs* 47 (2): 473-96.

Van Hear, Nicholas. 1998. *New Diasporas: The Mass Exodus, Dispersal and Regrouping of Migrant Communities*. Seattle: University of Washington Press.

WCD. 2000. *Dams and Development: A New Framework for Decision-Making: The Report of the World Commission on Dams*. London: Earthscan.

Wilkerson, Ray. 2002. "A Critical Time for Refugees and Their Environment." *Refugees* 217: 4-23.

Zerner, Charles. 1994. "Through a Green Lens: The Construction of Customary Law and Environment in Indonesia's Maluku Islands." *Law and Society Review* 28 (9): 1079-122.

Part 1
Displacement, Multinationals, and the State

Who Defines Displacement? The Operation of the World Bank Involuntary Resettlement Policy in a Large Mining Project

David Szablowski

Over the past decade, globalizing industries such as mining have witnessed an intensifying battle over the development of large-scale projects in [illegible] have been particularly successful in conveying the plight of many local and [illegible] communities faced with dispossession, environmental degradation, and impoverishment as a result of megaproject development. These critiques have done damage to the legitimacy of actors involved in developing these projects, including private sector corporations, financial institutions, multilateral development banks, and governments. As a result, a fiercely contested and many-sided debate is taking place concerning the [illegible] between such projects and local communities impacted by their operations. [illegible] be required of project developers [illegible] before their operations can be [illegible] social acceptability.

The concept of [illegible] is being deployed by certain actors [illegible] these debates. In particular, the World Bank has used [illegible] legal regime [illegible]. This chapter [illegible] its involuntary resettlement policy [illegible] development-induced displacement [illegible] in the global south. [illegible]

1
Who Defines Displacement? The Operation of the World Bank Involuntary Resettlement Policy in a Large Mining Project

David Szablowski

Over the past decade, globalizing industries such as mining have witnessed an intensifying battle over the development of large-scale projects in the global South. During this period, advocacy campaigns have been particularly successful in conveying the plight of many local and indigenous communities faced with dispossession, environmental degradation, and impoverishment as a result of megaproject development. These critiques have done damage to the legitimacy of parties involved in developing these projects, including private-sector corporations, financial institutions, multilateral development banks, and governments. As a result, a fiercely contested and many-sited debate is taking place concerning the principles that ought properly to govern relations between such projects and local communities impacted by their operations. This is a battle to define what will be required of project developers (often over and above state legal requirements) before their operations can be deemed to meet a new benchmark: "social acceptability."

Development-induced displacement (DID) is an important paradigm that is being deployed by certain actors involved in these debates. In particular, the World Bank has used the concept of DID as the basis for a transnational legal regime that it applies to projects for which bank agencies provide financial services. This regime is centred on a particular set of rules relating to its involuntary resettlement policy (IR policy). What promise does the development-induced displacement paradigm offer to those embroiled in the complex social conflicts that arise from large-scale project development in the global South? This chapter argues that, to answer this question meaningfully, norms and principles should not be considered in a vacuum. To understand what DID principles can mean to project-affected populations on the ground, it is important to examine the institutionalized means by which such policies are translated into practice.

Studying Legal Regimes

As has long been recognized in socio-legal studies, how legal regimes determine facts, define terms, and apply rules in practice depends greatly on how they are structured, on who has what kind of say in decision-making processes, and on how interpretive authority and power are distributed among different actors involved in the regime. Such regimes, whether or not they are managed by a state, are also social fields of action with their own internal rules and processes. A practical understanding of the operation of a legal regime requires an understanding of the rules of the game underlying the social universe within which the operation takes place (Bourdieu 1987).

This chapter offers an analysis of the operation of the transnational legal regime enforcing the World Bank involuntary resettlement policy in the context of mining development. This analysis will focus on the ensemble of actors involved in producing the regime's regulatory decisions, their structural roles in this process, and the nature of their contests over interpretive authority. The aim is to elucidate how the regime performs in the context of mining development: what form of regulatory influence does it exert over relations between mining companies and local communities? And to what degree does it legitimate these relations?

The World Bank Involuntary Resettlement Policy: Regulatory Architecture

The World Bank Group is made up of several agencies, the best-known of which are those engaging in public-sector development activities with governments, the International Bank of Reconstruction and Development (IBRD) and the International Development Association (IDA). However, the Bank Group also includes two agencies, the International Finance Corporation (IFC) and the Multilateral Guarantee Agency (MIGA), which deal with the private sector, providing financial services to facilitate investment in the countries of the global South. Created in 1957 and 1988, respectively, these latter two agencies are mandated to pursue poverty reduction in the developing world through the promotion of private-sector development. IFC acts as a banker and investor, providing equity and debt to private-sector investment projects. MIGA is a loan guarantor that provides political risk insurance.[1] Both agencies are involved in financing large mining projects. In a contract for financial services made with either IFC or MIGA, a client must covenant to comply with that agency's "safeguard policies" (formal policies designed to address project-related negative social and environmental impacts) and submit to the agency's supervision and enforcement procedures. Failure to comply constitutes grounds for termination of the contract.

Initially drafted in the 1980s, and revised several times over the past two decades, the IR policy is the first social safeguard policy created by the World

Bank (Fox 1998: 304). The relevant version for the purposes of this discussion is Operational Directive 4.30 on Involuntary Resettlement (hereafter OD 4.30 or the directive), which was in force from 1990 to 2001. Projects approved for IBRD or IDA assistance on or after 1 January 2002 are subject to a new version of the policy that is divided into two documents, the first dealing with policy and the second with procedure. These are Operational Policy 4.12 and Bank Procedure 4.12 on Involuntary Resettlement (OP/BP 4.12).[2] At the time of writing, IFC and MIGA had not adopted these new policy documents and were awaiting the results of an external review of their safeguard policies.[3] Although IFC continues to use OD 4.30, MIGA has adopted an interim IR policy pending the results of the review. Because the project presented in the case study was approved for MIGA assistance in 1998-99, the analysis provided here will focus upon the text of OD 4.30. However, in order to keep the analysis up to date, endnotes will refer to the corresponding provisions of the new policies (OP/BP 4.12) and will indicate where their content varies significantly from that of the previous text. The thrust of the critique presented here concerns a structural element found in all versions of the Bank Group's IR policies.

The policy on involuntary resettlement is an attempt to address a specific set of project-related social and economic impacts: those which arise from the appropriation of land without the informed consent of its owners, occupiers, and users. For local people, the forced sale of land can mean a loss of access to resources, income-earning opportunities, shelter, and/or the disruption of social networks that underpin vital production systems. Compensation schemes mandated by states frequently fail to provide either full or effective compensation for the physical and social resources lost by people with land-based livelihoods. Such systems restrict compensation to officially recognized forms of property, ignoring what is often a substantial part of the resource base underlying rural livelihoods (such as informal or de facto property rights recognized locally); they neglect entire categories of loss inflicted on disrupted communities (including lost access to social networks crucial to agricultural production systems and start-up costs faced by relocated people); they assume that cash is an uncomplicated form of compensation easily translated into new productive assets (disregarding local capacities and opportunities for money management, local inflationary effects, and cash as a form of property that can be appropriated by a single actor). The result, repeatedly documented in studies on the subject, is deepened impoverishment among people often already considered very poor (see Cernea 1988, 1997, 1999; Cernea and McDowell 2000; McDowell 1996; World Bank 1996).

The stated purpose of OD 4.30 is to "ensure that the population displaced by a project receives benefits from it" (para. 3).[4] This is to be achieved first by addressing the considerable risks of socio-economic harm that can arise to local populations from the forced acquisition of land by a project and, second, by assisting such populations with their efforts to "improve their former living standards, income earning capacity, and production levels" (para. 3).[5] The resettlement policy's central requirement is that those impacted by a project's land acquisition process should be *at least* as well off afterwards as before the project's intervention into their lives (para. 3).[6] To this end, the project sponsor (that is, the mining company) must structure land acquisition as a participatory development intervention. This intervention, called a "Resettlement Plan," must be designed, managed, and monitored by qualified experts (paras. 6, 22, 23).[7] Involuntary resettlement must be avoided where feasible, and otherwise minimized (para. 3[a]).[8] Effective compensatory measures must guard against the threat of impoverishment for displaced persons[9] and should permit them to improve their standard of living (paras. 3-5).[10]

At its core, the intention of the resettlement policy is similar to that of a far older regulatory mechanism employed by liberal states: the requirement for compensation for the expropriation of private property pursuant to the state's power of eminent domain. Under the doctrine of eminent domain, states reserve the right to force a sale of property that is required in the public interest. Sale is made at fair market value: a sum presumed sufficient to compensate a rational actor operating within a market economy (who will then be in a position to purchase a productive asset equivalent to the one sold). The doctrine of eminent domain recognizes that absolute freedom of contract and property could obstruct or impose unfair costs on certain desirable public goods (Rose 1994). Forcing a property holder to sell his or her land is deemed to be justified by the public importance of the good pursued and by the full compensation of the property holder according to liberal economic principles (that is, compensation for fair market value of legally recognized property interests) (Rose 1994: ch. 6).

IR policy, however, asserts a logic very different from the liberal, market-oriented paradigm used both by states and enterprises to frame property transactions. Instead, it reads like a version of eminent domain conceived by social scientists and rural development professionals. It seeks to base compensation on a more comprehensive socio-economic accounting of community assets and project-related impacts. It directs the project sponsor to treat formal and informal property equally;[11] it emphasizes the need to facilitate the reconstruction of damaged social components of local production systems; and it focuses attention on the impacts of lost income-earning opportunities and lost access to public services (paras. 2, 3, 7, 14, 17).[12] Given the seriousness of displacement, it requires that IR be avoided or minimized where feasible (para. 3[a]).[13] It emphasizes the need to tailor compensation carefully to the target population and to view the situation overall as a development opportunity. The basket of compensatory measures available for rebuilding and improving local living standards includes asset replacement, cash compensation, development projects to improve physical assets (such as land reclamation and irrigation projects), development projects to improve human capacities (such as training), and the provision of employment opportunities (paras. 13-19).[14] In the case of rural populations, the resettlement policy strongly favours land-for-land exchanges over exchanges of cash for land (para. 13).[15] Furthermore, it views the full remedying of harm (that is, the restoration of pre-existing livelihoods) as the *minimum* level of acceptable compensation (para. 3).[16] The resettlement policy also draws attention to equity issues, calling upon the project sponsor to identify "vulnerable groups" within the affected population (which may be women, indigenous people, landless peasants, and so on) and to ensure that such groups are properly included in the compensation framework (paras. 8, 16).[17] And finally, the resettlement policy requires that planning, execution, and follow-up of resettlement activities be conducted with the participation of both the affected population and any "host" communities to which it may be relocated (paras. 7-10, 13).[18]

The resettlement policy thus represents a considerable normative challenge to how business is conventionally transacted by a mining enterprise. First, it argues for much broader conceptions of property and compensation than those specified within liberal legal systems. Second, and more fundamentally, the policy calls for a wholesale reconstruction of the property transaction relationship. In a liberal legal framework, the responsibilities of the parties to one another usually end with the exchange of compensation for land. The resettlement policy, however, holds the project sponsor responsible for the *economic outcomes* of its transactions with local people. The company is directed to ensure that its compensation actually does "at least ... restore" to pre-project levels the "living standards, income earning capacity, and production levels" of "displaced persons." The company is cast into an unfamiliar role as a fiduciary with considerable paternalist responsibilities and (as we shall see) powers. This is a foreseeable site of normative conflict. The regulatory regime that emerges around the resettlement policy will have to respond to forces within (and perhaps external to) the mining company that seeks to maintain the logics and practices of "business as usual." We can predict that the result of this normative conflict will have a significant impact upon the overall regulatory influence of the regime.

Of course, terms such as "living standards," "displaced persons," and "participation" are far from self-defining, particularly when transplanted into different socio-economic environments. What forms of harm are compensable? When is a harm considered to be remedied? Who counts as displaced? What is a valid participatory process? The regulatory impact of the directive's legal regime will to a large extent depend upon the mechanisms through which the directive is interpreted and applied in the local environment. This regulatory architecture is set out in OD 4.30 itself, in the sponsor's contract with IFC or MIGA, and occurs in the planning and permitting processes that accompany project design and development.

Briefly, the project sponsor is charged with conducting the field research and participatory consultation necessary for its design of the resettlement plan. This material (in the form of written reports) and the plan itself are reviewed for approval by IFC or MIGA[19] in Washington DC and by an independent engineer (an environmental engineering consulting firm contracted pursuant to the financing agreement to act as an independent monitor of environmental and social compliance). In the case of a large mining project, staff from the bank agency will also typically arrange for a short visit to the project site. After any revisions, the plan is then implemented by the project sponsor, who is required to make ongoing progress reports to the bank agency. Since 2000, a Compliance Advisor Ombudsman (CAO) office has been established in Washington DC to address compliance issues respecting IFC- and MIGA-financed projects, including local complaints (CAO 2001).

What are the implications of this structure? One of the most striking is the marginalization of local people within the process of interpreting and applying the directive in their local circumstances. There is no requirement to provide local people with copies of the directive; nor is it mandatory that they be made aware of its existence as a body of rules binding company action with respect to compensation for their livelihoods and property.[20] Furthermore, there is no requirement to advise local people of the existence of IFC, MIGA, the independent engineer, or the CAO, or of the means of contacting them. Accordingly, local people are effectively shut out of any direct involvement in the IFC/MIGA review process. The form and extent of their involvement is determined by the company's participatory process, and their input is mediated to the supervising agency via the company's reports. In contrast, the bank agency has a positive duty to inform its customer of the directive (para. 24)[21] and to finance technical assistance to enable the customer to carry out its resettlement responsibilities (para. 23).[22] Without alternative input, the company's reports tend to become the only authoritative "legal facts" describing the local environment, its economic and social structures, the degrees of impact, and the needs and entitlements found to exist among local people. Reviewers at the bank agency and the independent engineer are able to check for reasonableness, methodological soundness, and consistency, but are largely faced with the facts as presented. Subsequent discussions regarding the application of the directive are conducted exclusively between the company and the reviewing agencies.

The resulting construction of the role played by local people is markedly different from that accorded to legal persons[23] by liberal legal systems. Liberal legal systems derive their legitimacy from a conceptualization of the individual as an active rights-bearing agent who is protected from arbitrary government action by the rule of law and by the principles of procedural fairness. A person is entitled to know the rules she or he faces and is also entitled not to be dispossessed without the opportunity to present a case that contests the facts and legal interpretations asserted by another party. Within the liberal legal framework, abuse of these rights delegitimizes the result. In contrast, the IR directive circumscribes the role played by local people as actors and casts them instead as passive subjects. Although they are to provide information and to be consulted as to their preferences, they are principally expected to act as the objects of expert study. Interpretive conclusions are drawn by experts who elicit and use the input of local people alongside other raw material. Under the recently created CAO complaint procedures, local people can gain some measure of active participation once something "goes wrong." However, initiating such a complaint requires a knowledge of the structure and procedures of the directive's legal regime, which can be quite difficult for local people to obtain and which the regime itself does little to facilitate.

Rather than granting concrete procedural rights to local people, the directive imposes a duty on the project sponsor to ensure their "participation" in planning and decision making.[24] Participation denotes a generalized form of procedural involvement that has become ubiquitous among development practitioners and within some circles of researchers. It is a flexible rather than formalistic approach. The practical content of participation is tailored by development and research professionals to be appropriate to local circumstances and the issues in question (Davis and Soeftestad 1995). Although a commitment to participation has become nearly universal within the development field, the question of what constitutes valid and effective means of participation remains highly contested. Durst (1994: 64), for example, calls it an ideology "devoid of a shared meaning and a common methodology." Furthermore, it is often argued that much participation is tokenistic, involving no real impact upon the decision-making process (Cooper and Elliot 2000; Lohmann 1998). Certainly, a wide spectrum of perspectives and practices is currently classed within the category of participation: participation may encompass a rigorous involvement in decision-making procedures or it may not (compare, for example, the approach set out in IFC Environment Division 1998 with the nuanced analysis suggested by Carter 1998 and the emphasis on accountability in Feeney 1998). The ambiguous requirement of participation also indicates a paternalistic framing of the role played by local people. Although World Bank IR policy affirms the need for special measures to ensure the effective compensation of local people, it offers limited respect for local agency. As a result, the degree and manner of local involvement in the process are other factors to be determined largely via the legal facts and interpretations developed by the project sponsor.

It is worth recalling that, for local people, there is a great deal at stake in the ways that IR policy is interpreted and implemented. The results of the processes of interpretation and implementation will determine whether the people are dispossessed of their livelihoods and provided – or not – with effective means for reconstruction or compensation. Furthermore, as will be discussed, the application of IR policy can have an important legitimation effect upon the land acquisition process, which, in turn, may impede the community's capacity to mobilize support from transnational allies. Given the importance of these matters to the lives of local people, the marginalization of local people within the process of interpreting and applying IR policy demands a very high burden of justification.

What, then, is intended to ensure the integrity and legitimacy of this process? It is the expertise and integrity of the professionals hired to run it (OD 4.30 paras. 22, 25).[25] In the regulatory regime of the directive, interpretation is presented as a technical activity rather than a political or contestable one. Specialized personnel are employed by both the mining company and IFC/MIGA. The research, analysis, participatory design, and resettlement planning are performed by the company's specialists and reviewed by the bank's specialists. These tasks are presumably assessed on the basis of a shared professional perspective on standards of practice, accepted procedures, and mutually recognized norms. The process is analogous to scientific peer review: the adequacy of the practitioner's credentials and methodology, the thoroughness of the procedures, and the reasonableness of her/his conclusions within the accepted parameters of a professional discourse all attest to the work's validity. In the same spirit, the interpretation of terms such as "participation," "displaced person," "living standards," and "resettlement" ultimately derives from the content of these shared professional practices, standards, and judgments. The integrity and legitimacy of these interpretations therefore rest upon the premise that they will be produced by disinterested and autonomous technical professionals applying scientifically validated professional norms and judgments.

Thus, as we have seen, World Bank IR policy inserts the development-induced displacement (DID) paradigm into a regime in which decision making is treated as the province of experts, apparently to the detriment of the rights of agency and self-determination of project-affected populations. How IR policy operationalizes DID as a framework for addressing project-related impacts and benefits on local populations is for these reasons bound up with the construction of this new form of professional specialization, its autonomy, interpretive authority, and the context within which it operates.

The Social Specialist

The term "social specialist" is used here to refer to expert professionals hired by mining companies and World Bank agencies to frame and address community issues. They play a key role in the construction of who and what is "the community": its geographical and political scope, its social, cultural, and economic character, its legitimate needs and entitlements. The conclusions of social specialists are invested with the authority of their individual academic and professional credentials. On the face of it, social specialists would appear to play a role analogous to that of lawyers within national legal regimes: they are the regime's specialized interpreters. Just as legal training is required in order to translate a controversy into the language and logic of a lawsuit (and to transform it in the process – Bourdieu 1987: 833), so it is the particular task of the social specialist to phrase project-related social conflicts within a "social acceptability" framework.

Social specialists do not exercise their interpretive functions in a vacuum. In the mining industry, their activities are integrated within the hierarchical planning and decision-making structure of the mining enterprise itself, typically under a department responsible for "community relations" which either employs them as staff or retains them as external consultants. Decisions taken by the department must be coordinated with other corporate departments and ultimately approved by senior management. Land acquisition and resettlement planning, for example, will also involve staff from departments responsible for legal compliance, environmental issues, operations, and so on, and must be structured within the overall budgeting and timetabling processes for planning and project development.

This suggests a series of related questions. What authority or influence is exercised by social specialists within this organizational structure? To what extent, and in what circumstances, do social specialists possess the authority required to assert interpretations and representations that will be carried out in practice? How strong is the interpretive authority of social specialists within their institutions as compared with that of other actors with competing interests? There are a number of compelling reasons to question the extent and depth of their influence and interpretive authority.

First, there is a lack of consensus within the mining industry concerning the legitimacy of social responsibility policies. Strong feelings exist throughout the industry that it has been the victim of unfair and misinformed criticism (Wilson 2000). According to this view, the creation of these policies and of community relations departments represents an unreasonable concession to political correctness. At their most extreme, proponents of this view contend that community activities should consist chiefly of public relations efforts rather than promotion of substantive change. A less extreme version of this line of thought places social issues at the periphery of a mining company's core concerns: they may have to be addressed but must not get in the way of "real" work.

Second, both mining companies and environmental consulting firms are dominated by professionals from physical science disciplines such as geology, biology, and engineering. Social scientists working on interdisciplinary impact assessment teams have identified among many physical scientists a tendency towards a "disciplinary chauvinism" characterized by a lack of understanding of or respect for the premises, methodologies, and results of social science inquiry. These attitudes, particularly when they are held by senior decision makers or "research brokers," may result in the underfunding of social research ("What is it you guys really do to use all that money?") and the failure to contract qualified personnel to address social issues ("anyone can determine the social consequences of development").[26]

Third, there are strong structural motivations in the industry for continuing with "business as usual" – particularly with regard to diminishing the impact of social responsibility requirements on the timing and cost of other operations. Strict control of production costs and timetables is a paramount value within the mining industry. Metals prices are established on volatile world markets, and the success of a mining enterprise depends on achieving production at the lowest possible cost. In addition, the need for considerable borrowing in order to develop a large mine places a high premium on the efficient use of time: the faster a mine can become productive, the less debt servicing will be necessary. These values are deeply embedded in a company's institutional culture as well as in the individual professional cultures of its staff. The capacity of social specialists to insist on action that increases costs or requires delays may be limited both by overt policy and by the "natural" dispositions of company personnel active in the decision-making process (including the social specialists themselves).

Finally, the profession of social specialist in the context of mining remains poorly institutionalized and offers little to bolster the interpretive authority of individual practitioners. It is not a professional category with accreditation, compulsory professional standards, or disciplinary self-regulation. It is not clear what qualifications are required for social specialists. Although many who are hired in this capacity are anthropologists or sociologists, others may be physical scientists or managers who have acquired some practical experience with community issues. In Peru, it is not uncommon to find Peruvian mining engineers ("old hands" at dealing with communities) or even former industry-side labour negotiators in senior positions in community relations departments. Not surprisingly, little foundation exists for the creation of the interpretive consensuses which help to consolidate a profession's specialized authority (see Burdge and Vanclay 1996: 66-70; for a contrary view, see Finsterbusch 1995;[27] for evidence of growing institutionalization of professional standards, see ICGP 1995 and IAIA 2002).[28]

These observations call into question two assumptions concerning the capacity of social specialists to ensure the integrity and legitimacy of regulatory decisions produced by the directive's legal regime. It is not clear that social specialists operating within the mining industry have a strong sense of shared professional standards and judgments to serve as authoritative and reviewable guidance in interpreting and applying IR policy (particularly with respect to such specialized terms as "displacement," "resettlement," and so on). In addition, these observations suggest that social specialists may have difficulty formulating or asserting interpretations (that are carried into practice) that conflict with dominant logics, assumptions, and practices within the company. In the words of a social consultant with substantial mining industry experience, "The difficulty for consultants of providing objective and complete assessments of the potential impacts from project development when they are being paid to assist a company to develop a project can be quite extreme" (Joyce and MacFarlane 2001: 8). In addition, the influence of individual social specialists can be diminished by those higher up in the decision-making structure. Consultants who collect field information can often be several steps removed from those who write the general conclusions of a study (Fearnside 1994). How these conclusions are drafted is typically subject to great scrutiny by corporate clients. We can expect that internal contests for interpretive authority and power are important issues with respect to how mining companies define and address social matters.

Insight into the dynamics of these contests may be derived from the trajectory of the introduction of social specialists within the individual agencies of the World Bank Group itself. The World Bank introduced its social safeguard policies and social departments in response to concerted outside pressures. Since the 1980s, advocacy networks connecting Northern NGOs with grassroots movements and NGOs in the South have waged sustained campaigns to promote change and accountability in bank-funded projects (Fox and Brown 1998). Although these pressures have scored significant successes in establishing or changing formal policies and procedures at the bank, changes in actual practice have been much more elusive. For example, the bank-wide review of public-sector projects carried out between 1986 and 1993 revealed a systematic and widespread pattern of non-compliance with the resettlement directive (World Bank 1996). Social specialists employed at the public-sector side of the bank have been free to write and publish as they wish; however, they have had to struggle against the marginalization of their influence upon actual practice (Fox 1998; Francis and Jacobs 1999; Gopinath 1996). Factors identified as contributing to this marginalization include the economist-led corporate culture of the bank and institutional disincentives to rigorous application of social safeguard policies.[29]

J.A. Fox and L.D. Brown (1998) have suggested that external pressure on the bank can help to increase the authority and reform opportunities available to social staff within the bank. During interviews they conducted in the social departments of the World Bank agencies, informants agreed with this suggestion: they felt that the presence of outside pressure helped to increase their standing within their organizations. As community issues become more important problems, those qualified to address them gain greater importance and authority. This dynamic is likely to apply as well to the social departments working within mining companies: that is, the authority of social specialists will be strongly influenced by the relative presence, absence, and form of outside pressure and scrutiny of the process.

Case Study: Compañía Minera Antamina

This case study concerns the initial phases of relations between a majority Canadian-owned transnational mining enterprise and local communities in a remote rural district in Andean Peru. More specifically, it focuses on corporate-community relationships during acquisition of land and introduction of project into local environment. This work is based upon field research undertaken in 2000 and 2001 at the mine site in the district of San Marcos, as well as in the departmental and national capitals. I conducted interviews with a wide range of informants including indigenous peasants, peasant leaders, municipal officials, townspeople, company staff and management, government representatives, and NGO staff. Additional interviews were conducted in Washington DC with NGO representatives and with social and environmental staff from the World Bank, IFC, and MIGA.

Compañía Minera Antamina and the District of San Marcos

The district of San Marcos is located in the Conchucos Canyon region, in the department of Ancash, in the central Peruvian Andes. Nationally, San Marcos is counted among the poorest and most marginalized of areas, with high levels of malnutrition and illiteracy, and a significant rate of permanent emigration. The majority of its residents are Quechua-speaking indigenous peasants who practise subsistence agriculture. Neither San Marcos nor the Andes generally lends itself to tidy, comfortable images of "community." Andean environments such as these are riven with a long history of opposing solidarities, internal divisions, and conflict – particularly with respect to conflicts over land.

Rural environments in the Andes have often been regarded as isolated pre-modern spaces in which traditional communitarian practices have persisted along with quasi-feudal forms of exploitation dating from the Spanish conquest. Over recent decades, a profound and ongoing series of transformations has disrupted the familiar classifications of traditional/modern, Andean/coastal (Diez 1999: 263). Land reform in the late 1960s and 1970s provided *campesinos* (indigenous peasants) with new freedoms and removed the linchpin of the existing system of dominance maintained by *mestizo* (mixed descent) local landlords and bosses. Large-scale emigration from the rural Andes to coastal urban centres was greatly accelerated in the 1980s and 1990s by the persistent crisis of the rural economy and by deepening political violence. The "modern" *criollo* (Creole)[30] coast has itself been transformed by the arrival of millions of Andean migrants vigorously engaged in informal urbanization and commerce and struggling with economic and social marginalization. The "traditional" rural Andes has experienced a constant flow of returning and visiting migrants, with profound and ongoing effects upon Andean social and political institutions (Paerregaard 1998; Diez 1999). As a result, even the most remote corners of the Andes are continuously articulated with the urban world. This articulation, and the spanning by migrants of spaces with different and changing rationalities, puts into question the meaning of Andean identities. It opens for Andean peasants the possibility of social and economic transformation, of greater access to the benefits of the modern metropolitan world, even as they experience marginalization in both rural and urban settings.

Rural livelihoods in the Andes are based upon a fragile balance. To whatever degree possible, traditional agricultural production and non-market exchange are supplemented by production for regional markets,[31] seasonal migration for salaried labour, and remittances from migrants. Diversified agriculture is managed across ecological zones that vary with altitude and microclimate. Families and communities ensure access to a mixed basket of goods by spreading their own production across various zones and by maintaining local networks involving both traditional and market forms of exchange.[32] However, the need created by demographic pressures far exceeds the productive capacity of these strategies, making emigration to the cities of the coast a necessary survival strategy for households and communities (Figueroa 1989).

The land sought by the Antamina project in San Marcos is located at an elevation above 4,300 metres and forms part of an important high-altitude pastoral production zone called the *puna,* which is chiefly used to pasture animals.[33] Legal ownership of this land was divided between two peasant communities (legal entities that hold communal title under Peruvian law)[34] and a number of families of peasant smallholders. These lands, whether privately or collectively owned, are relied upon by a relatively extensive group of users (which includes owners, extended family, renters, and retainers) for livelihood interests that vary from person to person and family to family – including cash income, goods, domicile, and employment. Small numbers within this group (often retainers or poor relations, but sometimes landowners) are either permanently or seasonally resident in the puna and act as shepherds tending the animals of others (GRADE 2000; Orlove 1977; Pinedo 2000; Rios Ocsa 1992).

In September 1996, the Peruvian government approved a joint bid by two Canadian mining firms to exploit the undeveloped Antamina copper-zinc deposit, awarding them the concession previously held by a state-owned company. Rights to the concession were vested in Compañía Minera Antamina (CMA), a Peruvian company created and initially owned by the two partners.[35] In 1996, at US$2.3 billion,[36] Antamina was the largest mine project financing ever arranged (Watkins 1999). The financial consortium that provides the project with debt and investment guarantees includes the World Bank's MIGA; accordingly, pursuant to its financing contracts, the project is obligated to comply with the World Bank involuntary resettlement policy.

The discussion that follows presents a compressed account[37] of the land sale and resettlement processes conducted in San Marcos between 1997 and 1999. It is divided into two parts, dealing with the processes of land acquisition and resettlement. It is followed by an account of subsequent events that took place in 2000.

Making the Deal: Persuading Peasants to Sell Land

CMA's community relations staff were given the task of acquiring legal title to lands required by project designers for the mine and its associated infrastructure. The project's land acquisition, resettlement, and development plans had been made in advance, pursuant to studies commissioned from social and development experts and pursuant to the company's assessment of its various legal and regulatory obligations (including Peruvian contract and property law, CMA's MIGA commitments, and environmental permitting).[38] Accordingly, in convincing landowners to sell, community relations staff were required to use a pre-set package of offers. Negotiations with the various landowners took place over roughly one year.

During the course of these negotiations, it is likely that CMA negotiating strategies evolved as staff discovered what tended to persuade peasants and what did not. In many ways, these discussions became a diffuse negotiation process in which peasants with the limited standing to do so engaged with company representatives regarding the terms upon which the mining project should be allowed entry into San Marcos. CMA and peasant negotiators did not restrict their discussion to the narrow issue of price: peasants wanted to know how the arrival of the mine would change their lives and the environment around them. Many peasants feared the destructive capacity of the project and its effect upon existing livelihoods. Foreign mining operations from the nineteenth and early twentieth centuries in Peru were well known in the country for their appropriation of peasant lands and their devastating environmental effects (CooperAcción 2000; Mallon 1983). Furthermore, the fragility of many livelihoods in San Marcos meant that few could afford to lose the lands being sought by the project. In addition, many peasants hoped that the mine would bring transformative economic opportunities, particularly in the form of work for the young, but also as a market for local agricultural goods.

CMA representatives were successful in inducing contracts of sale by responding to both the hopes and anxieties prevalent within peasant communities. With respect to transformative economic opportunities, CMA staff offered what was viewed at that time as a high purchase price for land[39] and the promise of a number of development projects for the benefit of local people. In addition, it appears that in many cases these offers were supplemented by misleading assurances that the mine would bring large-scale, secure employment for the local people of the region (GRADE 2000; Szablowski 2004). With respect to peasant fears of loss of access to the high-altitude pastures, CMA negotiators invoked the company's resettlement plans made pursuant to its resettlement commitments to MIGA. Landowners were told that purchased lands would be replaced in a subsequent resettlement process. The resettlement offer provided an assurance not only to owners but also to the larger community that depended economically on highland pastures that existing production systems would not be dismantled as a result of the sale (Szablowski 2004).

During my interviews, peasant informants reported that CMA negotiators also threatened intransigent peasants with the state's powers of expropriation in favour of mining development. Pursuant to Peruvian law, after initiating negotiations for the purchase of surface rights, a mining-concession holder can apply for and be granted an easement, at the state's discretion, essentially expropriating required surface rights in exchange for a nominal payment to their owner.[40] The threat of expropriation was used both to encourage reluctant vendors and to discourage those who sought to bargain for more than the company was offering.

Breaking the Deal: Redefining Resettlement

CMA's land acquisition strategy represented an initial success for the company. The project obtained title to the lands it required at a price that was kept under the company's control and in circumstances of relatively general local approval. This climate of approval, however, would be short-lived. Some five months after the land acquisition process was complete, it became apparent that CMA's operations department had appropriated those lands set aside by the company for resettlement purposes. Community relations was not aware of the change until it began resettling peasants into areas that soon became construction sites. Furthermore, driven by the substantial gains to be realized by early completion of the project's facilities, operations insisted upon an accelerated timetable for the clearance of required lands. Community relations was directed to accept these new arrangements. With the rainy season approaching and with no time to acquire replacement land, the land-for-land resettlement plan was dropped in favour of a faster cash-based program[41] (see GRADE 2000; Ian Thompson Consulting 1999: 9).

For local peasants dependent upon the purchased lands, the cash-based program represented a dramatic reversal of policy. Although the promise of land-for-land resettlement had been made to owners during the land acquisition process (in some cases in writing), cash-based resettlement was offered only to those identified as "permanent residents" of the high-altitude pasturelands. These relatively small numbers of shepherd families were pressured to accept very high levels of monetary compensation in exchange for their immediate departure.[42] Owners were no longer the targets of this negotiation process.

Distrust of company promises deepened as the other major commitments made locally by company representatives failed to materialize. At that time, little evidence was seen by peasants of CMA's plans for local development projects.[43] Furthermore, the hope of widespread employment with the mine was becoming increasingly faint. Accordingly, when the evictions took place in early 1999, many peasants found their principal hopes dashed (no stable employment, little results from development promises, a fleeting rather than steady access to income) and some of their worst fears realized (loss of productive assets underpinning household economies, deep community divisions sparked by differential levels of compensation). Many peasants raged against the company, which remained, at that time, deaf to their complaints. In the countryside, the company's identity was rapidly reconstructed in the popular imagination: transgressive, deceitful, and corrupt, it came to be regarded as a powerful destructive force which, many were convinced, would pollute and destroy their lands.

Since this time, a number of important events have once again significantly altered relations between the project and local communities. In early 2000, nearly a year after the evictions, local municipal, peasant, and civil society leaders drafted a long letter of complaint against CMA that was sent to a range of national and international authorities. Faced with the company's intransigence, these leaders sought outside help. Letters were sent to, among others, the national ombudsman, the office of the president, the national congress, the Canadian embassy, and (due to references by company staff to World Bank policies) the World Bank office in Lima. In contrast with the national authorities (who, according to my informants in the district municipality, offered no effective reply), the World Bank activated a swift regulatory response to the letter. This led to substantial correspondence between MIGA and CMA, followed by a visit to the mine site by MIGA staff, an independent compliance review commissioned from a Peruvian development research institute, and an extensively researched report identifying cases of non-compliance with the bank's involuntary resettlement policy. Furthermore, during and following these events, CMA restaffed and revitalized its community development office, initiated its first substantial local development projects for the population at large, promoted and financed the creation of a local development roundtable and a local environmental committee,[44] and began to settle claims based on its written promises of resettlement.[45]

Many of these developments represented important gains. In my interviews, CMA representatives reported that during the period of company silence following the evictions in the puna, a change in community relations policy and practice was already in the works. However, corporate behaviour suggests a period of uncertainty, indecision, and internal struggle regarding the appropriate character of community engagement. In any event, it appears that the community complaint to the World Bank played a key role in bringing out once again the socially responsible face of the company[46] in San Marcos or, at the very least, in shaping its character and accelerating and strengthening its return.

Analysis of the Case Study: Were the Objectives of World Bank IR Policy Achieved?

The purpose of the following analysis is to examine the effectiveness of the IR policy regulatory regime (as managed by MIGA) in accomplishing its stated objectives. In particular, the aim here is to evaluate the influence of the regime's key means for ensuring the accuracy, integrity, and legitimacy of its regulatory decisions: the delegation of fact-finding and interpretive discretion to company social specialists, and the supervisory role played by expert MIGA staff. Accordingly, for the purposes of this study, we must look at the regulatory decisions made before local actors in San Marcos succeeded in making direct contact with MIGA with their letter of complaint. Actors in San Marcos showed enough initiative and good fortune to stumble upon the means to activate a review process. We cannot assume that all local actors will be able to do so. The discussion that follows will look at the IR policy's economic and participatory objectives.

Did the IR policy's legal regime succeed in achieving the policy's fundamental goal of ensuring "at least" the restoration of the "living standards, income earning capacity, and production levels" (OD 4.30 para. 3[b]) of those displaced by CMA's land acquisition program? As stated previously, the high-altitude pasturelands were relied upon directly by relatively extended groups of persons (including formal owners, renters, relations, retainers, and employees) for a range of livelihood interests (including income, goods, employment, domicile, and savings).[47] Of these groups, only two received compensation from CMA: those identified as either legal owners (who received the sale price) or as permanent residents of the highlands (who received cash resettlement payments).[48] It goes without saying that, in the absence of other measures, those who were uncompensated suffered direct economic losses as a result of the land transactions.

But what about the others? Did the cash compensation received by owners and residents enable them to rebuild their previous standard of living? Due to the lack of effective pre-resettlement socio-economic baseline data, this is very difficult to assess.[49] A Lima-based development research institute subsequently contracted to evaluate the resettlement process has argued that the monetary payments offer no guarantee that medium- or long-term living standards have been maintained (GRADE 2000). Certainly, there is evidence to suggest that many recipients were not able to translate the payments they received into new productive assets. Local inflation, especially in prices for land and housing, sharply diminished the payments' value. For many, cash proved to be easily susceptible to appropriation, to claims made through family and social networks, or to simple consumption. Many of my peasant informants reported that after two years, both the money and the land were gone. The notion that many had experienced a net loss from the transactions was strongly asserted by peasant informants. Although it is very likely that some possessed effective money management skills, others (in particular the shepherds of the highlands) had no experience with large sums of money and had limited opportunities to invest them. It is likely that for many peasants, a form of productive property had been exchanged for one that would chiefly be consumed.

How well did the legal regime ensure the quality of local participation in regulatory decision making? To what degree were local people involved in the interpretation and application of the IR policy? The case study shows that this involvement took place over various stages. During the initial stages of resettlement planning, local people were studied by social specialists and were able to voice their concerns at informational meetings conducted by CMA. Subsequently, MIGA's review of the resettlement plan took place without active local input. To the extent that this review considered local perspectives, it relied upon accounts provided by the EIS and CMA reports. During the sale of land process, those identified as landowners were involved in negotiations with company staff. However, CMA negotiators took pains to ensure that these negotiations did not result in any change in the company's established plans. During the resettlement process, negotiations were initiated concerning potential relocation sites; however, as described above, this process was soon replaced by an ultimatum demanding near-immediate departure.

Throughout, CMA sought to retain unilateral control of the interpretation and planning functions of the regulatory regime. Its repeated modus operandi was to select the group which, according to its own criteria, was entitled to compensation, decide upon a compensation plan, then approach the group and seek to compel it to accept the plan without change. Local people were not provided with copies of OD 4.30; they were not provided with explanations of its contents; they were not provided with the technical and advocacy assistance necessary to understand and represent their own interests. CMA did refer publicly to the directive, but only as a voluntary policy that the company had elected to follow (see Klohn Crippen Consultants 1998: appendix 2). CMA did not advertise its binding commitment to implement OD 4.30; nor, as far as I have been able to ascertain, did it advise local people of the existence of potential complaint procedures through MIGA (or, after 2000, through the CAO).

As a result, the broad population of highland-dependent families (many of whom did not fall within CMA's categories of owner or permanent resident) were not engaged in the process of determining who would qualify as "displaced" by the land transactions, how they would be impacted, and what forms of resettlement would help to remedy the situation. What justifications can be forwarded for this state of affairs? Certainly not that the impartiality and expertise of CMA's social specialists made public engagement unnecessary. The marginalization of the affected population from active involvement in interpreting IR policy has served principally to limit community bargaining power.

The Autonomy of Corporate Social Specialists

CMA's social specialists were provided with a departmental organization, a set budget, and space within the construction timetable. The company committed personnel, time, and funds to community relations work in an overt strategy to win local hearts and minds. However, this case study has shown that, despite the platform given to social specialists within CMA, in many respects, their status has been quite limited within the organization. Over the period examined, the community relations department was subject to unexpected external revisions of its plans and budget, and it was excluded from important information-sharing and decision-making processes involving its key operations.

The case study also suggests that, in important ways, the interpretive logic used by CMA's social specialists in applying IR policy was strongly influenced by the demands of prevailing corporate imperatives. This is evidenced by the monetization of resettlement in contravention of the directions of OD 4.30; it is also shown in the shifting definition of "displaced person." During the land negotiations, the resettlement program was presented as a pledge to landowners (and perhaps to the greater highland-dependent community) to replace purchased land. However, resettlement was later reconceived by CMA staff as a right that belonged exclusively to permanent highland residents. Essentially, the term "displaced person," denoting entitlement to resettlement compensation under the IR policy, was redefined. This shifting conceptualization occurred in sync with the changing demands placed on community relations staff by core corporate priorities accompanying the step-by-step advancement towards mine development: first, the owners needed to be persuaded to sell; next, the occupiers needed to be persuaded to leave. The close alignment of policy interpretations with corporate objectives in this case suggests limits to the capacity of corporate-employed social specialists to act as the impartial guarantors of the application of IR policy.

The Supervisory Role Played by MIGA

As described earlier, social and environmental staff at MIGA are intended to play a supervisory role in the regulatory regime. During a project's evaluation and approval phase, they examine the documents generated by its social staff; in the case of large mining projects, MIGA staff also conduct a site visit in order to review the project's team and verify the bona fides of company efforts. MIGA staff conducted such a site visit at Antamina in 1999 (CAO 2001). After project approval, MIGA supervisors rely upon the reporting obligations set out in the contract of guarantee, which require project staff to provide compliance information on a regular basis (the task of reviewing these reports may be delegated to the independent engineer) and to notify MIGA with respect to special developments.

How effective were these structures at ensuring IR policy implementation? CMA's poor implementation record before the time of the community complaint does not speak well for these types of arrangements. Social staff whom I interviewed at World Bank agencies stated that they are usually left with the "legal facts" as presented by company specialists. A further complicating factor with respect to MIGA appears to have been a comparatively low priority assigned to social issues at that agency.

MIGA's department responsible for social and environmental assessment and monitoring is small. Only two persons – neither of whom is a social specialist – constituted the agency's core in-house review staff when research was conducted. As a result, MIGA regularly relies upon social specialists from IFC for project review (CAO 2002: 9, 14, 16). However, despite this arrangement, MIGA's treatment of social issues has been problematic. A study conducted by the Compliance Advisor Ombudsman (CAO) of MIGA's application of its environmental and social review procedures from 2000 to 2002 noted "major shortcomings" in MIGA's social review of projects (CAO 2002: 14). The study disclosed poor performance in identifying and reporting social issues, in contrast with environmental ones. The interviews I conducted at World Bank agencies in 2000 reinforced the idea that at MIGA there was little regard for social safeguard issues. At MIGA, OD 4.30 was frankly described as a "fundamentally flawed" document, largely inappropriate for the private sector. It is also noteworthy that, before the San Marcos community complaint was sent to the World Bank, no social specialists were assigned to the evaluation teams of MIGA or to the independent engineer responsible for the Antamina project (CAO 2001).

Concluding Remarks: World Bank IR Policy and Development-Induced Displacement

The events presented here lend support to the thesis advanced by Fox and Brown (1998), that the authority of "reformers" (such as concerned social specialists) to implement controversial new practices in institutions such as the World Bank and mining enterprises tends to increase with the presence of effective external pressure and diminish without it.[50] Before local actors in San Marcos succeeded in issuing a complaint directly to MIGA, social specialists appeared to exert a much less rigorous regulatory influence over the behaviour of their organizations than they would afterwards.[51] If Fox and Brown are correct, this would argue against structuring IR policy decision making in a way that privileges expert influence at the expense of effective public participation. Rather, strong and active public participation (backed, for example, by access to independent sources of advice, technical and financial assistance, and the standing to present arguments and negotiate agreements) may prove to be a necessary counterforce to the gravitic pull exerted on IR policy decision making by the business pressures involved in project development. In any event, the CMA case study suggests that the corporate expert-driven decision-making model does not possess clear advantages in accuracy and regulatory effectiveness that would justify denying to project-affected groups the right and the means to defend their own interests.

There is a further danger presented by the particular way in which World Bank IR policy has operationalized the development-induced displacement paradigm. Although the bank's expert-driven model may in a particular case fail to produce effective regulation on the ground (stopping, for example, at half measures), it may nevertheless exert a quite disproportionate legitimation effect, reaching far beyond the local community. Unless aggrieved community members are able to get their message out, the story that is heard outside of the local environment will be that which is conveyed by company reports. From the perspective of Lima, Washington, or Toronto, the details of issues and conflicts in a locality such as San Marcos tend to become indistinct. It is here that the expert reports provided by social specialists can be, perhaps, most valuable, as they outline interlinked processes of community participation, careful identification of displaced persons, and the provision of generous resettlement benefits. Equally, adherence to exacting World Bank policies and review procedures can be advertised as persuasive evidence of social acceptability. Meanwhile, disorganized community protests can be dismissed as the work of a few malcontents.[52]

In conclusion, it can be said that the development-induced displacement paradigm can hold promise for project-affected people to realize some rights to existing livelihoods and development benefits to which they may not otherwise have access. However, the case study suggests that the manner in which the paradigm is operationalized by the World Bank IR policy is seriously flawed and not at all guaranteed to achieve this goal. If the DID paradigm is to offer real solutions to social conflicts arising from project development, the existing IR policy decision-making model should be rejected in favour of an alternative that recognizes not only the economic rights of project-affected people, but also their right to active and effective involvement as parties to the regulatory processes through which these economic rights are given definition.

Acknowledgments
This is a revised version of a 2002 article entitled "Mining, Displacement and the World Bank" originally published in *Journal of Business Ethics* 39 (3): 247-73.

I would like to thank Harry Arthurs, Pablo Bose, Liisa North, D. Jane Pratt, and Peter Vandergeest for their insightful comments on earlier drafts of this work.

Notes

1 "About IFC," http://www.ifc.org/about/. "About MIGA," http://www.miga.org/screens/about/about.htm.

2 For an overview of NGO and World Bank correspondence relating to the consultation process leading to the adoption of OP/BP 4.12, see http://www.ciel.org/Ifi/wbinvolresettle.html.

3 See "Safeguard Policy Review," http://www.ifc.org/cao.

4 OP 4.12 para. 2(b) provides that "resettlement activities should be conceived and executed as sustainable development programs, providing sufficient investment resources to enable the persons displaced by the project to share in the project benefits."

5 OP 4.12 para. 2(c) states that "Displaced persons should be assisted in their efforts to improve their livelihoods and standards of living or at least to restore them."

6 OP 4.12 para. 2(c).

7 OP 4.12 para. 19.

8 OP 4.12 para. 2(a).

9 OD 4.30 does not define the term "displaced persons" and at times uses other phrases such as "adversely affected population." OP 4.12 is more precise with its terminology. Entitlement to assistance under the policy is restricted to "displaced persons" defined as those who suffer "direct economic and social impacts" that arise from the "involuntary taking of land" resulting in relocation or loss of shelter, loss of assets or access to assets, or loss of income sources or means of livelihood, whether or not the affected persons must move to another location. Within the meaning of the policy, persons may also be "displaced" due to adverse livelihood impacts resulting from the loss of access to legally designated parks (OP 4.12 para. 3, note 3). "Involuntary" is defined as "actions that may be taken without the displaced person's informed consent or power of choice" (OP 4.12 note 7).

10 OP 4.12 paras. 2, 3.

11 Unlike OD 4.30, OP 4.12 makes a distinction between holders of legal title and those with informal livelihood interests in land. Those with rights recognized by the state (or with a claim to such rights) are entitled to compensation for the land they lose and to other resettlement assistance. Those without state-recognized rights, who nevertheless count as "displaced people" due to their livelihood reliance upon the lands taken, are not entitled to compensation for land. Instead, they are provided with "resettlement assistance" and "other assistance, as necessary, to achieve the objectives set out in this policy" (OP 4.12 para. 16). However, restricting land compensation to holders of legal title does not affect the responsibility under the policy to ensure livelihood restoration and improvement for all displaced persons. Therefore, in theory, the distinction need not result in significant

differences in compensation between title holders and other displaced persons. The policy provides that "resettlement assistance may consist of land, other assets, cash, employment, and so on, as appropriate" (OP 4.12 note 20). It remains to be seen how the distinction is managed in practice.

12 OP 4.12 paras. 6, 13.

13 OP 4.12 para. 2(a).

14 OP 4.12 paras. 6, 11, 12, 13(b).

15 OP 4.12 specifies that land-based resettlement strategies should be preferred for both indigenous peoples with traditional land-based modes of production and for displaced persons whose livelihoods are land-based (OP 4.12 paras. 9, 11). Non-land-based options (involving both cash and employment or self-employment opportunities) may be considered where they are the preferred option of displaced persons, where provision of land would affect the sustainability of a park or protected area or where sufficient land is not available at a reasonable price (the lack of such land must be demonstrated to the bank's satisfaction) (para. 11). Paragraph 12 provides that cash compensation for lost assets may be appropriate where either livelihoods are not land-based, where active markets for land, housing, and labour exist, or where land taken for the project is a small fraction of the affected asset and the residual is economically viable.

16 OP 4.12 para. 2(c).

17 OP 4.12 para. 8 lists among potential vulnerable groups "those below the poverty line, the landless, the elderly, women and children, indigenous peoples, ethnic minorities, or other displaced persons who may not be protected through national land compensation legislation."

18 OP 4.12 paras. 6(a), 9, 13(a).

19 Depending on which agency is involved in the project's financing.

20 OP 4.12 para. 6(a)(i) does require that "measures" be taken to ensure that "displaced persons" are "informed about their options and rights pertaining to resettlement." This is an improvement. However, the case study presented here suggests that these provisions must be much more specific (at a minimum) if the intent is to mandate effective participatory rights that provide affected people with the information, standing, and capacity to play an active role in the decision-making process. What constitute appropriate "measures" is precisely the issue.

21 BP 4.12 para. 2.

22 OP 4.12 para. 32(b) provides that the bank may "at a borrower's request" supply "financing of technical assistance to strengthen the capacities of agencies responsible for resettlement or of affected people to participate more effectively in resettlement operations."

23 These are rights-bearing entities, including persons and corporations.

24 When OD 4.30 was drafted, the term "participation" was deliberately chosen in preference to the weaker alternative of "consultation" (D. Jane Pratt, personal communication 2001). This represented a victory for advocates of the social perspective within the World Bank, but, as the following discussion illustrates, the issue soon became one of defining what participation means in practice.

25 OP 4.12 paras. 19, 32; BP 4.12 para. 2.

26 The quotes, characterizations of "disciplinary chauvinist" attitudes, are from R.J. Burdge and P. Opreyszek (1994: 170) and R.J. Burdge and F. Vanclay (1996: 69), respectively. These studies, as well as A. Chase (1990) on the perspectives of engineers, are generally useful.

27 K. Finsterbusch (1995) states the case for the autonomy and institutionalized recognition of the field developed by social assessment practitioners. His argument differs chiefly from those of critical or reformist practitioners not in its substance but in its emphasis: after all, the cup that is criticized for being half empty is also half full. Finsterbusch stresses the profession's achievements, particularly in developing common methodologies and in obtaining recognition for the value of its work. Of course, he has to qualify these claims. Of the six methodological steps he identifies as "necessary for a *minimal but adequate* SIA [social impact assessment]," he points out that two are either mostly not done or "often neglected and shortchanged" (emphasis added; ibid.: 247, 242). Although he argues that "the field has matured and earned sufficient legitimacy to become a standard intellectual

tool for decision making," he also notes that "its acceptance, however, is still incomplete. SIA is opposed by some economists and engineers who are not convinced that its benefits will be greater than its costs" (ibid.: 243). His discussion also alludes to other problems faced by the profession with references to "the typical social impact assessor who is in the midst of an underbudgeted SIA" (ibid.: 244). As a principled practitioner, Finsterbusch holds that more needs to be done in the way of professional oversight and control. He advocates a deepened professionalization of SIA, arguing for a decision-making model that features external review of SIA work by outside experts and a greater reliance on professional standards and judgment in preference to rigid written requirements. He also stresses that it is "the obligation of the SIA community" to assert itself further in order to police the frontiers of its field of practice and "to use political and bureaucratic influence to attain the adoption of professional standards so that fraudulent SIAs are more difficult to get away with" (ibid.: 246).

28 There are also indications of development of a professional specialization in resettlement issues. Although much of this development has taken place within the World Bank, the International Network on Displacement and Resettlement (INDR) "provides a virtual, global communications network of scholars, practitioners, and policy makers attempting to prevent development-induced impoverishment" (INDR website, http://www.displacement.net, accessed 9 August 2002).

29 The bank's "culture of approval" rewards managers who get the most loans "out the door." Painstaking application of onerous social requirements tends to stand in the way of a manager's personal advancement (Gopinath 1996; Fox 1998: 320).

30 Whites of Spanish descent.

31 As a result of low prices, low productivity, and high transportation costs, it is common for Andean peasants to be priced out of regional and national markets. Many peasant informants in San Marcos reported that they produced for subsistence rather than sale because prices were below production and transportation costs.

32 It is also argued that production is distributed across various zones in order to manage the risk of disaster. Better a small and secure income than a larger one that is more prone to unacceptable risks. See Adolfo Figueroa (1989).

33 The animals kept in these high-altitude pastures play an integral role in Andean livelihoods. They are a source of important goods (chiefly meat and wool) used for consumption, barter, sale, and artisanal production. They also serve as a vital source of cash (typically very scarce in Andean peasant economies – Mayer and Glave 1999). The market for meat and animals ensures that money can be stored in animals until it is needed for immediate costs such as medicine or a child's education (Orlove 1977; Ríos Ocsa 1992).

34 *Ley General de Comunidades Campesinas* No. 24656 (enacted 13 April 1987).

35 The ownership of CMA has gone through a number of changes since the project's inception. The company was initially formed in 1996 when two Canadian mining firms, Rio Algom and Inmet, won a privatization bid to develop the Antamina mine. For financial reasons, Inmet dropped out of the project before it received government approval in 1998. Rio Algom was joined at that time by two other Canadian companies, Noranda Inc. and Teck Corporation. Subsequently, a Japanese company, Mitsubishi, joined with a 10 percent interest while project financing was being arranged. In 2000, Noranda made a takeover bid for Rio Algom, which failed when the latter arranged to be acquired by UK mining firm Billiton. In 2001, Billiton merged with the Australian mining giant BHP; subsequently, Teck merged with Cominco, another Canadian firm. Thus, at the time of writing, CMA was owned by BHP-Billiton (33.75 percent), Noranda Inc. (33.75 percent), Teck Cominco (22.5 percent), and Mitsubishi (10 percent) (see Antamina's website: http://www.antamina.com/01_antamina/En_empresa.html).

36 US$1.32 billion of which is debt.

37 For a fuller account, see D. Szablowski (2004).

38 Unfortunately, restrictions of space do not permit a full discussion of the requirements imposed on the Antamina project by Peru's environmental assessment regime. Very briefly, this regime required CMA to submit a comprehensive technical evaluation called an environmental impact study (EIS) of the project's likely environmental and social impacts.

The EIS must also set out proposed measures for mitigating the impacts identified. Government approval of this lengthy and highly technical document is required before a large mining project will be allowed to proceed (see, generally, *Código del Medio Ambiente y los Recursos Naturales* D.L. No. 613 and D.S. No. 016-93-EM as modified by D.S. No. 059-93-EM). This regime has serious deficiencies, including weak participatory measures and limited monitoring and enforcement capacity (see Pulgar-Vidal 2000 for a detailed commentary). In addition, the task of evaluating and approving the EISs of mining projects has been controversially delegated to the Ministry of Energy and Mines rather than to the Ministry of the Environment (*Ley Marco para el Crecimiento de la Inversión Privada,* D.L. No. 757, art. 51). The social chapter of the Antamina project's EIS represents a very superficial treatment of the relevant issues and fails to provide an effective baseline from which to assess local impacts. The chief social commitments made to secure environmental approval from Peru's Ministry of Energy and Mines were compliance with World Bank IR policy and investment of a total of US$6.2 million in local development projects in San Marcos and other areas over a period of three years (Klohn Crippen Consultants 1998).

39 CMA offered US$400 per hectare of pastureland and US$1,000 per hectare of cropland. At the time, this was significantly higher than both the level of compensation set by the Ministry of Agriculture and compensation paid for highland pastures by other mining companies. No real market for highland pastures existed in San Marcos. Very few exchanges had taken place, in recent decades, that were not inheritances (Pasco-Font et al. 2001).

40 Article 7, *Ley de Tierras* No. 26505 (enacted 17 July 1995) as modified by law No. 26570 (enacted 4 January 1996).

41 During my interviews, CMA representatives reported that the cash-based program was adopted when peasants refused to agree to vacate lands in exchange for the company's promise to provide replacement lands in the future.

42 Some sixty-eight families, identified as "permanent residents" of the purchased lands, were each offered sums up to US$33,000 in order to leave forthwith. In contrast, some two hundred owners sold land to CMA, the majority of whom received less than US$8,000 apiece (GRADE 2000: 11, Anexo 2).

43 My interviews with development NGOs that were negotiating with the company to be contracted for the expected development programs reveal that, during this period, CMA's development plans in San Marcos were suspended.

44 These bodies are intended to coordinate with CMA staff concerning local environmental and development issues.

45 Individual landowners with written promises of resettlement were paid US$5,000 apiece in settlement of their claims. Those who had not bargained for commitments in writing were not provided with this compensation by CMA.

46 It should be noted, however, that despite the company's efforts since 2000, trust has been notoriously difficult for the company to rebuild in San Marcos, and strong local suspicion has continued to problematize CMA's engagement with communities.

47 In keeping with the economistic perspective of World Bank IR policy, this list does not attempt to include spiritual, cultural, or "way of life" interests provided by the acquired lands.

48 The determination of who was a "permanent resident" was very poorly realized by the company. Community relations staff failed to take into account the seasonal pattern of residency in the highlands, particularly in circumstances where extended-family members would tend one another's herds on a rotative basis. Where three related households rotated these duties between them for four months at a time, all too often, CMA identified only one of them (or none of them) as permanently resident and thus entitled to resettlement compensation.

49 A key problem in this respect is the lack of an effective baseline study of the population economically dependent on the highlands. The baseline information prepared in CMA's EIS and resettlement plans is inadequate for this purpose (Klohn Crippen Consultants 1998; GRADE 2000). The failure to gather and maintain such data is in itself a serious breach of World Bank IR policy (OD 4.30 para. 11).

50 A number of social specialists whom I interviewed at World Bank agencies agreed that outside pressure on community or social issues increased their authority within their institutions.

51 It is worth noting that the risk of CMA's non-compliance with MIGA environmental policies or guidelines carried significant perils for both CMA and MIGA. For MIGA, non-compliance threatened a potential scandal akin to those that rocked both the IBRD and IFC in the 1990s (see Fox and Brown 1998; Friends of the Earth 2000). For CMA, the issue of non-compliance presented the risk of serious problems with its financial consortium. Potential non-compliance would have to be reported to the project's lenders and guarantors. Furthermore, non-compliance, if not corrected within a period set forth in MIGA's contract of guarantee, would entitle the agency to cancel its contract, thereby withdrawing its coverage – a risk unlikely to be appreciated by the project's financial stakeholders (*MIGA Environmental and Social Review Procedures,* para. 44; MIGA 2001).

52 The legitimation effect of the IR policy's legal regime may also help to distance project-affected groups from the allies they may need most: national and transnational advocacy networks. NGOs and advocacy campaigns thrive on simple paradigmatic stories of dramatic black-and-white struggles. Where stories are more complex, ambiguous, and difficult to access, linkages between local actors and national and transnational NGOs (or the media) can be much more difficult to create (Li 2000: 171).

References

Alberti, G., and E. Mayer. 1974. *Reciprocidad e Intercambio en los Andes Peruanos*. Lima: Instituto de Estudios Peruanos.

Antamina. http://www.antamina.com/01_antamina/En_empresa.html (accessed 12 February 2006).

Bourdieu, P. 1987. "The Force of Law: Toward a Sociology of the Juridical Field." *Hastings Law Journal* 38: 805-53.

Burdge R.J., and P. Opreyszek. 1994. "On Mixing Apples and Oranges: The Sociologist Does Impact Assessment with Biologists and Economists." In R.J. Burdge, ed., *A Conceptual Approach to Social Impact Assessment,* 167-74. Middleton, WI: Social Ecology Press.

Burdge R.J., and F. Vanclay. 1996. "Social Impact Assessment: A Contribution to the State of the Art Series." *Impact Assessment* 14: 59-86.

CAO. 2000. *Operational Guidelines*. Washington, DC: IFC/MIGA. http://www.cao-ombudsman.org/.

–. 2001. *Preliminary Audit Review of MIGA in Relation to Compania Minera Antamina S.A. – Public Report.* Washington, DC: IFC/MIGA. http://www.cao-ombudsman.org/.

–. 2002. *Insuring Responsible Investments? A Review of the Application of MIGA's Environmental and Social Review Procedures*. Washington, DC: Compliance Advisor Ombudsman. http://www.cao-ombudsman.org/.

Carter, A.S. 1998. *Community Participation as an Indicator of Social Performance at International Mining Projects*. MERN Working Paper No. 131. Bath: MERN.

Cernea, M.M., ed. 1988. *Involuntary Resettlement in Development Projects*. World Bank Technical Paper No. 80. Washington, DC: World Bank.

–. 1997. "The Risks and Reconstruction Model for Resettling Displaced Populations." *World Development* 25 (10): 1569-87.

–. 1999. *The Economics of Involuntary Resettlement.* Washington, DC: World Bank.

Cernea M.M., and C. McDowell, eds. 2000. *Risks and Reconstruction: Experiences of Resettlers and Refugees*. Washington, DC: World Bank.

Chase, A. 1990. "Anthropology and Impact Assessment: Development Pressures and Indigenous Interests in Australia." *Environmental Impact Assessment Review* 10: 11-23.

Cooper, L.M., and J.A. Elliot. 2000. "Public Participation and Social Acceptability in the Philippine EIA Process." *Journal of Environmental Assessment Policy and Management* 2 (3): 339-67.

CooperAcción. 2000. *Minería y Comunidades. Testimonios orales y gráficos*. Lima: CooperAcción.

Davis, S.H., and L.T. Soeftestad. 1995. *Participation and Indigenous Peoples*. World Bank Environment Department Paper No. 021. Washington, DC: World Bank.

Diez, Alejandro. 1999. "Diversidades, alternativas y ambigüedades: Instituciones, comportamientos y mentalidades en la sociedad rural." In V. Ágreda, A. Diez, and M. Glave, eds., *Perú: El problema agrario en debate,* 247-326. Lima: SEPIA.

Durst, D. 1994. "'Heavy Sledding': Barriers to Community Participation in Beaufort Sea Hydrocarbon Developments." *Community Development Journal* 29 (1): 62-74.

Fearnside, P.M. 1994. "The Canadian Feasibility Study of the Three Gorges Dam Proposed for China's Yangzi River: A Grave Embarrassment to the Impact Assessment Profession." *Impact Assessment* 12: 21-57.

Feeney, P. 1998. *Accountable Aid: Local Participation in Major Projects.* London: Oxfam.

Figueroa, Adolfo. 1989. *La Economia Campesina de la Sierra del Perú.* Lima: Pontificia Universidad Catolica del Perú.

Finsterbusch, K. 1995. "In Praise of SIA – A Personal Review of the Field of Social Impact Assessment: Feasibility, Justification, History, Methods, Issues." *Impact Assessment* 13: 229-52.

Fox, J.A. 1998. "When Does Reform Policy Influence Practice? Lessons from the Bankwide Resettlement Review." In J.A. Fox and L.D. Brown, eds., *The Struggle for Accountability: The World Bank, NGOs and Grassroots Movements,* 303-44. Cambridge, MA: MIT Press.

Fox, J.A., and L.D. Brown, eds. 1998. *The Struggle for Accountability, the World Bank, NGOs and Grassroots Movements.* Cambridge, MA: MIT Press.

Francis, P., and S. Jacobs. 1999. "Institutionalizing Social Analysis at the World Bank." *Environmental Impact Assessment Review* 19: 341-57.

Friends of the Earth. 2000. *Dubious Development: How the World Bank's Private Arm Is Failing the Poor and the Environment.* Washington, DC: Friends of the Earth.

Gopinath, D. 1996. "The Greening of the World Bank." *Infrastructure Finance,* September.

GRADE. 2000. *Evaluación del Proceso de Reubicación y del Programa de Post-Reubicación en Antamina.* Lima: GRADE.

IAIA. 2002. *International Association for Impact Assessment.* http://www.iaia.org/.

Ian Thompson Consulting. 1999. *Review and Assessment of the Resettlement Program, Community Development Plan and Community Relations Program of Compania Minera Antamina.* Vancouver, BC: Ian Thompson Consulting.

ICGP (Interorganizational Committee on Guidelines and Principles for Social Impact Assessment). 1995. "Guidelines and Principles for Social Impact Assessment." *Environmental Impact Assessment Review* 15: 11-43.

IFC Environment Division. 1998. *Doing Better Business through Effective Public Consultation and Disclosure.* Washington, DC: International Finance Corporation.

Joyce, S., and M. MacFarlane. 2001. *Social Impact Assessment in the Mining Industry: Current Situation and Future Directions.* MMSD Background document. London: IIED.

Klohn Crippen Consultants. 1998. *Environmental Impact Statement: Compañía Minera Antamina.* Lima: CMA.

Li, Tania M. 2000. "Articulating Indigenous Identity in Indonesia: Resource Politics and the Tribal Slot." *Comparative Studies in Society and History* 42 (1): 149-79.

Lohmann, L. 1998. *Same Platform, Different Train: The Politics of Participation.* http://www.icaap.org/inicode?400.4.

McDowell, Christopher, ed. 1996. *Understanding Impoverishment. The Consequences of Development-Induced Displacement.* Oxford: Berghahn Books.

Mallon, F.E. 1983. *The Defense of Community in Peru's Central Highlands: Peasant Struggle and Capitalist Transition, 1860-1940.* Princeton, NJ: Princeton University Press.

Mayer, E., and M. Glave. 1999. "Alguito para ganar (a little something to earn): Profits and Losses in Peasant Economies." *American Ethnologist* 26 (2): 344-69.

MIGA. 2001. *Standard Contract of Guarantee.* Washington, DC: MIGA.

Orlove, B. 1977. *Alpacas, Sheep, and Men: The Wool Export Economy and Regional Society in Southern Peru.* New York: Academic Press.

Paerregaard, K. 1998. "The Dark Side of the Moon. Conceptual and Methodological Problems in Studying Rural and Urban Worlds in Peru." *American Anthropologist* 100 (2): 397-408.

Pasco-Font, A., A. Diez, G. Damonte, R. Fort, and G. Salas. 2001. "Aprendiendo Mientras se Trabaja." In G. McMahon and F. Remy, eds., *Grandes Minas y la Comunidad,* 145-201. Washington, DC, and Ottawa: World Bank and IDRC.

Piñedo, Danny. 2000. "Manejo comunal de pastos, equidad y sostenabilidad en una comunidad de la cordillera Huayhuash." In I. Hurtado, C. Trivelli, and A. Brack, eds., *Perú: El Problema Agrario en Debate. SEPIA VIII*, 277-326. Lima: SEPIA.

Pulgar-Vidal, Manuel. 2000. *La evaluación del impacto ambiental en el Perú.* Lima: Sociedad Peruana de Derecho Ambiental.

Ríos Ocsa, Benicio. 1992. *Ganadería y Economía Campesina.* Cusco: Centro de Estudios Regionales Andinos Bartolomé de las Casas.

Rose, C.M. 1994. *Property and Persuasion.* Boulder: Westview Press.

Szablowski, D. 2004. "Legitimacy and Regulation in the Global Economy: Legal Mediation of Conflicts between Communities and Transnational Mining Companies." PhD diss., Osgoode Hall Law School, York University.

Watkins, M. 1999. "Private Insurers Come Out." *Project Finance* 197 (September): 19-21.

Wilson, Sir R. 2000. "The Global Mining Initiative." *ICME Newsletter* 8 (3): 3-4.

World Bank. 1996. *Resettlement and Development: The Bankwide Review of Projects Involving Involuntary Resettlement, 1986-1993.* Environment Department Paper No. 032. Washington, DC: World Bank.

2
Gendered Implications: Development-Induced Displacement in Sudan

Amani El Jack

> The women make the homes, the men make the wars. The whole of Africa, that's one big gender fight, man. Only the women do God's work around here.
>
> – John le Carré, *The Constant Gardener*

The lines of causality in the relationships between violent conflict and development have not been altogether clear. If determining whether violence and conflict are the sources or the consequences of development has been difficult, then, until quite recently, their relationship to gender has at best been blurred and at worst hidden. In fact, the almost complete silence concerning issues of gender and their nature as constants is a lamentable feature of many discussions of development-induced displacement (DID), the process of forcing or inducing communities to evacuate land needed for development projects. Indeed, we could go further and suggest that the invisibility of women in discussions about development and displacement is one of the symptomatic problems in current ways of looking at both DID and the attempts to mitigate it. Under certain prescribed conditions and procedures, mainstream DID discourse seeks to minimize the costs of displacement and encourages foreign investment in infrastructural projects as producing benefits that accrue from development.

Focusing primarily on the oil/energy sector in Sudan, I will contest the conceptual frameworks of development-induced displacement, arguing that gender-insensitive practices have had a negative impact on groups that have been marginalized because of gender, race, class, age, ethnicity, language, religion, and other identities. However, Sudanese women, who are already subordinated by the structural inequalities of male-dominated Sudanese society, tend to be very adversely affected by DID. These policies are particularly constraining and disadvantageous to Dinka, Nuer, and other groups of Sudanese women in the south and in the Nuba Mountains. Facing distinct disadvantages within their households and communities, increasing numbers of these women have become internally displaced within Sudan; others have fled to the Horn of Africa, particularly to Kenya and Uganda. With specific emphasis on the implications for Sudanese women, and with the important proviso that DID policies do not affect all women in the same way, this chapter attempts to engender the analysis of DID in the context of war and conflict. Specifically, it looks at the example of displaced southern Sudanese women refugees in Kenya and Uganda and closely studies the personal narratives of the displaced women, men, and children.

Between July and October 2001, I conducted interviews with forty-five Sudanese women, men, and children in Kenya and Uganda. Residing in various refugee camps, as well as in cities such as Nairobi and Kampala, the interviewees classified themselves as refugees or displacees.[1] They came from a range of socio-economic and ethnic backgrounds, but all lived close to or below the poverty line. Yet, as we shall see, both because of and despite their experience of DID, the women showed the need for a reappraisal of humanitarianism in general and the extant modelling of DID in particular. All were violently displaced from the expansion oilfield territories in southern Sudan under the brutal authoritarian supervision of the Sudanese Islamist state.[2] The contestation over this region and its resources lies at the centre of the twenty-year-old civil war in Sudan.

Because they are typically identified as refugees from a war-torn society, such displacees would not ordinarily be viewed as refugees from development; to be sure, at first glance the prolonged and vicious civil war in Sudan does not seem an obvious subject for a discussion of the engendering of DID. Rather, Africa's longest-running and sustained post-colonial conflict appears as a characteristic case of conflict-induced displacement. Home to the highest number of internally displaced people (IDPs) in the world, Sudan has approximately 4.5 million IDPs, 1.5 million of whom are in the southern sectors (Idahosa 2002). The degree of insecurity and the scale of population displacements[3] have been major obstacles to humanitarian relief efforts and have devastated most of the indigenous trading and production systems. An estimated two million people, or nearly 8 percent of the country's population, died from the consequences of fighting, which included widespread disease and famine, 3 percent alone between 1983 and 1998. By one estimate, displacees accounted for as much as 85 percent of Sudan's southern population (ibid.). Predictably, hundreds of thousands of Sudanese from all parts of the country, including the interviewees in this study, were forced to migrate and/or become refugees to countries of immediate proximity or beyond. Given this, Sudan would appear to be more suitable for an analysis of its many moral and practical issues, typical as they are of zones of conflict necessitating political and humanitarian intervention, than for normative questions regarding gender and development.

Standpoints, Invisibilities, and Male Biases

Methodologically, this work begins by adopting the "standpoint" (Harding 1987: 7-8) of those who are "excluded" or marginalized; it does so in the belief that, because they are unlikely to have a stake in maintaining the social reality from which they come, their perspectives can lead us to a stronger[4] understanding of it (Harding 1993: 9-10). My participatory research disposition, moreover, situated me in a dialectic between myself and the research subjects, and permitted me to pose some questions that deconstructed certain undifferentiated gender, class, and racial assumptions about displaced women and their responses to their predicament. As a result, I have countered some common-sense assumptions and stereotypes concerning women in circumstances of both conflict and displacement. Furthermore, this research identified my own intersecting identities, those of a privileged Muslim and Arabic-speaking woman from northern Sudan, which have influenced the research project and shaped its analysis and results. I have had to confront that, by birthright, I have benefited from being part of a dominant, oppressive system that has violated women's *and* men's basic rights in different regions of Sudan.

Central to this project is "making the invisible visible, bringing the margin to the centre, rendering the trivial important, putting the spotlight on women as competent actors, understanding women as subjects in their own right rather than objects for men" (Reinharz 1992: 248). If women's experiences have been judged as salient only to the extent that they relate to those of men, then one needs to pose questions that relate specifically to women's experiences. This does not exclude their relationship to men. Quite the contrary, since in order to reveal how differences and boundaries are constructed, we must create appropriate cultural understandings of DID processes by relocating them within a relational understanding (see Mohanty and Torres 1991) that identifies their often mutually reinforcing and dependent links to each other. This, as we shall see, is true not only at the local level but also at the global level, where the fact of displacement is tied to global processes, and also where global discourse approaches to displacement's discontents are inappropriately phrased in masculinist terms.

Invisibility here refers to the lack of recognition of women within the processes of social reproduction in livelihoods lost due to war but induced by oil development projects. One use of this term, of course, derives from the work of feminist scholars who employed it to identify the many ways in which the rewards of women's labour remain unrecognized, and how their efforts invested in the production of commodities, based on the cost of production, go unrewarded. In the distribution of the proceeds, women remain invisible because their labour is essentially unrecognized. Clearly, invisibility is about both the lack of recognition *and* its distributional effects, but as we shall see, it is about more than that.

Tacit within the preceding discussion is the notion that *male bias* is fundamental to women's experience of development (Elson 1995: 1-8). Through differential rights and resources, men are systematically privileged over women in the development process and are favoured through entrenched prejudices and discrimination both at the "conscious level" and through "unconscious perceptions" (ibid.: 7). It is within and through institutions, practices, and policies, and in the application and use of neutralizing theoretical categories such as the "household" that bias is effectively normalized, thus rendering gender relations, and the conflicts within them, invisible. So much so, in fact, that women's work relations between production and reproduction within the household, and contestation over the unrecognized kinds of work, such as childrearing, also limit women's capacity to seek alternative forms of productive activity and to negotiate different spaces within the family. However, such an analysis points not only to structures of subordination but also to agency, and to the appropriate resources and institutions required to transform or at least mitigate this bias. The remediation offered by DID cannot do that. Yet those who have charged themselves with depicting DID as a process (McDowell 1996) and/or with mitigating its consequences (Cernea 2000; McDowell 1996) do so in ways that exactly describe what has taken place in Sudan, even if it does not appear to be derived *directly* from development projects. If, as Michael Cernea (2000) claims, displacement is multi-dimensional, then, in Sudan, all of the particular pieces connected with it are acutely omnipresent: landlessness, joblessness, homelessness, marginalization, food insecurity, increased morbidity, loss of access to common property resources, and community disarticulation. As this last category implies, socio-economic consequences cannot be the only yardstick with which to measure the effects of war and displacement. There is also the inflicting of significant socio-cultural costs, the devastation of complex systems of social integration involving participation in networks of relations and kinship ties as well as the reciprocity embedded within complex trading and welfare systems within and across ethnic groups. In short, the long-drawn-out conflict has exacted an extraordinarily high toll. These circumstances of acute change and human suffering, and the psychological and social damage that occurs when people lose their sense of place due to displacement, require, beyond the usual infrastructure of humanitarian efforts and relief, a sensitivity to the specificity of people's needs and cultural and social values, including, and most especially, those of women.

Although detailing the many humanitarian and political relationships embedded within the Sudanese conflict is beyond the scope of this chapter (see Ramsbotham and Tom 1996), some central questions need to be asked and some entanglements need to be sorted out. What is the context in which forced displacement occurs? What is the relationship between development and displacement in circumstances of sustained, violent civil conflict and war, and what are the specific ways in which development projects stimulate violence in oilfield territories?[5] How do national and global processes affect local conditions leading to the forcible uprooting of communities? More specifically, how are the burdens of these effects placed upon displaced communities and women in particular, and how is the experience of displacement assessed differently by women, men, and children? Moreover, how do Sudanese women challenge narratives of victimization and assert their own agency in resolving conflict and displacement? To answer these questions, we must first briefly set out the approach that informs this chapter. I seek to provide a framework for analyzing and critiquing DID through combining the three overlapping feminist perspectives of standpoint, invisibility, and male bias, and by drawing together the two sets of literatures on the forced migration of women in conflict zones and gender and development.

What does DID scholarship specifically have to tell us about these? Unfortunately, the evident limitation of the DID literature (Drydyk 2000; Cernea 2000; Cragg 1999; McDowell 1996; and Parasuraman 1999) lies precisely in its lack of an integrative gender analysis. The acknowledgment that women's economic needs differ from men's and that, consequently, women's needs require further attention counters much established (neo)liberal development policy and economic theory. Development theorists typically view the household as a place of homogeneous interests in which resources are shared equally by women and men (Cernea 2000; McDowell 1996). However, women face distinct disadvantages within their households and in their communities because, globally, they have less access to power, resources, and decision-making processes than do men.

The rare instances in which gender is actually taken into account typically describe women's "traditional" roles within the family rather than addressing the gendered relationship of power embedded in the social construction of production and reproduction. When we examine DID in the context of gender, however, it is important to articulate gender as a social construct, rather than simply giving an account of women's prescribed social function. Gender is based not in biology but in social and cultural expectations defining the behaviour and attitudes of women and men (El-Bushra 2000; Kabeer 1994). As well as setting gender-aware contexts within the study of DID, we should, at the same time, ensure that gender does not exclude a consideration of race, class, ethnicity, religion, culture, and nationality. Gender should, therefore, be part of a shifting, open-ended framework that takes into account the fact that women, men, and children experience displacement and subsequent impoverishment differently. This framework should avoid "vulnerable group" and "victim" characterizations, thus allowing women and men to exercise their agency in challenging gendered relationships of power (El Jack 2003: 6-7).

"Development" projects that involve displacement are often justified because they will provide important benefits to the larger community if they are carefully planned, executed, and managed (Cernea 2000: 28). Development projects such as dams, infrastructure construction, irrigation, and oil and mining concerns, "even if carried out adequately," cause the dismantling of societies, kinship systems, and local culture, and result in certain trade-offs and conflicts (Cernea 1996; McDowell 1996; Muggah 2000; Parasuraman 1999). Although some development-induced displacement projects can and should be avoided, others cannot. Cernea argues that, in these cases, developing societies must balance benefits such as safe water supplies, irrigation projects, efficient transportation systems, and oil and mining development with the cost of forced displacement and resettlement. However, Cernea (1996: 28) also believes that such a balance has not been achieved: "Long-term national or regional interests served by these programs often cut across the interests of smaller groups, local communities or some individuals. National interests and needs usually prevail. Conflicts emerge because the gains expected from these projects in the long term impose hard-to-bear losses in the short-term. As one resettler in India summarized it, 'For their tomorrow we are giving up our today'"(ibid.).

Not just "today" but tomorrow also for many groups of people, usually the most vulnerable. The loss of home distinctly and harshly impacts women since the home is where many women live out their lives and carry out their gendered responsibilities. That being said, it is important to emphasize that displacement does not affect all women in the same way and that women's experiences vary depending on race, ethnicity, sexual orientation, class, religion, and language. Disadvantaged groups of women face distinct disadvantages within their households and communities. During the process of displacement, these groups face unique problems within their communities and households due to the disintegration of communities and kinship and support systems. The added responsibilities that women have in terms of productive, reproductive, and community work are often transferred to daughters and other younger women within the family. These young women must assume more responsibilities, such as the burden of domestic work as well as caring for children, the elderly, and the sick. As my fieldwork revealed, this shifting of responsibility has both a short-term and a long-term impact on the welfare and future of female household members.

Evidence from a number of countries shows that, in comparison with women, men of non-dominant groups are more adversely affected by displacement because they have lost the socio-economic and political roles of breadwinners, decision makers, and protectors of their families. The significant shift in men's socially constructed roles marginalizes them, leading to depression, alcoholism, and an escalation of violence against women in public and private spheres (El-Bushra 2000: 6).

Ultimately, women and men who are most severely impacted by DID do not have a say in the decision-making process concerning such projects. This is due to lack of negotiation with those who are being displaced. Peter Penz (1999: 4) argues that people's perception of the "harm" imposed upon them by development-induced displacement should be integral to the normative evaluation of development goals. Normative approaches would, consequently, emphasize the importance of consultation, free negotiation, and ongoing public participation in the management of development projects. However, the question of how to enforce such normative evaluations remains unanswered. Many countries in which development-induced displacement is implemented lack the mechanisms that would ensure appropriate, fair assessment of displacement conditions, intervention on behalf of the displaced, and the involvement of women and men in political decision making and the planning of DID projects. Although some programs of DID are governed by national and international guidelines, displacement occurring in zones of conflict and under authoritarian regimes tends not to be strictly monitored and has therefore led to mass impoverishment and human rights violations.

Impoverishment as a consequence of DID impacts the most vulnerable. Development theorists have proposed an impoverishment risks and reconstruction (IRR) model as a conceptual construct that claims to predict and reverse the impoverishment process resulting from various forms of forced displacement and resettlement (Cernea 1996: 22-23). However, the IRR model is gender-blind: that is, it does not address how gendered relations of power affect women and men differently because women in many parts of the world do not have equal access to land, credit, employment, and education, and are especially vulnerable to food insecurity and death in childbirth.

If, on the whole, DID targets the most vulnerable, most marginalized, and least powerful groups in Sudan, the oilfield project itself targets ethnic minorities living in the south and the Nuba Mountains. In this case, the displaced have been left out of negotiations involving the planning and execution of projects that will disempower them by destroying their communities.

The Roots of Displacement: Oil and "Development" in Sudan

Oil and its exploitation continue to be, and will remain, central to understanding the conflict, its satisfactory resolution, and the future of Sudan in general. Oil was a major basis for the war, and for displacement and development. Often somewhat hidden from the consciousness of the world, the Sudanese conflict occasionally bursts onto the global media stage and is often cast, somewhat simplistically, as a struggle between the oppressing "Arab," Muslim north and the Christian, "animist," black African south.[6] I will further address this below; suffice it to say for now that not only do these religio-cultural portrayals often elide complex histories and ignore local political-cultural constructions about nation, identity, space, and resources, but they also remain fundamentally masculinist, hiding complex gender relationships and exclusions. If simple depictions inform misunderstandings of the complexity of the conflict, what remains unquestionable, however, is the fact of a historically inegalitarian, oppressive state, the origins of which go back to pre-colonial times, even prior to the late-nineteenth-century Madhist regime that sought, inclusive of slavery, to impose itself upon non-Muslim populations. From paternalist colonial times[7] to the present, uneven development and a political economy of maldistributed resources have continued to intertwine with the religio-cultural patterns of oppression, inequality, and mistrust. It is important to articulate that DID cannot be studied in isolation from the armed conflict in Sudan. This conflict has shifted from what has been described by historians as a "war of visions" over contested identities – northern/southern, Muslims/Christians, Arabs/Africans (Deng 1995) – to what is now, I contend, a resource-driven war. Oil exploration and development is indeed central to any understanding of the armed conflict. This is not to say that the ethnographical and anthropological construction of competing identities in Sudan is no longer important. Indeed, historical constructions have empowered one particular group (Arabs/Muslims/men in the north) while marginalizing others (Africans/Christians/women in the south). In fact the gendered and racialized construction of the southern Sudanese as "black," "cannibalistic," "heathen," and "primitive" (Seligman 1932) is significant because it reflects how Dinka and Nuer have been perceived as less than human and, therefore, exploitable. It is in this context, I believe, that southerners who reside on land rich in resources are not considered as humans when development occurs on it. This dehumanization is used to legitimize violence against southerners and the militarized practices of oil-induced displacement.

Conflict came quickly to Sudan, even just prior to, and not long after, independence in 1956, the subsequent military coup in 1958, and the succeeding southern violence in 1963.[8] Since the late 1970s, skewed resource allocation has compounded the conflict and further fuelled the war through the discovery, expansion, and exploitation of southern oil by a partnering of the Sudanese Islamist state with transnational oil companies, first with Chevron until 1983 and, more recently, with a consortium of oil companies.

In Sudan, oil and control of the rich oil territories in the south have been central to the "civil war" between the north and the south that has been waged on and off since 1955 (Kebbede 1999: 44; Madut 1999: 429). War was caused by inequitable development in the south, the cheap productive and reproductive labour of southerners, and competition over the control of economic resources, mainly oil. Disputes over oil, moreover, were the main cause of the resumption of the war in 1984. Since that time, those disputes have resulted in the displacement of communities, communities that have not received compensation or been given the opportunity for resettlement negotiations in areas earmarked for oil pipelines running from the oilfield in the south to oil refineries in northern and eastern Sudan (Amnesty International 2000: 1).

The main on-stream oil concessions in Sudan are administered by the Greater Nile Petroleum Operating Company (GNPOC), a Sudanese parastatal, which, in partnership with various multinational corporations,[9] develops oil deposits in Heglig, a region south of Kordofan, as well as in the Unity State, a region around the Western Upper Nile. These corporations included the China National Petroleum Corporation, Petronas (the national petroleum company of Malaysia), Sudapet (Sudan's state petroleum company), and Talisman Energy[10] (Canada's largest independent oil and gas exploration company). Talisman's partnership with the Government of Sudan began in October 1998; until recently, it was the most influential company in the country. However, in November 2002, it sold its 25 percent interest in the consortium to ONGC Videsh Ltd., a subsidiary of India's national oil company.[11]

Between 1999 and 2002, the GNPOC's oil investment, mainly by Talisman, was directly implicated in intensifying the war in Sudan, as well as in causing extensive oil-induced displacement that was enforced by the military (Amnesty International 2000: 9; Harker 2000: 17). Various reports (Gagnon and Ryle 2001; Harker 2000) documented that gunships regularly flew sorties from Heglig (the oil project's base), attacking civilian settlements as part of an ongoing campaign to control territory that could be used for oil development. Oil is not only causing the war, it is also increasing the scale of the conflict because oil revenues are reinvested into the war. In fact, oil revenues, greatly increased by Talisman-provided technology and expertise, make up half of Sudan's annual war budget (Idahosa 2002; Macklin 2004).

Beneath the oppression of the militarist Islamist state, and amidst the violence of civil war, the oilfield project was proposed as a "development" project that would enhance Sudan's socio-economic and political conditions, spreading prosperity throughout the country. It was often further argued that oil investment in Sudan would be a "catalyst for economic and social development that [would] ultimately improve the standard of living in the Sudan" (Harker 2000: 15). In reality, however, the militaristic, violent practices of oil production and development induced displacement by destroying harvests, looting livestock, and setting up the military occupation of the oil region in order to prevent the return of the displaced population (Amnesty International 2000: 8).

Indeed, P. Idahosa (2002) argues that, beginning in 1998, when displacement increased due to intensified oil exploration and drilling in Western

Upper Nile territories, along with the shipping of crude oil to the Red Sea, oil development and counter-insurgency came together. As stated above, approximately 85 percent of southern Sudan's population was forcibly displaced, destroying much of the region's indigenous production and trade infrastructure (Idahosa 2002: 11). Areas near oil installations became targets for southern insurgents, whose actions escalated the struggle and expanded its zones, all of which increased human displacement and exacerbated parallel conflicts among rival rebel groups. In turn, this led directly to an oil-induced famine in the Western Upper Nile region in February 2001. In short, such DID has created socio-economic chaos in its destruction of established trade and production patterns of various ethnic groups, leading to massive human rights violations and human insecurity (Idahosa 2002: 11). Clearly, the oilfields project is not a "catalyst for development" but rather a mechanism for serving the interests of the Sudanese government through the oil companies' goal of securing global capitalist interests (Amnesty International 2000; Macklin 2004).

One would certainly expect violent upheavals and the displacement of peoples to go together; one might also anticipate that, along with children, women would be the most vulnerable in war zones and the most affected by the consequences of displacement. If armed conflict negatively affects both men and women, it does so for women through gender-specific disadvantages that are not always recognized or addressed by mainstream, gender-blind understandings of conflict and reconstruction (see El-Bushra 2000; El Jack 2002). So, for example, the conflict in Sudan is compounded by the political-legal context of violence: significantly, the Sudanese state is not party to the Convention on the Elimination of All Forms of Discrimination against Women (CEDAW) (see Gagnon, Macklin, and Simons 2003). Such indifference to what many consider a fundamental protocol of human rights clearly draws upon a complex history of women's subordination in Sudan; its impact upon gender inequality in so many different spheres of life reflects power imbalances in social structures that predate conflict periods, though armed struggle and its aftermath often exacerbate it. Such unconcern equally leads to a disregard for violence against women, such as the indiscriminate aerial bombing and razing of communities where women pursue their livelihoods, through to their abduction and rape, and their being killed as non-combatants. When gender issues are not foregrounded in the analysis of such situations, assessing those affected by violence becomes impossible and accessing the views of those caught between the costs and benefits of the projects that displace them becomes problematical.

Within large marginalized ethnic groups in Sudanese society, such as the Dinka and the Nuer, who in general have been most adversely impacted by DID policies, there has been a rejection of the idea that oil operation is legitimate economic development. Among them, women have been articulate in voicing this rejection. One of the women whom I interviewed near the Sudanese/Kenyan border described the attitude of those affected by the oilfields project: "If they [the oil companies] are giving us development, they must make sure that we have an equal share in it. They must make sure that the southern Sudanese are also benefiting from development. But where are we now? ... Nobody thought of us ... For any development to happen, we must see that we obtain peace. You cannot have development when war is taking place, and while there is fighting and bombardment" (interview with Dinka woman, August 2001).

The acute sense of the macro causes of the displacement process is intensified by frustration, itself a result of the fact that many communities have been displaced several times over extended periods. Certainly, those who have suffered forcible displacement not only believe that they have been harmed but also know that they have been excluded from considerations of development that are often cast in terms of the "national interest." Realizing that the military government obtained power illegally, they also perceive the GNPOC and Talisman as tools by which this government sustains its power through exploiting the oil in the south for the benefit of the north. A Dinka woman whom I interviewed made the connection between oil and displacement clear: "The government and oil companies are displacing us to use our land. The people here resisted. They refused to leave their homes. In my presence, twenty-one of them were shot dead. When the rest saw the twenty-one people dead, they were forced to flee the land ... we walked for fourteen days without food; most of the children lost their lives. Oil production is causing these problems. Now northern Sudanese governments with the help of oil companies are forcibly displacing and killing us, and that is not fair" (interview with Dinka woman, August 2001).

The GNPOC, Talisman, and the military government of Sudan viewed the population of the south, particularly those people in close proximity to oil-rich regions and to oil infrastructure such as pipelines, with suspicion. They see southern men as either directly or indirectly involved in fighting, and southern women as offering food and support to opposition groups. Since they are regarded as potentially jeopardizing the government's oil operation, Dinka and Nuer men and women have become targets of violence and forcible displacement. One of the interviewees articulated that "this oil is for the southern Sudan; it is in the land of the southern Sudanese. We are forced to leave our land and our resources. The land is raped and sold to some of the other countries [Canada], and our people [Dinka and Nuer] are killed by the gunships of those who are claiming to be our saviours" (interview with Nuer man).

Since 1984, about two million people have been killed and over 4.5 million men and women have been displaced in the oilfield territories in Sudan (Amnesty International 2000: 7; Idahosa 2002: 15), challenging the core premise of development as an enhancement of human well-being. Despite the claims of mainstream DID discourse, which, under approved circumstances and practices, promotes development projects because they generate benefits to displacees, the Sudan case illustrates that displacement, rather than being the inevitable outcome of oil "development," is a deliberate strategy of oppression surrounding the oilfield project.

Gendered Implications of Development-Induced Displacement in Sudan

We have seen, then, that forced displacement has been used as a strategy of war in Sudan, one that aims at marginalizing and excluding non-dominant segments of the population, namely, the Dinka, Nuer, and people from the Nuba Mountains. Yet, though displacement is a source of human rights violations and insecurity for women, men, and children, displaced Sudanese are not passive victims. Rather, they are active agents who have shown tremendous courage in resisting DID, the outgrowth of northern ethnocentrism, and its imposition of uneven development upon the south. Northern Sudanese ethnocentrism and racism, predating British colonialism and having been sustained systematically through Sudan's institutions, has favoured the politically dominant Arabic, Muslim peoples of the north. On the other hand, the non-Arab people of southern and western Sudan, including women, have been considered "pagan" and "powerless" (Hale 1996: 44). Indeed, the north-south dichotomy has not merely highlighted the geographical differences between the two parts of Sudan but, more importantly, it has also led to the subjugation of southern Sudanese communities, namely Dinka and Nuer, to an institutionalized sense of "otherness" and inferiority. The inaccuracy of such stereotypical depictions simply reinforces what feminist analysis tells us: that "woman" is not a homogeneous category and that women's experiences vary depending on class, ethnicity, religion, and language. Feminist scholarship on forced migration also stresses that displacement and relocation involve the "reordering" of gender relations within different societies (Babiker 1999; Indra 1999). Such reordering, however, is largely based on previous culturally inscribed notions of "maleness" and "femaleness." Therefore, because gender-structured beliefs typically predate displacement, we recognize that women's experiences of DID will vary in accordance with gendered assumptions about their roles within the family and society (Indra 1999: 2-3).

My fieldwork revealed that, depending on their ethnic, cultural, and religious belief systems, southern Sudanese who were displaced to Kenya and Uganda exhibited differing perceptions about gender as a category of analysis. Unsurprisingly, interviewees often misconceived or rejected gender analysis because it was a Western construct and, therefore, considered culturally inappropriate. As a result, both southern Sudanese women and men resisted gender-aware frameworks. Some men resisted them because they believed that they advocated absolute equality between the sexes and consequently threatened men's power and control over women. Some of the women I interviewed were concerned that gender frameworks, as they are often defined by development and humanitarian agencies, divert scarce economic resources away from programs that focus specifically on women and girls in order to focus more broadly on women and men. These women stressed the need to concentrate on economic and political institutions and structures in which women were underrepresented.

Unlike the interviewees, I do believe that gender analysis contributes to the study of DID in Sudan. First, it should point out the structural imbalances of power relations between the north and the south. For this reason, a gender-sensitive approach should not exclude other dynamics of armed conflict, specifically ethnicity, religion, and culture. Second, a gender-sensitive approach could also deconstruct the view of a community as a homogeneous group of women, men, and children. It should highlight the different ways that women, men, and children are constructed within communities as well as how they are differentially affected by this construction (El Jack 2002). Gender analysis could, therefore, not only articulate gendered differences but, more significantly, address the inequalities between women, men, girls, and boys that exist in those parts of Sudan that have little access to power, resources, and decision-making processes.

DID certainly does initiate a change in gender relations, but it reinforces stereotypes and practices that discriminate against women. Often, "appropriate" gender roles and behaviours tend to be redefined in ways that constrain women's activities and activism. Gender analysis is significant here because it can reveal how gender roles are defined in ways that suit and privilege male-dominated structures while, at the same time, subordinating women. Whether it is caused by development or war, displacement is a particularly harsh experience for women. During the displacement process, they disproportionately face violence in the form of rape, forced prostitution, spousal abuse, and other forms of hardship that arise from the disintegration of community, kinship and support systems, and the reorganization of age and gender identities (Colson 1999: 23-24).[12]

Dams, agricultural schemes, and other modes of economic "development" in Sudan have historically resulted in both voluntary and involuntary patterns of displacement. The construction of the Aswan Dam in southern Egypt created Lake Nasser, which extended into northern Sudan and resulted in the displacement of large communities of Sudanese Nubians. To clear the way for the project, they were forcibly evicted from their homeland along the Nile and resettled through the New Halfa irrigation scheme.

Both Nubian men and women were impoverished (Colson 1999: 26). Yet, Nubian women were disproportionately affected: after the displacement and resettlement processes, they not only lost traditional support systems within their extended families and communities but also their rights to land around the Nile. Furthermore, Nubian women lost independent sources of income, namely, subsistence food production; as a result, they became dependent on their husbands, who gained strict control over cash-crop production of cotton for export and consequently monopolized household income and resources in New Halfa (ibid.).

Throughout the present oil-induced displacement in southern Sudan, another pattern of gender imbalance is occurring, even though the violence characterizing the oil project has set it apart from DID that occurred in the past. One of the interviewees stated that "Most of the men are taken to the war. They are forced to fight, and the majority of them are dead. To be frank, most of the women here have lost their husbands and are left with kids who do not have access to schools. There is not enough food and no shelter for those kids. We are supposed to feed them, shelter them, and at the same time, we remember we don't have jobs" (interview with Nuer woman, September 2001).

As her comment illustrates, women have increasingly become heads of households as a consequence of DID. This has resulted in changes to demographic patterns and to the division of labour, intensifying marginalization for both women and men. Furthermore, the difficulty of accessing healthcare, education, and other basic goods and services has led to insecurity and human rights violations.

Sudanese women who have been internally displaced within Sudan, as well as those displaced in the Horn of Africa, particularly in Kenya and Uganda, have suffered most through enduring the traumas of relocation caused by the conflict. Other research has identified the cultural trauma associated with this displacement, pointing to the deep attachment to place that many Nuer and Dinka people, and women in particular, feel, and to the shame that accompanies the compulsion to move: "To a Dinka, his [sic] country with all of its deprivations and troubles is the best in the world. Until recently going to a foreign land was not only a rarity, but a shame" (Deng, quoted in Abusharif 2002: 54).

Because they are traditionally agriculturalists and agro-pastoralists, many women cannot transfer their skill sets in ways that ensure their survival in urban centres or as refugees. For these groups of women, the fallout in terms of the disintegration of community results in an understandable lament for their loss of traditional support systems within their extended families and communities, as well as for their customary rights over land. Women, therefore, have lost independent sources of income, namely, subsistence food production and, as a result, have become more vulnerable.

Today, however, these marginalized, displaced women are assuming more responsibility for themselves and their families, if not always in ways that are deemed acceptable by government authorities. In Sudan, both men and women in Dinka and Nuer communities are at a disadvantage when it comes to meeting their "responsibilities" as fathers/husbands and mothers/wives. Some of the men join the armed forces; others seek work in neighbouring countries or large cities, while women are left behind to care for children, the elderly, and the sick, with little or no support after the dispersal of family and communal networks.

For families in which the couple remains together, as is the prevalent pattern among those displaced in northern Sudan, the gendered dynamics of displacement mean that once men lose either their land or their jobs, women are expected to take up the burden, finding ways to provide for themselves and their families. Dinka and Nuer women's economic activities in their homeland include cattle rearing and breeding, cultivating food products, and brewing and selling traditional liquor. When they arrive in the camps/shantytowns around Khartoum, these women find themselves economically vulnerable. As a result, they may turn to brewing as a means of income generation, despite the fact that liquor is prohibited by the Islamic law strictly imposed by the National Islamic Front government in northern Sudan. Moreover, since the law does not recognize the rights of non-Muslims, these displaced women are often harassed, detained, and persecuted (Macklin 2004: 89). In major urban centres in Sudan, especially Khartoum, the social anomie has often been acute and profound, and "sexual abuse, prostitution, harassment, and other social practices that hitherto were virtually absent among [displaced groups]" are extensive (Abusharif 2002: 54).

The south has suffered a variation of forcible displacement in that all displacees are consolidated in government-controlled areas ironically called peace camps. A. Macklin (2004) states that in the Pariang peace camp she visited, people were coerced to stay in the camp by the promise of limited food security or basic healthcare. The real purpose of the camps, however, is to monitor the activities of the displaced so that oil exploration and oil-drilling areas remain secure. A women interviewed in 2000 described the reality of these violent camps: "I came here in May. The government of Sudan would not let us leave Pariang camp. The government forces mistrust us. We were not given any services, we have to find our own food and make our own living. When the women would go to gather wood and cut grass to build shelters, the Arab militia follow us to take what we had and rape us. I tried to escape with three others from the camp. The government of Sudan shot at us. The others were killed. I was hit in the leg but managed to escape" (Harker 2000: 84).

Indeed, though a peace camp may sound like a refuge from the battlefield, these camps are a degrading form of forced displacement for both men and women. Women are, however, disproportionately affected in the camps because of the sexual abuse inflicted upon them by the militia, male relatives, and their husbands (Macklin 2004). Sexual violence against women damages both their physical and mental health. This is seen in high rates of adolescent pregnancy, sexually transmitted diseases, and maternal mortality (Madut 1999: 433).

Dinka and Nuer men who are suffering through displacement and are therefore demeaned, humiliated, frustrated, and unable to play their "protector" and "breadwinner" roles tend to violate and sexually abuse "their" women. These women most often experience rape, beatings, and other forms of gender-based violence from their husbands and close male kin. Husbands rape wives who refuse to bear the children who would grow up to defend their territories from oil companies and from national and international aggression. Dinka and Nuer women not only experience gender-based violence within their households but are increasingly subjected to it in their communities and in public spaces. The recent prevalence of this abuse was reiterated by interviewees: "Women are raped by both government officials and opposition groups, especially at the border when they are crossing. This is how women are really affected, and I am sure some of the women I know are now experiencing stress recalling what happened. I don't think that they are mentally stable because of that" (interview with Dinka woman, September 2001).

Another recently raped woman stated that

> women are stressed and traumatized simply because of repeated rapes we experienced inside and outside our homes ... Rape is not only directed towards us but young girls: even seven-year-old children are raped. In our camp, a woman who had just given birth to a child (about seven days old) and had no food at all, went to the bush with some other women to collect food and firewood; all were raped more than three times ... you ... never expected to have HIV/AIDS but [you contract it] because you are just raped, or you are forced to have sex with men. Many of the women here and their children have the disease, which is spreading very fast all over the place. (Interview with Dinka woman, September 2001)

Although it is morally important to emphasize the severe impact of violence on women and girls, and their victimization by means of a process generated by DID, one should not fall prey to the understandable conclusion that all men and boys are privileged in Sudan. Men are also targeted in armed conflicts and, as a result, experience specific vulnerabilities. They make up the majority of casualties caused by violent displacement; the fact that women-headed households dominate refugee populations is a graphic illustration of this. As well, during violent displacement, men and boys are often subjected to rape, a form of assault designed to shatter their power and masculinity. In fact, almost all the men I interviewed were reluctant to speak about their experiences of rape because of the stigma of male rape. Our growing knowledge that men, too, are victims of sexualized violence also illustrates the need to interrogate the cultural constructions of masculinity/femininity and to establish a gender-relational framework that articulates how women, men, and children are differently constructed and violated as a result of DID.

Although there is much documented evidence of the adverse impact of DID, I think it is important to emphasize that, in a few instances, women have benefited from displacement. For example, educated women displaced in big cities in Kenya and Uganda have access to healthcare, education, employment, and other resources through local or international NGOs and, therefore, appear to be in a relatively better position than women who are in refugee camps or internally displaced in Sudan. One of the women I interviewed stated that "We have suffered a lot as a result of DID. However, those of us who made it to big cities 'alive' are in relatively better shape than when we were in Sudan. Look at me, I am employed with one of the international NGOs in Nairobi, and my daughter is entering secondary school next year. So, yes, we are better off than before leaving Sudan" (interview with Dinka woman, Nairobi, October 2001).

Women's work in leadership roles within various NGOs has to some extent strengthened women's self-esteem and allowed them to develop social and political awareness, providing them, therefore, with the ability to enhance significantly their gender roles. At least on a superficial level, giving opportunities to women in assistance programs in countries such as Kenya and Uganda has lessened their disadvantaged status, allowing them to make increasingly significant contributions to their households and communities. However, such independence hardly challenges, even less transforms, patriarchal ideology; nor does it seek to realize equity with even a modicum of social and economic justice for both women and men. To attain this, it is urgent, Judy El-Bushra (2000: 4) notes, for both women and men to "participate as active partners" in negotiating to eventually change oppressive gender ideologies and practices. The necessary resources are scarce or not available for such a program of negotiated partnerships; where they do exist, they are either insufficient or not sufficiently sustainable to make a difference.

Conclusion

One might think that it would be important for DID discourse to stress the need to acknowledge, negotiate, and re-evaluate questions of gender. To be sure, the process of negotiating gendered relations of power is never an easy one, and it appears to be especially unpropitious in Sudan, given the current uncertainties of the Comprehensive Peace Agreement and the turbulence of the newly formed Sudanese government. If displaced women are coping and resisting under difficult circumstances through daily survival strategies, it is not, however, because of the contributions of those who would promote the ameliorative facets of DID. For that, we must look at, as it were, the auto-negotiations and agency of the women who are victimized by it. Yet, though southern women have been depicted as passive victims of war, famine, and disease, I have highlighted how they play an instrumental part in holding together the social and economic fabric of their communities. Southern Sudanese women's exuberant exercise of public agency is reflected in their insistence on brewing traditional liquor despite the risk of imprisonment. Such cultural resilience in the context of overcrowded refugee camps, and in the face of the homelessness wrought by displacement, points to poignant remnants of a practical activity that speaks to community and familial roles under changed circumstances. It speaks not only to their capacity to assert their authority, and the pride they take in being able to do so, but also to the practical necessity of economically and socially reproducing themselves and doing so in ways that have become far more visible than previously imaginable.

Indeed, the inability to identify, let alone understand, the importance of social reproduction to DID and its mitigation reinforces many of the gender invisibilities that feminist scholars have been locating and profiling for over three decades. The conflict in Sudan is, in fact, a clear example of the salience of gendered, racialized, and culturally specific systems of oppression, as well as the struggles to negotiate and redefine those systems. Just as gender analysis has contributed to the mainstreaming of development studies, it can also make contributions to the study of DID. It is time that DID scholarship mainstreamed gender. Until that has been achieved, it cannot fathom development-induced conflicts such as those in Sudan, and it cannot understand how to genuinely ameliorate the conditions of the women and men caught up in them.

Notes

1 I also undertook extensive interviews with representatives of political, religious, and women's civil society groups. Interviewees here included commanders in the Sudan People's Liberation Army/Movement (SPLA/M) as well as members of various Sudanese groups who were displaced in Kenya and Uganda. The interviews, conducted in either Arabic or English, were recorded and translated, or, as required, transcribed into standard English by myself.

2 As I write this, an uncertain Comprehensive Peace Agreement (CPA), signed between the Government of Sudan and the Sudan People's Liberation Movement in Nairobi on 9 January 2005, is at risk after the tragic death of Dr. John Garang. Former commander-in-chief of the SPLA, Garang served as the vice-president in the newly formed government in Sudan and was to be president of the (yet to be formed) government of southern Sudan. He played the central role in negotiating the CPA, which is expected to pave the way towards establishing

peace and promoting development in all parts of Sudan, with specific emphasis on power sharing, security, and arrangements about the division of oil revenues (Prendergast and Mozersky 2004). However, conflict and brutal dispersal continues in western Sudan, and the United Nations continues to appeal for nearly half a billion dollars to support some 3.5 million displaced Sudanese. Human Rights Watch (2003) has released an extensive new report documenting the continuing complicity of oil companies with human rights abuses in Sudan, warning, moreover, that disputes over oil revenue have the potential to prolong the conflict (Human Rights Watch 2003).

3 Current statistics estimate that, including the recent IDPs in Darfur region in western Sudan, five million people have been displaced; up to two million may have died.

4 Harding (1993) defines "objective" approaches as those which strive for strong and robust understandings but which also recognize that the individually situated knowledge and interests of researchers will drive them to take a stand regarding those whose conditions they interrogate. Nonetheless, and as will be shown, this does not reduce my analysis to the assumption that a group of women is in some way homogeneous, irrespective of a number of other identities and relationships (see Hill Collins 2000), and are simply oppressed and without volition.

5 There is, of course, neither paradox nor unusualness in these questions. Few countries in the world have not experienced some kind of conflict induced by contestation over resources, with state or companies having argued that resource extraction or "development" will improve the well-being of those in whose name they are invoked but who are in fact often at the short end of both. In the case of Sudan, as elsewhere, the issue is less about the positive or negative nature of development (though only the most flagrant apologists, such as the oil companies themselves, would claim that development has been positive in Sudan) than about the use to which these resources have been put: keeping a government in power through force of arms. One need only think of Colombia (see Chapter 6 in this volume), Nigeria, and numerous other places throughout the South to reach the obvious conclusion that where development projects occur, there will be beneficiaries but not always true development, and that people who are obstacles to the resource utilization defined self-servingly as "development" are often displaced with the most brutal of violence. None of this undermines a truism about development – that it is not only contested but also very unequal.

6 Many scholars, including Francis Deng (1995) Sudan's most eminent Southern scholar, have noted that the two visions of Sudan – North and South – do not necessarily refer solely to geography. Northern Sudan here does not so much designate a geographical north as an ideological North, one whose geographical confines are limited to Muslim, Arabic-speaking, central riverine Sudan.

7 The British colonial state, for example, sought partial protection for southerners by insisting, often at the behest of Christian missionaries, that no Arabic or Islamic presence exist in the south. Although this "Southern Policy" was ostensibly intended to encourage indigenous growth, it in fact diminished cultural contact between north and south and undermined southern *economic* development (see Deng 1995).

8 For example, a rebellion of Southern soldiers, and the precipitation of violence against northerners in 1955, came about partly because of the fear of apparent collusion between the Egyptians and sectors of the Sudanese political elite to establish formal relations with Egypt and control of the south by the Arab-Islamic north. This period also saw the migration of people near the southern borders, who fled into Uganda and Congo. Mistrust, violence, expulsion, and migration have been endemic in Sudan.

9 Oil exploration in the contested oil territories of southern Sudan began in 1975 when Chevron was granted a concession to construct an oil pipeline running from the southern oilfields to northeastern oil refineries located at Port Sudan, on the Red Sea coast. Chevron was forced to stop drilling for oil in 1990 after the murder of three of its workers by armed opposition groups. The Canadian company Arakis Energy explored for oil between 1990 and 1998.

10 Other companies involved in the GNPOC include National Iranian Gas Company; Gulf Petroleum Company, Qatar; Royal Dutch Shell; Agip Italy; and Total Fina, France (Amnesty International 2000: 11).

11 At the time of writing, Talisman had not yet fully left Sudan: it preserved its links by retaining technical consultants on the ground.

12 For a discussion in which the current situation is compared with those of the past, see J. Bacher (2000). Especially in terms of its impact upon marginalized, vulnerable groups, and women in particular, and despite the distinctly militarized nature of the current oil-induced displacement in southern Sudan, this "development" project, as previously intimated, shares continuities with previous DIDs, such as the colonial and post-colonial Gezira cotton development schemes and Egypt's Aswan Dam project of 1964.

References

Abusharif, R. 2002. *Wandering Sudanese Migrants and Exiles in North America*. Ithaca: Cornell University Press.

Amnesty International. 2000. "Sudan: The Human Price of Oil." AFR 54/001/2000.

Babiker, F. 1999. "The Gender Impact of War, Environmental Disruption and Displacement in Sudan." In Mohamed Suliman, ed., *Ecology, Politics and Violent Conflict*, 45-58. London and New York: Zed Books.

Bacher, J. 2000. *Petrotyranny*. Oxford: Dundurn Press.

Berger, I. 2003. "African Women's History: Themes and Perspectives." *Journal of Colonialism and Colonial History* 4 (1). http://muse.jhu.edu/journals/journal_of_colonialism_and_colonial_history/v004/4.1berger.htm.

Cernea, M. 1996. "Understanding and Preventing Impoverishment from Displacement: Reflections on the State of Knowledge." In Christopher McDowell, ed., *Understanding Impoverishment: The Consequences of Development Induced Displacement*, 13-32. Oxford: Berghahn Books.

–. 2000. "Risks, Safeguards, and Reconstruction: A Model for Population Displacement and Resettlement." In M. Cernea and C. McDowell, eds., *Risks and Reconstruction: The Experiences of Resettlers and Refugees*. Washington, DC: World Bank Publication.

Colson, E. 1999. "Gendering Those Uprooted by 'Development.'" In Doreen Indra, ed., *Engendering Forced Migration: Theory and Practice*, 23-38. New York: Berghahn Books.

Cragg, W. 1999. "Mapping Values, Descriptive Axiology and Applied Ethics: Lessons from Environmental Ethics Case Study." Paper presented at SSHRC Workshop on International Development Ethics and Population Displacement, York University, April 2000.

Deng, F. 1995. *War of Visions: Conflicts of Identities in the Sudan*. Washington, DC: Brookings Institution.

Drydyk, J. 2000. "Not Another Set of Guidelines: Towards a Framework for Ethical Evaluation of Development-Induced Displacement." Paper prepared for Shastri/SSHRC and presented at SSHRC Workshop on International Development Ethics and Population Displacement, York University, April.

El-Bushra, J. 2000. "Gender and Forced Migration: Editorial." *Forced Migration Review* (9): 4-7.

El Jack, A. 2002. "Gender Perspectives on the Management of Small Arms and Light Weapons in the Sudan." In V. Farr and K. Gebre-Wold, eds., *Gender Perspectives on Small Arms and Light Weapons*. Brief 24, 51-57. Bonn International Centre for Conversion, Bonn. http://www.bicc.de/publications/briefs/brief24/brief24.pdf.

–. 2003. *Gender and Armed Conflict: Overview Report*. BRIDGE Institute of Development Studies, University of Sussex, Brighton, UK. http://www.ids.ac.uk/bridge/reports_gend_CEP.html.

Elson, D. 1995. *Male Bias in the Development Process*. Manchester, UK: Manchester University Press.

Gagnon, G., A. Macklin, and P. Simons. 2003. *Deconstructing Engagement: Corporate Self-Regulation in Conflict Zones – Implications for Human Rights and Canadian Public Policy. ND.*

Giles, W., and J. Hyndman. 2004. *Sites of Violence: Gender and Conflict Zones*. Berkeley, CA: University of California Press.

Hale, S. 1996. *Gender Politics in Sudan: Islamism, Socialism and the State*. Boulder, CO: Westview Press.

Harding, S. 1987. "Is There a Feminist Method?" In Sandra Harding, ed., *Feminism and Methodology*, 1-15. Bloomington: Indiana University Press.

–. 1993. "Rethinking Standpoint Theory: 'What Is Strong Objectivity?'" In Linda Alcoff and Elizabeth Petter, eds., *Feminist Epistemologies,* 49-82. New York: Routledge.

Harker, J. 2000. "Human Security in Sudan: The Report of a Canadian Assessment Mission." Department of Foreign Affairs and International Trade, Government of Canada, January. http://www.web.ca/~iccaf/humanrights/sudaninfo/harkersummary.htm.

Hill Collins, P. 2000. *Black Feminist Thought: Knowledge, Consciousness and the Politics of Empowerment.* New York and London: Routledge.

Human Rights Watch. 2003. "Sudan: Oil Companies Complicit in Rights Abuses." http://hrw.org/english/docs/2003/11/25/sudan6528.htm.

Idahosa, P. 2002. "Business Ethics and Development in Conflict (Zones): The Case of Talisman Oil." *Journal of Business Ethics* 39 (3): 227-47.

Indra, D. 1999. *Engendering Forced Migration: Theory and Practice.* New York: Berghahn Books.

Kabeer, N. 1994. *Reversed Realities: Gender Hierarchies in Development Thought.* London: Verso.

Kebbede, G. 1999. *Sudan Predicament: Civil War, Displacement, and Ecological Degradation.* Dartmouth: Aldershot.

McDowell, C. 1996. *Understanding Impoverishment: The Consequences of Development Induced Displacement.* Oxford: Bergharn Books.

Macklin, A. 2004. "Like Oil and Water, with a Match: Militarized Commerce, Armed Conflict and Human Security in Sudan." In W. Giles and J. Hyndman, eds., *Sites of Violence: Gender and Conflict Zones,* 75-107. Berkley, LA: University of California Press.

Madut, J. 1999. "Militarization and Gender Violence in South Sudan." *Journal of Asian and African Studies* 34 (4): 427-42.

Mohanty, A. Russo, and L. Torres. 1991. *Third World Women and the Politics of Feminism.* Bloomington: Indiana University Press.

Muggah, R. 2000. "Through the Developmentalist's Looking Glass: Conflict-Induced Displacement and Involuntary Resettlement in Colombia." *Journal of Refugee Studies* 13 (2): 133-64.

Parasuraman, S. 1999. *The Development Dilemma: Displacement in India.* London: Macmillan.

Penz, P. 1999. "Draft Framework Paper for the Two Projects on the Ethics of Development-Induced Displacement." Centre for Refugee Studies, York University.

Prendergast, J., and D. Mozersky. 2004. "Love Thy Neighbor: Regional Intervention in Sudan's Civil War." *Harvard International Review* 26 (1): 70-73.

Ramsbotham, O., and W. Tom. 1996. *Humanitarian Intervention in Contemporary Conflict: A Reconceptualization.* London: Polity Press.

Reinharz, S. 1992. *Feminist Methods in Social Research.* New York: Oxford University Press.

Seligman, C.G., and B.Z. Seligman. 1932. *The Pagan Tribes of the Nilotic Sudan.* London: Routledge.

3

Uprooting Communities and Reconfiguring Rural Landscapes: Industrial Tree Plantations and Displacement in Sarawak, Malaysia, and Eastern Thailand

Keith Barney

> Wherever the plantation has arisen or wherever it was imported from the outside, it always destroyed antecedent cultural norms and imposed its own dictates, sometimes by persuasion, sometimes by compulsion, yet always in conflict with the cultural definitions of the affected population.
>
> – Eric Wolf (quoted in Stoler 1985)

As the succession of logging booms has now come and gone for many of Southeast Asia's resource-rich nations, the promotion of commercial fast-growing-tree plantation projects now represents an important strategy through which regional governments are promoting development in rural and upland zones. Embedded in this observation, however, lies a rather fundamental problematic: one that logging operations often initiated but that agro-industrial plantation development very sharply intensifies. For, in Southeast Asia, the very notion of an empty, "unclaimed space," readily available for forestry development projects, is most often mistaken. Due to the extent and complexity of non-formalized, overlapping, and customary resource claims and long histories of village forest, swidden, and non-timber forest product management regimes, the majority of large-scale rural development projects in the region are likely to impinge upon and transform local resource access in one form or another. As industrial tree plantations signify a prime example of territorially extensive development, it is particularly useful to analyze how such projects attempt to reconfigure rural landscapes – to "de" and then "re"-territorialize – to carve out plantation space in a region with very deep and unresolved contestations over rural resource rights. As explained below, the roots of these very modern forestry conflicts in the region stretch back into history, often well into the colonial period (see Peluso and Vandergeest 2001).

This chapter draws from ethnographic research conducted in Bintulu Division, Sarawak, and in eastern Thailand, over eleven months from 2000 to 2001. I will argue that there are two underlying processes which act as facilitators of plantation-linked rural displacement in the region: the first is a modern reworking of the colonial legacy of legal and informal land tenure arrangements; the second is an intensified commercialization of land markets. In both Sarawak and Thailand, plantations represent an important sector of the rural economy, and yet both are also sites of vigorous rural mobilization and opposition. In both countries, powerful conglomerate corporations, integrated into global supply chains and international financial markets, are spearheading plantation production. Yet, the national-institutional contexts in which these global economic forces are played out diverge in a number of crucial aspects. National down to local forces frame the way in which forest territory is demarcated and the strategies through which plantations are designed and implemented. This in turn has implications for how community informants in Sarawak and eastern Thailand tended to view the displacement effects arising out of these projects.

In conceptualizing local responses to plantation development in Thailand and Sarawak, I view development, and its attendant displacements, as a "problematic, contested, political *process* of domination and struggle," most often achieved through a "complex unity of coercion and consent" (Roseberry 1996: 77, original italics). A challenge for normative analysis of development-induced displacement is to incorporate complexities, both in terms of an understanding of the different geographical spaces and scales driving displacement, and of the relationship between coercion and persuasion, as well as local acquiescence and local resistance, in its achievement. This conclusion connects strongly with the difficult questions of the production of "voluntariness" (see Introduction, this volume), and the broader relationship between coercion and consent in development-induced displacement.

A Political Economy of Pulpwood Plantations and Land Tenure in Sarawak and Thailand

My research focused upon plantation projects in two localities: in Bintulu Division, Sarawak, involving the Borneo Pulp and Paper (BPP) project, and in the eastern Thai provinces of Chachoengsao and Sra Kaew, involving the Thai paper firm Advance Agro. There are a number of structural forces specific to the regional pulp and paper industry which are here important to recall. First, the industry has undergone a rapid expansion in Southeast Asia in the last decade. This is not only because countries such as Malaysia, Thailand, and Indonesia have optimal climates, low labour and fibre costs, and an available land base for the hybrid species of fast-growing trees favoured by the industry. The East Asian region, and China in particular, is experiencing rapid manufacturing-led development, which leads not only to increased domestic paper consumption, but requires large volumes of paper and packaging materials for export industries.[1] Second, to be globally competitive, modern pulp and paper projects must achieve very large economies of scale, often entailing billion-dollar upfront investments in state-of-the-art pulping and paper machines. Paper firms therefore require access to international debt markets and institutional investors. In the instance of Asia Pulp and Paper (APP), an Indonesian firm targeted by environmental groups as causing widespread tropical deforestation and displacement, billions in corporate bond offerings were underwritten by the premiere New York financial houses, facilitated through company listing on the New York Stock Exchange (Shari 2001) and further leveraged through subsidies and loans provided by Northern export credit agencies.[2] Although the case of APP stands out in many ways, the globalization of production, consumption and, particularly, of investment, is thus a key driver of the Southeast Asia pulp industry and the displacement that is resulting.

Sarawak

With an economy dependent on resource-based extraction (particularly in the logging, oil and gas, and hydroelectric sectors), Sarawak faces an imminent and sharp decline in state revenues as a result of three decades of intensive overharvesting of forest resources (Anonymous 1991). Economic and political incentives are in place for a diversification from tropical hardwood logging into agro-industrial estate crops – largely oil palm and short-rotation tree plantations – through which upfront investments may be recouped as quickly as possible. Indeed, state plans call for 1.4 million hectares of forest plantations (*Reuters* 2001) and 1 million hectares of oil palm (Chek 1999, cited in Anonymous 1999) to be established within the next fifteen years, a program which would potentially cover 20 percent of Sarawak's total land area in tree crop estates. Even if these targets are only partially realized, such a vision would have serious implications for ecological sustainability and rural resource rights in Sarawak.

The BPP project was initiated in a 1996 joint venture proposal between the Sarawak state government and Singapore-based Asia Pulp and Paper – the largest pulp and paper producer in ex-Japan Asia. As then conceived, the project would involve a total investment of US$1.53 billion, producing 750,000 tonnes a year of bleached hardwood kraft pulp from 200,000 hectares of tree plantations. These would be managed in intensive seven-year rotations, using selectively improved provenances of an exotic tree species, *Acacia mangium*. The project is situated within a 600,000-hectare concession of logged-over, swidden-based, and high canopy/high diversity dipterocarp forests in Bintulu Division. In recent years, the BPP project has fallen well behind schedule, due to a financial crisis engulfing the APP group, resulting from an astounding US$13.4 billion debt load. Vigorous judicial challenges and road blockades from Native longhouses have also resulted in delays in plantation establishment. Fifteen thousand hectares of *A. mangium* had been planted as of March 2002, but the start-up for the pulp mill is now described as "unclear" (*Paperloop* 2002a). The Sarawak government has since moved to revoke the forestry licence awarded to APP, placed BPP into receivership, and is now attempting to proceed with new investors (*Malaysiakini* 2002). Investors in the plantation portion of the project are thought to now include three large-scale Sarawakian timber companies: Samling Group, Rimbunan Hijau Group, and KTS Sdn. Bhd. (ibid.).

Thailand

In Thailand, unlike in Sarawak, debates and conflicts over the establishment of pulpwood plantations are by no means new. With respect to eucalyptus plantations, forced evictions and land seizures accompanied the rise of the industry in the mid-1980s and have since been widespread in forest reserve areas throughout Northeast Thailand (see *Bangkok Post* 1988). Following the revocation of a number of poorly conceived eucalyptus projects, which threatened to displace large numbers of peasant farmers, and a general increase in environmental (and specifically anti-eucalyptus) consciousness in Thailand through the 1990s, there was a tangible degree of media surprise concerning the announcement of a new joint-venture eucalyptus megaproject, negotiated in part by then Thai deputy prime minister (and subsequent head of the World Trade Organization) Supachai Panitchpakdi and then Chinese president Jiang Zemin (see *Bangkok Post* 1999). The Chinese–Advance Agro project was to include a contiguous concession area of 250,000 rai[3] and contract eucalyptus farming on 500,000 rai. A 700,000 tonne per year pulp and paper mill with a combined investment of approximately US$1 billion would promote substantial export sales of pulp to China. Although, in February 2000, the Thai cabinet approved in principle the proposal to secure land in the east or northeast region (*Nation* 2000), by 2001, media reports suggested that projected compensation costs to displaced farmers, designated a Chinese responsibility, had stalled the joint project, with Chinese negotiators threatening to relocate the project to Malaysia (*Bangkok Post* 2001a). Latest reports envision the plantation and pulp mill project under the auspices of the parastatal Forest Industry Organization, in possible association with Advance Agro (*Bangkok Post* 2001b), although it remains unclear which areas in eastern Thailand are under consideration, what the present land use is, or whether any farmers might already be settled there.[4] NGO and village organizations were immediately concerned about the new proposal, as the existing Advance Agro eucalyptus plantations in eastern Thailand were viewed as causing widespread ecological degradation, social conflict, and rural displacement.

Agrarian Livelihoods and Land Tenure in Sarawak and Thailand

The history of legal and informal land tenure in Thailand and Sarawak is critical to understanding present-day displacement processes due to projects such as I have outlined above. Nineteenth-century colonial governments throughout Southeast Asia enacted a series of land laws, creating a completely novel administrative system over rural space. N.L. Peluso and P. Vandergeest (2001) refer to this as the creation of a "political forest," abstract, mapped territory (not necessarily with forest or without people) controlled de jure by the new state bureaucracies. In the Dutch East Indies and in Sarawak, a simultaneous system of "Customary Rights," representing a limited subset of pre-colonial local practices, was also interpreted and enshrined in law. There were significant divergences between the colonial states in their institutional and political capacities to claim control over rural space (ibid.: 771), and also differences in how multiple local resource tenure and livelihood practices were recognized and reorganized by state governments into "village territory" (ibid.: 776).

The Brooke regime[5] was the most active of the colonial Southeast Asian governments in enshrining village territorial land rights, influenced by a legal pluralist discourse of customary rights *(adat)* from the Dutch East Indies (ibid.: 779). However, due to the dispersed nature of Native settlements in Sarawak and the sizeable extent of territory claimed as Native Customary Land (estimates range from between 13 to 25 percent of the state), local adat holdings are now viewed by Sarawak state agencies primarily as obstacles to the implementation of resource extraction and rural development projects. Customary lands still have not been officially demarcated from state land in much of Sarawak, while megaprojects such as the recently restarted Bakun dam and the BPP project, as well as many smaller, more extensive, oil palm projects and timber-harvesting operations, have involved a substantial expropriation of land from customary tenure. Accompanying Malaysian rural development strategies are increasing limitations on both the legal and de facto recognition of native adat, as enshrined in the 1958 Land Code (see Bian 2000; Hong, 1987). Since the first wave of logging protest in the mid- to late 1980s, serious instances of rural conflict in Sarawak (involving blockades, arrests, and, at times, police violence) have tended to coalesce around local responses to large-scale development initiatives. This appeal to the legalized and formalized version of adat enshrined in the original 1958 Land Code now represents the major means by which local communities in Sarawak are attempting to reclaim control over customary land.

For Siam/Thailand, there was never recognition of a native or customary landownership system that remained outside of state domain, nor was there a pluralist concept of native/European law (Peluso and Vandergeest 2001). The Thai Forestry Department mapped and claimed control over substantial portions of national territory, a move that P. Vandergeest (1996) locates historically as characteristic of the emergence of modern state power via strategies of internal territorialization. Eventually, nearly half of the total geographic area of Thailand was considered as forest reserve, although the ability of the state to enforce these claims over the political forest remained tenuous (ibid.). For the approximately five to ten million Thai farmers thus currently settled within forest reserves, secure, full title land documents often remain unavailable. A substantial number of farmers in forest reserves have no ownership documents at all, increasing the risks of land seizures and evictions. As well as having security implications for immediate livelihood, this lack of official land title serves to block access to institutional credit services. Influential research conducted by G.T. Onchan Feder, Y. Chalermwong, and C. Hongladarom (1988) concluded that this situation served to discourage investments in agricultural productivity. Rural extension and infrastructure development programs are often not expanded to include people living without title in forest reserve areas, disadvantaging these farmers even further.[6]

As will be described below, even with respect to the legally more secure areas outside national reserve forests, small-scale farmers in rural Thailand are often positioned precariously on the edge of insolvency. Historical burdens of agricultural debt (see Hirsch 1990), often to multiple institutional and informal creditors, increased dramatically in the years following the Thai financial crisis of 1997-98. Farmers in my research site in Chachoengsao province thus come to view the sale of land (for example, to forest plantation companies) as one of their few remaining options. This process of land speculation and consolidation is by no means a story of the rationalizing and disciplining forces of the market, however. In addition to the massive subsidy distortions that characterize global agriculture, and a general underinvestment in effective agricultural extension and marketing programs in Thai development priorities (see Office of Agricultural Extension 1998), there is also opportunity for an array of coercive and intimidatory tactics by companies and speculators seeking to increase production areas in desirable districts (see Lohmann 1995).

Case Study 1: Bintulu Division, Sarawak

Village surveys conducted by R. Cramb (1992) and V. King, M. Parnwell, and D. Taylor (1998) in Bintulu Division, Sarawak, assist in describing some of the nuances of the experiences of longhouse people in this part of Sarawak with modernity. King, Parnwell, and Taylor (1998: 12), for instance, emphasize a view towards Sarawak's ethnic Dayak groups that would include "a more active involvement of these people in their current situation and future, rather than a view which would see them as passive victims, and as traditional societies under threat from the modern world." Native communities in Sarawak are continuing in a long history of navigation through the forces of modernization and development, positioning themselves at different political moments between alignment and disengagement. In this discussion, however, it is important to recall that the state-sponsored logging companies which extensively degraded forests and Native Customary Lands in Sarawak most often negotiated settlements with local communities, and that timber harvesting operations did not often result in the permanent removal of land use rights from longhouse communities. A historical appreciation of active responses to change should thus be maintained, but also considered in light of arguably more severe developments, in the form of a rapid transformation of the rural landscape due to monoculture plantation establishment, through which villages lose all access to customary land and resources.

In the ethnic Iban communities I visited in Bintulu Division, the primary commercial crops remained pepper and rubber and, for a few with sufficient start-up capital, small-scale oil palm. Hill paddy is still planted for subsistence, supplemented by fruit trees, vegetable gardens, fishing, hunting, and the gathering of forest products. However, most young people now find employment with timber companies and palm oil estates or with the manufacturing and service industries located in the coastal cities of Bintulu, Miri, Sibu, and as far away as Brunei and the Malay Peninsula. For informants with whom I spoke in Bintulu city, the longhouse represented a place to which they travel for weekends or holidays, where they might raise children or return to in times of financial difficulties, or where they plan to retire after working in the city. Longhouse culture in Sarawak is in the midst of rapid transformation, although, even for many people working in urban areas, it yet provides what could be termed as a critical socio-cultural and economic "safety net."

Plantations and Dispossession

Key to the social conflict surrounding the BPP project is that approximately 28 percent of the concession area is claimed by Native longhouse communities under Native Customary Rights (NCR) status (IDEAL 1999: 65). This will potentially affect over twenty thousand people, largely ethnic Iban Dayak (BPP-EIA 1996). Perfunctory environmental and social impact assessments have been prepared separately for the plantation and pulp mill components of the project, the latter involving an annexation of land from approximately eighteen hundred Iban villagers living in twelve longhouses along the Sungai (river) Tatau. Three of the Sungai Tatau longhouses are to be relocated entirely, to a resettlement area located 150 kilometres away at Samarakan, a road-accessible township constructed to house plantation employees. Two other distinct coalitions of Native longhouses have been active in opposition to the BPP project – the first group at the River Sekabai and the second from longhouses along the Bawang and Kemena rivers – citing a lack of consultation, land clearing in violation of customary practices, and inadequate land compensation packages. In this effort, these groups continue to be aided by concerned Native Sarawakian civil rights lawyers and a number of Sarawakian NGOs. Each of the above longhouse groups has filed challenges with the Sarawak High Court, alleging unlawful seizures of NCR land by BPP and the Sarawak Lands and Survey Department.

Consultation for the initial environmental impact assessment (EIA) of the BPP plantation project was undertaken in the form of a socio-economic survey in 1996, covering 124 household heads from eleven longhouses in the area of the project (BPP-EIA 1996: sec. 3, p. 62). The initial EIA identifies the early concerns of longhouse inhabitants: "Most of the long house people are not clear [on] the impact of the proposed project on their well-being. The people are especially apprehensive with regard to their NCL lands that they claimed and have constantly inquired from the district office for more explanation on the project and its impact on them. The reactions are general [sic] categorized into 'fear of being cheated' of their land. There is need for assurance to be given that they will not lose their land and to address their concern regarding compensation issues" (ibid.: sec. 3, p. 63).

In practice, BPP did not engage in any consultations with longhouses at Sekabai before land-clearing activities began. Longhouses from Bawang/Kemena were able to meet with company officials and request customary financial settlements (*pelasic menoa*), although no agreement has been reached to date.

For the Iban longhouse communities living along the River Tatau, the resettlement scheme was initiated through a company-led program in which, though the subject of regular visits by company negotiators, the longhouse inhabitants feel they have little control or negotiating position. Indeed, longhouse residents were required to sign an "unconditional" resettlement package, which, in effect, has served to rally them into forming protests and road blockades, and launching court proceedings. The longhouses to be relocated to Samarakan Township would be allocated RM50,000 (approximately US$13,150) per family to cover the construction of new longhouses, a relocation fee of RM1,500 per family (approximately US$400), and, in accordance with the resettlement procedures established from the nearby Bakun hydroelectric project, "the Superintendent [of the Land and Survey Department] shall use his best efforts to procure an allocation of three acres of land with provisional lease per door [family] for farming purposes to the Longhouse Inhabitants after they have moved into the longhouse" (Borneo Pulp and Paper 2000). Longhouse residents to be resettled were given two weeks after receiving their compensation packages to evacuate the longhouses (ibid.).

Ten longhouses in the Sungai Tatau group are affected by the BPP project. At the time of my fieldwork, in September 2000, three longhouses faced immediate resettlement; the others were confronted with a loss of customary land. Each longhouse has an elected headman, who is responsible for responding to the resettlement and/or land compensation plans. The Sungai Tatau longhouses were divided over the issue, which also led to discord among families within the longhouse; there was an impassioned debate over the issues. One of the three longhouses targeted for resettlement had accepted the BPP program, and the longhouse families, along with some individual families from a second longhouse, moved their homes. Other longhouses and families agreed to the pulp mill project in principle but sought better land compensation or improved terms of resettlement. However, the majority of the Sungai Tatau longhouses and families refused the resettlement scheme and/or the land compensation packages in it's entirety (longhouse meeting, 30 September, 2000).

A major issue of contention for members of the three longhouses facing immediate resettlement was the future security of their landholdings on the opposite bank of the river. One *tuai rumah* (headman) in particular feared that once they accepted the resettlement plan and moved to Samarakan, they would be unable to maintain their dispersed *pulau* holdings (often high-quality longhouse forest reserves, managed for local timber, non-timber, and hunting purposes). The longhouses claimed that timber companies had already extracted much of the timber from the *pulau* without paying compensation *(penti pemali).* Others feared that the remaining lands might be seized by other oil palm plantation companies if they were forced to leave. The fact that the Land and Survey Department entered and surveyed land belonging to the longhouse groups without permission, and the company then cleared land without first agreeing upon compensation, both in violation of longhouse adat, has resulted in a serious loss of confidence concerning the good faith of state agencies and company negotiators.

In response to intrusions into customary lands, concerns voiced at the inter-longhouse meetings I attended ranged from fears of a loss of identity due to erosion of the adat rituals that govern various aspects of daily life – including birth, growing up, hunting, planting rice, old age and death – to fears, for those remaining on the Sungai Tatau, of damage to water quality due to pulp mill effluent. In the language of longhouse meetings, and in the broader discourse of Native challenges to development projects in Sarawak, customary land is consistently related to an explicitly Sarawakian *indigenous* identity, that is, a localized, identity-based counter-territorial strategy (Peluso 2003). At one meeting, a longhouse spokesman compared accepting the resettlement scheme to willingly entering into hardship and suffering. Another elder related his conviction that "they [BPP] will leave us once we are alone." In this language, removal from the environment of the riverside longhouses becomes equated with an encompassing sense of separation and isolation from place and home.

What the communities requested was a form of "development which actually develops the communities" (longhouse meeting, 30 September 2000). In this notion, they included roads, schools, health clinics, piped water, and extension assistance with agricultural crops. Despite the claims of numerous Sarawakian media reports and the assertions of state politicians, the longhouses did not position themselves along "anti-development" lines. Rather, a leading NGO in the region convincingly portrays Native struggles over state resource-development activities in Sarawak as articulating a distinction between "development and theft" (see IDEAL 2001).

After a series of longhouse meetings in September-November 2000, a majority of the headmen of the Sungai Tatau decided, in consultation with their longhouses, to block the pulp mill access roads and to file a case in the Sarawak High Court challenging the right of the government to seize NCR lands for the purpose of a provisional lease. Their challenge was based upon the loss of *temuda* (cultivated secondary forests), *menoa* (communal land), and *pulau* to company bulldozers, and the failure of the Land and Survey Department to properly notify or consult with the longhouses prior to these actions. The case of the Sungai Tatau longhouses was initially strengthened by an unexpected and potentially precedent-setting decision in 2001 by the Sarawak High Court in Kuching, which ruled in favour of the land claims of Rumah Nor and against the BPP plantation project in the neighbouring area of Sungai Sekabai (High Court at Kuching, 2001). Based on community mapping exercises undertaken with the assistance of a local NGO, the High Court ruled that the land cleared by Borneo Pulp Plantation and the Sarawak Department of Land and Survey was Native Customary Land, and had thus been cleared unlawfully.[7] The Sarawak state government responded to the 2001 High Court decision by introducing the Land Surveyors Bill (see Sahabat Alam Malaysia 2001). The bill proposes an unprecedented piece of legislation that would outlaw cadastral mapping by unlicensed surveyors and ciminalize community-based countermapping exercises. The status of this bill was unclear at the time of writing (Sahabat Alam Malaysia, 2001).

Because they had agreed to resettlement before the court case was launched, the three Sungai Tatau longhouses facing resettlement were assured of only three guarantees: these included the provision of a new longhouse, with piped water facilities and internal wiring, for each family; a relocation subsidy of RM1,500 per family; and transportation to the resettlement site. The longhouses at the Sungai Tatau face land seizures with an unconditional compensation package for what the Land and Survey Department has deemed as their customary rights territory. The three longhouses at the Sungai Tatau are to be relocated and organized into plantation villages; integrated into the plantation labour force, they will work upon lands that they formerly cultivated as their own. At the time of research, plantation labour in Sarawak was heavily comprised of migrant workers from Kalimantan, earning an average daily income of RM8-10 (US$2.10 to $2.63) at the sawmills of nearby Tatau town (BPP-EIA 1996: sec.4, p. 45).[8] For longhouse inhabitants deemed by company officials to be unable to work productively, displacement will dramatically heighten risks to well-being and livelihoods. As the BPP resettlement plan is modelled after the problematic Bakun dam resettlement scheme, it is likely that resettlement would result in similar social stresses for villagers: a removal of food security; an increase in incidence of poverty; and a complete loss of access to traditional livelihood strategies and culturally relevant activities for life on the river longhouses, including the farming of hill rice and other cash crops, collection of products from the forest, as well as hunting and fishing (Coalition of Concerned NGOs on Bakun 1999).

Justifications for Displacement

> My vision for the next 20 years is to see modern agriculture development along the major trunk road, with rows of plantations and villages well organized in centrally managed estates, with a stake of their own in them.
>
> – Former chief minister Abdul Taib Mahmud[9]

> One of the most conspicuous functions of the Malaysian state has been its mediating role in an ethnically divided population. In the face of potent and enduring sub-national identities, centralised planning has become the principal device in the much-publicized pursuit of "National Unity."
>
> – A. Robertson (in King 1988)

There are a number of generalized development justifications that appear in the Sarawak media or that may be gleaned from government or private-sector policies and reports. The first is what may be considered the Sarawakian "package approach" to rural development. P. Brosius (2000: 10) views post-colonial rural interventions in Sarawak as based around three broad strategies: the promotion of the timber industry; the creation of large-scale plantation estates; and an associated push behind the resettlement and consolidation of longhouse communities into centralized villages, thereby facilitating access by state development organizations. Alongside the latter strategy is a political effort to discredit the commercial and ecological viability of common property holdings and production methods. NCR landowners, especially those engaged in swidden-based agriculture, are often spoken of as "unproductive," or "mediocre" (see, for example, *Borneo Post* 2000b), backward, and as barriers to development. Former Sarawak chief minister Abdul Taib Mahmud's comment above presents the idea that profitable, efficient agricultural production is not to be found within the mixed household/common property organization of Native agricultural systems. Agricultural productive efficiency instead becomes conflated with the consolidation of customary lands, partnerships between state and private sector, and plantations of oil palm and other estate crops.

The BPP project is situated within these primary justifications for development in Sarawak, based on state-led projects and centralized political control. The initial BPP-EIA report (1996) frames the justifications for the project largely in terms of national economic development, the capturing of foreign exchange, rural employment, and skills development. The notion of local people as being without useful *training* surfaces in the report, which is in keeping with the notion that customary land management, particularly swidden practices, are backward, environmentally destructive, and unconducive to both capital accumulation and state building.

At an international conference promoting the forest plantation industry in Sarawak, Barney Chan (1998: xi) of the Sarawak Timber Association neatly captured a primary set of justifications for forest plantation projects, linking the economic interests of the forest industry directly to issues of "rural development" in Sarawak: "The move into more and bigger plantation development and operation is presenting the State Authorities with the golden opportunity of a holistic approach towards rural development. It seems that many social issues of the local people can be addressed at the same time: phasing out of shifting agriculture, bringing job opportunities to the rural poor, consolidating settlements for better health and educational services, economic use of Native Customary Rights (NCR) land which otherwise would have no returns, and so on."

The critical relationship between the production of plantation space and "rural development" is here made explicit. Indeed, according to Chan, large-scale plantation projects represent the very *method* through which officials might successfully enact the modernist state visions of rural development which have to date met with so much resistance in Sarawak. This strategy of development necessarily attaches the provision of basic needs such as healthcare and education to the consolidation of NCR territory and the displacement of rural people from customary lands.

Media reports of the BPP resettlement scheme in Sarawak consist primarily of public exhortations by state politicians for the longhouse inhabitants to unconditionally accept the government's development and resettlement plan. In the *Borneo Post* (1999: 2), Sarawak deputy chief minister Alfred Jabu adopts a typical rhetorical style, raising the concerns of longhouses, seemingly in their entirety, only to summarily dismiss any possible substantive basis: "They should not be influenced by groups whose agenda is to frustrate the implementation of the [BPP pulp mill] project, by claiming that their resettlement would affect their lives and result in a loss of their culture, traditions and customs. And they should not attempt to delay the process by making claims on state land."

Through the state-controlled news media, the Malaysian leadership often articulates challenges to development projects in terms of a destabilizing "racialization" of the issues. Rural communities in Sarawak who do raise substantive challenges to megaproject development on the basis of cultural identity or traditional resource rights and practices may be marked by politicians as in need of a "radical mind overhaul" (*Borneo Post* 2000c: 4), or as "influenced" by opposition parties or by foreigners (see *Sarawak Tribune* 2000: 3), and potentially find themselves removed from rural assistance programs (*Borneo Post* 2000a: 6). The rather ironic balance that is maintained in Malaysia is that state efforts to suppress opposition to development, on the basis of maintaining ethnic stability, are continually undermined by the tensions generated in part by state policy. Racialized national development policies, though redistributing wealth and opportunity with some success, continue to favour some ethnic and religious groups (such as Malays and Muslims) and to disempower others (particularly the Tamil and Orang Asli minority in the Peninsula, and rural indigenous communities in Sarawak and Sabah). National and state-level politics in Malaysia thus continues to be negotiated in part through an official racialized discourse, itself a legacy of pluralist colonial administrations.

In Sarawak, this racial discourse takes form in the perceived urgency to bring rural Dayak communities into the "mainstream" of Malaysian society (Brosius 2000: 9). The consolidation of customary rights and swidden holdings into "land banks" amenable to large-scale initiatives comes to represent a simplified, more rational, and hence potentially profitable use of land, which will serve the high-modern drive towards development (see Scott 1998). It is then primarily through participation in partnerships between government and the private sector, achieved through the consolidation and development of NCR territory, that Native groups can be lifted out of their preconceived state of poverty and projected into Malaysia's grand modernist future. In a document distributed to longhouses throughout the state, urging the natives to relinquish customary land for joint venture oil palm development, Sarawak deputy chief minister writes: "A community that accepts challenges and able [sic] to overcome the challenges will be strong and able to compete, while a community that does not accept challenges will be left behind and remain backward ... We must prepare ourselves for the greater challenges of the future so that our State of Sarawak and the

Country will forever be in the forefront of development ... This new strategy is purely based on efficiency and commercial viability" (Ministry of Land Development 1997).

Brosius (2000: 23-24), drawing upon J. Short (1991), relates Malaysia's futuristic development paradigm to the ongoing creation of a civic identity. Malaysia's nationalist-modernist vision of achieving developed-nation status by the year 2020[10] is epitomized through urban architectural projects in Kuala Lumpur: the "Multimedia Supercorridor" (Cyberjaya; Bunnell 2004) that connects the gleaming new KL international airport to the twin Petronas towers. Cultural discourses of modernity are not inscribed only upon Malaysian cityscapes, however (see Goh 2002): in Sarawak, spatial inscriptions of modernist ideology also take form in state-sponsored rural development programs (see Majid Cooke 2002) and resource development megaprojects, including the recently restarted Bakun hydroelectric project and Borneo Pulp and Paper.

Given the reality of semi-authoritarian Malaysia, where the primary source of political legitimacy is economic growth and stable ethnic relations, further justifications for development policies are rarely required. Indeed, Brosius (2000: 9) writes, "The development paradigm exists today as one of the few uncontested domains of Malaysian political discourse. The particulars of what constitutes development, and what it might have to do with ethnicity, religion or the environment might be questioned, but the ultimate valorization of the concept is virtually unchallenged."

Excluded from Malaysian development ideology is then any substantial conception of the inherent value or historical/ecological appropriateness of customary agricultural production practices under adat or of the possibility that rural communities might become "economically productive" and contribute to national development goals while maintaining management over customary lands. This high-modernist vision pervades state bureaucratic approaches to rural development and serves as a further rationale for development practices that benefit primarily a corporate and political elite. What makes the initial 2001 Sarawak High Court ruling in favour of Rumah Nor's claims to customary land so interesting is that it was a rare instance of a successful challenge to this development ideology from within the apparatus of Sarawak's semi-authoritarian political system. Although this case is ongoing, it could conceivably open the door for broader challenges to the state and private-sector interests, which have run roughshod over Native Customary Land claims for decades.

A strong case can be made that dispossession and relocation of Iban communities under projects such as BPP are not only unjust, but represent a serious threat to livelihood and to their continued viability as dynamic rural communities. I will submit two qualifying aspects to conceptualizing local opposition movements to displacement-inducing development projects in Sarawak. The first is forwarded by King, Parnwell, and Taylor (1998) and implies the underlying tension between coercion and persuasion in how displacement and resettlement are achieved. Longhouses in Bintulu Division exist within a process of increasing integration with commercial markets: of their own volition, some villages have moved physically closer to markets. In general, young people of the area have been quick to take opportunities in local labour markets and participate widely in the urban and estate-based workforce, including those at the oil palm plantations, logging operations, sawmills, and pulp and paper projects that have at times displaced their own communities.

State-backed plantation and agri-business projects in Sarawak are not often achieved through the deployment of extreme force, although instances of suppression and police violence against local people have clearly occurred. In between the rhetoric of politicians, the aggressive land-clearing practices of companies, and highly visible acts of local resistance and road blockades, there are also attempts by state agencies to negotiate, to persuade and coopt longhouse leaders, to offer written contract agreements and enhanced resettlement programs, to provide conditional health and education services and employment, to undertake (however poorly researched) environmental and social impact assessments, and so forth. Some villagers are interested in these development offerings. And there also exists political recourse – to bargain, to block, to protest, and to challenge – through negotiation and use of the legal system. It is vital to understand that these relationships are negotiated through the widely diverging power relations characteristic of a semi-authoritarian developmental state. Yet, in the midst of these highly visible political struggles, the subtle combination of persuasion and subversion acts in other political moments, adding layers of local complexity to rural land and resource struggles. In this sense, A. Stoler's (1985: 8) description of the phenomena of coercion and persuasion "existing side by side (in stronger or lesser relief) in different moments of economic crisis and political repression," and T.M. Li's (2002: 47) formulation of the "significance of local histories in shaping a range of responses not reducible to the antinomies of accommodation or resistance" allude to the complexity of plantations-linked displacement in Sarawak.

A second process of modern subject formation and governmentality here emerges in that, throughout this broader process, Dayak longhouses are further enmeshed and constituted as political subjects in the Malaysian state. The very act of resisting land seizures through the technological mapping of village boundaries is simultaneously the deployment of another form of modern territorialization. This time, however, the elusive goals of state bureaucracies are accomplished by state subjects themselves, via the use of a mapping technology that promotes rationalization of land use and access, and a spatially and temporally fixed conception of space and resources (see

Peluso 2003). In the next case study, the complexity of scalar interactions driving displacement, the tension of local responses, and the problem of voluntariness is further highlighted through an analysis of displacement from eucalyptus-pulp forestry.

Case Study 2: Chachoengsao Province, Thailand

I next discuss a case study of plantations and rural displacement with regard to private-sector development in Chachoengsao province, involving the Thai pulp and paper firm Advance Agro and one of its subsidiaries, the Suan Kitti Company. Lohmann (1995), among others, has argued that the problems – including land seizures – associated with tree plantations are part of a larger struggle occurring in rural Thailand over both legal and de facto security of land rights for farmers situated within the system of forest reserves administered through the Royal Forestry Department (RFD). But there have also been expansions in eucalyptus forestry outside the reserve system, where legal land tenure is somewhat more secure. In these areas, I argue, local people tend towards a more varied response to plantation establishment and the resulting speculative, market-led displacement from their commercial rice and cassava farms.

Village *(ban)* Laem Yai,[11] situated near the town of Phanom Sarakham[12] in Chachoengsao province, is a farming community of approximately a hundred households. Most landowning villagers plant wet rice in the low-lying regions and cassava and corn in the higher areas; others maintain plots of vegetables in sites accessible to small irrigation ponds. A number of families with larger plots of land have entered into contract eucalyptus-farming agreements with the nearby Suan Kitti Company. The landscape is sloping, with the cassava fields interspersed with small patches of tall trees. Company eucalyptus plantations, which now almost completely encircle the village, are monocultures arranged in neat rows and harvested in five- to seven-year rotations; they feature an extremely dry, humus-deficient soil and negligible herb or shrub understory development, which is typical of intensively-managed, short-rotation eucalyptus farms.

Their close access to markets in Bangkok, and a higher level of rainfall than in the northeast, would suggest a greater opportunity for value-added crop mixtures for farmers in Chachoengsao. However, almost all higher-value-added crops, including fruit trees and vegetables, require not only irrigation canals but also pumps and equipment for accessing the water in the canals. This restriction, along with high upfront costs and requirements for expensive fertilizer/pesticide inputs (and thus a greater level of financial risk), results in a situation whereby most villagers engaged in agriculture in Ban Laem Yai remain in low risk, low return "traditional" farming of rice and cassava. Landless villagers work as hired labour, and it is common for villagers to hire local help with the planting and harvesting of cassava. Much of the younger generation no longer engages in farming as a primary livelihood, taking up opportunities to work in either the Suan Kitti pulp mill, in company plantations (with holdings of approximately 200,000 rai in Chachoengsao), or in industrial estates located in the western area of the province, now the outskirts of greater Bangkok. Many others have left the village for employment or education opportunities in the urban centres of the eastern seaboard.

Reactions differ within Ban Laem Yai towards the ubiquitous eucalyptus plantations surrounding the village. One high-profile incident involving an elderly woman, Mrs. Kham, required particular interventions by a local NGO. In this instance, an unscrupulous neighbour sold land held by Mrs. Kham, but which was undemarcated, to the Suan Kitti Company without her consent. The legal battle to resolve this conflict with the company continued for approximately six years and was made possible only through financial and organizational NGO assistance. Mrs. Kham places blame for her present alcoholism on the stress of dealing with the company and the police enforcers sent to intimidate her during this period. The neighbour implicated in the dispute subsequently sold all his land due to debt problems and was later murdered. This situation left his spouse, Mrs. Phan, who now also has problems with alcohol, with little means with which to support herself. Presently, Mrs. Phan is dependent on remittances from her children and the (illegal) sale of rice alcohol to other villagers. She lives in a dilapidated shack on the edge of the village, adjacent to the eucalyptus plantations which cover her former fields.

The structural issue of farmer debt in rural Thailand is clearly a driving factor behind sales to the Suan Kitti Company. In the period from the late 1980s to 1997, corresponding with the economic boom in Thailand, land prices rose from approximately 4,000 baht per rai, to 60,000 baht (approximately US$2,300 in 1997 dollars) and even 80,000 baht per rai (US$3,100) for land with accessible surface water (village interviews, 2001). Meanwhile, debt loads of informants in Ban Laem Yai – to the state Agricultural Bank and private banks, as well as to informal creditors – ranged upwards of 400,000 baht (US$15,600). For those who could reach a deal with Suan Kitti for the sale of land, it was often a gainful venture. Some villagers allegedly sold land in Laem Yai and then moved on to purchase farmland at a cheaper price elsewhere. Others even wished that they had sold when the prices were high, as the onset of the economic crisis in 1997 marked the end of the company's land acquisition strategy. Persuasion through economic circumstances has played a key role in local displacement, yet there are hints of coercion in the process also. Villagers suggested that the company did not employ direct force but that, at times, spatial access to irrigation water or a road was cut off by company plantations. This situation sometimes leaves villagers with little choice but to sell their land, presumably, on such occasions, with reduced bargaining power.

An attitude that stood out in numerous interviews was one of resignation. When asked to give his views on the "fairness" of the process that has seen Suan Kitti expand its holdings, one middle-aged farmer summed up the views of many: "The land already belongs to the company; it is an impossible question, there is no need to talk about it." During interviews, a number of villagers did take a firmer stand against plantation companies; however, most adopted a more cautious approach, commenting, for instance, that "The company gives opportunities for employment, but damages the environment." With regard to villagers who sold their land to Suan Kitti, other informants responded with statements such as "it is not my business" or "it depends on each person."

Most, however, agreed that much of the money gained from the sale of land by villagers disappeared into non-productive consumption. A village Tambon council member provided the following perception: "All farmers spent the money; I did it too. Afterwards, there was nothing left. It depends – some people think they made the right decision, some the wrong." Those who sold land assets but did not purchase other farmland usually entered the local or urban-based wage labour economy.

Although this complex view of the land consolidation process was, perhaps, the dominant theme running through the interviews, it is important to recognize the "ideal visions" that villagers articulated. Villagers expressed sadness that farmers were being displaced from their lands and from rice and cassava fields, with one suggesting that "If I had enough money, I would buy the land from the company and then rent it back to the villagers." One woman compared the land consolidation process to "cutting the future for the next generation." A second, the village Tambon council representative, stated: "Some feel guilty and upset they have to sell the land; people at that time had no idea of the problems to follow; the money was not worth enough. Things have not improved, because after a salary almost all money is spent on food. In the old days, when farmers had their own land, they could harvest rice, but now we have to pay for everything." A representative consensus from the interviews was that "If the people had no debt and no company, the people would not go anywhere and would continue farming cassava and rice."

The case study reveals what is perhaps a typical instance of how rural displacement through land commercialization occurs as a result of tree plantation development in areas outside the Thai national reserve forest system, with fairly secure landownership in place. There are instances of coercion and intimidation on the part of the company and also examples of shrewd business dealings by villagers who have waited for advantageous offers before selling. The villagers may be, above all, pragmatic in the face of increased land commercialization, but still retain what they consider as an ideal vision for their communities. For almost all villagers, this vision is one that does not include the extent of eucalyptus plantations seen today but that does desire more viable livelihood opportunities for people on their own farms. Displacement as occurring in this village of Chachoengsao is complex, in part because plantation development here was not a coherent, spatially contiguous project. Rather, it more resembles an ongoing process of poorly regulated land purchases by an industry, purchases that are facilitated through smallholder debt, the economic imbalances of cash cropping, land commercialization, and the macro-forces of economic transformation during the Thai boom and bust of the late 1990s. In this sense, farmers in Ban Laem Yai tended to accept the economic and political realities in which they were enmeshed, but they nevertheless challenged the fairness of how these forces were played out, in the village and for their neighbours. The concept of "voluntary" displacement here becomes submerged and substantially muddied in the realities of rural life in eastern Thailand.

Justifications for Displacement

In the same manner as with BPP in Sarawak, the proposed Advance Agro expansion project is often presented in terms of a promotion of "rural development," the creation of employment, money for local farmers, and the generation of export income for the Thai government (see *Bangkok Post* 2001c). Declining commodity prices for annual crops such as cassava then provide a subtext for the official promotion of eucalyptus.[13] That the proposed Thai-Chinese project would be situated within "degraded forest reserves" and in areas deemed ecologically marginal for other crops serves as a strategy addressing the environmental concerns (ibid.). The Thai Forestry Department has a particular fixation with meeting national goals for increasing forest cover. As recently tabled, this involves expanding the current forest cover, which is now probably under 20 percent, to a mix of 30 percent natural forest and 10 percent economic forest (plantations). In aid of this process, the Forestry Department's Office of Private Reforestation situates itself as a facilitator for entrepreneurship in forestry, from big industry to small growers. Interviews with representatives from its Reforestation Division highlighted potential economic returns for farmers through paid employment with companies, the alleviation of rural-urban migration, and the ecological characteristics that enable eucalyptus to adapt to poor soil conditions (interview, 23 April 2001).

A provincial RFD official similarly positioned the proposed Advance Agro–Chinese pulp mill project in terms of creating economic benefits for rural villagers, while at the same time distancing the RFD from responsibility for the provision of compensation to displaced families, stating that compensation would be the responsibility of the company (interview, 20 April, 2001). The Agricultural Land Reform Office (ALRO) also sought to distance the organization from responsibility towards displaced farmers: "If there is compensation [suggested as between twenty and thirty thousand baht per rai] and the Chinese take the [local] farmers to work in the area, it would be okay. But if the Chinese give money but then take workers from another place, there is a big problem."

A further, more subtle subtext to this project relates to the continued jockeying for territorial control by competing institutions and ministries within the Thai state. Tensions have often formed between those agencies responsible for forests (e.g., RFD) and those responsible for rural farmers (e.g., ALRO). In Chachoengsao province, 94 percent of the nearly one million rai currently under the jurisdiction of the ALRO was land formerly controlled (de jure if not de facto) by the RFD. The RFD tends to release land to the land-reform program only reluctantly, under directives from the Ministry of Agriculture. The RFD also seeks to attach various conditionalities to the land reform, for example, requiring that 20 percent of the land allocated to farmers be converted from agricultural uses back to a form of tree cover. According to the RFD, the smallholder contract eucalyptus farming component of the Thai-Chinese plantation project would be secured through such mechanisms. This would coerce those farmers living in former forest reserve territory who qualify for land reform titles into planting eucalyptus on 20 percent of their holdings. The Thai forestry department has come to view itself as the embattled protector of any possible remaining forest cover in Thailand: "There are other departments who ask the government to give parts of their land, not only ALRO. A lot of departments need forest area, but it still belongs to the RFD" (Chachoengsao RFD official, 20 April 2001).

Referring specifically to a historical instance of forceful plantation-induced displacement by the state-owned Forest Industry Organization in nearby Tha Takiab district, this Chachoengsao forest officer partially justified it through the notion that most of the settlers within the province's forest reserve were migrants from other provinces. Displacement issues were also reduced by the provincial RFD officer to the proper enforcement of land laws: "Villagers in this area, maybe they live there 'outlaw,' so when the company rents land from the government some villagers have to move away, because of the law."

A member of the National Economic Social and Development Board responsible for the project again situated the Advance Agro proposal within the broader reforestation goals of the country: "[The] Advance Agro project is a small piece; to increase forest area is the goal, but by whom? By community forests, small farmers, or big projects? If it is the last one, where? What area? This is the problem." According to this informant, the economic requirements for companies to secure large, contiguous, tracts of land for plantation development were a primary obstacle. Almost inevitably in rural Thailand, this type of development would lead to local displacement and demands for compensation by small farmers. He noted: "After the Pak Mun dam,[14] no one will enter into these projects, due to the cost of the compensation required" (interview, 8 January, 2001).

With respect to the processes of land commercialization and consolidation, a member of a local Chachoengsao NGO described the problems with eucalyptus plantations as involving intersections of local and national politics, the lack of an effective and participatory rural democracy, traditions of patronage/clientism, and the real-life, pragmatic livelihood choices with which rural people in the region are faced:

> Behind every politician is a private company. For Suan Kitti, why, they were established because at that time [the late 1980s] Mr. Sanan [Khajornprasat] was the minister of agriculture, so Suan Kitti gives money to the Democrats, and this is why Suan Kitti can establish plantations. The problem may be also traced through the voting system and vote buying. The villagers do not understand that if they elect someone with new laws to help them, it will be a better life. They think if illness befalls them, or if they are in trouble with the courts or the police, they can go to a politician and ask for help ... The villagers have no choice, and don't know the impacts of electing corrupt politicians because they know today they can get the money they need. They do not, or cannot, look to the future. (Interview, 21 April 2001)

For villages outside the reserve forests, the commercialization of agricultural production has led to opportunities and new stresses as well as the onset of increased economic stratification. For local people in areas of Chachoengsao, the market-led consolidation of land under forestry production has had wide-ranging impacts that may not always correspond to those invoked by "anti-plantation" villagers. A process most akin to persuasion thus facilitates displacement in many areas, acting side by side with other instances of coercion and rural resistance strategies.

This research also suggests that displacement-inducing development projects are becoming increasingly unacceptable in Thailand's political climate. As the false starts of the proposed Thai-Chinese joint venture demonstrate, political-economic or bureaucratic imperatives by themselves are at times not enough to impose controversial development projects, even when involving the top echelons of political power. New social movements and the political realities of democratizing and decentralizing Thailand have rendered the "moving" of rural people through the landscape increasingly difficult. The failure (to date) of the Advance Agro–Chinese project to move forward may represent a political recognition of this sea-change, in Thailand if perhaps not in the rest of Southeast Asia.

The Thai case study also highlights a key problematic for efforts to fully account for the range of development-induced displacement processes, as many rural communities in Southeast Asia are not based on relative positions of power, and the concept of "voluntary" is fully framed within lived realities. The case shows how development projects often affect the value of local land markets. Highly indebted rural communities – a structural feature in much of rural Thailand – and particularly highly indebted individuals within communities, may experience economic windfalls as the price of their land rapidly increases. Although many community members surely benefit from such opportunities and are quick to take advantage of them, negative displacement effects can also result, as, for instance, from inter-community competition over what are often poorly demarcated family land holdings. As with the examples of Mrs. Phan and Mrs. Kham above, economic displacement can also run through gendered power relations within households. Finally, windfall revenues gained from land sales may simply be spent on unproductive investments or consumer goods, which can serve to saddle farmers with further problems. In Thailand, it is also common for land speculators with access to inside information to enter such situations. Although these issues are extremely complex and locally contingent, one could yet imagine a situation where the likely effects of development projects on land markets could be foreseen. Here, one could even envision a role for public education workshops, to provide information and advice to rural communities located adjacent to planned development projects, in preparation for the economic opportunities and drawbacks which may lie ahead. In Thailand, as in much of Southeast Asia, the extent of entrenched imbalances in political power between city and countryside, urban speculator and peasant farmer, would render the implementation of such policies a formidable task. However, various "pro-poor" and anti-speculatory safeguards built into land titling programs and the 1958 Thai Land Code could yet be envisioned (see Leonard and Ayutthaya 2003).

Uprooting Communities and Reconfiguring Rural Landscapes in Southeast Asia

Development-induced displacement in the plantation industry operates through a range of processes occurring across scales. In Thailand and Sarawak, this involves an international political economy of forest products, the structure of national property regimes, inter-bureaucratic competition, discursive deployments of national development priorities, and local histories of settlement and livelihoods. The "thickness" and complexity of these networks, ranging from the high finance of global bond markets down to micro-level issues of land demarcation and farmer debt in rural Southeast Asia reveal the multiplicity of forces that combine to drive the process of development-induced displacement. The relative strength of these networks also shapes how state institutions and industries proceed in justifying plantation development and how tree plantations are experienced and contested by rural communities.

Central to this process in Sarawak is the allocation of concession rights in forests to political-business interests without regard for overlapping local property claims. Native communities are contesting these spatial strategies and challenging high-modernist state development strategies through recourse to colonial-implemented laws of adat and an explicitly indigenous notion of customary rights. This recourse remains tenuous, however, as the legal definition of customary lands can be and has been altered by the Sarawak government, and local strategies such as community mapping may be declared invalid. The de facto recognition of customary land depends on the ability of the judiciary to actually uphold the law, and, in this sense, the recent High Court decision will be a critical test case for shaping the relationship between rural communities and the state in Sarawak.

In Thailand, a more "open" political system,[15] which includes a greater potential for the involvement of rural and Bangkok-based NGOs, has meant that Thai villagers and civil society organizations have mounted very successful protest campaigns that have effectively acted to delay and even immobilize projects involving widespread displacement. State institutions in Thailand are also under pressure to achieve greater reform and decentralization, a fact that decreases their capability to implement the centralized, high-modernist development ideology characteristic of Malaysian-style resource megaprojects. In the non-reserve-forest areas of Chachoengsao province, land purchases have often represented the means by which plantation companies have gained access to rural space. Plantation development and displacement have thus become embedded within ongoing, seemingly inexorable processes of land and agricultural commercialization. Thailand lacks distinctive grounds for basing a claim to resources on "indigenous" status and has little in the way of a historical legalization of customary rights resource tenure; therefore, recourse to collective ownership has been largely absent from responses to development-induced displacement in its eastern seaboard. In two very different social, historical, and geographical contexts, and via diverse political mechanisms, rural displacement from plantations development is proceeding apace.

My research suggests that multiple interpretations of the "fairness" and criticality of these changes exist between and within villages and that there is a range of potentials and capabilities for voicing protest and resistance in differing political contexts. I suggest that this exploration of the multiple routes to large-scale plantation displacement in Southeast Asia, and of the heterogeneous responses by villagers, means that any approach to systematically addressing development-induced displacement from an ethical standpoint, even within a single-commodity sector, must attempt to incorporate this complexity. When gauging local responses to displacement, as, for instance, via the concept of "voluntariness," ethical analyses must adopt a highly nuanced conception of how displacement is most often achieved; here it is discussed as involving a range of processes operating in different political moments, from coercion and repression to persuasion and cooptation. An appreciation of this complexity, which is rooted in the marginality of many rural communities, should not blind us to the underlying injustice of these displacements. Second, analyses of displacement must be nested within different observational scales, recognizing how patterns of displacement arise out of both projects and market processes. This suggests the need to widen the scope of attention to development-induced displacement from individual megaprojects, definitive though these are, to include broader state policies such as market reforms and land reform. The complex matrix of linkages between historical and global to local processes, as they articulate with state modernist and developmentalist ideologies, makes development-induced displacement a powerful and insidious *process*, requiring ongoing, detailed attention to the trajectories of rural and agrarian transformation in the global South.

Acknowledgment

A version of this chapter was published in 2004 as "Re-encountering Resistance: Plantations Activism and Smallholder Production in Thailand and Sarawak, Malaysia" in *Asia-Pacific Viewpoint* 45 (3): 325-39.

Notes

1 According to conservative growth estimates of 3 percent per year, Chinese consumption of paper and packaging materials will increase from 36 million tonnes in 1999 to 165 million tonnes by 2050, or one-half of the present-day global market (Rusli 2001: 5).

2 International creditors of APP include the respective export credit agencies of Germany, Austria, Sweden, Finland, France, Denmark, Spain, Italy, and Canada (*Paperloop* 2002b).

3 One hectare is equivalent to 6.25 rai.

4 At the time of publication, no further progress had been made on this project, although there is continued interest of Thai pulp companies in plantation expansion within both Thailand and neighbouring Laos (see Barney 2004).

5 The Brookes were a British "family empire," governing Sarawak from 1841 to 1946.

6 This exclusion of the livelihood challenges faced by Thai farmers manifests itself not only in land consolidation and displacement but also in land degradation. The Thai Office of Agricultural Extension (1998) writes that "The land degradation process is continuing unabated, and community based land-use plans do not exist that could contribute to the reversal of this process."

7 The Sarawak state government has responded to the High Court decision by introducing an unprecedented piece of legislation that would ban unlicensed computer-assisted community mapping, although the status of this bill was unclear at the time of writing (Sahabat Alam Malaysia 2001). The Sarawak state government has responded to the High Court decision by introducing an unprecedented piece of legislation that would ban unlicensed or unapproved computer-assisted community mapping.

8 Barney Chan (1998: xi) of the industry-funded Sarawak Timber Association makes explicit reference to the reliance on foreign labour: "Investors in tree plantations, like investors on other crop plantations, will require a massive input of labour. It is expected that a big percentage of this labour will be foreign. Investors need assistance by the Authorities to bring in such labour to develop tree plantations ... investors are concerned at the tight control put on [labour immigration] by Federal Authorities."

9 *Sarawak Tribune,* 9 December 1984, quoted in Cramb (1992).

10 As represented in Prime Minister Mahathir's *Wawasan* [Vision] *2020* program, which Beng-Lan Goh (2002) calls Malaysia's "Grand Narrative of Modernity."

11 All village and personal names in the Thai case study are pseudonyms.

12 The small provincial town of Phanom Sarakham, near Bangkok, has a fascinating hidden history, which demonstrates vividly that even "traditional" and "rooted" communities can represent outcomes of extensive mobility and that sweeping programs of displacement, resettlement, and integration are not exclusively modern phenomena. In the late nineteenth century, the Kingdom of Siam was struggling to manage instability along its outer zone of control, against key rival principalities based in Hue, Vietnam, and south China. The Phuan principality, centred on the Plain of Jars in Xieng Khouang (present-day Laos), was the focus of repeated Siamese depopulation campaigns aimed at depriving invaders of foodstuffs and potential conscripts. From 1876 to 1878, Siamese soldiers force-marched approximately six thousand Phuan villagers deep into Siam. According to accounts, the villagers endured such horrendous conditions en route that half of them perished due to hunger, exhaustion, and neglect. The remainder were resettled in Siam's Chao Phraya basin and the town of Phanom Sarakham. Today, the Phuan of Thailand are integrated politically into mainstream Thai society, although in ethnic terms many still consider themselves to be Phuan (not Thai and not Lao) and work to retain distinctly Phuan cultural traditions (see Smuckarn and Breazeale 1988).

13 Even so, the actual returns from eucalyptus for small-scale farmers are variable, and most area farmers to whom I spoke thought that planting rubber trees (which may be both tapped and then harvested for the growing rubberwood furniture industry) would produce higher returns. This general perception has indeed been borne out by a rubber boom under way in East Asia (*Bangkok Post* 2005).

14 The Pak Mun dam was a controversial dam project on a tributary of the Mekong in Ubon Ratchathani province, northeast Thailand, which attracted international attention and served as a case study in the high-profile World Commission on Dams (2000) report.

15 This chapter was written in a time of greater optimism, before the authoritarian tendencies of the current Thaksin Shinawatra administration in Thailand became fully apparent.

References

Anonymous. 1991. "Forest Resources Status and Timber Supply Planning for the Future." Annex 1 to Strategies for Sustainable Wood Industries in Sarawak. Report on ITTO Project PD 107/90(I).

–. 1999. "Environmental Impact Assessment of the Proposed Samling Plantation at Kuala Tatau." Bintulu Division, Sarawak: Final Report. Prepared by Ecosol Consultants Sdn. Bhd. for Samling Reforestation (Bintulu) Sdn. Bhd.

Bangkok Post. 1988. "Fell Blow for Forest Reserves." 16 June. http://www.bangkokpost.com.

–. 1999. "Pressure Groups Up In Arms against Eucalyptus Scheme." 22 September. http://www.bangkokpost.com.

–. 2001a. "Land Problem Sets Back Pulp Plant Plan: Chinese Put Off by Likely Compensation." 6 March. Available at http://www.bangkokpost.com.

–. 2001b. "Plant Suggested to Supply China with Pulp Products." 22 May. http://www.bangkokpost.com.

–. 2001c. "White Forest Arouses Strong Debate." 18 June. http://www.bangkokpost.com.

–. 2005. "Rubber Prices Likely to Soar Higher: Rising Demand from China, India Expected." 18 March. http://www.bangkokpost.com.

Barney, K. 2004. "Re-encountering Resistance: Plantations Activism and Smallholder Production in Thailand and Sarawak, Malaysia." *Asia-Pacific Viewpoint* 45 (3): 325-39.

Bian, Baru. 2000. "Native Customary Rights: Imaginary or Real." Advocate and Solicitor, High Court of Malaya and Borneo. Manuscript.

Borneo Post. 1999. "Some RM 11m Claims Paid in Pulp Mill Project." 19 May, 2.

–. 2000a. "Government Warns Those Who Raise Racial Issues." 7 September, 6.

–. 2000b. "Discard Mediocrity, Robert Tells Baram Farmers." 23 September, 5.

–. 2000c. "Orang Ulu Mind Overhaul Vital, Says Robert." 29 September, 4.

Borneo Pulp and Paper. 2000. "BPP Memorandum of Understanding." Sent to Tuai Rumah [village headman] Entika, Tatau River Iban Longhouse, Bintulu Division, Sarawak, and the Superintendent of Land and Survey, Bintulu Division. Unpublished translation from Bahasa Malaysia.

BPP-EIA. 1996. "Preliminary Environmental Impact Assessment for Proposed Forest Plantation at Bintulu and Sibu Divisions, Sarawak, East Malaysia." Prepared by Tanjong Manis Logging Sdn. Bhd. in association with EPR (Kuching) Sdn. Bhd.

Brosius, P. 2000. "Bridging the Rubicon: Development and the Project of Futurity in Sarawak." Paper presented at the Borneo 2000 Conference, Kuching, Sarawak, 10-14 July.

Bunnell, T. 2004. *Malaysia, Modernity and the Multimedia Super Corridor: A Critical Geography of Intelligent Landscapes.* London: Routledge Curzon.

Chan, B. 1998. "Concerns of the Industry on Tree Plantations in Sarawak." In B. Chan, P. Kho, and H. Lee, eds., *Proceedings of Planted Forests in Sarawak: An International Conference.* Kuching: Forest Department Sarawak, Sarawak Timber Association, Sarawak Development Institute.

Chek, Abdullah. 1999. "Socio-economic Considerations of Peat Land Development." Paper presented at the Working towards Integrated Peat Land Management for Sustainable Development workshop, State Planning Unit, Kuching, Sarawak.

Coalition of Concerned NGOs on Bakun. 1999. *Empty Promises, Damned Lives: Evidence from the Bakun Resettlement Scheme.* Final report of the fact finding mission, 7-14 May. Kuala Lumpur: Suaram Komunikasi.

Cramb, R. 1992. "The Evolution of Property Rights to Land in Sarawak: An Institutionalist Perspective." Agricultural economics discussion paper 3/92, Department of Agriculture, University of Queensland.

Feder, G.T. Onchan, Y. Chalermwong, and C. Hongladarom. 1988. *Land Policies and Farm Productivity in Thailand.* Baltimore: Johns Hopkins University Press.

Goh, Beng-Lan. 2002. *Modern Dreams: An Inquiry into Power, Cultural Production and the Cityscape in Contemporary Urban Penang, Malaysia.* Ithaca, NY: Southeast Asia Program Publications.

High Court at Kuching. 2001. *Judgment in the High Court in Sabah and Sarawak at Kuching. Suit No. 22- 28-99-1.* Justice Datuk Ian H.C. Chin. 12 May. http://www.rengah.c2o.org/news/article.php?identifer=de0200t and subject=6 (accessed 24 January 2005).

Hirsch, P. 1990. *Development Dilemmas in Rural Thailand.* Singapore: Oxford University Press.

Hong, E. 1987. *Natives of Sarawak: Survival in Borneo's Vanishing Forests.* Penang: Institut Masyarakat.

IDEAL. 1999. *Tanah Pengidup Kitai* [Our Land Is Our Livelihood]. Sibu, Sarawak: IDEAL TIME Sdn. Bhd.

–. 2001. *Not Development but Theft: A Testimony of the Penan Communities of Sarawak.* Sibu, Malaysia: IDEAL Time Sdn. Bhd.

King, V. 1988. "Models and Realities: Malaysian National Planning and East Malaysian Development Problems." *Modern Asian Studies* 22 (2): 263-98.

King, V., M. Parnwell, and D. Taylor. 1998. "Socio-economic Responses to Change among Iban Communities in the Bintulu Region of Sarawak, Malaysia." *Sarawak Development Journal* 1 (1): 1-27.

Leonard, R., and K.N. Na Ayutthaya. 2003. *Monitoring Paper: Thailand's Land Titling Program.* Chiang Mai: Land Research Action Network. http://www.landaction.org/display.php?article=133 (accessed 8 February 2006).

Li, T.M. 2002. "Local Histories, Global Markets: Cocoa and Class in Upland Sulawesi." *Development and Change* 33 (3): 415-37.

Lohmann, L. 1995. "Land, Power and Forest Colonization in Thailand." In M. Colchester and L. Lohmann, eds., *The Struggle for Land and the Fate of the Forest*, 198-227. Penang: World Rainforest Movement.

Majid Cooke, F. 2002. "Vulnerability, Control and Oil Palm in Sarawak: Globalization and a New Era?" *Development and Change* 33 (2): 189-211.

Malaysiakini. 2002. "Company Bankrupt, Sarawak's Mega-Paper Mill in Trouble." http://brimas.www1.50megs.com/BPP-Malaysiakini-26-8-02.htm (accessed 24 January 2005).

Ministry of Land Development Sarawak. 1997. *Handbook on New Concept of Development on Native Customary Rights (NCL) Land*. Kuching: Ministry of Land Development.

Nation. 2000. "Plantation Secured for Joint Paper Mill Project." 2 February, Bangkok edition.

Office of Agricultural Extension. 1998. *Thailand Agricultural Sector Needs Assessment Study, Vol. 1: Draft Final Report of TA-3002-THA*. Bangkok: Ministry of Agriculture.

Paperloop. 2002a. "Borneo Pulp and Paper Hits Hurdle as Sarawak Government Awaits APP Decision." 5 March. http://www.pponline.com (accessed 24 January 2005).

–. 2002b. "Financial Restructuring Experts Do Not Rule Out APP Asset Sales." 4 April. http://www.pponline.com (accessed 24 January 2005).

Peluso, N.L. 2003. "Territorializing Local Struggles for Resource Control: A Look at Environmental Discourses and Politics in Indonesia." In P. Greenough and A. Lowenhaupt Tsing, eds., *Nature in the Global South: Environmental Projects in South and Southeast Asia*, 231-52. Durham and London: Duke University Press.

Peluso, N.L., and P. Vandergeest. 2001. "Genealogies of the Political Forest and Customary Rights in Indonesia, Malaysia and Thailand." *Journal of Asian Studies* 60 (3): 761-812.

Reuters. 2001. "Startup of Borneo Pulp and Paper Mill Delayed to End of 2004." http://www.paperloop.com (accessed 24 January 2005).

Robertson, A. 1984. *People and the State: An Anthropology of Planned Development*. Cambridge: Cambridge University Press Studies in Social Anthropology 52.

Roseberry, W. 1996. "Hegemony, Power and Languages of Contention." In E. Wilmsen and P. McAllister, eds., *The Politics of Difference*, 355-66. Chicago: University of Chicago Press.

Rusli, F. 2001. *Asia Paper Sector*. Hong Kong: Credit Suisse First Boston. 16 January.

Sahabat Alam Malaysia. 2001. "New Law Will Make Community Mapping Illegal." Press statement, 31 October. http://www.rengah.c2o.org/ (accessed 24 January 2005).

Sarawak Tribune. 2000. "Resolve NCR Land Woes Amicably: Dr Wahbi." 17 July, 3.

Scott, J. 1998. *Seeing Like a State: How Certain Schemes to Improve the Human Condition Have Failed*. New Haven: Yale University Press.

Shari, M. 2001. "Asia's Worst Deal." *Business Week Online*. 13 August. http://www.businessweek.com/magazine/content/01_33/b3745003.htm (accessed 8 February 2006).

Short, J. 1991. *Imagined Country: Environment, Culture and Society*. London: Routledge.

Smuckarn, S., and K. Breazeale. 1988. *A Culture in Search of Survival: The Phuan of Thailand and Laos*. New Haven: Yale University Southeast Asia Studies Monograph Series 31.

Stoler, A. 1985. *Capitalism and Confrontation in Sumatra's Plantation Belt: 1870-1979*. New Haven: Yale University Press.

Vandergeest, P. 1996. "Territorialization of Forest Rights in Thailand." *Society and Natural Resources* 9: 159-75.

Wolf, E. 1959. "Specific Aspects of Plantation Systems in the New World: Community Subcultures and Social Classes." In V. Rubin., ed., *Plantation Systems of the New World*, 136-47. Washington, DC: Pan American Union.

World Commission on Dams. 2000. *Dams and Development: A New Framework for Decision Making*. London and Sterling: Earthscan. http://www.dams.org/report/ (accessed 8 February 2006).

Part 2
Displacement and Neoliberalism

4
Enforcement and/or Empowerment: Different Displacements Induced by Neoliberal Water Policies in Thailand

Michelle Kooy

Deconstructing Displacement Discourse

The [illegible] development agencies [illegible] some of the [illegible] cation of thousands of people for hydroelectric dams or the destruction of slums in the name of urban redevelopment – has led to the identification of a set of processes now labelled as "development-induced displacement" (DID). The many examples of physical displacement [illegible] of people from land, from homes, and from communities are, however, only one facet of the development-displacement nexus [illegible] and power (Robinson 2002). [illegible] a variety of displacements [illegible] the [illegible] redistribution of resources and power [illegible] program.

[illegible]

4
Enforcement and/or Empowerment? Different Displacements Induced by Neoliberal Water Policies in Thailand

Michelle Kooy

Deconstructing Displacement Discourse

The increasing recognition within development agencies of some of the dilemmas caused by international development projects – such as the relocation of thousands of people for hydroelectric dams or the destruction of slums in the name of urban redevelopment – has led to the identification of a set of processes now labelled as "development-induced displacement" (DID). The many examples of physically enforced and often violent removal of people from land, from homes, and from communities are, however, only one facet of the development-displacement nexus. Understanding development itself to be the actual process of respatializing resources, people, and power (Robinson 2002) illuminates a variety of displacements that, though they often contain the possibility for harmful outcomes through the inequitable redistribution of resources and power, fall outside the purview of current DID analysis, leaving the consequences of particular development interventions relatively unproblematized[1] and limiting the amount of self-examination that development agencies institutionalize within their programs.

This chapter examines a set of displacements initiated in Thailand through the development of irrigation water policies by the Asian Development Bank (ADB) and describes the variety of ways in which water and people are being reorganized through the development intervention, an intervention that is not open to any self-criticism regarding its possibly inequitable consequences. The project, grounded in the neoliberalization of water policies, respatializes water resources between productive and unproductive agricultural producers; the subsequent movement of rural households into/out of irrigated farmland and rural livelihoods does hold "harm" for certain populations. However, this cannot be mitigated (within the project policy and implementation) until the development intervention and the displacements it sets in motion are acknowledged as two-edged – holding possibilities for both positive and negative experiences among differently empowered development participants. The question of how this particular program of development comes to be empowering for some but enforces the displacement of resources from others should, I argue, be part of its design and implementation, as it is with the accepted and identified examples of DID. However, the definition of displacement as currently codified within DID discourse (see Cernea 2000), as a pre-identifiable negative movement of populations and/or resources connected at only one point in time to the development intervention (the building of a dam, the enclosure of a forest), fails to allow for the indeterminate nature of development processes that flow through different socio-economic dynamics to affect different experiences of displacements, for different actors, in different places in society. The continual and contingent processes by which resources, people, and power are reordered into new configurations, beneficial to some but detrimental to others, through neoliberal water policy are concealed. Such concealment denies the fundamental implications of development as a process of connected displacements, depoliticizes the development intervention that itself might seek to justify inequities through the rhetoric of impersonal market processes, and therefore ultimately deflects responsibility for any inequitable outcomes away from the development agency.

The intervention I investigated as an example of DID resulted from a rural program launched by the Asian Development Bank (ADB) for implementation in Thailand. Set within a broader development program of modernized agriculture and rural poverty reduction, the bank's Irrigation Sector Reform Program (ISRP) works to reregulate water supply according to neoliberal conceptions of economic efficiency,[2] through policies of decentralization and commercialization. I try to highlight the tensions inherent within this development intervention by focusing on the differing experiences of those involved in the project and following how policies designed to be empowering end up being enforced on particular populations. Currently, the application of neoliberal policy to irrigation water supply carries potential for both positive and negative displacements of farmers, water, and power: decentralization policies might induce both negative displacements of economically "inefficient" users and a positive displacement of power from the state to local communities. As the rearrangement of responsibility between the state and society induces the reorganization of local resources into commercial, competitive, and efficient agricultural production, the costs and benefits of this development are likely to be differentially distributed between and among rural and urban water users. Disagreements among local non-governmental organizations (NGOs) regarding their campaigns of resistance to or acceptance of the irrigation water policies have highlighted the potential for both empowered and enforced displacements proceeding from these new policies. Some fear the physical displacement of small-scale, low-income rice farmers from water access as irrigation water becomes (prohibitively) priced. Others anticipate an increase of on-farm income and local resource control made possible through agricultural diversification and reordered water-use priorities. However, because current discourses of DID (reliant upon definitions of "forced versus voluntary") fail to capture how these experiences are part and parcel of similar processes acting upon people with differing resources, and because the development project itself is designed to conceal the ways in which potentially harmful displacements of rural households away from access to water resources will occur, the investigation into how and why participants might be inequitably affected is prevented.

The remainder of this chapter contextualizes the spaces in which development processes are taking place in Northeast Thailand, briefly describes how the reregulation of irrigation water policy works to respatialize resources, people, and power, and then looks in more detail at how these displacements might operate within the specific context of two case study sites. My field research was conducted in 2000, when the Asian Development Bank (ADB) was planning for the implementation of new irrigation water management practices within eight pilot project areas in Thailand. In examining both the planning process and the early implementation of these new practices, I divided a total of ten months of study between Bangkok-based development agency headquarters, central government offices, and two of the pilot irrigation projects – Thum Samrit and Huay Luang – in the northeast of Thailand. Having analyzed the implementation of the policies within these projects, I conclude that the opportunistic or oppressed nature of DID depends upon the ability and/or desire of current water users to adopt a new "ethic" of water use predicated upon economic efficiency *and* that these abilities and/or desires are themselves mediated by power relations existing between and among rural water users, urban water users, state departments, and the Asian Development Bank.

Defining, and Denying, Displacements within Neoliberal Development

The DID processes that I studied in Thailand stem from a series of irrigation water policy reforms made conditional to a US$600 million agricultural sector restructuring loan from the ADB and the Japan Bank for International Cooperation (JBIC).[3] In a move reflecting the logic of the ADB's neoliberal ideology and its new mandate to fund only those projects in line with its reregulated water policy,[4] the Thai government intends to reorient the relationship between farmers and the state and to raise the economic efficiency of irrigation water use through decentralizing and commercializing what were previously state-supplied water services (see Halcrow and Partners 2001). Embedded within the rhetoric of community resource management, the devolution of fiscal responsibility from the state to citizens imposes the burden of cost recovery directly onto water users. This process of "development" of more efficient water resource policy works through the "development" of water users into more economically rational resource users, gradually internalizing an economically rational ethic of water use within the newly empowered water user while simultaneously working to exclude those economically inefficient users/uses by raising irrigation water supply costs. Water users who do not or cannot realize greater profits from their water use will eventually be unable to afford the increased cost of its supply. Eventually, water allocation will be respatialized according to economic productivity, legitimizing the flow of water to higher-value commercial agriculture and industrial urban centres. A technical assistance grant attached to the loan funds the Irrigation Sector Reform Program, which promises over a six-year timeframe to transfer full responsibility for infrastructural and operational management as well as rehabilitation, and partial responsibility for any future capital financing,[5] from the state Royal Irrigation Department (RID) to rural water users organized into corporatized Water User Associations (WUAs).

Attempts to increase the economic efficiency of irrigation water are set within efforts to increase the economic efficiency of agriculture, which is itself set within the broader national development discourse of the state. Relating the reprioritization of irrigation water allocation to national development plans is important in that it indicates the impossibility of restricting understandings of DID within the specific time/space boundaries of individual development interventions. For, if we set Thailand's irrigation reforms, and the displacements they simultaneously promise and threaten to induce, within the broader framework of national development, the targeting of "inefficient" irrigation water uses becomes more clearly connected to the ecological crises and water scarcities produced as costs of previous development pathways. Decades of promotion of industrialization and economic export policies by the Thai state during the period of rapid growth marvelled at by the World Bank (World Bank 1993) have increased confrontations over scarce dry-season water allocation between and within economic sectors and geographical regions (Christensen and Boon-Long 1994; Sethaputra et al. 1990; Rigg 1996; Molle, Chompadit, and Keawkulaya 2000). Recent crises highlight the importance of water to continued national economic growth;[6] concerns that water scarcity will impede such growth prompt the reprioritization of water use according to economic efficiency. Thus, the reregulation of irrigation water to enforce increased economic efficiency within the rural sector and the implementation of mechanisms to facilitate future transfer of water out of the countryside and into the city are propelled by concerns over the continued modernization and economic development of the country. Situated within the broader development discourses promoting one pathway to economic growth, the displacements resulting from the irrigation sector reforms have their causal moments quite outside the project limits, illustrating how the promotion of policies far beyond the boundaries of individual development projects is implicated within "direct" displacements.

In the case of the temporal and spatial boundaries of the development project's actually affecting patterns of water use, the relation between irrigation policy and agricultural reform also illustrates the connections of specific displacements to broader neoliberal development designs. Attached as a conditionality to the agricultural-sector restructuring loan, the restructuring of agricultural water use is quite visibly situated within the transformation of the sector towards higher-value, export-oriented commercial agricultural production. According to an ADB agricultural "needs assessment" study, the vision of Thai agriculture's future involves reduced reliance upon state subsidies and increased dependence upon and integration into global food markets and export production; this necessitates "reforms to ensure that the country's natural resources are used efficiently and that its export competitiveness is not eroded" (ADB 1999: 1; MOAC 1998: 4). Included within the ADB's plans for the reformation of Thai agriculture are new irrigation water policies designed to enforce economically efficient uses of water, demand higher levels of profits from farmers, and encourage more profitable production of higher-value crops. Although the sector is already dominated by agri-business conglomerates, whose vertically integrated and value-added agri-food production has been transforming the countryside since their emergence in the 1980s, total farm earnings have been declining since the 1970s, and restructuring is thought to be necessary in order to maintain competitiveness in increasingly global markets[7] (Goss and Burch 2001).

What might prove problematic for the sector's transformation into large-scale commercial operations is the presence of individual household producers, whether at the small-scale or subsistence-oriented level, who do not promise the same potential for increased productivity as do commercial operations. Recent studies by the World Bank (2000a) state that although 63 percent of Thailand's population lives in rural areas and 92 percent of that population is involved in at least marginal agricultural activities, farming, on average, contributes a mere 36 percent to rural household income. With the slow and/or declining rate of growth of agricultural export earnings being blamed on water scarcities (Poapongsakorn, Ruhs, and Tangjitwisuth 1998), one might legitimately wonder whether the motive behind the irrigation reforms is to decrease water consumption by these small-scale producers. Through the irrigation reforms, and the agriculture assistance components included within them, farmers are encouraged to move into production of commercial crops with lower water requirements and higher export value than current rice crops. Because some farmers will fail (for reasons explained below) at efforts to diversify into higher-value, less water-consumptive crops, therefore also failing to raise on-farm profits to match increased water supply costs, the gradual displacement of these households from farming is induced. Removal of less efficient and less productive farming households from land within irrigated areas will then, conveniently, make more land and water available to the more productive commercial operations.

The Irrigation Sector Reform Program (ISRP) emerges as the product of these national development concerns over water scarcity, sustained economic growth, and agricultural export earnings. Employing the new technology of power described by D. Slater (1989, 2002), policies of decentralization and privatization are set in motion within this development program to facilitate the release of water currently "locked in low-value uses" (as worded by World Bank 2000a: xvi). The restructuring of irrigation water policy decentralizes fiscal responsibility to alternately encourage and enforce efficient use by farmers, imposing a mandate to either increase their production values or decrease their use of water. The policies used to facilitate the transfer of water to more profitable agricultural producers and, later, to non-agricultural uses, embody the tensions described in both the Introduction to this volume and this chapter – tensions between empowerment and enforcement that seem to be particular to neoliberal projects. The ISRP reflects this paradoxical nature: irrigation policy reforms hold potential for both the liberation of populations from poverty and state control while also threatening their increased marginalization and/or elimination should they stray outside of prescribed pathways of development.

The restructuring of Thailand's irrigation water supply through policies of decentralization, commercialization, and private-sector participation illustrates the aforementioned contradictions, since, as relations of rule between the state and its citizens are reworked and reassessed, power is redistributed (Ferguson 1990). Set within the national restructuring of state/society relations, the irrigation reforms are simultaneously connected both to reforms imposed by the $37 billion IMF bailout after the 1997 financial crisis[8] but also to the more credible attempts of the government to foster accountability of local governance and to curtail corruption. The national program promoting the decentralization of state functions and decision making is viewed as a positive step taken to redress the historically over-centralized style of the Thai state (Apichart 1999); for some, the ADB-imposed irrigation reforms are seen as a complementary agenda for facilitating the state's decentralization of power to local communities. Farmers who are able to increase their profits from production might be excited by the new relations of power around water. However, there are others who will probably not benefit from redistribution of power through the market-based system currently envisioned by the ADB. As the cost of "sharing" responsibility for water supply services gradually increases, farmers within irrigation areas who either cannot or will not alter production patterns to raise on-farm profits will be forced to choose between abandoning farming or moving to solely rainfed agricultural land.

Decentralization, Commercialization, Private-Sector Participation

Protests over the IMF loan conditionality by a group of NGOs, anti-globalization activists, and academics drew widespread public attention to Thailand's water policy reforms; the conditionality enforcing changes to irrigation water policy became the cornerstone of a much larger protest against ADB development that threatened the fate of the entire loan and the legitimacy of the Thai government (*Bangkok Post* 1999a-1999e; *Nation* 1999). The public's interpretation of the policy as a direct tax on irrigation water use resulted in uproar, for taxing the poorest citizens of the nation – rice farmers – was perceived to be unethical. Given the increasingly disproportionate concentration of poverty within rural areas,[9] and the continuing decline of agriculture's ability to provide for the needs of the average family (Rigg 2000), many fear that added financial pressures need not be very great to tip the scales in favour of abandoning farming altogether. The questions over the continued marginalization and/or elimination of small-scale farmers tied into broader anti-development campaigns through which local NGOs protested the unequal distribution of costs and benefits of previous development projects.[10]

The potential of the irrigation policy reforms to directly, physically displace small-scale rice farmers was what prompted my original investigation of this project under the EDID project's focus on DID as defined by mainstream discourse. However, after having observed the ongoing debates within and between advocacy groups, local and national irrigation department officials, ADB project staff, Thai consultants, and farmers within the pilot projects, I find it difficult, if not impossible, to describe the movements motivated within the project as any form of "direct," forced, DID. There are not, or at least not yet, any immediate causal displacements linked to the imposition of a direct tax on water via cost-recovery fees but rather a multiplicity of interconnected processes reallocating power, respatializing water, and redirecting rural livelihoods. More importantly, the changes in livelihoods and water-use priorities, and the opportunities these processes involve, are given differing interpretations by differently situated actors. Displacements of power and water and people were considered as either positive or negative, depending on which point of the process I examined and to whom I spoke, since the physical movements of water and farmers according to the priorities of economic efficiency occur within socio-economic, cultural, ecological, and political frameworks that affect the relative distribution of costs and benefits of this development process.

Examining the three policies key to the reregulation of irrigation water supply – decentralization, commercialization, and private-sector participation – proves that the progression of the policy measures is by no means a smooth prediction of actual outcomes. Policies of decentralization, commercialization, and private-sector participation intersect with specific sociopolitical power structures, ecological conditions, cultural relations, and economic realities to produce unforeseen results.[11] Focusing on the implementation of these policies within Thailand provides insight as to how they become contextualized at national, regional, and local scales to impact particular groups of rural water users in particular ways. In the proceeding sections, I follow the unfolding of "structures, mechanisms, and events that actually constitute these processes [reregulation] in different places" (MacLeod and Goodwin 1999: 515) to identify the different types of displacements induced by each of these policies.

Decentralization

Decentralization of fiscal and operational management of irrigation supply services to local users initiates the first phase of the ISRP program. In concurrence with broader national reforms withdrawing the state from its involvement in public-service provision, the Thai government is shifting responsibility for selected duties in irrigation water management to both the private sector and the corporate community of water users. Duties remaining in the realm of the state (control over dams and main canals) will be reorganized to operate on a corporate model; water users will enter into service contracts with both the state and private-sector providers who take over tasks seen as less crucial for state control (Halcrow and Partners 2001). Although a cynical analysis of the reorientation of the relationship between the state and farmers could interpret the policy as a tool to legitimize the elimination of state subsidies,[12] the decentralization of responsibility and the contractualization of accountability must also be analyzed in light of the historical relationship between a paternal, authoritarian state organization and farmers who were kept as permanent supplicants. Farmers' awareness and resentment of their place at the bottom of this hierarchical relationship are reflected in the commonly heard complaints that "the RID project staff never come to our fields; we must always go to their offices." Reactions to a reorientation in the state-farmer relationship were therefore ones of positive anticipation: the replacement of state-citizen relationships with an employer-employee relationship elevates farmers into new positions in relations of power. If a displacement of traditional relations around water provision allows "farmers to no longer be considered beneficiaries, but rather, clients" (ibid.: 6), the state will be legally bound to fulfill farmers' requests, its obligations to farmers-as-clients now cemented in service contracts exchanging services for money.

However, though the transfer of responsibility from public to private does appear to allocate more power over local resource decisions to local communities, it must be pointed out that this power will probably be transferred only to certain kinds of water users, certain (paying) members within newly constructed WUAs. For, as fiscal responsibility is devolved, participation in the "community" decision-making body will be made conditional upon payment of "cost-sharing"[13] fees, effectively excluding those not able to make payments. Other exclusions from access to water, and/or access to decision making regarding the timing and volume of water supply delivery, are also induced as the WUA becomes responsible for enforcing cost-recovery principles within the community. Any failure to do so will result in the gradual disintegration of the local water supply system. "Empowering" the WUAs to "share" the costs of infrastructure and operation in order to ensure the future of local water supply services gives them little choice but to increase the payments of each water user and to enforce payment and/or exclusion for previously subsidized and perhaps "inefficient" water uses. Marginal water uses/users will probably be made to pay or be excluded from water services, as the common-property water previously provided by the RID to the "general public" within the irrigation project boundaries becomes restricted to the privately serviced "paying public" members of the WUA.

The questions of who within the WUA will be making decisions as to what constitutes "efficient" versus "inefficient" use and what appropriate subsidy, if any, should be granted to more marginal water users raise the issue of internal power conflicts common to any community organization. Presently, project planners seem simply to assume that co-operation will exist among all "equal" members of the WUA. However, as echoed by D. Mosse (1997), the influence of power relations between differently positioned water users holds great potential for internal conflict and varying interpretations regarding "the common good." Within the ISRP projects, issues of class, gender, and rural/urban location are factors likely to complicate operations of a "communal" water users' association that typically amalgamates small-scale farmers growing five rai[14] of subsistence rice crops with successful commercial operators of eighty rai, not to mention local industry and tourism concerns.[15]

Commercialization

The commercialization of irrigation water services sets into motion a different set of displacements. The establishment of service contracts between farmers, the RID, and the private sector means an increase in the production costs of farmers, who will, after all, be paying for these services. To match the increase in costs with an increase in profits, farmers will be encouraged to adopt production patterns based on their commercial profit potential, involving the replacement of lower-value/subsistence crops and the reorganization of livelihood priorities so as to maximize agricultural production.

The ability of farmers to justify the financial and opportunity costs of participating in WUAs – granting access to irrigation infrastructure and water – will be determined by the economic profit returned by irrigation water use, leading to diversification into higher-value crops and/or increased intensity of rice production. The farmers who will not or cannot alter production patterns to raise on-farm profits will be involved in yet another set of displacements as they make choices regarding their future. Those not able/ willing to abandon farming as either the focus of, or supplement to, their current livelihood strategies and yet unable to diversify into higher-value crops may migrate to solely rainfed agricultural land. Others may rearrange their livelihood strategy, remaining on the land but perhaps renting out parts of it and engaging in more off-farm labour; yet others may completely move off rural land into urban areas and wage-labour employment.

However, as with decentralization, certain aspects of the displacements induced by commercialization exist in tension with the above scenarios, preventing the conclusive identification of these policies as instances of negative DID. The benefits of irrigation development programs are evident to a certain population of farmers who do wish to diversify into higher-value agriculture, raise on-farm incomes, and perhaps achieve some of the commercial success of their counterparts in other regions of the country. As chronicled by J. Rigg (1997), the rapid modernization of the countryside in Thailand has raised the expectations and demands of rural households, and the development desires of many Northeastern farmers cannot be ignored or minimized, as perhaps they tend to be by some anti-development campaigns.

Therefore, if, as promoted in the ISRP program, the involvement of private-sector operators helps to raise the production capacities and on-farm income of farmers by providing better water service, the commercialization of irrigation supply services might involve a positive displacement of responsibility. If commercial contractors are driven by financial incentives to adapt their services in response to the needs of commercially oriented farmers, the resulting improvement in the timing and volume of water delivery might make feasible the production of higher-value crops, whose water application needs require both a more reliable and more specific delivery schedule than is currently in place (Halcrow and Partners 2001). Catering to their "customers," and competing with other service providers, private-sector operators are presented as promising a more reliable delivery of water to farmers' farm gates, something never guaranteed by the state, which places farmers at the end of the line for dry-season water allocation (Molle, Chompadit, and Keawkulaya 2000).

Private-Sector Participation

Difficult to distinguish as a distinct policy phase since it is so intimately implicated in both decentralization and commercialization, private-sector participation (PSP) does hold particular ramifications for the ways in which it secures the rescription of citizens into clients. PSP itself is the least emphasized aspect of the ISRP because it serves as a symbol for the anti-privatization campaigns of local NGOs and because it represents what is currently the worst fear of farmers – an increase in irrigation fees. PSP does not come into play until the final phase of the project, when the proportions of costs shared by the state and the farmers becomes borne almost completely by farmers, and the RID has all but completely withdrawn from former service provision. The anxiety expressed by farmers around the cost-sharing fees prompted project promoters to reduce the initial contributions from 210 to 120 baht (from approximately US$5 to US$3) per rai (Molle 2001; Halcrow and Partners 2000), so, of course, the reality of needing to achieve WUA profits great enough to offer attractive fees to private-sector operators is downplayed. Also, in efforts to minimize emphasis on financial contributions of farmers, the project plans stress the possibility of contributing "in kind." Lower-income water users are given the option of paying (at least part of) their fees through contributing labour for daily operational duties and monthly rehabilitation. Regardless of whether or not they choose this option and, by performing such "poor people" tasks, advertise their lesser (economic) status in the community, the fact remains that members of the WUA will simply not be able to take over all the daily duties of operation previously fulfilled by RID staff. Farmers will probably not be able to "donate" enough time to meet daily management requirements, and/or they may lack the capacity to conduct technical engineering work. The contracting out of both heavy labour and skilled management will be necessary, and this labour will need to be paid for by the profits of the WUA, essentially enforcing payments (in kind and/or in cash) for access to water.

The payment of cash for access to water concludes the process initiated in the very first phase of the project: water supply is transformed from a public to a private service, and rights of access shift from one's status as a citizen to one's purchasing power as a client. However, despite the overwhelmingly negative analysis of these citizen/client rescriptions for equity in urban water supply (Bakker 2001; Bond 1999), the case seems more complex for rural water users in Thailand. It is problematic to label the reconfiguration of rights as either an entirely positive or an entirely negative displacement within state-society relations. What is certain is that the transformation of water supply services from a state to a commercial contract means that farmers must now pay for rights that were formerly granted them, albeit somewhat imperfectly, as citizens under the state. Those unable to afford the new articulation of rights, unable to afford participation in the WUA and access to water supply infrastructure, will probably be negatively affected through the displacement of accountability from the state (upon whom, as citizens, they can always make claims) to a private sector operating according to economic imperatives. As cost-sharing fees eventually increase, those able to afford participation in the corporate public sector (WUA) and services from the private sector might come to have more rights to water than do those who cannot. Ostensibly, the question of which particular farmers will determine the affordability of, and authority over, local irrigation water resources will rest simply upon the achievement of the highest "economic efficiency" of water use. In actuality, policies allowing such farmers to concentrate power over local water supply will probably reinforce existing inequalities: farmers able to achieve the higher returns are most likely to be aided in this endeavour by prior advantages of superior soil quality, favourable parcels of land with accommodating topography and advantageous locations along the canal, and surplus capital to invest in farm inputs.

However, what is for the economically and socially marginal water users a decidedly negative ideological displacement from their rights as citizens is held in tension with a more positive interpretation of commercial contracts as representing guaranteed water rights. Farmers' dissatisfaction with their permanent state of dependence upon a sometimes unresponsive state organization and their chronic desire for a more reliable timing and volume of water delivery attract interest in legal guarantees: the right to the delivery of a specified amount of water as guaranteed by a legal financial contract (CUSRI 2001). The historical state-citizen relationship has not always guaranteed delivery of water at a reliable time or volume, and, as stated above, state prioritization of water allocations to urban, industrial uses leaves farmers last in line to receive scarce dry-season water (Molle, Chompadit, and Keawkulaya 2000). Also, though the state construes the water supplied by its planning, financing, operating, and maintaining of irrigation management as a "gift" to farmers, the giving of this gift rests all power with the giver (Vandergeest 1991). The Thai state has never relinquished its authority over setting conditions under which the "gift of water" is bestowed, allowing for negligence, corruption, and unequal allocation between regions (Halcrow and Partners 2001; Molle 2001). Therefore, water users who are willing and able to pay increased fees for access to water view their new power as clients as a positive development.[16]

As is evident from the differing reactions of farmers to aspects of each of the above policies, there is more than one interpretation of displacements induced by this development program; they can be seen as empowering or enforced. Farmers who fit the mould of the neoliberal vision for agricultural development and whose socio-economic status will allow increased diversification into commercial agricultural production, might stand to benefit from the transfer of water rights into economic contracts. However, farmers with less access to capital, and who do not reorient their livelihood practices according to "modern" rationales, might be physically displaced as their rights as citizens are displaced through the commercialization of the water supply.

The potential for *all* of the displacements outlined above to occur in partnership with each other needs to be acknowledged within any analysis of DID, for what is empowered development for some water users might come only at the expense of other users/uses. Were analysts to accept this decidedly less rosy outcome, project planners could then begin to look more closely at factors involved in determining the differential outcomes. If the process of DID holds the potential for effecting such divergent experiences, the questions of how, why, and where these differences are produced must be the first "development dilemmas" to be accorded attention. Those who consider how development policies come to be enabling for some people and disabling for others might look more closely into the contexts of the particular places where development processes are set in motion – at the matrices of political-economic and social relations that help determine the nature of the displacement experience.

Experiences of Displacement: Determinants in Northeast Thailand

The questions of how, by whom, and why the various displacements induced by the irrigation water policy reforms would be experienced were set into the context of two ADB pilot projects in the northeast of Thailand. I chose these specific projects because the region's particular ecology, hydrology, and socio-cultural environment present significant challenges to achieving the type of intensive, year-round, high-value, market-oriented agricultural production necessitated by water policy reforms. Agricultural production techniques and livelihood strategies developed in response to the region's environment limit the level of efficiency and productivity that some farmers can or want to achieve from on-farm production (Rigg 1985), leaving doubt about their future existence on the farm in the face of the irrigation reforms.

Farmers located in the Huay Luang irrigation project, in the province of Udon Thani, and the Thum Samrit irrigation project, in the province of Nakhon Ratchasima, are particularly vulnerable to the more negative aspects of the DIDs outlined above. Historically, the northeast has been the poorest region of the country (Parnwell 1996); it suffered the highest rate of increased poverty after the 1997 financial crisis.[17] In part, the region's poverty results from fluctuations between extreme drought and extreme flooding: 80 percent of the northeast's average rainfall (1,400 millimetres) occurs during five months of the year and is variable in both timing and amount (Parnwell 1988). Coupled with unpredictable water supply, the extremely poor soil quality (acidity, salinity, and poor drainage) keeps agricultural productivity markedly lower than that of other regions; the region comprises

40 percent of the country's total agricultural land area but contributes less than one-quarter of national output (World Bank 2000a). Recording the chronic difficulties of agricultural production in the northeast, M.J.G. Parnwell and J. Rigg (1996) date the beginning of the region's marginalized participation in commercial export agriculture to 1855, when the signing of the Bowring Treaty marked Thailand's first integration into the global agricultural market. Efforts since then to raise the region's rice yields and rural income have involved decades of state- and foreign-funded projects (TDRI 1995; Parnwell, Webster, and Wonsekiarttirat 1986), but the success rate is questionable; 90 percent of the farmers in the region still manage only one rice crop per year, and with 20 percent of households under the poverty line, the region is still the poorest in the country (World Bank 2000b).

The challenges posed by the area's environment to securing stable rural livelihoods have led households to develop agricultural production practices and livelihood strategies that minimize the risks and maximize the benefits of household investments into farming. Uncertain crop yields due to unreliable weather patterns are countered with less intensive production practices and low-risk crop selection, minimizing the investment of capital and labour resources into what are often uncertain outcomes. Livelihood diversification strategies spread household energy between other income-generating endeavours, and on- or off-farm wage labour helps supplement low agricultural incomes for a large percentage of households in the northeast (Jones and Pardthaisong 1999). Perversely, it is these very strategies allowing rural households to survive in a difficult environment that are now threatening to increase probabilities of negative displacements. Examples given below illustrate the development dilemma.

Low-Value, Low-Risk Agriculture: Reliance upon Rice

Low-risk production strategies adopted in response to uncertain yields and fluctuating market profits offer a partial explanation for the hesitation (and perhaps the unwillingness) of farmers to diversify away from rice production into higher-value crops, as called for by the ISRP project. Since poor soil productivity and an unreliable water supply rarely guarantee high yields, cropping choices and production methods requiring minimal labour and capital resources are seen as preferable, allowing farmers to maximize returns for time spent in on-farm activities and leaving more time to be spent in other, less risky income-generating activities. Because rice can be seeded and maintained with relatively little labour until its harvest, has a guaranteed market and established price supports,[18] and supplies the subsistence food requirements of the family, it holds a low risk for not returning the costs of investment by farmers. The role of rice production is most important for low-income families; their dependence upon small-scale production to meet subsistence needs might make the costs of replacing rice with higher-value and higher-risk commercial crops incompatible with their interests in survival.

However, although they are seemingly logical in such a high-risk environment, when inserted into the ISRP framework, the same low-risk production strategies and crop choices are seen as irrational and inefficient uses of irrigation water. Not only does the logic of these local survival strategies fail to match neoliberal goals for economically efficient water use but the low-risk mandates also preclude involvement in a commercially oriented agriculture demanding risky investments in higher-value crops. "Modern" agriculture requires intensive labour and high capital investments for agricultural inputs such as seed, fertilizer,[19] and pesticides,[20] requirements that explain why many small farmers are becoming contract farmers (Goss and Burch 2001; Siamwalla et al. 1992) for the larger agri-businesses that can afford these investments and offer farmers guaranteed prices as well as the technical support of agricultural extension agents. Among households that continue as independent producers, the labour and capital demanded by higher-value agriculture will guarantee neither adequate yields nor adequate prices; for such farmers, the displacement of traditional production strategies by those in line with the logic of economic efficiency will bring much greater risks for future physical displacement as on-farm losses increase.

Pluri-Activity Livelihoods versus Purely Agricultural Profits

The second local livelihood strategy impeding participation by Northeastern farmers in the ADB's vision for agricultural development is, ironically, the voluntary (temporary) displacement of household members. Seasonal migration, family members' moving back and forth between regional, national, and international wage-labour employment, supplements low, unreliable on-farm incomes, making agricultural activity only one (albeit an important) part of a pluri-activity livelihood strategy for most rural households. It is historically characteristic of the region (Parnwell 1988) that it is uncommon to find a rural household without at least one absent member contributing remittances to the family income (Pongsapich 1993). In fact, the number of such households is growing as the rising consumer expectations of rural people increase their desire for and dependence upon wage labour as a source of cash income with which to purchase modern conveniences (Rigg 1997). Currently, with the World Bank (2000a) reporting that average on-farm incomes constitute only 36 percent of total household income, maintaining the ability to spread household energy between multiple income-generating endeavours is crucial for farming families in the northeast.

The problem (for project planners) with what seems to be both a historically established livelihood pattern and a common trend in the transformation from agrarian to industrial economies is that substantial involvement in the off-farm activities precludes increased on-farm investments that constitute the intensive production requirements of higher-value crops. Farmers who are engaged in "part-time" farming merely to guarantee subsistence production might find it difficult to revise the current distribution of household energies in order to cultivate higher-value crops demanding frequent irrigation and time-consuming fertilizer and pesticide applications. The dependency of many families upon off-farm income, combined with their economic and/or cultural refusal to completely abandon their agricultural identities, means both that *current* subsistence-oriented on-farm activities are not economically efficient uses of water and that *future* transformation into more efficient commercial agricultural production is prevented by the diffusion of household labour. The choice of many rural households in the northeast to remain somewhat involved in agricultural production, despite their reliance on and/or preference for more stable and profitable wage labour, deviates from the general urbanization process laid out in development models. As has been noted by many researchers concerned with international development, these deviations present very real problems to development plans (Mosse 1997); in this case, they are proving a definite obstacle to prescriptions that the agricultural sector "will continue to shed resources in the future to fuel the growth of more productive parts of the economy" (World Bank 2000a: xvi).

Whatever the motivation of Northeastern families who still value their attachments to rural livelihoods,[21] the fact that such values run counter to those of neoliberal economic efficiency foreshadows disciplinary action. In order to straighten out these problems for neoliberal development designs, "undeveloped" households will need to be taught how to farm, how to use water – how to become efficient, productive members of society. For, as new irrigation policies begin to demand increased levels of investment into what are now low-value, subsistence-oriented crops, households will be forced to decide whether they are willing/able to use off-farm income to support rising on-farm production costs. Resources for livelihood activities will be displaced to new areas of concentration: farmers will either move labour/capital back to the farm to increase the return on costs of irrigation water use or they will move labour/capital completely off-farm, abandoning low-value production that demands unsustainable investment costs. The question as to whether or not these DIDs are ethical (that is, whether the displacement is coerced or voluntary) hinges on the ability of households to *locate themselves* into new spatial concentrations. The differing abilities of families to *transform themselves* into efficient rural or urban citizens are referred to by the Ministry of Agriculture itself. As stated by an official, "The process of reforming the agricultural sector carries financial risk for the farmers: less income, less cash flow, more expense on new raw material and technology" (*Bangkok Post* 2001). Increases in economic efficiency require not insubstantial amounts of capital for investment into inputs as well as the financial ability to withstand those years when commercial crop prices slump. Given the poverty levels in the northeast, which continue to rise in comparison with those in the rest of the country (World Bank 2000a), and the current level of farm debt among rural households,[22] it is unlikely that the majority of farmers either possess or can avail themselves of the capital necessary for these investments. The likelihood that rural households with less social and financial capital will be more constrained in their ability to increase on-farm investments *or* pursue off-farm labour while meeting household subsistence requirements suggests that, through this development program, the already marginalized might become more marginalized in order to advantage the already advantaged. If, as stated by Mosse (1997: 267), development projects "either open up possibilities for emancipatory change and new access to resources for the disadvantaged, or affirm dominant structures and interests," perhaps ADB project planners should become more concerned with the specific socio-cultural, economic dynamics into which potentials for positive/negative displacements are inserted.

In conclusion, an examination of only two of the eight particular contexts within which Thai farmers will experience DIDs of irrigation management power and water-use priorities suggests that the empowered or enforced nature of these displacements will be determined by how households can react to the respatialization of resources (water, labour, capital, and livelihoods). Ultimately, how they can react will be based upon the social status and socio-economic potential they currently hold. The characteristic neoliberal tension within these policies means that, though a movement out of the agricultural sector and/or pluri-activity livelihoods might not be such a bad thing for *some rural households* who meet certain criteria of class, income, education, skill level, age, and gender, other rural households will suffer decreased access to resources and increased vulnerability to risk. Using the concept of "increased risk" from Michael Cernea's (2001) development-agency-oriented definition of DID, the ADB might at least consider whether this development increases current states of marginalization, widening the gaps between rural households and entrenching existent income inequalities to certainly enhance the potential for a real, physical, direct, forced displacement to occur.

Conclusion: The Ethics of Development-Induced Displacement

The concluding discussion examines some aspects of the relationship between neoliberal development policies and the displacement highlighted within this case study. It foregrounds the ways in which displacements are currently justified through the rationale of neoliberalism but are simultaneously concealed through project processes that work to displace responsibilities for inequitable outcomes away from the development institution. The ADB's rural development program in Thailand, intended to respatialize resources and rural populations, does hold potentials for "harm" in that it both encourages and enforces the eradication of livelihoods and resource use practices that are incompatible with neoliberal development goals. Nonetheless, the project's processes of displacement operate within and through neoliberal policies in such a way that the issue of "potential harm" is denied, as the project itself works to conceal possibilities for inequity.

In Thailand, displacement lies at the very heart of the larger development goal that is moving water resources away from less economically efficient uses/users to more efficient uses/users. Securing national economic development through the "forward movement" of the agricultural sector into high-productivity export-oriented production entails the regional redistribution of sometimes scarce water resources in the name of economic efficiency. The reorganization of water resources, agricultural producers, and water-use opportunities within the rural landscape is therefore at the centre of the development intervention, making displacement both the goal and the means through which "development" will be achieved, as the project itself works through multiple types of displacements. The devolution of power over water resource management from the state to newly enscripted neoliberal citizens, the reallocation of irrigation water according to agricultural production potentials, and the physical movement of the non-competitive rural households out of rural livelihoods and/or out of areas of access for newly commodified irrigation water resources are all processes of displacement through which development goals are to be achieved.

The complexity of these processes, and the ways in which they are mediated through local relations of power to distribute costs and opportunities differentially, means that these displacements are both positive and negative, depending on how the project participants negotiate new identities as market-driven agricultural producers and water customers, how they manage their own "development" from small-scale subsistence rice farmers and citizens of a paternalistic state into citizens exercising their "rights" through market mechanisms. As I have shown in my case study of project sites in Northeast Thailand, some farmers will benefit from new irrigation policies but perhaps only at the cost of marginalizing other farmers who are not as well situated within socio-economic and/or socio-cultural hierarchies. The possibility that the advantages gained by some through the commercialization of water resource management might be achieved only by disadvantaging others produces a paradoxical situation: as we will see below, this intervention into rural livelihoods and resource use, rationalized as "poverty reduction," may actually make particular rural populations even more susceptible to impoverishment.

The ways in which the ADB has negotiated this paradox provide interesting insight into the contradictions inherent within neoliberal development policies and subsequent strategies of development interventions. To begin with, one might ask why the ADB has so far not acknowledged any issues of potential harm that might result from the displacement of water resources from "less efficient" to "more efficient" producers, thus addressing the potential discrepancies through DID-type policies that seek to mitigate "harms." Displacement is, after all, the purpose of the bank's project; not acknowledging the potential for the harmful displacement of those producers who are currently identified as "inefficient" carries a large assumption that all households will be equally able to negotiate the transition to new water use, agricultural production, and livelihood strategies geared towards increasing economic efficiency. This assumption as to ability, as argued in the main body of this chapter, can be interpreted as either – at best – overly optimistic in the face of decades of "failed" agricultural development programs in Northeast Thailand or – at worst – ill-informed about the particularities of local socio-economic, socio-cultural, and ecological contexts currently complicating both desire for and ability to complete the transformation. Why, then, does the ADB not address the potential for harmful displacement of those small-scale, subsistence-oriented producers who fall outside its development trajectory? Why does it not follow up this contradiction within its development intervention by addressing how those "harmed" by the processes of displacement can be assisted and their inequities remediated?

Ethically, the ADB justifies these displacements as necessary for a number of related development goals – efficient water use is crucial in sustaining national economic growth and transforming the agricultural sector – and rationalizes them according to the logic of economic efficiency. The redistribution of water resources according to economic productivity is justified through the ethic of economic efficiency, the set of values within which the project is based. Therefore, the potential harm that the application of this neoliberal management model might hold for households unable and/or unwilling to become more efficient and productive users is a perhaps unfortunate but necessary outcome of a development project that aims to achieve the "greater good," as displacements are codified within DID policies. Those who cannot become more productive farmers are justifiably excluded from access to water resources and eventually pushed to the boundaries of irrigated agricultural areas, continuing to exist but only in ways that do not constrain the operation of a more market-oriented agricultural sector. According to its own set of ethics, then, the ADB is justified in its action or has rationalized the displacement as necessary because it is crucial to development.

The problem for the ADB is that it has also justified this development intervention on the grounds of its "poverty alleviation," arguing that the application of more economically efficient water policies and a more efficient distribution of water resources will lift rural households out of poverty (see ABD 1999; MOAC 1998). Therefore, if the ADB were to admit to the potential for harmful displacement through its project, such an admission would highlight the paradox central to its ideology of development: the ethics of economic efficiency are not always equitable, and neoliberal development policies enforcing economic efficiency might actually contradict goals of poverty reduction. As mentioned earlier, NGOs opposed to both this particular project and ADB operations in Thailand in general hit upon this central contradiction in their campaigns against development policies that prioritize economic efficiency above equity. The project became the cornerstone upon which NGOs questioned the development ideology promoted by the ADB for Thailand and the Asia Pacific region after the 1997 Asian financial crisis. As a result, it was vulnerable to political derailments from its very genesis. Pressured by such opposition, which utilized an entirely different set of ethics through which to assess its justifications for displacements, the ADB could not continue to justify its project to the public on the basis of economic efficiency alone. Because it could not afford to admit to potentially inequitable outcomes of the displacements, it had to construe the project as a "success for all," maintaining to this day a "win-win" scenario for all rural households and the agricultural sector as well as for the other sectors of national economic development that depend on the water currently supplied by irrigation.

There will therefore be no "harmful" displacements experienced as a result of this project, at least not directly, as the potential contradictions in the pursuit of poverty reduction through market-based mechanisms are obscured through political technologies of decentralization and privatization. Denying the potential for both harmful displacements and further impoverishment of particular rural populations, as a result of poverty-reduction strategies, is made possible by a project design that devolves the duties of exclusion and displacement of water users to the project participants themselves. Such an approach deflects blame for any harmful outcomes from the policy to the participants, whose exclusion from water means only that they have "failed" in this development project. Within the ADB's project, the distribution of the costs and benefits of displacement is construed as dependent upon the actions and reactions of project participants: any eventual inequitable distribution of resources and/or harmful displacements become the responsibility of the individual project participant. In this way, it is one's own failure to negotiate new circumstances, one's "stubborn," "ignorant," or "childish" continuation of "irrational" water use practices, agricultural production, or livelihood patterns that transform one into "development's loser." The ways in which water resources and agricultural opportunities might be inequitably distributed among rural households are not therefore the responsibility of the development intervention: they are the "natural outcome" of competition, which determines winners and losers and rewards those who are both willing and able to adopt what the ADB determines are appropriate new identities as market-oriented, high-value agricultural producers.

Notes

1 That is, unproblematized by the development institutions themselves, not by the broader development community.

2 Economic efficiency can be defined broadly as the rational allocation of the resource to its most profitable use; specifically, it also refers to the ability of water use to recover the costs incurred in its provision. The prioritization of economic efficiency within water management results from the recategorization of water from a public to a private, tradable good. The basic assumption that, for the allocation of scarce resources, the market is more efficient than the government means that water provision becomes viewed as a business, which should have as its primary goal the maximization of economic efficiency rather than social equity or security of supply (see Bakker 2002). The World Bank and the ADB have encouraged neoliberalization of the Thai water sector since the early 1990s, funding private-sector participation studies for urban water supply and research into establishment of rural water markets and efficiency analyses (Binnies and Partners 1997; Kaosa-ard 1997).

3 The ADB and JBIC each contributed US$300 million; the loan document was signed in 1999.

4 According to its own website, "The ADB will selectively support programs based on a country's water action agenda. Projects in the pipeline will be reviewed and supported if they conform to ADB's broad water policy principles." http://www.adb.org/documents/news/2001 (accessed 16 January 2001).

5 Following six years of transition and staggered increase of costs borne by farmers, farmers will pay 100 percent of operation and maintenance (O and M) and construction costs of on-farm infrastructure, 100 percent of sub-lateral canal O and M costs, 100 percent of lateral canal O and M costs, 50 percent of main canal O and M costs, and will contribute a minimum of 20 percent for all future capital costs. See Halcrow and Partners (2001) for more details regarding proportions of O and M and future capital costs to be shared between the state and water users.

6 Development of industry, tourism, and commercial agriculture, as well as the expansion of urban areas, demands an ever-larger percentage of Thailand's water supply. This is reflected in the fact that national water use doubled within one decade, going from 20,530 cubic metres per year in 1980 to 43,000 cubic metres per year in 1990 (World Bank 2000a).

7 The contribution of agriculture to the national GDP has declined from over 30 percent in the early 1970s to 11 percent in 1997 (World Bank 2000a). Rice, the main export crop, accounted for only 3.7 percent of all exports in 1997, dropping to one-quarter of its proportional contribution in 1976 (Goss and Burch 2001).

8 As is typical with IMF loans, a number of state reforms were made mandatory. The reforms included those normally associated with structural adjustment programs: reducing the state budget and facilitating increased involvement of the private sector. For more on IMF loan conditions in Thailand, see J. Chomthongdi (2000) and W. Bello (1998).

9 Inequality between urban and rural wages has been rising steadily, and poverty is increasingly concentrated in rural areas: in 1975, 42 percent of the nation's poor lived in rural areas; by 1997, this had increased to 94 percent (Poapongsakorn, Ruhs, and Tangjitwisuth 1998).

10 Many NGOs involved in the campaign against the ADB loan had been or are still involved in campaigns for reparations from displacements induced by dam development (see *Watershed* 2001).

11 For details regarding how these policies, working within programs of irrigation management transfer, have unravelled in other contexts, see D. Hall (2001) for Ghana, R. Meinzen-Dick (1996) for India, R. Meinzen-Dick and M. Sullins (1994) for Pakistan, C.J. Perry (1996) for

Egypt, D. Vermillion (1997) for Mexico, D. Vermillion and M. Samad (2000) for Indonesia, and D. Mosse (1999) for Sri Lanka.

12 As a result of the post-1997 IMF-enforced state budget cutbacks, the Ministry of Agriculture saw a $772 million budget cut. Irrigation financing suffered the largest losses among the ministry's budget items (Goss and Burch 2001).

13 Political sensitivity over the term "cost recovery" prompted the ADB to come up with this new term, which is supposed to reflect more accurately the collaborative nature of the transfer of management responsibilities from the state to farmers (Halcrow and Partners 2001). However, although "cost-sharing" programs do not aim to collect sunk capital investment costs of irrigation infrastructure, their principles are essentially identical to those of cost recovery – elimination of state subsidies.

14 One hectare is the equivalent of 6.25 rai.

15 The existence of extremely heterogeneous water users/uses within the proposed WUAs was a dilemma for project planners, who, while calculating "cost-sharing" payments of members according to land area (baht per rai) (and for problems with this method of calculating contributions, see Molle 2001), had not yet established just how, or at what percentage, non-agricultural users would contribute costs. Given that the regional urban centre of Udon Thani relies upon the Huay Luang irrigation project to furnish its entire municipal water supply, this is no small oversight.

16 The willingness and/or desire of farmers to purchase water rights is especially prevalent among, and perhaps actually restricted to, specific populations of commercially successful farmers: rice farmers in the Central Plains as well as fruit and flower farmers around urban areas. Although these groups definitely cannot be considered representative of farming households in general, they were repeatedly cited by ADB stakeholder surveys seeking to document the "willingness" of (a certain population of) farmers to pay the cost-sharing fees if doing so would guarantee their access to water (Molle 2001; *Bangkok Post* 2000).

17 Poverty rates in the northeast rose from 19.4 percent of the population in 1996 to 30.8 percent in 1999 (World Bank 2000a).

18 Although there is no official rice price support, rice production is so political that the price is somewhat guaranteed, unlike that of other market products: for example, the price of chilies dropped from thirty to two baht per kilogram in one year (Molle 2001). See A. Siamwalla, D. Patamasiriwat, and S. Seboonsarng (1992) for a discussion of the Thai government's rice stabilization program, in relation to other crops.

19 Farmers' concern over fertilizer costs is illustrated by their conversion of the state-imposed Water User Group organizations (set up in the 1990s as a mandate from central RID but existing primarily on paper) into a group for the coordination of fertilizer purchases. "Collective" fees that were supposed to fund canal maintenance went instead to the buying of fertilizer, cheaper when done in large quantities that allow the farmer some leverage with the input supplier.

20 N. Poapongsakorn, M. Ruhs, and S. Tangjitwisuth (1998) list rice as the least pesticide intensive Thai crop (1.1 kilogram per hectare) and high-value vegetable and fruit crops as the most pesticide intensive (6.4 kilogram per hectare).

21 Rigg (1997) emphasizes rather practical economic reasons for why giving up agriculture altogether is still seen as a risky strategy to be avoided whenever and wherever possible. S. Ekachai (1990) and others (see, for example, H.W. Dick 1985) advance socio-cultural foundations to explain why agricultural livelihoods are still valued.

22 J. Goss and D. Burch (2001) report 52 percent of farm households in debt during 1996, in comparison to 27 percent in 1971.

References

ADB (Asian Development Bank). 1999. "ADB Loan to Increase Thailand's Agricultural Productivity." News release No. 083/99. 23 September. http://www.adb.org/documents/news/1999/nr1999083.asp.

Apichart, Anukularmphai. 1999. "Integration of Water Resources Management into Economic and Social Development: An Overview of Experiences in Thailand." *Water Resources Journal* 203: 14-23.

Bakker, K. 2001. "Paying for Water: Water Pricing and Equity in England and Wales." *Transnational Institute of British Geographers* 26: 143-64.
–. 2002. "From State to Market: Water Mercantilizacion in Spain." *Environment and Planning A* 34: 767-90.
Bangkok Post. 1999a. "Activists Oppose Loan Plan." 15 February, http://www.bangkokpost.com (accessed 1 March 1999).
–. 1999b. "Challenge to Terms of $600m Farm Loan." 16 February, http://www.bangkokpost.com (accessed 1 March 1999).
–. 1999c. "Chuan Takes Firm Line on Loan Terms." 17 February, http://www.bangkokpost.com (accessed 1 March 1999).
–. 1999d. "Farmers Won't Be Charged for Water." 19 February, http://www.bangkokpost.com (accessed 1 March 1999).
–. 1999e. "Irrigation Charge Dropped, ADB Loan Decision Today." 23 February, http://www.bangkokpost.com (accessed 1 March 1999).
–. 2000. "Farmers Not Opposed to Water Charge." 1 July, http://www.bangkokpost.com (accessed 2 July 2000).
–. 2001. "Big Break for Farmers." 8 April, http://www.bangkokpost.com (accessed 9 April 2001).
Bello, W. 1998. "Back to the Third World? The Asian Financial Crisis Enters Its Second Year." Focus on the Global South news-serve. 22 July. http://www.focusweb.org.
Binnies and Partners. 1997. "Chao Phraya Basin Water Management Strategy." Report prepared for the World Bank, Bangkok.
Bond, P. 1999. "Basic Infrastructure for Socio-Economic Development, Environmental Protection and Geographical Desegregation: South Africa's Unmet Challenge." *Geoforum* 30: 43-59.
Cernea, M. 2000. "Risks, Safeguards, and Reconstruction: A Model for Population Displacement and Resettlement." In M. Cernea and C. McDowell, eds., *Risks and Reconstruction: Experiences of Resettlers and Refugees,* 11-55. Washington, DC: World Bank.
–. 2001. "Development Economics, Sociology, and Displacement: A Vexing Dilemma under Interdisciplinary Dialogue." Paper presented at Moving Targets: Displacement, Impoverishment and Development Processes Workshop, Cornell University, New York, November.
Chomthongdi, J. 2000. "The IMF's Asian Legacy." Focus on the Global South news-serve. 15 September. http://www.focusweb.org.
Christensen, S., and A. Boon-Long. 1994. *Institutional Problems in Thai Water Management.* TDRI Working Paper, Natural Resources and Environment Program. Bangkok: TDRI.
CUSRI (Chulalongkorn University Social Research Institute). 2001. "Stakeholder Consultation Reports, Final Report for the Social Impact Assessment of the ADB TA 3260-THA." April, Bangkok.
Dick, H.W. 1985. "The Rise of a Middle Class and the Changing Concept of Equity in Indonesia: An Interpretation." *Indonesia* 39 (April): 71-92.
Ekachai, S. 1990. *Behind the Smile: Voices of Thailand.* Bangkok: Thai Development Support Committee.
Ferguson, J. 1990. *The Anti-Politics Machine: "Development," Depoliticization, and Bureaucratic Power in Lesotho.* Cambridge and New York: Cambridge University Press.
Goss, J., and D. Burch. 2001. "From Agricultural Modernization to Agri-Food Globalization: The Waning of National Development in Thailand." *Third World Quarterly Review* 22 (6): 969-86.
Halcrow and Partners, ARCADIS/Euroconsult. 2000. "Capacity Building in the Water Resources Sector Project ABD-TA 3260-THA." Vol.9, "Sharing the Cost of Irrigation." Draft Final Report prepared for the Asian Development Bank.
–. 2001. "Capacity Building in the Water Resources Sector Project ABD-TA 3260-THA." Vol. 3, "Component C: Reorienting and Reorganizing Service Delivery Operations in Irrigation." Final Report prepared for the Asian Development Bank.
Hall, D. 2001. *Water in Public Hands.* Public Services International Research Unit in University of Greenwich, London, June. www.psiru.org/reports/2001-06-W-public.doc.

Jones, H., and T. Pardthaisong. 1999. "The Impact of Overseas Labour Migration on Rural Thailand: Regional, Community and Individual Dimensions." *Journal of Rural Studies* 15 (1): 35-47.

Kaosa-ard, M. 1997. *Formulation of the Chao Phraya Basin Water Resource Management Strategy.* Bangkok: TDRI.

MacLeod, G., and M. Goodwin. 1999. "Space, Scale and State Strategy: Rethinking Urban and Regional Governance." *Progress in Human Geography* 23: 503-27.

Meinzen-Dick, R. 1996. "Reform Options in Indian Canal Irrigation." Paper presented at Workshop on Institutional Reform in Indian Irrigation, New Delhi, November.

Meinzen-Dick, R., and M. Sullins. 1994. *Water Markets in Pakistan: Participation and Productivity.* EPTD Discussion Paper No. 4, International Food Policy Research Institute, Washington, DC. www.ifpri.org/divs/eptd/dp/papers/eptd04.pdf.

MOAC (Ministry of Agriculture and Cooperatives), Office of Agriculture Economics. 1998. *Agriculture Sector Needs Assessment Study.* Draft final report of TA 3002-THA, prepared under technical assistance provided by the Asian Development Bank. Bangkok, November.

Molle, F. 2001. "Water Pricing in Thailand: Theory and Practice." Draft Research Report No. 7, DORAS Center, Kasetsart University, Bangkok.

Molle, F., C. Chompadit, and J. Keawkulaya. 2000. "Dry-Season Water Allocation in the Chao Phraya Basin: What Is at Stake and How to Gain in Efficiency and Equity." Presented at the Chao Phraya Delta: Historical Development, Dynamics and Challenges of Thailand's Rice Bowl, Kasetsart University, Bangkok, Thailand, December.

Mosse, D. 1997. "The Ideology and Politics of Community Participation: Tank Irrigation Development in Colonial and Contemporary Tamil Nadu." In R.L. Stirrat and R. Grillo, eds., *Discourses of Development: Anthropological Perspectives*, 255-91. New York: Berg.

–. 1999. "Colonial and Contemporary Ideologies of 'Community Management': The Case of Tank Irrigation Development in South India." *Modern Asian Studies* 33 (2): 303-38.

Nation. 1999. "Last-Minute Change Jeopardises Farm Loan." 1 April. http://www.nationmultimedia.com (accessed 2 April 1999).

–. 2000. "Groups against Farmers Paying to Use Water." 21 April. http://www.nationmultimedia.com (accessed 22 April 2000).

Parnwell, M.J.G. 1988. "Rural Poverty, Development and the Environment: The Case of North East Thailand." *Journal of Biogeography* 15 (1): 199-208.

–. 1996. *Uneven Development in Thailand.* Aldershot, UK: Avebury.

Parnwell, M.J.G., and J.Rigg. 1996. "The People of Isan: Northeast Thailand Missing Out on the Economic Boom?" In Denis Dwyer and David Drakakis-Smith, eds., *Ethnicity and Development*, 215-48. Chichester, New York: J. Wiley.

Parnwell, M.J.G., C. Webster, and W. Wonsekiarttirat. 1986. *Rural Development in North-East Thailand: Case Studies in Migration, Irrigation, and Rural Credit.* Occasional Paper No. 12 Sub-series of South-East Asian Development. Hull, UK: Centre for South-East Asian Studies.

Perry, C.J. 1996. *Alternative Approaches to Cost Sharing for Water Service to Agriculture in Egypt.* International Water Management Institute (IWMI) Report No. 2. Colombo: IWMI.

Poapongsakorn, N., M. Ruhs, and S. Tangjitwisuth. 1998. "Problems and Outlook of Agriculture in Thailand." *Thailand Research Development Institute Quarterly Review* 13 (2): 3-14.

Pongsapich, A. 1993. *Sociocultural Change and Political Development in Thailand, 1950-1990.* Bangkok: Thailand Research Development Institute.

Rigg, J. 1985. "The Role of the Environment in Limiting the Adoption of New Rice Technology in Northeastern Thailand." *Transactions of the Institute of British Geographers* 10: 66-86.

–. 1996. "In the Fields There Is Dust." *Geography* 80 (1): 23-32.

–. 1997. *South East Asia: The Human Landscape of Modernization and Development.* London: Routledge.

–. 2000. *More than the Soil: Rural Change in South East Asia.* Harlow, Essex: Pearson Education.

Robinson, J., ed. 2002. *Development and Displacement.* Oxford: Oxford University Press.

Sethaputra, S., T. Apanayotou, and V. Wangwacharakul. 1990. *Water Shortages: Managing Demand to Expand Supply*. Research Report No. 3. Bangkok: TDRI.

Siamwalla, A., D. Patramasiriwat, and S. Seboonsarng. 1992. "Public Policies toward Agricultural Diversification in Thailand." In S. Barghouti, L.Garbus, and D.Umali, eds., *Trends in Agricultural Diversification: Regional Perspectives, World Bank Technical Paper No. 180*, 199-214. Washington, DC: World Bank.

Slater, D. 1989. "Territorial Power and the Peripheral State: The Issue of Decentralization." *Development and Change* 20 (3) : 501-31.

–. 2002. "Other Domains of Democratic Theory: Space, Power and the Politics of Democratization." *Society and Space* 20 (3): 255-76.

TDRI (Thailand Development Research Institute). 1995. *Agricultural Diversification/ Restructuring of Agricultural Production Systems in Thailand.* Paper prepared for the Food and Agricultural Organization of the United Nations. Bangkok: TDRI.

Vandergeest, P. 1991. "Gifts and Rights: Cautionary Notes on Community Self-Help in Thailand." *Development and Change* 22: 421-43.

Vermillion, D. 1997. *Impacts of Irrigation Management Transfer: A Review of the Evidence.* International Water Management Institute (IWMI) Report No. 11. Colombo: IWMI.

Vermillion, D., and M. Samad. 2000. *An Assessment of the Small-Scale Irrigation Management Turnover Program in Indonesia*. International Water Management Institute (IWMI) Report No. 38. Colombo: IWMI.

Watershed: People's Forum on Ecology. 2001. "Forum: The Politics of Irrigation." 6 (3) (March-June): 10-24.

World Bank. 1993. *The East Asian Miracle: Economic Growth and Public Policy.* New York: Oxford University Press.

–. 2000a. *A Strategy for Renewing Rural Development in Thailand.* Rural Development and Natural Resource Sector Unit, East Asia and Pacific Region, April 2000. Bangkok: World Bank.

–. 2000b. *Thailand Country Dialogue Monitor.* September, Bangkok.

5

Displacements in Neoliberal Land Reforms: Producing Tenure (In)Securities in Laos and Thailand

Peter Vandergeest

Development in all its forms is inherently a spatial activity. From the most grandiose megaproject employing armies of development to the smallest-scale community-based resource management plan, all development projects involve reorganizing the meaning and control of space. Even the provision of basic infrastructure such as roads, health services, schools, or credit is a spatial activity – some areas gain access to these services and others do not. In this sense, the massive reorganizations of space and lives produced by megaprojects such as large dams are only the most obvious examples of a broader process of the redefinition of space that is inherent to development.

Because development is inherently about reorganizing space, all development has the potential to cause displacement, with most of that displacement taking indirect forms. Indirect displacement occurs when people are not physically forced to move, but when development planning and policies undermine or constrain livelihoods to such degree that people decide to move, seemingly of their own free will, but in a larger context in which their livelihood choices are constrained by development policies. This can happen in many ways. For example, zoning regulations may place people in areas where the state will not provide resource tenure security, or infrastructure and services may be distributed in such a way that people need to move if they want to access them.

If we tie these approaches to development and displacement together, we begin to see the wide range of ways in which development can produce displacement. Even small-scale, locally initiated development can produce displacement insofar as it means reorganizing the meaning and use of space. The literature on common property, for example, has made it clear that exclusion is necessary for common property institutions to be effective and, indeed, the imposition of new boundaries between village forests is one of the major problems plaguing the widespread application of community-based forest management.[1] My focus in this chapter, however, is on the kinds of development pursued by state agencies and large international aid organizations and, specifically on the displacement effects of what I am calling the new land tenure reform agenda. I will illustrate my arguments through an account of land tenure reform in Laos and Thailand.

Land tenure policies are best understood as an aspect of state territoriality. Modern states are defined in part through their claims on jurisdiction over a bounded territory. This involves not only the creation and policing of external territorial boundaries, but internal territorialization (Vandergeest and Peluso 1995) through multiple, overlapping, and contested zoning projects. It also involves claiming the exclusive right to adjudicate access to land and other resources, most often through what governments frame as the allocation of land to individuals or households under land laws. Zoning and land allocation usually have multiple objectives – they cannot be reduced to something simple such as increasing the economic product or making what people do visible as a way of enhancing state power (Scott 1998), although both of these are often important. The main point is that all states to a greater or lesser degree use zoning and land policy to create political spaces and to shape how these spaces are used. Because they are central to the remaking of space, zoning and land allocation policies almost always have displacement effects.

This approach can be used to understand some of the specific mechanisms through which development is systematically linked to displacement. The debates and academic literature on development and displacement seldom address these more systematic processes, focusing instead on direct displacement as exceptional situations that need special justification and appropriate measures for reconstructing lives (see, for example, Cernea 1997; Cernea and McDowell 2000; McDowell 1996). The exception to this emphasis on direct displacement is found among activist groups and academics who now regularly invoke the term *displacement* to criticize the disruptive effect of neoliberal trade, pricing, and privatization policies (see Via Campesina 2000). The policies discussed here can also be described as neoliberal, but my interest is less in trade and markets than in how neoliberal land tenure policies contribute to reorganizing space and resources.

Land tenure reforms demonstrate well the inherent potential for displacement in development in that they are often seen as driven by objectives that seem opposite to those that cause displacement. These include improving access to land for poor farmers or facilitating security of tenure and productive investments through the clarification of property rights (Deininger 2003). How can land tenure reform cause displacement? I will show that the land tenure reform programs of the last two decades in Thailand and Laos should not be seen in isolation, as projects for allocating or titling land, but as part of a broader project that also includes the consolidation of state control over land and the attempt to force farmers out of swidden and subsistence agriculture into permanent and commercial farming. This broader project has clear displacement effects, most obviously in the case of land allocation policies in Laos but also in land titling and land allocation in Thailand.

Context: From Redistribution to Neoliberalism

A comparison of land tenure reform policies in Thailand and Laos since the 1970s shows some surprising similarities in how these policies have changed over time, despite the political differences between Lao socialist and Thai capitalist development policies during this period. In both countries, the most striking change has been a shift from land reform as the redistribution of land from the land wealthy to the land poor, to land reform as the clarification of property rights. Both agendas have been justified partly in terms of their potential for alleviating poverty.

Until relatively recently, neither country has had significant areas of land under the control of large absentee landowners, as found in Latin America and the Philippines (Onchan 1990; Evans 1995). At the same time, landownership within villages is often highly skewed, although there is considerable regional variation within both countries in the degree of inequality. In this context, redistributive land reforms have usually been at the expense of local landowners, producing intense conflicts and resistance within villages (see Ganjanapan 1989). But the dispersed landownership patterns have also facilitated the formation of a common front against external threats to a village's access to land. This helps explain why programs to redistribute private land have generally failed in the face of local opposition, while rural mobilizations to defend a village's land rights as a whole have sometimes been successful.

Both Thailand and Laos created programs to redistribute access to land during the 1970s and 1980s. In Thailand, land reform efforts initiated in the 1970s were a response to growing rural support for the insurgent Communist Party of Thailand and for rural mobilization from 1973 to 1976. Important legislation included the Land Rent Control Act of 1974 and the Agricultural Land Reform Act of 1975. The former contained a variety of provisions regulating and limiting land rents, but opposition from landlords and local officials prevented widespread enforcement (Ganjanapan 1989). The latter established the Agricultural Land Reform Office (ALRO), with a mandate to allocate land to poor farmers. This land was to be obtained in one of two ways: first, by buying land from private owners holding in excess of legally prescribed amounts, determined according to use; and second, by making public land available to the ALRO (Onchan 1990: 83; Chirapanda 2000). But any possibility of significant redistribution of private land or enforcement of land rent controls was effectively ended by a military coup in 1976. The ALRO has instead become an agency for allocating public land to farmers under the new land tenure reform agenda.

In Laos, the collectivization campaigns initiated in 1978 were supposed to redistribute access to agricultural land as well as to make it possible for farmers to be more productive (Evans 1995). But most landowning farmers were not eager to transfer some of their wealth to land-poor villagers through participation in these co-operatives. Collectivization was never made mandatory, and by the mid-1980s, less than 40 percent of farmers had joined cooperatives. Many or most co-operatives, moreover, existed in name only (Evans 1995: 58-63). The government gradually lost its commitment to collectivization, and by the late 1980s, all co-operatives had dissolved, with the original landowning families retaining control of their family lands.

A new approach emerged in both Laos and Thailand during the 1980s, which played down the redistribution of land in favour of the clarification of property rights and tenure security. This new approach can be understood as an expression of neoliberal development policies, in this case, dropping the idea that land reform should reduce rural poverty through state-enforced redistribution of land and replacing it with the concept of land reform as creating appropriate institutions for facilitating private investments in productivity improvements. A lack of tenure security is understood by World Bank lenders as a significant obstacle to private investment and, thus, to improvements in productivity. They argue, moreover, that it is the poor whose property rights to land and resources are least likely to be formally recognized (World Bank 2005a). The World Bank and other development agencies have therefore rapidly expanded their support for projects concerned with clarifying land tenure (ibid.).

As in many countries, only a small proportion of agricultural land in Thailand and Laos was held under registered and legally alienable land titles during the 1980s. In Thailand, most land was held under various kinds of use certificates or land tax receipts, most of which were based on rudimentary forms of cadastral mapping (Vandergeest and Peluso 1995). Millions of cultivators, moreover, farmed land demarcated as state land, most importantly, that in reserve forests and protected areas. In Laos, most cultivators held no official documents at all, as these had been destroyed in 1975 after the war. Legally, all land was owned by the state, but the distribution of use rights was based on informal village-level institutions. There have therefore been two major components to the current land tenure reform policies: first, the extension of land titling and, second, the allocation of state land to households or village collectives. I will briefly discuss land titling before moving on to land allocation.

Land Titling

Both Thailand and Laos have embarked on major programs to extend full land titles to all rural areas. In Thailand, this program has been in place since the 1980s and is based on simplified mapping using aerial photographs.

The Lao program, developed in the mid-1990s, was modelled on the Thai program. It is supported by the World Bank and has so far been extended primarily to urban and peri-urban areas. The long-term intention is to extend it throughout the country, following completion of the Land and Forest Allocation Program (hereafter LFAP), discussed below.

Thailand has had an aggressive program for accelerated land titling since the 1980s, which has allowed it to be treated as a kind of laboratory for studying the effects of these programs. Already by the late 1980s, research conducted in Thailand (Feder et al. 1988) claimed to provide empirical support for the idea that secure and clear land rights would induce cultivators to make productive investments in their land, research that helped justify current World Bank land titling projects around the globe (Deininger 2003; World Bank 2002: 36). However, according to Daniel Maxwell and Keith Wiebe's (1999: 831) review, the evidence supporting this link outside much-cited research in Thailand is mixed: other studies have shown that land titling may not in fact be all that important for increasing productivity or food security. Recent World Bank (2002; Deininger 2003) publications have accepted arguments that the security necessary for encouraging investment can be provided by a variety of tenure arrangements, including customary tenure.

The World Bank has had projects to support land titling in Laos since 1996. The program is modelled on that in Thailand and was initially focused on the urban and peri-urban regions (World Bank 2005b). In the second project, approved in 2003, land titling would be extended to lowland agricultural areas. The project specifically excludes extending land titling to upland areas or areas inhabited by indigenous minorities (Deininger 2003: 38) – although these are the groups who are arguably the poorest in Laos, and who are most vulnerable to tenure insecurity. The exclusion is justified by what an appraisal document calls weakness in the legal and policy framework for land management (ibid.: 21). This allows the bank to claim that the project will not have significant adverse social or environmental impacts (ibid.: 32), easing the approval process. However, the project does include studies and "appropriate measures" that will facilitate future land titling among ethnic minorities (ibid.: 38).

Land titling has been widely criticized for the way in which titles might lead to loss of local control of land and growing class inequalities as small farmers are forced to sell their land due to debts. There is considerable case study evidence that titling has facilitated the sale of rural land to urban buyers in some parts of Thailand (see, for example, Ritchie 1996), especially during the economic boom years of the 1990s when there was widespread land speculation. For example, in Songkla province in the south, the area of my fieldwork, land titling preceded the purchase by urban-based people of almost all the land along the coast as well as of large areas along the Songkla

Lake lagoon. Some of these investors subsequently converted this land into intensive shrimp grow-out farms, especially after the drop in land prices during the Asian economic crisis made it impossible for them to recoup their investments through sale of the land

It is not clear, however, that sale of land to non-local buyers does in fact cause impoverishment or displacement in these two countries. Jonathan Rigg (2001), citing Mark Ritchie (1996) as well as his own fieldwork in villages near Chiangmai, for example, argues that access to non-farm work and education has become much more important than land in shaping rural differentiation. Ritchie and Rigg both go so far as to suggest that those who took advantage of land price inflation by selling land may be among the new village rich. Some of these conclusions may not be generalizable through the rest of Thailand, but in my research in the south of Thailand I also did not find evidence of impoverishment or displacement due to the way that titling facilitated the sale of land.

The most important displacement impacts of land titling may lie less in the way that it facilitates the sale of land than in the way it reshapes the definition and control of space. These effects can be produced in at least two ways. First, land titles clarify and protect individual or private property rights inside the spatial boundaries delineated through cadastral mapping but do not make provisions for protecting common property resources outside these boundaries. Even in intensive agricultural zones, there are many important common property resources. Shrimp farming, for example, has had major impacts on surface and ground water, collective pastures, and fisheries (Vandergeest, Flaherty, and Miller 1999). In Songkla province, thousands of rice farmers have found their water supplies and fields salinized by shrimp farming; hundreds of other villagers raising sea bass in cages along the shore of the lagoon blame fish die-offs on the disposal of polluted shrimp pond sediments in public waterways. Although there have been widespread protests and conflicts over these problems, villagers and local government officials repeatedly cite the landowners' right to do as they please with their private property as a reason for not trying to stop shrimp farming. In shrimp-farming areas, in other words, the exclusive focus on the clarification of household property rights without attention to local inequalities and common property rights has led to indirect displacement of important livelihood activities.

Second, land titling is incorporated into broader zoning processes which divide land into that suitable and that not suitable for agriculture. Land zoned not suitable for agriculture is often placed under the jurisdiction of state agencies, most commonly the forestry departments. In Laos, this link is explicit: the titling project is supposed to follow successful completion of the Land and Forest Allocation Program (LFAP), currently the most important means for implementing this kind of zoning. Specifically, the land titling project includes a component for studying the "modalities" through which Temporary Land Use Certificates issued under the LFAP can be converted to land titles and foresees an extension of land titling to upland areas when these modalities have been developed and adopted by the government. The bank's current exclusion of upland areas is no doubt a reaction to the criticisms of the LFAP that are now circulating among donor agencies, and it is thus linking expansion of the land titling project to reforms in this program. An examination of the LFAP in Laos and of land allocation programs in Thailand will illustrate how land allocation processes can lead to massive displacement.

Land Allocation

In both Laos and Thailand, large numbers of farmers occupy land classified as non-agricultural, or non-arable, and claimed by state agencies – most importantly, by their respective forestry departments. In these areas, the clarification of property rights has meant resolving these conflicting claims to land and forest resources.

In many ways, the Lao approach looks like the kind of program promoted by grassroots development organizations, community forestry advocates, and good-governance theorists. The LFAP provides villagers with collective rights to both forest and agricultural land. The allocation of collective forests, in particular, compares favourably with that of other governments in the region, who often claim all so-called natural forests as the exclusive preserve of state management agencies (Peluso and Vandergeest 2001). The "eight-step" allocation process in use since 1996 was developed through the Lao-Swedish Forestry Program (2001) and adopts what looks on paper like a highly participatory approach to negotiating village boundaries and village zoning. By 1999, agreements had been completed with about 6,900 villages, 50 percent of all the villages in Laos (Lao PDR Prime Minister's Office 2000). The entire process demonstrates that neoliberal programs to clarify property rights can be compatible with land allocation processes that mix individual and collective rights to resources and use participatory processes that draw on techniques developed by community-based NGOs.

The goals of this program include not only the clarification of property rights but also poverty alleviation through extension activities, and the promotion of community-based forest management, forest conservation, and the so-called stabilization of swidden agriculture. The central importance of the last goal, however, is indicated by the alternative name for the program – the "Shifting Cultivation Stabilization Program" – used by both the Forestry Department and by the Asian Development Bank pilot project, which is supposed to be the basis for a revamping of the allocation process to make it even more "holistic" and "participatory" (Asian Development Bank 2002). The World Conservation Union (IUCN) is also using the LFAP to contain swidden agriculture in the twenty National Biodiversity Protection Areas declared in 1993, which cover about 14 percent of national territory (Galt, Sigaty, and Vinton 2000: 50).

Notwithstanding the language of participation, decentralization, and community rights, evidence is growing that this program is a primary cause of displacement and impoverishment in Laos. Although it is impossible to determine how many people have moved, whether entirely or partially due to the allocation program, their numbers probably dwarf those displaced by controversial and internationally contested dams. In village-based studies by researchers at the National University of Laos (NUOL), in which I was involved (Silakone et al. 2001; Sannhavong et al. 2001), preliminary data show that, after the land and forest allocation, substantial out-migration occurred from both of the sites in which villagers practised swidden agriculture. In a Hmong village, for example, after the LFAP, over a third of the sixty-two Hmong families left the village for various other locations (Sannhavong et al. 2001). Reports on other sites around the country confirm these results. In 2004, when this chapter was written, the most convincing documentation was a participatory poverty assessment conducted in ninety villages through the State Planning Committee (2000). It found that the most commonly cited cause of poverty was land problems, mostly attributable to the LFAP. The report described, using quotes and examples, how the allocation process forced villagers to shorten fallow cycles, which in turn caused soil depletion and declining rice yields (ibid.: 7, 8, 12; for a more recent review see Baird and Shoemaker 2005).

More indirect evidence of the displacement and impoverishing effects of the program is presented by a UNESCO/UNDP study (Goudineau 1997) of resettled villages in Laos. According to this study, one-third of all villages had moved due to direct and indirect pressure to resettle and stop swidden agriculture; in some areas, the figure could be as high as 50 to 85 percent (ibid.: 20). In many cases this pressure was exerted by the restrictions introduced through land allocation. Resettlement, moreover, did not necessarily eliminate swidden agriculture, as many sites did not have land suitable for permanent farming. Villagers' ability to continue producing food was thus seriously compromised: the pressure from government policies, combined with population concentration, forced them to work with short fallows; in the first years after the move, draught animals had to be sold, partly to enable villagers to buy rice, resulting in a shortage of livestock; villagers did not have sufficient knowledge about farming in their new ecological environments; and villagers' health and capacity to work were often seriously affected.

At the same time, the LFAP has been welcomed by many farmers. The sense of tenure security derived from the documentation of village territories is very important in a country that has seen much instability during the past half century. For example, villagers in the single ethnic Lao village included in the NUOL research had twice lost paddy land due to dam construction, for which they had not been compensated; they hoped that the land allocation would prevent further uncompensated losses. In addition, they believed that restrictions introduced by the program on the swidden agriculture practised by the neighbouring Hmong village would improve water supplies to their wet rice fields.

The NUOL studies, together with other studies (State Planning Committee 2000), show that the non-Lao ethnic groups, which comprise about 45 percent of the population, are most at risk of displacement and impoverishment and that ethnic Lao are most likely to benefit from the program. Non-Lao ethnic groups are more likely to have lived in upland areas in the past and to have responded to government pressure to move to lowland sites. When they arrive in these sites, they often find that existing residents – typically ethnic Lao – already control most land suitable for permanent cultivation. They are thus forced to rely on swidden agriculture, livestock raising, and forest product collection (Hirsch 1997). This was the case for the Hmong village in the NUOL study, which was established in the early 1980s in response to government requests that it move to a lowland area: upon relocating, the Hmong found that the best paddy land was already occupied by ethnic Lao villagers. For many ethnic minorities, then, the land and forest allocation process provides not tenure security but new insecurities as their agricultural practices are rendered illegal.

When the LFAP was initiated, there was widespread support for a program of this nature among a broad spectrum of officials, development aid organizations, NGOs, and academics, all of whom cited the need to resolve ambiguity and conflicts over resource tenure and to base resource management on village-level needs and institutions (Australian Mekong Resource Centre 2002; Pravongviengkham 2000). A number of economic and demographic processes have created conflicts over access to resources as well as rapid resource degradation in some areas. These processes include increased integration of rural Laos into a market economy, increased demands on valuable forest and water resources by Thailand, the resettlement of people displaced by war, and internal migration induced by government policies to concentrate rural people in "focal sites" for development (Pravongviengkham 2000; Goudineau 1997). The resolution of the conflicts over access to land and resources that have emerged since the war cannot be achieved without some claimants' giving up their claims on at least some resources. A certain amount of indirect displacement of access to livelihood resources, in other words, may be unavoidable and justified, especially where the demarcation of village boundaries is achieved through inter-village negotiation and mutual consent.

All of which leads to the question of how a land tenure reform program that seems to incorporate so many of the currently popular approaches to grassroots development and community-based resource management can have so many deleterious effects. The answer lies within the context of the government's larger efforts to reorganize the use of space in Laos. The LFAP not only allocates land to farmers but also designates as state-owned large areas of forest land outside the new village territories, although much of this land has long been used by rural people. Today, the program is justified through managerial forms of environmental knowledge produced by (or, more accurately, recycled by) newly greened development agencies such as the World Bank (Goldman 2001) and the Asian Development Bank (ADB). The drive to reorganize space in this fashion was not introduced by international aid agencies: it was part of Pathet Lao policies almost from the moment they were able to control territory (Evans 1999: 127-28). What the international aid agencies have done is to help the Lao government systemize this reorganization into a national program and rationalize it through combining scientific discourses around biodiversity, land classification, and watershed protection. These are linked through a program drawing on the standardized toolkit for participation that circulates through development agencies as well as on neoliberal ideas about the importance of tenure security for enhancing productivity. The net result of this reorganization of space is supposed to be the concentration of productive farmers into clearly demarcated lowland areas and along major transportation routes, leaving most space uninhabited, covered by forest, and administered by state agencies.

Scientific rationalization is provided in part by land capability assessments that find that most land in Laos is unsuitable for agriculture and should be maintained as, or converted to, forest. A series of organizations have made separate assessments of the amount of land suitable for agriculture, with considerable variation in the results. According to the IUCN, only 3.3 percent of land in Laos is arable, though 34.3 percent of land in Thailand is arable (Chape 1996). The 1998-99 Lao agricultural census gives the total arable land as 3.7 percent of national territory. The Strategic Vision for the Agricultural Sector (Lao PDR MAF 1999) uses criteria such as slope and soil fertility to arrive at a figure of 15 to 32 percent. Although the results differ according to how different agencies view upland agriculture, all these figures rely on research and knowledge produced by non-Lao development agencies such as the World Bank, the ADB, or the Food and Agriculture Organisation (FAO)(ibid.: 20), and all of them classify most land in Laos as non-arable, although calculation of the percentage of non-arable land in these studies ranges from 68 to 96 percent. The LFAP is supposed to contribute to the objective of eliminating agriculture on non-arable land, where the primary forms of agriculture include swidden or rotational cultivation as well as grazing for livestock. The focus, however, is on stopping swidden cultivation. The primary means for doing this has been to demarcate village boundaries, zoning village land so that swidden cultivation is permitted only on land without "secondary" or "primary" forest cover, and, most controversially, enforcing a three-year maximum rotation period, much shorter than necessary for sustainable upland agriculture. According to an author interview conducted with the chief of the Ministry of Agriculture and Forestry's Shifting Cultivation Stabilization Office, the goal is to completely eliminate swidden agriculture by the year 2010. Local officials are required to report the area under swidden agriculture on an annual basis; officials who do not report decreases or meet targets may have their figures changed so that the appearance of success is maintained (personal communications 2001). The net effect is to compromise a participatory process with very restrictive rules and the need to meet targets, all to enforce the new organization of space based on environmental management criteria.

This attack on swidden agriculture is based on four assumptions, all of which have been challenged by research in Laos and in the wider literature on swidden agriculture. These are that swidden causes poverty, is becoming unsustainable given increasing population densities, destroys forests, and reduces water available for lowland agriculture.

First, with respect to poverty and swidden, the studies I have cited above indicate that the causality should often be reversed. Farmers make swidden fields for a variety of ecological and cultural reasons, but NUOL and other research (State Planning Committee 2000) indicates that they are not necessarily adverse to abandoning swidden for permanent agriculture. They fail to make this transition because they lack access to land suitable for permanent cultivation. That is to say, it is poverty, understood as lack of legal access to suitable land for agriculture, that is the cause of new poverty; this was the key finding of the State Planning Committee's (2000) participatory poverty assessment.

Second, my reading of the development literature on Laos, available both in published form and in project documents, suggests that the impact of population increase on swidden cultivation in Laos is often exaggerated. Data on the decreasing period of fallows and falling yields in swiddens often play down the fact that these changes are the result of government restrictions on swidden, attributing them instead to increasing population density (see, for example, Roder 1997). In many cases, population density and resource scarcity have become a problem, not because of an overall shortage of land, but because of population concentration due to migration and government policies encouraging people to settle in lowlands (see Thapa

1998; Australian Mekong Resource Centre 2002; Pravongviengkham 2000; Goudineau 1997). Consider that the overall population density of Laos is only about twenty-two persons per square kilometre (compare to about 250 in Thailand and 1,000 in Vietnam); in addition, because the population is concentrated in urban and lowland areas, densities in upland areas are even lower than the national average. The point is that these low population densities suggest that it would be very difficult for swidden agriculture to be a major cause of deforestation. This conclusion is reinforced by the agricultural studies cited above. For example, the 1998-99 agricultural census reports that the total land used for agriculture, including land under swidden fallow, was only 10,000 square kilometres, out of a total land area of 236,800 square kilometres – 4.2 percent of national territory. The Strategic Vision for the Agricultural Sector draws on its more optimistic assessment of arable land to estimate that the average area of land suitable for agriculture per family (including lowland wet rice cultivation) is between five and ten square hectares – which is enough to allow for a considerable area of swidden and swidden fallow.

Third, and related to the sustainability question, there is a sizable international literature that argues that swidden may transform or manage forests but does not necessarily destroy them. Jefferson M. Fox (2000; Fox et al. 2000), for example, draws on fieldwork in various mainland Southeast Asian sites where population densities are much higher than those in Laos to argue that swidden may often be the best means of preserving forest biodiversity and the most suitable land use for meeting the needs of local communities. With respect to Laos, both local case studies (Thapa 1998; Fujisaka 1991) and countrywide analyses (Anonymous 2000) suggest that commercial logging, rather than swidden, has been the primary cause of deforestation. Case study research also provides many instances of situations where swidden has not had a major impact on forest cover (for example, Thapa 1998; Sandewall et al. 2001).

Fourth, the notion that deforestation or swidden agriculture invariably decreases lowland water supplies finds little support from researchers who have studied the hydrological effects of different land use systems (Forsyth 1996; Walker 2003; Saberwal 1997). This assumption, nevertheless, pervades discussions of the benefits of the program, from official documents to village-level negotiations. In the NUOL research sites discussed above, for example, district officials used the promise of increased water for lowland agriculture as a way of convincing villagers to agree to restrictions on swidden. The preparatory report for the ADB pilot project (Asian Development Bank 1998: 8) is particularly indicative of how this assumption justifies the reorganization of space and livelihoods, even in the face of contrary evidence in the same report. According to its Annex 4 on forestry, the improved protection and management of forest watersheds should make it possible to irrigate the 92 percent of lowland rice fields that were not yet irrigated in the target provinces as well as to generate more hydroelectric power. These are astounding assumptions; the idea that eliminating swidden could somehow better regulate water supply is contradicted in the next paragraph, which observes that fallows in the project area regenerate into woody growth; that the mountain landscape is, as a result, not one large open area but a mosaic of cultivated patches surrounded by wide fields of forest fallows; and that, in this situation, adverse ecological impacts have not occurred. Surprisingly, the report goes on to conclude optimistically that this will make high-cost reforestation of old swidden fields unnecessary when or if swidden farmers reduce or stop their slash and burn activities. The obvious alternative conclusions – that swidden agriculture in this area is an ecologically benign or even beneficial form of cultivation (Fox 2000) and that stopping swidden will not produce more irrigation water – are not considered in the report.

The problems with the current LFAP are now widely recognized; as a result, some government officials and development aid organizations have begun to search for an alternative, more flexible, process. Examples include the ADB project and reports produced for the Lao-Swedish Forestry Program before it ended in 2001 (for example, Jones 1998). But the ADB project remained committed to the overall objectives of "stabilizing" shifting agriculture and reorganizing space into separate agricultural and forest zones. Policies in at least some areas have become more flexible: according to P.P. Pravongviengkham (2000: 80), Lao head of the ADB pilot project, the Ministry of Agriculture and Forestry discontinued its strict enforcement of limitations on swidden in areas lacking sufficient land for permanent agriculture. As I write this, it is unclear whether this loosening up of the program will fundamentally change the policy of using the land and forest allocation to reduce and eventually eliminate swidden cultivation.

Although there are some important differences between Laos and Thailand, the Thai government's basic approach to the cultivation of land claimed by state agencies is based on a vision and framing assumptions similar to those of Laos. The method is to divide reserve forests into land that can be removed from the Forestry Department's jurisdiction and allocated to farmers by the ALRO, and land that will remain under the Forestry Department's control.[2] By 1997, about 37 million rai of primarily public land (11.5 percent of national territory) had been declared land reform areas, and about 10 million rai (160,000 square hectares) had been allocated under ALRO land documents to about 500,000 families (Chirapanda 2000). The government sets annual targets for declaring land as land reform areas, and the ALRO negotiates boundaries with the Forestry Department. The limits on the land reform areas are based on a variety of criteria, including slope and existing land classifications. The most important is that land classified as a protected area, a class 1A watershed, or "conservation" forest cannot be turned over to the ALRO (author interviews in Southern Thailand; Chirapanda 2000). As part of its reconstitution as a conservation organization, and to stave off pressure to legalize cultivation on reserve forest land, the Forestry Department converted large areas of reserve forest into protected areas and began implementing watershed zoning regulations. As of 1999, there were 266 protected areas covering about 17 percent of the land area (87,696 square kilometres), with another 57 proposed, which would cover an additional 24,610 square kilometres, for a proposed total of about 22 percent of the land area. In addition, the ALRO program does not allow for the allocation of collective forest lands to villagers – unlike the Lao program.

The impacts of these limits on land reforms were apparent in my upland research site in Satun province, Southern Thailand. The primary livelihoods in this area were rubber and fruit cultivation; the rubber had been planted during the 1960s and 1970s on former swiddening land. Almost all the rubber smallholdings and many of those devoted to fruit had been demarcated as reserve forests. One village had part of its territory incorporated into a wildlife sanctuary. The ALRO land allocation program coincided with a redemarcation of the boundaries on the wildlife sanctuary; as a result, most villagers were in effect allocated their rubber plots through these two processes. The land reform documents provided them with tenure security, gave them access to benefits available through government programs such as the rubber replanting program, and facilitated investments in intensification. The latter occurred, for example, in the expansion of fruit orchards, a result that, in this case, supports World Bank arguments about the benefits of tenure security. Intensification, in turn, has decreased pressure for further expansion of rubber planting into the forest.

But land at higher elevations was not included in the ALRO land allocation program: this land was classified as conservation forest by the Forestry Department, and some of it remained in the wildlife sanctuary. It was the poorest villagers – recent migrants or young families who did not have land nearer the villages – who were most affected by these exclusions. In most cases, they continued to tap rubber with the implicit consent of local forest guards. However, the guards were not so lenient with respect to cutting down rubber trees in the wildlife sanctuary. Villagers with rubber in the sanctuary who wanted to replace it with higher-yielding rubber varieties or fruit trees were forced to clear existing rubber surreptitiously (at night). Outside of the wildlife sanctuary, villagers without land documents were not monitored as closely, but they found that they no longer qualified for government replanting assistance and that they were excluded from access to infrastructure such as roads and electricity.

Although the land use zoning implicit in the land reform process constrained the ability of some villagers to pursue their livelihoods in the Satun research site, no one was threatened with eviction or resettlement during my research (1998-99). The situation in the north of Thailand is more difficult – large numbers of people have been completely enclosed within protected areas, and the government has frequently threatened them with forced relocation. The underlying justifications are the same as those used in Laos – that upland agriculture destroys forests, is unsustainable with increasing population pressure, and reduces water available for lowland agriculture. As in Laos, upland ethnic minorities are most likely to be enclosed in protected areas, as many of them live in areas that are not part of the land reform program. So far, the government has not been able to evict many villagers. Affected villages have mobilized collectively through influential networks to resist these policies (Laungaramsri 2000), and there have been disagreements among government agencies about the appropriate approach. Government agencies are, however, finding ways of putting indirect pressure on upland minorities enclosed in protected areas and conservation forests, as, for example, through exclusion from roadbuilding and electrification (Maniratanavongsiri 1999). Ethnic minorities are also subject to violent harassment, signalling that their right to live in the uplands remains in question (Vandergeest 2002; Lohmann 1999).

In recent years, resistance to these policies has coalesced around demands for a community forest law that would permit community forests inside protected areas (Laungaramsri 2000), although land use in these zones would still be subject to many restrictions. As I revised this chapter in 2005, community forest laws continued to be debated but seemed at the moment to provide the most promising way of shifting some control over spatial reorganization and land management to those who are most directly impacted.

New Directions?

People throughout the mountainous zones of mainland Southeast Asia have long exhibited high levels of mobility due to war, the search for more productive environments, tax evasion, and so on (Goudineau 1997). What makes the land tenure reforms and associated resettlement programs of the last few decades distinctive is the fact that they are the outcome of development policies that seek to systematically reorganize space into two broad zones: the first is state land, usually uplands, covered by forests and used either for logging or conservation; the second is private or community land, typically in the lowlands and characterized by intensive commercial agriculture. This has involved moving people out of the ecological spaces to which they are accustomed and into spaces that they probably would not have chosen on their own. The dramatic effects of these policies are particularly apparent in the Lao case. The displacement impacts of the new land tenure reform policies are largely due to the way in which they reinforce this reorganization of space.

I am not arguing that land tenure reform programs should be discontinued. I have been careful to note in this chapter that many people do benefit from these programs: beneficiaries obtain legal recognition of resource rights in situations where they have previously been subject to uncompensated expropriations; they are able to use land rights as security for credit; they are more able and willing to make investments that improve incomes; they obtain better prices for their land, and so on. In other words, some of the basic tenets of neoliberal approaches to land reform cannot be dismissed. These benefits are important and could provide adequate justification for pursuing these policies – if they were subject to significant changes.

In Thailand and Laos, land tenure reform policies produce displacement and impoverishment when they are incorporated into national-level land use policies that enclose resources in state property and try to reorganize space in ways that deprive some people of their ability to maintain their livelihoods. Land titling programs can also create difficulties for poor people because they allocate private property rights without any constraints on how the use of this property might affect common property resources. There are other ways in which land tenure reform can lead to displacement, but my review of these programs suggests that, for the Thai and Laotian sites, enclosure/reorganization and land titling play the most important roles.

It is possible to correct these problems, but only with significant changes to the assumptions that guide current land tenure reforms. In the case of land titling, these programs could include provisions that constrain the ability of landowners to destroy common property resources and that allow for local collective regulation in the use of private resources. More importantly, land titling could be framed as only one of a series of legal channels through which people can gain land tenure security, with local people participating in the definition of which approach is most appropriate. In Thailand, the passage of a flexible community forest law would be a first step in this direction. In the case of land allocation, policies to eliminate swidden and reorganize space into distinct forest and agricultural zones need to be reconsidered. Swidden and other upland land uses, such as grazing livestock, could be treated as a viable and flexible farming system that could accommodate intensification and investment in the right circumstances. All of this comes down to the importance of opening up the process so that villagers can participate not just in implementing a land allocation model but also in choosing which kind of land tenure security and management system is most appropriate, as well as how much land they may use and manage.

With respect to the broader question of development and displacement, this chapter is in part an argument that our focus should expand beyond debates over megaprojects such as large dams to a consideration that any kind of development contains within it the potential to cause displacement. By linking neoliberal land tenure reforms to land use zoning, I have highlighted what turns out to be a fairly obvious example of how development involves the spatial reorganization of people and what they do, often without their participation in anything other than implementation of an approach generated by government agencies and development aid organizations. The essential understanding that displacement is inherent in development policies could be extended to many other forms of development activity. This implies that all development programs need to be assessed for their possible displacement impacts and that provisions concerning population displacement, such as those currently debated in the World Bank, could be applied to all development projects, programs, and policies.

Acknowledgment

This is an expanded version of "Land to Some Tillers," originally published in *International Social Science Journal* 55 (155) (March 2003): 47-56.

Notes

1 General models developed by common property theorists always indicate that groups that manage common property need to be able to exclude non-members – who would otherwise be considered free-riders benefiting from the management work and restrictions invested by members – from accessing commons resources. Extensive literature is available through the website for the International Association for the Study of Common Property: http://www.iascp.org/resources/articles.html.

2 After I completed the research upon which this chapter is based, the Forestry Department was split up, with jurisdiction over protected areas moving to another department. This change has not affected my basic approach or lines of contestation.

References

Anonymous. 2000. "Aspects of Forestry Management in the Lao PDR." *Watershed* 5 (3): 57-64.

Asian Development Bank. 1998. "Annex 4." In *Lao PDR Shifting Cultivation Stabilization Project Preparation Report.* Rome: FAO/Asian Development Bank Cooperative Programme.

–. 2002. "Lao PDR Shifting Cultivation Stabilization." http://www.adb.org/Documents/Profiles/LOAN/29210013.ASP (accessed 15 October 2002).

Australian Mekong Resource Centre. 2002. "Resource Management in the Nam Ngum Watershed, Lao PDR." http://www.mekong.es.usyd.edu.au/case_studies/nam_ngum/a_multi.htm (accessed 15 October 2002).

Baird, Ian G., and Bruce Showmaker. 2005. "Aiding or Abetting: Internal Resettlement and International Aid Agencies in the Lao PDR." Toronto: Probe International. http://www.probeinternational.org.

Cernea, Michael. 1997. "Risks and Reconstruction Model for Resettling Displaced Populations." *World Development* 25 (10): 1569-87.

Cernea, Michael, and Christopher McDowell, eds. 2000. *Risks and Reconstruction: Experiences of Settlers and Refugees.* Washington, DC: World Bank.

Chape, Stuart. 1996. *Biodiversity Conservation, Protected Areas and the Development Imperative in Lao PDR: Forging the Links.* Vientiane: IUCN.

Chirapanda, Suthiporn. 2000. "The Thai Land Reform Programme." http://www.seameo.org/vl/landreform/index1.htm (website for ALRO).

Deininger, Klaus. 2003. *Land Policies for Growth and Policy Reduction.* World Bank Policy Research Report. Washington, DC: World Bank.

Evans, Grant. 1995. *Lao Peasants under Socialism and Post-Socialism.* Chiangmai: Silkworm Books.

–. 1999. "Ethnic Change in the Northern Highlands of Laos." In Grant Evans, ed., *Laos: Culture and Society,* 124-47. Chiangmai: Silkworm Books.

Feder, G., Tongroj Onchan, Yongyuth Chalermwong, and Chira Hongladarom, eds. 1988. *Land Policies and Farm Productivity in Thailand.* Baltimore: Johns Hopkins University Press.

Forsyth, Timothy. 1996. "Science, Myth, and Knowledge: Testing Himalayan Environmental Degradation in Thailand." *Geoforum* 27 (3): 375-92.

Fox, Jefferson M. 2000. *How Blaming "Slash and Burn" Farmers Is Deforesting Mainland Southeast Asia.* AsiaPacific Issues 47. Honolulu: East-West Center.

Fox, Jefferson M., Dao Minh Truong, A. Terry Rambo, Nghiem Phuong Tuyen, Le Trong Cuc, and Stephen Leisz. 2000. "Shifting Cultivation: A New Old Paradigm for Managing Tropical Forests." *BioScience* 50 (6): 521-28.

Fujisaka, S. 1991. "A Diagnostic Survey of Shifting Cultivation in Northern Laos: Targeting Research to Improve Sustainability and Productivity." *Agroforestry Systems* 13: 95-109.

Galt, Annabelle, Todd Sigaty, and Mark Vinton, eds. 2000. "Executive Summary." In *The World Commission on Protected Areas, 2nd Southeast Asia Regional Forum, Pakse Lao PDR, 6-11 December 1999.* Vol. 1. Vientiane, Lao PDR: IUCN.

Ganjanapan, Anan. 1989. "Conflicts over the Deployment and Control of Labor in a Northern Thai Village." In Gillian Hart, Andrew Turton, and Benjamin White, eds., *Agrarian Transformations,* 98-124. Berkeley: University of California Press.

Goldman, Michael. 2001. "The Birth of a Discipline: Producing Authoritative Green Knowledge, World-Bank Style." *Ethnography* 2 (2): 191-217.

Goudineau, Yves, ed. 1997. *Resettlement and Social Characteristics of New Villages.* Vientiane: UNESCO and UNDP.

Hirsch, Philip. 1997. "Seeking Culprits: Ethnicity and Resource Conflict." *Watershed* 3 (1): 25-28.

Jones, P.R. 1998. *Options for Forest-Land Use Planning and Land Allocation.* Vientiane: Laos-Swedish Forestry Program.

Lao PDR MAF (Ministry of Agriculture and Forestry). 1999. *The Government's Strategic Vision for the Agricultural Sector.* Vientiane: Government of Lao PDR.

Lao PDR Prime Minister's Office. 2000. *National Environmental Action Plan.* Vientiane: Government of Lao PDR.

Lao-Swedish Forestry Program. 2001. *Experiences from the Lao Swedish Forestry Program 1995-2001.* Vientiane: Swedish International Development Agency (available on CD-Rom).

Laungaramsri, Pingkaew. 2001. *Redefining Nature: Karen Ecological Knowledge and the Challenge to the Modern Conservation Paradigm.* Chennai: Earthworm Books.

Lohmann, Larry. 1999. *Forest Cleansing: Racial Oppression in Scientific Nature Conservation.* Corner House Briefing 13. http://www.thecornerhouse.org.uk/item.shtml?x=51969.

Maniratanavongsiri, Chumporn. 1999. "People and Protected Areas: Impact and Resistance among the Pgak'nyau (Karen) in Thailand." PhD diss., Ontario Institute for Studies in Education, University of Toronto.

Maxwell, Daniel, and Keith Wiebe. 1999. "Land Tenure and Food Security: Exploring the Dynamic Linkages." *Development and Change* 30: 825-49.

McDowell, Christopher, ed. 1996. *Understanding Impoverishment: The Consequences of Development-Induced Displacement.* Oxford: Berghahn Books.

Onchan, Tongroj, ed. 1990. *A Land Policy Study.* Research Monograph No. 3. Bangkok: Thailand Development Research Institute.

Peluso, Nancy, and Peter Vandergeest. 2001. "Genealogies of the Political Forest and Customary Rights in Indonesia, Malaysia, and Thailand." *Journal of Asian Studies* 60 (3): 761-812.

Pravongviengkham, P.P. 2000. *A National Advocacy for a Holistic and Decentralised Approach to Forest Management in Lao PDR.* Bangkok: FAO and RECOFTC. Mekong Resource Centre online library. http://www.mekonginfo.org.

Rigg, Jonathan. 2001. "Embracing the Global in Thailand: Activism and Pragmatism in an Era of Deagrarianization." *World Development* 29 (6): 945-60.

Ritchie, Mark. 1996. "From Peasant Farmers to Construction Workers: The Breaking Down of the Boundaries between Agrarian and Urban Life in Northern Thailand." PhD diss., University of California at Berkeley.

Roder, W. 1997. "Slash-and-Burn Rice Systems in Transition: Challenges for Agricultural Development in the Hills of Northern Laos." *Mountain Research and Development* 17 (1): 1-10.

Saberwal, Vasant. 1997. "Science and the Desiccationist Discourse of the 20th Century." *Environment and History* 3: 309-43.

Sandewall, Matts, Bo Ohlsson, and Silavanh Sawathvong. 2001. "Assessment of Historical Lnd-Use Changes for Purposes of Strategic Planning–A Case Study in Laos" *Ambio* 30 (1): 55-61.

Sannhavong, Kamnhin, Manisoth Lienpaseuth, Montha Namsena, and Thongsay Sichanh. 2001. "Impact of Land Allocation on Agricultural Production." Interim Report, National University of Laos, July.

Scott, James C. 1998. *Seeing Like a State.* New Haven: Yale University Press.

Silakone, Boungheng, Sisouvanh Douangmany, Fongkeo Boualapha, and Anoulom Vilayphone. 2001. "Impact of Traditional Land Tenure System of Different Stakeholders on Food Security." Interim Report, National University of Laos, July.

State Planning Committee. 2000. *Poverty in the Lao PDR: Participatory Poverty Assessment.* New York: State Planning Committee.

Thapa, Gopal. 1998. "Issues in the Conservation and Management of Forests in Laos: The Case of Sangthong District." *Singapore Journal of Tropical Geography* 19 (1): 71-91.

Vandergeest, Peter. 2002. "Racialization and Citizenship in Thai Forest Politics." *Society and Natural Resources* 16: 19-37.

Vandergeest, Peter, Mark Flaherty, and Paul Miller. 1999. "A Political Ecology of Shrimp Aquaculture in Thailand." *Rural Sociology* 64 (4): 573-96.

Vandergeest, Peter, and Nancy Lee Peluso. 1995. "Territorialization and State Power in Thailand." *Theory and Society* 24: 385-426.

Via Campesina. 2000. "Bangalore Declaration of the Via Campesina." 6 October 2000, Bangalore, India. http://viacampesina.org.

Walker, Andrew. 2003. "Agricultural Transformation and the Politics of Hydrology in Northern Thailand." *Development and Change* 34 (5): 941-64.

World Bank. 2002. *World Development Report 2002: Building Institutions for Markets.* New York: Oxford University Press.

–. 2003. Project Appraisal Document, Second Land Titling Project. World Bank Website: http://web.worldbank.org/external/projects (under Home > Countries > East Asia & Pacific > Lao People's Democracy > Projects & Programs) (accessed 26 March 2005).

–. 2005a. "Land Policy and Administration." Agriculture and Rural Development. http://lnweb18.worldbank.org/ESSD/ardext.nsf/11ByDocName/TopicsLandPolicyandAdministration (accessed 26 March 2005).

–. 2005b. Second Land Titling Project. http://web.worldbank.org/external/projects/main?pagePK=104231 and piPK=73230 and theSitePK=40941 and menuPK=228424 and Projectid=P075006 (accessed 26 March 2005).

6

Contested Territories: Development, Displacement, and Social Movements in Colombia

Sheila Gruner

Displacement in Colombia is a dramatic and traumatic reality lived by increasing numbers of people throughout the country. However, in research on the subject performed outside of Colombia, the analysis and experiences of the people most directly affected by displacement often receive inadequate consideration or are missing altogether. Nonetheless, these perspectives are crucial for an understanding of the historical origins, trends, and, more importantly, adequate responses to the problem of displacement. This chapter aims at making these perspectives more explicit, emphasizing those that reflect organized social movements engaged in land struggle to remain in their areas of origin. At the same time, it is intended to contribute to a growing area of interest concerning the relationship between violence, development, and displacement.

Policy research on displacement at the global level generally lacks analyses regarding the underlying and *historical* determinants of violence and, more specifically, of how this violence relates to global development principles and trends. The tendency towards intensification of violence and displacement in areas strategic to national and global development interests raises important questions about this interrelationship.

Colombia provides one of the most explicit cases in which historical as well as current (neoliberal) economic policies coincide with violence and displacement. Armies, and indeed Colombia's ongoing war itself, are systematically used to secure access to and control of valuable lands and resources; the subsequent displacement of people can be understood as one direct and intentional result. A principal objective of this chapter is thus to explore the links between development, violence, and displacement as they are historically situated and currently expressed in Colombia.

The continuing armed struggle in the country reflects not only internal problems and tensions but also global trends towards increased conflicts over land and natural resources. Now in a critical phase, Colombia's armed conflict – the longest-standing in the Americas – is rooted in multiple problems, including inequitable land distribution, growing poverty and exclusion, and a lack of state legitimacy, meaningful political participation, and mechanisms for political negotiation. It is further deepened by foreign political, economic, and military involvement, all significant to increased violence leading to displacement. As will be explored below, Colombia's cultural and ecological diversity, geographical location, and abundance of natural wealth have made it important for transnational economic and strategic interests.

Throughout world history, the demand for resources such as water, oil, gas, and forests has often coincided with internal conflicts and displacement. Within the current stage of advanced capitalist development, and as scarcity worsens, it is likely that the desire for control and ownership of natural resources will increasingly generate conflicts (Schwarz and Singh 2000: 9). As the homogenization of trade regulations and the transcontinental liberalization of trade promote the concentration of resource control and ownership, further struggles will probably arise, subsequently resulting in increased displacement of people (Klare 2001).

In a country suffering from pervasive historical conflict, violence related to development can be invisible to the outside world. This violence stems in part from the normalization of capitalist principles and values in the North. Through the use of media and with the support of vast military power, these principles are increasingly exported south within "trade and development" strategies. Three interrelated hegemonic strategies are used primarily to gain access to resources and to assert political control or influence in Colombia; these, I will argue, are related to the ongoing displacement of people. First is the implementation of legal/economic rules, regulations, and policies; second is the organized and systematic employment of violence; and third is the use of ideological tools, including development discourse, the media, and so forth. I will explore the connection between these three elements as they relate to displacement.

Although the media is not a main focus of this chapter, it nonetheless significantly influences policies that may relate or lead to human displacement and thus merits reflection. The mainstream global media image of Colombians – as incurably violent drug traffickers, mafias, and militias – perpetuates mistaken and biased beliefs concerning the causes of internal conflict. These media portrayals serve to convince the US public, for example, that military policy and actions are a correct and acceptable form of addressing such "evils." A clear instance of this type of military policy is Plan Colombia, which is, in effect, a US-Colombia military-development strategy that provides mostly military funding from the US to fight the "war on drugs" and to promote investment in the country. The media stereotyping leading up to and following the articulation of Plan Colombia in 2000 glossed over or omitted key socio-economic and contextual conditions surrounding the drug trade and armed insurgencies.[1] These conditions include inadequate agrarian reform and increasing concentration of landownership, lack of local economic alternatives to drug crop production, ongoing marginalization of the popular sectors, and lack of spaces for meaningful political participation (Álvarez 2001, Spanish-to-English translations are my own). These contextual realities are ignored in the extreme vilifications of Colombians, stereotypes and misrepresentations that have played an important role in gaining public support in the United States for Plan Colombia.

More importantly, significant alternative responses to the growing problems of war and displacement have largely been ignored by mainstream media, arguably leading to the general intensification of both. Vital cultural, class-, and gender-based movements do not often make headlines or figure into international public opinion. Nonetheless, based in both rural and urban areas, local, regional, and national popular organizations have developed strategies with which to face ongoing conflict and its determinants. These projects are elaborated by women, indigenous people, Afro-descendants, small-scale farmers, organized workers, and urban and rural displaced, who together arguably represent the country's majorities (Archila and Pardo 2001). Numerous groups, each sharing similar points of departure, have converged, thereby gaining the status of movements and generating important spaces for political expression. They enjoy significant support, especially among poor and middle-class sectors of Colombian society, because they represent an alternative voice to that of elite rule, which has brought ongoing and degenerative war, exploitation, and the systematic violation of cultural, land, and gender rights. According to many social leaders and academics, these movements come into direct confrontation with a type of "development logic" that responds to global imperatives. As will be explored below, this logic is linked to a vast military complex that views the movements as obstacles to predefined economic plans and goals. Movement leaders and members are finding themselves under increasing pressure, which leads to their victimization through human rights violations, forced displacement, and violence.

Another principal objective of this chapter is to explore perspectives of displaced people, particularly those of the organized social groups that have developed a critical understanding of displacement. Here my main source of reference is the land-based movements of southern Colombia that have engaged in critical analyses regarding displacement. These perspectives underscore the importance of land rights, livelihood security, ethnicity, gender, and nature to the debate on displacement, as elements of locally informed responses to the problem.

Research for this study was carried out in Colombia from 2000 to 2002. Over one hundred people, including social movement leaders, members of displaced communities, academics, and representatives of government and non-governmental organizations attending the displaced were interviewed for this project. My interest lies in how unarmed movements and people aim at achieving class, ethnic, and gender vindications as a way of (re)appropriating territories and political spaces under conditions of aggressive development, violence, and displacement. I also wish to understand how their unique position as popular social organizations and movements – as local defenders of territory, identity, and rights – places them at the forefront of the contestation of globalization and its consequences. I have thus focused on social and ethno-territorial groups that have achieved a significant level of organization and that engage in critical analysis concerning the determinants of displacement in the global context, as well as on non-governmental organizations and academics who have researched the subject. It is important to stress that the Colombian situation merits careful attention and committed analysis, given the precarious conditions faced by displaced people and those who work with them.

In sum, this chapter is divided into interrelated areas of reflection aimed at furthering an understanding of displacement as it relates to violence and development, with emphasis on the perspectives and experiences of territory-based people. In the first section, I overview the relationship between economic goals, violence, and displacement as it is historically situated within a global context and expressed in the recent past. I then explore the link between development, violence/conflict, and displacement, looking specifically at how violence is systematically used to coerce migration in order to access strategic lands and productive resources and to assert political control. I then focus more specifically on the experience and views of displacement of organized ethno-territorial groups, emphasizing the indigenous and Afro-descendent people and movements of southwestern Colombia. In this section, I touch on some key concepts and alternative ideas about territory and outline local perspectives concerning development, violence, and displacement. In the final section, I present a case study of a rural Afro-descendent community, illustrating causes, trends, and effects of displacement as it relates to violence and development, and drawing general conclusions about the violence-development-displacement relationship that is grounded in this specific local experience. I aim to support the argument that much greater attention should be paid to local organized social movements, in particular to ethno-territorial groups, with regard to their perspectives on and approaches to addressing displacement.

Before presenting a historical overview of displacement in Colombia, however, I would like to reflect on some key terms used for this study, including "development," "conflict," and "violence." *Development* is a contested term: for some, it refers to community-based improvement; for others, it entails exploitative practices that are in direct conflict with local community interests. Local communities, for example, engage in what is sometimes referred to as sustainable, local, or small-scale development, which, for them, implies an improvement of living conditions. Local development tends to be carried out by local residents in the areas in which they live; the residents themselves must face the consequences of their practices.

Large-scale development, in contrast, often has to do with aggressive extractive projects such as mining, the building of hydroelectric dams, the construction of petroleum pipelines, transnational or intercontinental transportation routes, and so forth. These projects, generally controlled and operated by private owners, are often carried out in areas in which they do not reside. More importantly, this development is increasingly articulated with neoliberal policy, bilateral and multilateral trade pacts, resource legislations, structural adjustment policies, and global macro-development plans, all of which receive growing support from national governments and all of which feature an increased concentration of *private ownership*.

Through the appropriation of local discourse, development terminology is often used and reproduced to justify large-scale exploitative practices and the "national project." In the end, development discourse reinforces the larger historical project of capitalism and modernity, a project built upon centuries of exploitative and imperialist practices, that is, in its current phase, labelled globalization. Although it would be more accurate, perhaps, to avoid the word *development* altogether, I will nevertheless use it here to refer to capitalist and hegemonic discourse and practice.

The literatures on development-induced displacement and conflict-induced displacement are generally distinct (Cernea 1999; Muggah 2000). However, research – especially by Colombian authors – increasingly explores the complex relationships between, and issues related to, development, violence, and displacement (Escobar 2001; Cubides and Domínguez 1999; CODHES 1999). I aim to further explore this relationship, basing my approach on the conviction that a key to understanding this enormous problem lies in making this link more visible outside Colombia.

In defining *conflict* and *violence,* it is important to distinguish between these concepts whenever possible. Disagreements over territories and resources are arguably often inevitable; such disagreements may be termed conflicts when mechanisms may be found through which to resolve them. Violence may thus be avoided and local people are not forced to flee. However, when war becomes profitable, as many argue is the case in Colombia, there is an interest in preventing the development of viable mechanisms of negotiation (Caicedo 2001: 95; Caycedo 2001). This is particularly important for Colombia: the lack of viable space for real negotiation addressing the ongoing conflicts over land, resources, and political representation is a crucial factor in the persistence of displacement in the country. Addressing the problem of displacement is rooted in a much deeper need for building equitable conditions for negotiation between all sectors of Colombian society, thus challenging the very model of development currently in place in the country and, indeed, across the Americas. Because there are no real spaces for negotiation, Colombia's crisis will probably worsen, especially for those most vulnerable to displacement. As Carlos Rosero (interview, March 2001), a social movement leader from the Colombian Pacific, remarks, "Conflict and violence are the extension of development, and this leads directly to the displacement of our people."

A Historical Overview of Displacement: Towards Globalization

A few key questions guide this inquiry into the history of displacement in Colombia. What are the historical trends of violence against and displacement of land-tied people? How have these patterns related to external economic goals and interests, and how are they currently expressed within globalization? Conflict and the threat of violence are understood to be primary causes of displacement in Colombia – what, then, are the determining factors of the ongoing conflict in Colombia, and how might they respond to macro economic interests? What lessons can be derived from the experience of displacement of land-tied people in Colombia?

It is important to recognize the current stage of displacement within Colombian history as the intensification of global trends and interests in the region. This section will aim at briefly exploring key historical stages and the general experience of displacement of territorial or land-tied people within each stage. The history of Latin America is in many ways one of displacement and violence perpetuated by external economic and capitalist interests in coordination with national elites (Galeano 1997).[2] The visible or written history of Colombia is one of conquest and violence, extraction and exploitation by national and transnational elites, beginning with the Spanish conquest (Ospina 1999: 175; Borda and Agudelo 1983). This history can be divided into three broad periods:

1 the Spanish conquest and colonialism (sixteenth century to mid-nineteenth century)
2 independence and establishment of the nation-state (mid-nineteenth century to mid-twentieth century)
3 economic globalization (mid-twentieth century to today).

These three periods can be generally defined and differentiated by qualitative and quantitative changes in the character and location of ruling elites, forms of territorial exploitation, production processes, and markets. Violence and displacement, however, are pervasive elements for all three.

During the conquest and colonial period throughout Latin America, the ruling elites were Spanish subjects who acted on behalf of the Spanish Crown and extracted natural and agricultural resources from the region. Although the Crown colonized an enormous portion of the continent, often using violence and coercion, Spanish subjects, in fact, occupied small territories and organized the colony in enclaves. Some of the products extracted during this period included gold, silver, tobacco, sugar cane, cotton, precious woods, and spices. The products and their accessibility largely determined which territories were occupied and often cleared of people.

This process coincided with the first forced displacements in Colombia – a process most often carried out with the use of violence. Where valuable products were available, local people were subjugated and often forced into slave labour. Many Afro-descendants articulate their historical experience of displacement as beginning with the forced exit from Africa to work as slaves in the Americas. Slave labour was essentially made up of historically land-tied peoples – indigenous peoples, Afro-descendants, and later, to a lesser extent, *mestizo* (mixed-blood) peasants.

During the industrial revolution, direct Spanish control, slave labour, and many of the products of the colonial period became obsolete due to changes in the global market and the political climate. The eventual outcome was national independence for Creole (Spanish-descent) elites and their constituencies, and the establishment of the nation-state. These local, regional, and national elites maintained strong links with European markets, while also creating new national markets. Slave labour was gradually, although not completely, abolished and replaced by wage labour. This period led to the expansion of the agricultural frontier as well as the creation of a large peasant-based economy that took the form of extractive projects in the Andean ridge and the inter-Andean valleys. Although Colombia developed into a nation-state, these projects and policies reflected elite interests and goals, at the profound expense of indigenous and African-descendent peoples.

Still, over two-thirds of the country's territory remained almost completely neglected by national elites until recently. In the forest regions of the Amazon and the Pacific, as well as in the Eastern Plains, indigenous peoples and escaped slaves continued to live in a generally autonomous way, distant from urban centres. Exceptions to this included sites where natural resources were identified for extraction. In these areas, indigenous people, African-descendants, and peasants were forced into extractive labour activities and often made to work in deplorable conditions.

The qualitative and quantitative changes that recurred during the early twentieth century were results of industrialization and the new processes of mass production. Elites, supported and guided by the multinational networks in which they were integrated, developed new plans to incorporate rural areas into the global agri-business sector and to create a large population of surplus labour in the urban centres. This transformation was undertaken through aggressive legal and illegal strategies. A decade of violence beginning in the late 1940s, a period known as la Violencia, was crucial in displacing the majority of rural Colombians into cities and concentrating landownership in the hands of a few wealthy people (Valderrama and Mondragón 1998: 23; Braun 1987). Areas of monoculture crops and masses of surplus labour in the impoverished cities were established. Attempts at urban and rural popular resistance through peaceful political means were met with unrestrained violence and repression. The rural population either rapidly became urbanized or moved deeper into forested areas along the Pacific Coast and on the Eastern Plains.

It was during this period of capitalist expansion that diverse armed insurgency movements appeared as forms of agrarian armed resistance (Sánchez 1991). In response to the growing insurgency organizations, paramilitary groups were created and financed by national elites. Illegal trade also expanded as an alternative to the inadequate or nonexistent legal income-generating activities in impoverished areas, advanced by large national and multinational cartels. Concentrations of economic, military, and political power thus emerged throughout the country, coming into conflict with one another.

This history of colonization, expansion, exploitation, and conflict has developed into the current period, which is characterized by neoliberalism, globalization, and the opening of economies and privatization. Structural adjustment policies introduced through the World Bank and the International Monetary Fund (IMF) during the late 1980s coincided with the national economic and development policies that were implemented into the 1990s and that promoted the further penetration of multinational and transnational corporate activity. Colombian regional and national elites, as well as the government itself, have, generally, avidly supported linkages with foreign economic interests.

It is within the recent global context that much of Colombia has become a country of contested territories. The push to access and control remote areas and to promote private ownership is a process as yet unfinished in Colombia. As international trade rules increasingly facilitate the concentration of private ownership, and the demand for natural resources for global markets takes on unprecedented dimensions, large-scale development projects – as well as illegal multinational activities – reach formerly remote regions. As will be discussed below, one such area is the Colombian Pacific in the southwest, a once forgotten "jungle region" that entered into national and global economic plans in the 1970s.

Unemployment and unemployability are on the rise, together with all forms of violence and the deepest and most comprehensive crisis in the country's history. Colombians are forced into an ever-increasing "race to the bottom" as territories, resources, and labour are delivered at low cost to both legal and illegal multinational interests.

Within this context, insurgent groups, appearing on the scene since the mid-twentieth century, have grown in number, territorial presence, and strength, sometimes coercing or convincing the poor and disenfranchised to join forces with them. Drug production and trade have increased, and a dirty war has been launched where paramilitary forces act in tandem with the government's armed forces. The United States has increased its military aid to Colombia's army and government as part of its "war on drugs" and its more recent "war on terrorism." The situation of permanent war, together with structural adjustment policies, bilateral and continental free trade agreements, and aggressive privatization of public services, defines the current period, setting conditions for the further incorporation of the country into the global economy.

This "visible" history of violence, capitalist exploitation, and displacement vastly overshadows and, in many senses, eliminates, the lesser-known but vibrant history of land-tied peoples. Nonetheless, their responses to displacement, forced slavery, poor working conditions, and lack of adequate land bases, together with their determination to build autonomous cultural and economic networks and models, demonstrate a vigorous history of resistance (Pardo 2001). As many territorial peoples in Colombia traditionally opted out, or were left out, of national development plans and strategies until relatively recently, distinct and rich histories, little known to outsiders, have flourished among many ethnic groups (Escobar and Pedrosa 1996).

Consequently, social and economic practices that differed from the logic of accumulation developed in these regions. These practices include traditional land use models that give priority to local customs, needs, and plans, inherently emphasizing sustainability. Recognition and support for historically rooted, locally based social and economic models are important for building strategies to address displacement, giving priority to strengthening local autonomies and cultural and ecological diversity rather than to continued, uncontrolled, and aggressive monoculture-based development. This, as part of a broader strategy to address the determinants of displacement, confronts the essence of the problems generated by large-scale aggressive capitalism, and it is from the lesser-known history of land-tied peoples that some of the most relevant lessons are still to be learnt.

Colombia: Setting Conditions for Development

Colombia is strategically located as an entrance to South America: through its border with Panama, it is the only link by land between Central and South America. Important natural resources found in Colombia include oil and gas, fresh water, biodiversity, minerals, and precious metals. These make it an especially lucrative region for national and global economic interests. This, along with a tradition of governing elites who have strong political relationships with the United States, makes Colombia important in setting conditions for the promotion of free trade in South America and furthering the goals of the proposed Free Trade Area of the Americas (FTAA).

Policies aimed at facilitating the integration of Colombia into hemispheric trade relations have been enforced in the country through a plethora of mechanisms. Aggressive structural adjustment strategies implemented through the World Bank and the IMF in the early eighties, nineties, and into the twenty-first century provided a framework for privatization and foreign investment. The creation of "special economic zones," "special port zones," and free trade zones (which provide tax and other incentives to national, transnational, and multinational companies) has provided a testing ground for the promotion of trade liberalization within the country ("Special Economic Zones and Free Trade Zones of Colombia" n.d.). Since then, bilateral trade agreements have been advanced, leading Colombia towards eventual incorporation into the far-reaching FTAA.

A more explicit expression of global development interests in the country is contained in Plan Colombia, first introduced in July 2000 in Colombia. Ironically, this military-development plan was originally a peace plan aimed at insurgent groups (Anzola 2001: 94-95). Its current character was conceived during the Clinton administration and approved by the US Congress before it was made known to the Colombian people. George W. Bush developed it and subsequently introduced the Andean Regional Initiative, a similar but much more far-reaching policy that incorporates Andean countries into a broader and coordinated "development" strategy for the Andean region (US Department of State, 2001b).

Plan Colombia combines military strategies with the promotion of foreign investment, primarily aimed at accessing key resources. Moreover, it seeks to align development initiatives, opening up new territories and setting conditions for attaining larger development goals. Smaller regional development plans are also incorporated within Plan Colombia. One example is Plan Pacífico, aimed in part at opening the Colombian Pacific to foreign economic interests and military control. Colombia thus experiences profound foreign influence over development planning and military strategies at diverse levels.

National Governments and Liberalization of Trade

In the early 1990s, the Gaviria government (1990-94) took measures to internationalize and liberalize the economy. Later, the Pastrana administration (1998-2002) deepened and accelerated these neoliberal policies. This liberalization of Colombia's economy led to a huge increase in the presence of multinational companies and foreign investment throughout the country. For example, a document published by CENSAT Agua Viva (2001) registered a 90 percent increase in the presence of Canadian-registered oil

Table 6.1

Displacement tendencies in Colombia, 1986-2000

Year	Number of displaced
1986	36,000
1991	110,000
1996	181,000
2000	317,000

Source: CODHES 2001: 41.

companies in Colombia in the second half of the 1990s. Moreover, the economic aperture led to an estimated increase of 700 percent in imported foods, drastically reducing productive regions and debilitating rural economies (Valderrama and Mondragón 1998: 56).

Table 6.1 provides information on the scale of population displacement in Colombia since the mid-1980s, based on data collected by CODHES (Consultancy on Human Rights and Displacement), a non-governmental research institution dealing with displacement.

Figures continue to skyrocket in the twenty-first century. CODHES (2001) data put the number of Colombians displaced between January to March 2002 at 90,179. According to the Social Solidarity Network (see UNHCR 2003), a governmental organization, 168,000 Colombians were displaced between January and June 2002.

According to many Colombian academics, the increase in foreign investment has also coincided with conflict and poverty. As Libardo Sarmiento Anzola (2001: 88) writes:

> The regions of highest poverty, of wealth in biodiversity and [which are] strategic for the purposes of capitalist development, coincide with areas of higher levels of conflict, specifically in terms of armed confrontations and displacement. However, it is towards these areas that the model of accumulation expands. In other words, these are spaces that concentrate the large macroprojects of development ... In these areas, the complex intertwining of the conflict of national interests, the strategies of war, the actions of an excluding and authoritarian economic modernization and the infrastructure promoted by multinationals, by the state, and the regional elites takes place. Globalization, projects of nation [building], modernization of the economic apparatus, petroleum, and cocaine animate the territorial dynamics of the war and the portfolios of investment.

The view that territories where land-tied people live are generally being cleared and reorganized in response to the goals of economic interests is shared by many Colombian researchers and social leaders. For instance, María Theresa Uribe (interview, March 2002), a professor at the University of Antioquia in Medellín, emphasizes that the maps of capitalist development interests, violent conflict, and population displacement coincide. Colombian economist Hector Mondragón recently stated, in an August 2001 presentation to a Canadian human rights delegation in Bogotá, "There are not only displaced people because there is war, but rather there is war in order that there be displaced people."

Jorge Rojas of CODHES stated in an interview that peasants fleeing terror during 2001 had abandoned what probably amounted to more than three million hectares of land. And, unlike in previous decades, he states, speculation has come to play a large role in displacement: "Land, as well as territory, have acquired specific values that relate to, among other aspects, natural resources and a geostrategic condition that go beyond traditional agricultural exploitation" (interview, 2001).

During the past three decades, many programs and incentives were developed to entice small "inefficient" farmers from the countryside. Early development experts, such as the Canadian-born economist Laughlin Currie, influenced these policies. As development advisor to the Colombian government during the 1960s, he suggested that war would accelerate urban emigration in the event that economic incentive programs did not work (Currie 1968: 95). The direct or indirect influence of Currie is the subject of debate in Colombia, although the oft-cited justification for paramilitary violence in rural areas coincides with his position. The general goal suggested by Currie, following other development experts of the time, was a reduction of 4 percent annually in the number of people dedicated to agriculture. For Colombia, this translates to about 800,000 inhabitants in fewer than ten years – about the same quantity of people who were displaced by violence between 1987 and 1997, Valderrama and Mondragón analyze this thinking alongside official policies put in place to depopulate the region at the time, strategies that, in the end, did not entice small-scale farmers off their land at rates suggested by Currie (Valderrama and Mondragón 1998: 58-59). The numbers proposed by Currie were eventually achieved through violence. According to economists Valderrama and Mondragón and others who research displacement, Currie's earlier policies directly influenced the goals set out by governments and elites through the subsequent decades, targets that coincide with a systematic depopulating of regions through the use of violence.

Violence and Its Relationship with Development and Displacement

The relationship between development, violence, and the forcible displacement of people in Colombia is perhaps the most revealing key to understanding Colombia's political turmoil. The view that armed actors are used directly and indirectly as tools of economic interests in order to access territories and resources, and to secure investment and political control, is shared by social leaders and academics alike. According to Carlos Rosero (interview, March 2001), a prominent Afro-descendent leader, "Every time a large 'development' project is implemented, our people have to leave. And they use legal or violent methods to expropriate our land from the population. It is a history that continues to repeat itself, as you can see happening in the Pacific Coast, in Northern Cauca, in the Caribbean. In a context of war where certain armed actors serve the interests of business – these actors in the end, voluntarily or not, are necessarily linked to these business interests and work against the rights and interests of our communities."

Paramilitary forces have also revealed development-related motivations behind violent acts, through explicit and public statements. For example, the following comment by Carlos Castaño, leader of the paramilitary AUC (United Self-Defence of Cordoba), in a June 2002 interview with Colombian weekly magazine *Semana,* is telling. When asked what threat Kimy Pernia Domico, an indigenous leader of the Embera Katio people, who had been abducted and disappeared, could pose to his group, Castano said: "The dam! He is stopping the functioning of the dam!"

Americas Update also outlined, in its 2001 report, those points at which paramilitary violence and military complicity are made evident (Ismi 2000: 2):

> Extending the Pan-American Highway is part of the Colombian government's aggressive development plans for the Pacific Coast. Plan Pacífico calls for oil exploration, mining, large-scale agriculture, commercial fishing, and tourism and the building of two super-ports, hydroelectric and energy plants, more roads, telecommunications networks, an oil pipeline, a railway and a military base. Much of this will be done in collaboration with multinational corporations. It is in this resource rich area (Uraba) that two thousand people were massacred by paramilitaries during 1995 and the first half of 1996. Following this carnage, General Rito Alejo del Río Rojas, commander at that time of the Colombian army's 17th Brigade, remarked "the region is now safe and you can invest." According to the Washington Office on Latin America (WOLA), del Río facilitated one of the most ruthless paramilitary campaigns in the country.

The relationship between capitalist development and violence has become well known in Colombia, although it has not been adequately addressed at a policy level, either inside or outside the country. To the contrary, the United States has continued its development and military policies and practices in Colombia, seeking to limit its own international legal liability and supporting a government known for violence with impunity. For example, despite ample evidence of human rights abuses being perpetuated with impunity by the Colombian government and of its links with paramilitary groups, US president Clinton signed a "human rights waiver" shortly before the implementation of Plan Colombia, ensuring that the military strategy would go ahead. This increased financial support for the Colombian military included military equipment, training, aerial sprays for crop fumigation, and so forth. Moreover, though many countries have signed on to the International Criminal Court (ICC) agreement, a global pact that allows for the prosecution of government officials charged with war crimes, the United States has refused to do so. Significantly, though Colombia did sign the ICC agreement, it has exempted US personnel from prosecution at the ICC for potential war crimes committed in the country (Arrington 2002).

The current Uribe administration is building on the trend of past governments towards further articulating the economic-military Plan Colombia with the United States–led "war on terrorism." This plan counts on intersecting development and military or violence-oriented strategies that will probably produce further displacement. These strategies include the creation of conditions for the promotion of increased foreign investment, the securing of key zones for access to important resources and territories, the implementation of an externally funded counter-insurgency war, and the ongoing repression of dissenting voices and social organizations. Uribe has focused on creating civilian "informant networks" as well as on promoting free trade in key "special economic zones"[3] and strengthening military control in what are called "zones of rehabilitation and consolidation," areas considered by the government to be under guerrilla influence or control (Global IDP Database n.d.). Many Colombians across the social and political spectrum have criticized the Uribe approach as overtly promoting US interests in the country and compromising national sovereignty (Leech 2002).

Development and the "War on Drugs"

The illegal drug trade is presented in the media as an industry of "subversive" actors – mostly mafiosi and guerrillas who are slotted into a single category and increasingly referred to as "narco-terrorists" within this new discourse (Fairness in Reporting 2000). Because of the real involvement of guerrillas in drug trafficking and other illegal activities such as kidnapping, the political character of the insurgency project is continually reduced to terrorism by the establishment. Less reference is made in the media to the involvement of paramilitary groups in drug trafficking, despite the fact that the leader of these groups publicly stated in a March 2000 television interview that over 70 percent of paramilitary operations is funded by the drug trade (Reuters 2000). Even less mention is made of corrupt officials, elites, and beneficiaries from North America and Europe, where the main markets are located and principal profits generated.

Paramilitary groups, in contrast to guerrilla groups, gain increased attention as political actors, despite their nature as illegal, violent extensions of the Colombian army and their expression of elite repression against the poor. New efforts have been made to promote "peace talks" with the paramilitaries, and settlement with them would probably include their reintegration into society, with key economic benefits. Ongoing collaborations between the ruling elite, global economic interests, and the most violent and illegal armed factions are perhaps most indicative of the systematic relationship between development and violence-induced displacement in Colombia. This is a relationship that demands much deeper scrutiny by the international institutions that continue to send development aid through Plan Colombia.

Moreover, media depictions of the drug issue do not address long-standing structural problems within crop-producing regions. Inadequate agrarian reform, lack of sufficient access to legitimate markets or initiatives for local economic independence, subsequent poverty, and external interest in extractive resources are some crucial factors that have led many small-scale farmers within these regions to become dependent on the coca crop as a means of subsistence. Although I do not intend to go into detail about the complex drug issue, it is important to note a few elements that play a central role in the perpetuation of violence and displacement as it relates to development goals and practices. I will briefly examine this relationship, touching on important underlying goals of Plan Colombia's "war on drugs," the determinants of illegal drug production, and the role of armed groups. I will explore the idea that the drug problem is an expression of deeper "development"-related problems that have been caused in part by agrarian inequity, poverty, and marginalization, intensified or advanced by underlying development interests and linked to systematic violence and displacement.

As Ricardo Vargas and S. Barragan (1996: 4) explain, "Illegal cultivation in Colombia is a part of a conflictive scenario that should be seen as part of the so-called 'agrarian problem.' This is characterized by, among other things, an unequal distribution of land ownership, which has been the historical cause of frustrated attempts at agrarian reform. This is expressed in part by an unequal distribution of resources in the poorest rural areas, making the legitimacy of the state throughout the country – and especially in the countryside – ever more fragile."

Local crop substitution programs have been promoted in the past by local governments, particularly in southern Colombia (such as in Cauca, Putumayo, and the Amazonas). These programs have aimed at saving productive lands, developing markets for alternative crops, and preventing the displacement of indigenous and peasant communities. However, they gained insufficient support at the national and international levels, and failed to deter military plans for aerial fumigation and military action. The fumigation of coca plants equally damages food crops, with well-documented detrimental effects on human health and the natural environment, and is directly linked to displacement (Mutis 1999: 240-73). Multiple health problems have been reported, as has been the destruction of ecologically sensitive areas (Romero-Medina 2001; Vargas 1999; Constanza, Vargas, and García 2001: 121-40). Increased military action has spread throughout the region, intensifying levels of violence overall. Numerous people have subsequently been displaced to Ecuador and other areas.

Plan Colombia, in sum, uses the discourse of "war on drugs" as well as of "national development" to implement military strategies that further political and economic objectives. The plan is aimed at regions of guerrilla influence, where illicit crops are targeted and fumigated and local small-scale farmers are displaced. Notably, these areas contain significant quantities of petroleum, biodiversity, and other important natural resources (Anzola 2001: 89). In the Putumayo region, where Plan Colombia's military and fumigation strategies were first implemented, a number of contracts for oil exploration projects were granted to foreign oil companies, including various Canadian companies. As Mondragón (2001: 10) describes, "In the years 1999 and 2000 heaps of contracts were signed which distributed national territory between US transnationals like Chevron and Occidental, English transnationals B.P. and Shell, and Canadians – Oxy, Alberta, and Mera-Mills – and the Spanish Repsol and Hocol. It is incredible to see the maps of Ecopetrol [Colombian national oil company]. They gave, millimetre by millimetre, the western Amazon and the department of Putumayo, which, not coincidentally, is the initial stage of Plan Colombia. What remains is the distribution of the river basins of the Pacific and the Southeast Amazon."

It is in this sense that paramilitary-driven, violence-induced displacement is considered by many to be a reflection of hegemonic power structures and a tool through which to access key resources, with or without the direct complicity of transnational companies. A conviction shared by numerous researchers is that "the direct control of territories by [these multinational] companies is vital, explaining their participation in the expulsion of the population, supported by the creation and financing of paramilitary groups" (Maldonado 2001: 10).

A comparison of illegal drug industry practices with those of legal capitalist projects demonstrates a similar extractive logic and pattern, involving the clearing of land and the transformation of peasant farmers into wage labour (Molano 1987: 126). As Arturo Escobar (2003) further describes, "From the perspective of movement organizations and organizations of the displaced ... all of the external actors including guerrillas, paramilitaries, capitalist developers and the state share the same goals of the appropriation of territories for radical reconfiguration ... along the lines of the capitalist modern project of extraction and exploitation of natural resources ... This project is a planned process and not something that happens spontaneously."

Although estimates vary, depending on their sources and other variables, overall, they do strongly show that the paramilitary groups are responsible for displacing the highest numbers of people by violence, especially by means of assassination and massacre (CODHES 1999: 16). The relationship between the Colombian military and paramilitary forces, moreover, has also been well documented (Human Rights Watch 2001). According to the US Department of State's own US Country Report on Human Rights in Colombia 2001 (US Department of State 2001a), "members of the security forces sometimes illegally collaborated with paramilitary forces. Members of the armed forces and the police committed serious violations of human rights." More troubling is that, according to official Colombian state documents, the paramilitaries, or the AUC (United Self-Defence of Cordoba), have grown in number, from an army of 1,500 combatants in 1998 to 8,150 in 2000 (Government of Colombia n.d.). The US Department of State suggested that their numbers might have reached as high as 11,000 (US Department of State 2001a).

Written as the first phase of Plan Colombia was being implemented, this US Department of State report coincided with the increased growth of armed groups, including paramilitaries, insurgency, and militias, as well as with increasing human rights violations and displacements. Such trends appear to form the basis of the kind of development planned for Colombia – large-scale, extractive, and aggressive. A key question left for researchers concerns the level of "inevitable eventuality" of violence and displacement within advanced capitalism, particularly as conflicts over territories and demand for resources increase.

Caught in the middle of unwanted conflict, unarmed indigenous, Afro-descendent, and peasant communities struggle to remain on their ancestral lands. The drug problem, violence, and displacement are perhaps the greatest concerns for land-tied peoples in regions affected by Plan Colombia and its severely detrimental social-cultural, economic, health, and environmental effects. The production of coca crops by peasant farmers is linked to the underlying determinants of the conflict itself, socio-economic problems that merit much fuller and more appropriate analysis than what currently informs national and international policies. Lack of support for a negotiated solution to the armed conflict, aggressive development strategies such as Plan Colombia, and a lack of will to replace military and fumigation activities with local autonomy and crop substitution programs are clear contributing factors related to increased displacement in the region.

Conflicting Logics: Territory and Ethnicity versus Displacement for Development

> For us, this relationship between violence, displacement, and development is a direct one; it has been a constant not only in the present but always in the past. And I think that, ultimately, what lies at the heart of the issue is a clash between two different ways of observing and relating to time and space. Our communities think about time and space in a way that differs from that of advanced capitalism. In the Pacific, people take thought for the *"renaciente"* – those "who are to come" – and strive to create conditions so that the renaciente can survive. For this reason, resource use among our communities is not as intensive or aggressive as that which is now prevalent in these zones. Nonetheless, one must also recognize that the aggressive notion of development has permeated many communities and that this today constitutes a major difficulty. In certain parts of the Colombian Pacific, displacement has already forced our people out, allowing for the arrival of others who subscribe to totally different cultural logics and a different use of natural resources.
>
> – Interview with Carlos Rosero, March 2001

Diverse land-tied peoples and ethno-territorial movements in Colombia share this perspective. Ethno-territorial movements are organizations of local actors – generally representing and made up of people from rural indigenous and Afro-descendent communities – who struggle for territorial and cultural rights based on a historical claim to land and the right to self-representation (Grueso, Rosero, and Escobar 1996). Although many of these movements have gained new recognition and political status over the past two decades, they often represent much older historically rooted efforts. Rural movements also include mestizo farmers who have engaged in long-standing struggles for human and land rights as well as resistance to displacement and globalization.

The term *territory* in the context of ethno-territorial movements, refers to a historically rooted *place* where a distinct cultural group lives and expresses its identity. It denotes a historical connection to an ecological area where communities have organized, managed, or related to land in culturally specific ways (Restrepo 2001). It makes reference to a distinct "way of being" that is economic, cultural, and politically engaged. Territory in this sense is intimately tied to identity. The significance of territory or "place" is paramount in the struggle of these movements against the forms of displacement that many authors associate with globalization (Escobar 2000). Although "globalization" often refers to diaspora, displacement, or deterritorialization, "place" and "territory" refer to culture, land, tradition, and so forth (ibid.). It is the contrast between local forms of social and economic organization and large-scale development plans that brings to light major differences in ways of conceptualizing, managing, and relating to land and territory.

The importance of territory is reflected in the fact that black communities have been working towards titling collective territories and administering them autonomously in accordance with traditional practices and values. The Colombian Constitution recognizes this right through Law 70 of 1993 (Restrepo 2001).

Although titling is important, the process presents some contradictions. It does offer the possibility of recognizing of historical rights to ancestral lands after centuries of exploitation and abandonment, but it can also cause land disputes and, in some cases, a reduction of territory. Moreover, the process of titling coincided with the liberalization of the economy in 1991, sparking new conflicts between foreign development interests and local actors who were given limited time to complete the titling process. In some instances, titling became an obstacle to the implementation of development projects; as a result, Afro-descendent leaders perceive in titling an explanation for the entrance of paramilitaries and the use of violence against their communities.

Perhaps one of the most significant issues facing ethno-territorial movements is that they face threat of displacement and violence specifically *because* they are organized. These movements are targeted because of their vocal and public rejection of development projects that they argue are against their interests. They become obstacles to development as they vocally protest and resist the multiple threats of displacement, violence, and other human rights violations perpetuated against the communities they represent. In their own words (PCN 2000):

> The Black Communities of the Colombian Pacific [PCN] have been struggling for the right to legalize their collective territories along with the right to administer them in an autonomous manner, and in accordance with their traditional practices and values. The Colombian Constitution recognizes this right through Law 70 of 1993. The community "base" organizations of River Anchicayá have carried out an advanced process of land titling. Collective appropriation by the Black Communities of the Colombian Pacific is seen as a threat for those who maintain an interest in capitalizing on

> the enormous wealth of the region, which includes: precious highly marketable tropical woods, gold and the potential for establishing commercial intensive cultivations.

As these organized local groups engage in alternative sustainable economic practices, they enter into tension with the goals of large-scale capitalist development. These contested territories become the sites of some of the worst paramilitary aggression and forced displacements.

Organized social groups that actively engage in alternative social and economic programs in Colombia are numerous, growing out of both need and conviction. Ethno-territorial movements and other popular social organizations share similar experiences in regard to the determinants of displacement and the violent effects of globalization. These groups include mestizo rural communities, organized labour, women's groups, and organizations of the displaced, among others. Their distinct and local forms of expression and practice in the face of dominant development thinking, are under constant threat of violation, destruction, or displacement (Anzola 2001: 83).

The Americas Update Report of November 2000 (Ismi 2000: 4) notes that "to attract foreign investment, the Colombian state has resorted to large-scale privatization of key sectors of the economy ... State repression has been most severe against those unions resisting these privatizations." Anzola (2001: 84) further underscores the fact that one of the fundamental elements of Colombia's economic program of liberalization has been the repression of social and labour unrest. This is true for both rural and urban movements that contest current economic and political policies. In the case of rural movements, US State Department documents (US Department of State 2001a) record that over 1,200 rural peasant, indigenous, and Afro-descendent leaders were murdered during 2001 alone.

For an ethno-territorial movement, as for social movements in general, the loss of one leader is a shock to the overall organizational process. To suffer multiple losses debilitates the movement and can lead to its disintegration. Many movement leaders and those who work with them suggest that this is the intention behind the systematic assassinations. Paramilitary groups often view social movement leaders and members as guerrilla collaborators because they are organized and they contest state policy and actions. Guerrilla groups have also been criticized for threatening, killing, or displacing unarmed social leaders and community members, which has occurred in cases where local, indigenous, or Afro-descendent autonomy is perceived as a threat to guerilla goals for territorial or political control. However, paramilitary violence, because of its clear links with national and global business elites, can be seen as a direct expression of the development-violence-displacement relationship.

As a result of assassinations, social movement groups often weaken to the point at which they may succumb to pressure from an armed group, ceding territorial or political power, or they may be forced to flee. The goal of armed groups appears to be the reduction or elimination of social actors vying for legitimate representation within a given territory. In this sense, the attempt by both sides of the armed conflict to subdue or eliminate the "weaker" or unarmed movements responds to a military-development logic.

Ethno-Territorial Movements: Proposals in the Face of Displacement and Globalization

In the face of this onslaught, many rural, indigenous, and Afro-descendent organizations have developed resistance strategies based on systematic analysis, coordinated action, and solid historical roots in an ethno-territorial project. Such movements have mobilized vast amounts of energy and resources to maintain a position of unarmed resistance, while advancing territorial claims and promoting community interests within their traditional areas. They argue that without an organized voice representing the territorial rights of communities, local residents have little or no political clout, or protection from displacement and development. Movements have created room to manoeuvre by entering into dialogue with government and coordinating with other social and territorial organizations and by putting out early-alert notices about pre-announced, threatened displacements, demanding protection, and mobilizing national and international opinion. The latter is an increasingly effective tool for the prevention of displacement, as pressure is aimed at both national and global sources of threat and advocacy.

More significantly, movement organizations have engaged in land reappropriation and titling processes, have developed local economic models based on traditional agricultural systems, and have undertaken important cultural projects, part of what indigenous and Afro-descendent organizations in southern Colombia refer to as Life Plans and Projects. Through their articulation and promotion of local autonomy and productive social and ecologically sustainable projects, Life Plans play an essential role in protecting people against large-scale development and subsequent displacement. Activities may include efforts to develop small-scale industries such as community fishing and shrimp harvesting (Escobar and Pedrosa 1996: 144-75). Moreover, the Life Plans construct food sovereignty as people reclaim traditional seed sources and diversify crops for local consumption and sale at local markets, rather than adopt external economic programs that insist on the production of monocrops for global markets. These strategies also focus on creating the organizational capacity to protect communities: initiatives here include human rights training, the promotion of legitimate local authority and socially respected institutions, and, during periods of conflict, evacuation and return plans, as well as the maintenance of food and health security. In other words, development-induced and violence-induced displacement can be addressed in numerous ways at the local level, provided that local initiatives are indeed recognized, supported, and given priority over large-scale development objectives.

The Colombian Pacific: A Brief Case Study Overview

The Colombian Pacific is one of many regions of Colombia in which ethno-territorial movements have developed important social and political processes during the past few decades, processes that reflect centuries of history and organized existence in the region. It is also one of the many areas in which conflict, development, and displacement coincide and are on the increase. The Colombian Pacific is a zone of significant ecological and cultural diversity, where indigenous, black, and peasant communities have long lived in a distinct and integral relationship with the surrounding ecological systems. However, violence arose in the area during the 1970s, when the government sought to incorporate the Pacific into national development strategies (Escobar and Pedrosa 1996: 13-18; Ismi 2000: 2; CUSO 1994).

The region has thus experienced a rapid transition from relatively peaceful inter-ethnic coexistence, as well as governmental neglect, to increasing involvement by the Colombian government as it pursues national and international economic interests. Many are convinced that the violence in the Pacific is a premeditated strategy. According to Escobar (2003), "it is a strategy that has to do with firstly, the economic interests surrounding the appropriation and exploitation of the natural resources and secondly, with the plans for development, the so-called mega-projects, that exist for the region."

Naya-Yurumanguí: Forced Displacement on the River

The link between development, violence, and displacement on the Pacific Coast is manifest in the Naya and Yurumanguí river basins.[4] Since the first violent episode in 2001, approximately seventeen thousand indigenous, Afro-descendent, and mestizo peasants live under the constant threat of further displacement. A sequence of massacres began with organized AUC paramilitary attacks on the Afro-descendent communities of the Lower Naya during April 2001. Violence included the massacres of hundreds of inhabitants and the subsequent displacement of thousands more. These atrocious acts of brutal violence became known as the Easter Week Massacres, as they took place during the religious holiday, when the country's attention was elsewhere. The massacres, carried out with chainsaws and axes, were intended to terrorize and displace the immediate and surrounding communities. They occurred despite the fact that the Colombian government had received prior warning through the "early alert system," to which it did not respond, according to local leaders and the national commission that subsequently investigated the situation (Comisión Interinstitucional 2001).[5]

After carrying out these massacres, the AUC announced a plan to invade the neighbouring Yurumanguí River district, a threat again denounced in advance to authorities by the Yurumanguí inhabitants. As in the case of the Naya massacres, nothing was done, as has been reported by local leaders. Two weeks later, the AUC entered the fishing village of El Firme on the Yurumanguí, killing seven Afro-Colombian peasants. The entire community subsequently fled to neighbouring communities; from there, some tried desperately to reach Buenaventura, the closest port city.

According to a report by the investigating commission, the area in which the massacres and displacements occurred contains significant strategic interests: "[the region is] important for hydro and forestry reserves, its proximity to the ocean turning it into a geostrategic zone and an important point for communication for the Andean region with the rest of southwestern Colombia and Ecuador. Control of the river basins that connect with the Pacific Ocean is without a doubt one of the factors that position the region as lucrative for diverse actors" (Comisión Interinstitucional 2001: 4).

The Afro-descendants of the Yurumanguí River region had gained collective title for 57,000 hectares, a title that, for black activists from the river, symbolized recognition and vindication of their historical territorial and cultural rights. However, according to social leaders, the land title turned them into military targets, due to the natural wealth contained within the region. Land title is, at the same time, the only protection these communities have in the face of development's onslaught. Despite this contradiction and violence, as one local leader stated, "my people, my community, have made the decision to resist within our territory. We know that if we leave it ... our collective title would no longer have meaning, and outside of our territory, neither would we have meaning" (interview with anonymous PCN leader, 21 August 2001).

Afro-descendants, as well as indigenous people, place great importance on land, often stating that they would rather die than permanently leave their territory. According to local testimony, they could always guarantee themselves some basic food in their territory, however incomplete, since "they had their farms, their river and their forest, their homes" (ibid.). The territory is considered their place in which to build meaning and culture; without it, as an Afro-descendent leader said, "we are nothing" (interview with anonymous PCN leader, 21 August 2001).

After the El Firme massacre, the people of the Yurumanguí did experience a brief displacement to Buenaventura, where they suffered hunger, sickness, and general neglect. In the city, with little or no food and no land upon which to grow it, they felt helpless and as if they "did not exist." Moreover, some were exposed to the possibility of further violence, were followed and threatened with death because they came from the displaced village. For these reasons, the people of the Yurumanguí, as well as those of the Naya, made the collective decision to return and remain within their territories. Titling of this land creates a sense that outsiders will eventually have to recognize it as theirs, though the general feeling is that the violence may yet worsen.

Rural leaders now based in Buenaventura perceive a clear link between what is happening in their home communities and the exercise of policies that establish "special economic zones" and "special port zones." They assert that these zones are intended to give businesses and companies access to key resources in the countryside, including minerals, oil, and water. One PCN leader stated that "business interests use the [paramilitaries] as instruments to implement these [special economic zone] policies, which uproot local and family economies for the benefit of the multinationals" (interview with anonymous PCN leader, 21 August 2001).

Currently, the residents, again surrounded by paramilitaries, consider that they are "displaced within," as the river routes they normally use for the transportation of food and fuel have been entirely cut off by road and river blocks. This has led to a new perception of displacement. Because they can no longer follow their traditional routes for food gathering and fishing, they feel trapped or "kidnapped" in their own lands. According to Carlos Rosero (interview, September 2002), "[our] way of life, within these conditions, is being displaced and will have the same impacts on us in the medium to long run if they starve us out of our lands."

Effects of Displacement on Local Communities

The effects of violence and displacement on local communities and ethnoterritorial movements are overwhelming.[6] Cultural, social, economic, and environmental damage is often permanent. In its yearly reports, CODHES emphasizes the multiple effects of violence and displacement in indigenous reserves and Afro-Colombian communities, and has placed increasing emphasis on this theme as the problem worsens. In the Naya-Yurumanguí region, the effects of displacement are evidenced through testimonies of displaced residents and the physical state in which villages have been left. Impacts are severe and are felt on multiple levels including

- the loss and threatened loss of ancestral lands, the destruction of the environment and biodiversity, and the depletion of natural resources
- the systematic elimination of community members and social leaders, resulting in social fragmentation and the deterioration of organizational processes

- the psychological and physical deterioration of individuals and communities due to traumas evoked by fear, massacre, rape, torture, and disappearance
- the diminishment of food and social security, and the increase of hunger, poverty, sickness, and illiteracy
- the rupture or deterioration of local cultural practices and the relationship with the environment, leading to subsequent cultural-environmental deterioration
- the weakening or destruction of sustainable economic models and strategies for building local economic autonomy and well-being.

Overall, in Colombia, women and children are without a doubt the most heavily affected by displacement. According to a report by Paula Andrea Rossiasco in the Colombia Journal Online (2003), "many Colombian women, after first surviving the armed conflict, must then confront a longer and more difficult struggle, fighting for their own survival and that of their families in new locations. In addition to confronting fear, war and the loss of loved ones (sons, husbands, fathers, etc.), these women are forced to take on the role of head of household, assuming economic responsibility as well as providing social and psychological support for their family. The opportunities for these women are limited, given that few are educated or possess the resources to initiate economic activity." There are particularly traumatic consequences for women and, subsequently, for the social fabric of black communities of the Pacific. After losing their male counterparts to the conflict or violence, many women end up as heads of households, with little or no income, and are forced into a life of urban misery. In general, rural women from ethnic communities are affected in distinct ways by displacement, as they confront multiple additional shocks related to rural-urban migration. During actual displacement, women must also respond to family needs in the midst of crisis. These include organizing families for rapid flight, designing itineraries, installing families in new locations, and overseeing the physical and emotional survival of those under their care. Women are more likely than are men to solicit help from governmental and non-governmental organizations and to more quickly find remunerated, generally, domestic work in cities (CODHES 1999: 127; Bello, Cardinal, and Arias 2000: 227-322).[7]

The community councils in the Pacific tend to possess a high percentage of women members, which is indicative of the significant leadership role they play in the reappropriation of territory and the promotion of local autonomy. Traditionally, the socialization of Afro-Colombian youth is a responsibility that falls largely upon women. It is alongside their mothers that children begin to construct their identities and associate with their surrounding environments. The depopulation of women from Afro-descendent territories is fatal to the political-cultural organizational process of Afro-Colombian communities.

Conclusion: Violence, Development, and Displacement in Colombia

Displacement in Colombia is a problem that is both growing and systemic in nature. It is not a recent problem: instead, it is deeply embedded in a historical process of pervasive exploitation and violent uprooting. From colonization to industrialization to present-day globalization, the specific characteristics of displacement have shifted throughout history; nonetheless, all these periods have seen the use of violence against rural or land-tied people in order to access key resources for accumulation by external interests.

This history underscores a need to systematically explore the link between development, violence, and displacement in modern Colombia, in order to understand and effectively approach the problem of forced migration. Violence and the conflict itself in Colombia can be understood as methods used by multiple armed actors to displace people in order to gain access to territories and resources, or to impose political control.

Current levels of displacement are likely to increase under the new Uribe government as it moves to further align itself with the United States and foreign multinational economic interests. Strategies to remove opposition through military force, to secure territories, and to promote foreign investment are central elements of the new government's plans, to be implemented co-operating with its northern partner. The United States has particularly aggressive development plans for the country and region, as is exemplified by Plan Colombia, the US-Colombia Free Trade Pact, the Andean Regional Initiative, and the proposed Free Trade Area of the Americas. As these trade and development plans and pacts advance in the region, the underlying causes of internal conflicts will become more difficult to address, and, thus, violence will probably worsen, leading to further forced migration. Displacement is a problem that has steadily increased since Colombia's move towards economic liberalization in the early 1990s.

National and regional development plans such as Plan Colombia and Plan Pacífico are typical examples of "development" in Colombia in that they reflect interrelated global economic and military interests and goals. The "war on drugs," the "war on terrorism," and the discourse involving development and foreign investment are key elements that promote the use of military violence to achieve economic objectives. Plan Colombia focuses largely on military training, the provision of military equipment, the fumigation of crops, and related activities. Grave social, ecological, and economic consequences result, including the destruction of forests and food crops and increased poverty and violence, forcing people to move to other parts of the country or to bordering areas.

Plan Colombia thus clearly expresses the interrelationship between development, military violence, and the displacement of rural Colombians. It follows a pattern of mixing and employing military violence, political-legal instruments, and ideological strategies to seize control of districts and resources for national elites and global interests. Paramilitary violence leading to displacement has intensified, specifically in areas strategic to development. Thus, paramilitary violence appears to be a significant factor within the hegemonic development process.

It is vital that a redefinition of the conditions upon which "development" is practised is given serious attention. A critical appraisal of development paradigms and policies would have to consider the linkage between development, violence, and displacement. It is important that actors involved in any conflict-ridden zone make their interests explicit and that consequences for perpetuators of such conflict are made substantial enough to serve as a real deterrent. In order that violence leading to displacement is prevented in the short term, incentives for foreign investment in areas of resource and land conflicts should be reduced or eliminated after careful reflection and critical appraisal that involves local leaders.

Pressure to adhere to the International Human Rights code and the International Criminal Court (ICC) system is an important measure that can be taken towards eliminating some of the human rights violations that lead to displacement. The reversal of foreign exemptions from the ICC would be a step towards addressing the lack of state legitimacy as well as the deepening internal conflict in Colombia.

The employment of "militaristic" or "violence-oriented" logic for the sake of accumulation and territorial control is perpetuated by numerous armed groups, aand that logic tends to coincide with goals of development based on intensive exploration, extraction, and short-term accumulation. This is so in both legal and illegal spheres of capitalist accumulation. Moreover, this military-capitalist logic demonstrates a specific way of viewing land that conflicts with local ethno-territorial uses and conceptualizations. Land-tied or territorial people have been most severely affected by this process throughout history, but displacement increasingly affects people in urban centres, which have become sites of reception and expulsion of the displaced as conflicts increasingly enter cities, uprooting individuals and families, in some cases, more than once.

Notably, violence and displacement are aimed at leaders and members of social organizations who have developed analyses, strategies, and methods to remain on traditional lands; who struggle to protect human, cultural, territorial, or labour rights; and who promote autonomous local development. The very condition of being socially organized is seen as a threat to many armed groups who view territorial movements as potential obstacles to political, economic, and/or territorial interests. If unarmed social organizations do not side with a given armed group, they are often perceived as serving the interests of an opposing group. Social and ethno-territorial movements are also seen as obstacles to "progress" and "development," and are targets of paramilitary violence, which aims to secure areas for state and elite control.

Rather than ceding lands in response to threatened violence, however, ethno-territorial movements are becoming increasingly organized, with clear ethnic, gender, and class analyses, and lines of action. These diverse social processes persistently build movements in response to a problem that they see as inherently linked to structural inequities that produce racial and gender discrimination, ecological and cultural deterioration, marginalization, and exclusion. In this context, leaders and members of these social movements feel that they have no alternative but to defend land and human and cultural rights, thus imperilling their lives. They often become military targets and are increasingly the objects of threat, disappearance, and assassination – or of forceful uprooting along with families and, in some cases, entire communities.

Despite the enormous difficulties facing leaders and members of ethno-territorial and other social movements, the strengthening of organizations in regions affected by displacement constitutes an important response to violence and forced removal. Social organization in and of itself offers a strategy with which to confront and prevent displacement. Through organizational activities, rights are more easily secured and global visibility generated. For many groups that share cultural and historical experiences, such as indigenous people, women, workers, rural farmers, or Afro-descendants, the choice to organize despite the threat of violence is often perceived as the only option. Moreover, among indigenous and many Afro-descendent communities, the tendency to remain in or return to traditional territories is the norm, despite the ongoing possibility of violence. This tendency or "right of return" is a basic principle of the ethno-territorial organizations that work to maintain integral relationships between local people and land in the face of actual or potential displacement.

Finally, ethno-territorial movements should be recognized and supported as stewards of natural resources within their titled areas. Unfinished titling should be completed as quickly as possible. The right to consultation for ethno-territorial communities must be respected in a meaningful way. Rights gained by indigenous and Afro-descendent peoples under the Constitution of 1991, promoting local autonomy and control over natural resources, should be further strengthened at a policy level and genuinely protected. Moreover, the definition and integrity of the ethno-territorial entity within the 1991 Constitution must be protected against proposed changes to the Constitution that would facilitate a new surge in multinational activity in indigenous territories. Local needs and rights should be continually strengthened for all rural peoples, including the right to remain in territories or to return after displacement has occurred. In essence, the protection and promotion of local organized groups and social processes that maintain cultural and economic ties within given territories is crucial for rebuilding place-based strategies to prevent and reduce displacement in Colombia.

Notes

1 One example of such stereotyping occurs in *Collateral Damage,* an Arnold Schwarzenegger film featuring citizen revenge in response to Colombian terrorist attacks against the USA; strongly criticized, it was the focus of street protests in Canada and the United States. It was released after Plan Colombia came into effect and, as it attracted increasing criticism in the United States and elsewhere for its militaristic character, was often compared to earlier war policies for Vietname and Central America. The movie also came in the wake of the 11 September 2001 terrorist attacks in the US, when the American public felt a heightened sense of insecurity.

2 On the history of violence as related to economic interests in the Americas, Galeano (1997), first published in 1973, is a classic work.

3 Special economic zones are open to national or foreign investment, which is encouraged through special tax breaks and other incentives. Among other areas, these zones include the port city of Buenaventura in the Colombian Pacific, Cauca in southwestern Colombia, and the Atlantic region, where indigenous, Afro-descendent, and small-scale farmers have traditionally lived.

4 The city closest to the communities living in the Naya and Yurumanguí river basins is the port city of Buenaventura. Villages are one to six hours away by motorized canoe.

5 Participating in the Comisión Interinstitucional were the Association for Alternative Social Promotion (MINGA), Consultancy on Human Rights and Displacement (CODHES), Juridical Corporation for Active Humanity, Inter-Congregational Commission for Justice and Peace, National Association for Solidarity Aid (ANDAS), Centre for Popular Research and Education (CINEP), Lawyers Collective "Jose Alvear Restrepo," and the Committee Foundation for Solidarity with Political Prisoners (FCSPP). Other participants in this process included the ombudsman, the Office of the High Commission of the United Nations for Human Rights, and the Office of the High Commission of the United Nations for Refugees. The commission delegates interviewed local administrative officials, church authorities, social leaders, and members of indigenous, black, and *campesino* [peasant] communities who were victims of the paramilitary attack. Interviews were also carried out with military authorities in the region.

6 See CODHES bulletins and reports on displacement as well as website archives at http://www.codhes.org.co.

7 There is an important and growing body of research concerning the effects of displacement on women in Colombia, the work of both Colombian and non-Colombian authors.

References

Álvarez, Jairo Estrada, ed. 2001. *Plan Colombia: Ensayos Críticos* [Plan Colombia: Critical essays]. Bogotá: Universidad Nacional de Colombia.

Anzola, Libardo Sarmiento. 2001. "Conflicto, Intervención y Economía Política de la Guerra [Conflict, intervention and the political economy of war]." In Jairo Estrada Álvarez, ed., *Plan Colombia: Ensayos Críticos,* 63-91. Bogota: Universidad Nacional de Colombia.

Archila, Mauricio, and Mauricio Pardo, eds. 2001. *Movimientos sociales, Estado y democracia en Colombia* [Social movements, state and democracy in Colombia]. Bogota: ICANH.

Arrington, Vanessa. 2002. "Colombia Opts Out of Sending Suspected War Criminals." *Associated Press,* 4 September, via University of Buffalo listserv.

Bello, Martha Nubia, Elena Martín Cardinal, and Fernando Jiovani Arias, eds. 2000. *Efectos Psicosociales y Culturales del Desplazamiento* [Psychosocial and cultural effects of displacement]. Bogotá: Universidad Nacional de Colombia.

Borda, Juan Gustavo Cobo, and Dario Jaramillo Agudelo. 1983. *Manual de Historia de Colombia* [Handbook of Colombian kistory]. Bogotá: Círculo de Lectores.
Braun, Hebert. 1987. *Mataron a Gaitán* [They killed Gaitán]. Bogotá: Universidad Nacional de Colombia.
Caicedo, Daniel Libreros. 2001. "Nuevo Modelo de Dominación Colonial [New model of colonial domination]." In Jairo Estrada Álvarez, ed., *Plan Colombia: Ensayos Críticos,* 93-106. Bogotá: Universidad National de Colombia.
Caycedo, Germán Castro. 2001. *Con las Manos en Alto* [With your hands up]. Bogotá: Planeta.
CENSAT Agua Viva. 2001. *Report on Canadian Oil Interests in Colombia.* Bogotá: CENSAT.
Cernea, Michael, ed. 1999. *The Economics of Involuntary Resettlement: Questions and Challenges.* Washington, DC: World Bank.
CODHES. 1999. *Un País que Huye: Desplazamiento y violencia en una nación fragmentada* [A country that flees: Displacement and violence in a fragmented nation]. Bogotá: CODHES.
–. 2001. *Informa #3,* April 2001. Bogotá: CODHES.
Comisión Interinstitucional. 2001. *Verificación de los Hechos de las Cuencas del Naya y Yurumanguí en los Departamentos de Cuca y Valle del Cauca Mayo 2-5, 2001* [Verification of the Events Taking Place in the River Basins of Naya and Yurumanguí in the Departments of Cuca and Valle del Cauca 2-5 May 2001]. Bogotá: Comisión Interinstitucional.
Constanza, Mery, García Vargas, and Nubia Mejía García. 2001. "El Impacto de las Fumigaciones Aéreas [Impact of aerial fumigations]." In Jairo Estrada Álvarez, ed., *Plan Colombia: Ensayos Críticos* [Plan Colombia: Critical essays], 121-40. Bogotá: Universidad Nacional de Colombia.
Cubides, Fernando, and Camilo Domínguez, eds. 1999. *Desplazados, Migraciones Internas y Reestructuraciones Territoriales* [Displaced, internal migrations, and territorial restructuring]. Bogotá: CES.
Currie, Lauchlin. 1966. *Accelerating Development: The Necessity and the Means.* New York: McGraw-Hill. Repr., Mexico: FCE, 1968. Citations are to the FCE edition.
CUSO. 1994. *Plan Pacífico: Colombia and the Canada Connection.* Kingston: Community Publishing.
Escobar, Arturo. 1996. "Camaroneras Comunitarias ¿Alternativas al Capital? [Community shrimp farmers, alternatives to capital?]." In Arturo Escobar and Alvaro Pedrosa, eds., *Pacífico ¿Desarrollo o Diversidad? Estado, Capital y Movimientos Sociales en el Pacífico Colombiano* [The Pacific: Development or diversity? State, capital and social movements in the Colombian Pacific], 144-74. Bogotá: CEREC.
–. 2000. "El Lugar de la naturaleza y la naturaleza del lugar: ¿Globalización o postdesarrollo? [The place of nature and the nature of place: Globalization or post-development?]." In Andreu Viola, ed., *Antropología del Desarrollo,* 113-43. Barcelona: Paidos.
–. 2003. "Displacement and Development in the Colombian Pacific." *International Social Science Journal* (175) (May): 157-67.
Escobar, Arturo, and Alvaro Pedrosa, eds. 1996. *Pacífico: Desarrollo o Diversidad? Estado, capital y movimientos sociales en el Pacífico Colombiano* [Pacific: Development or diversity? State, capital and social movements in the Colombian Pacific]. Bogotá: CEREC.
Fairness in Reporting. 2000. "Colombia's Cocaine Shell Game: Media are Leading the U.S. into a Civil War in the Name of the 'War on Drugs.'" May/June. http://www.fair.org/index.php?page=1030.
Galeano, Eduardo. 1997. *Open Veins of Latin America.* 1973. Reprint, New York: Monthly Review Press.
Global IDP Database. N.d. "President Uribe's Military Solutions to the Conflict Do Not Improve Security." Global IDP Database. http://www.idpproject.org.
Government of Colombia. N.d. "Estrategia del Estado Colombiano contra las Autodefensas Ilegales [Strategy of the Colombian state against the illegal self-defence groups]." Unpublished document.
Grueso, Libia, Carlos Rosero, and Arturo Escobar. 1996. "El Proceso de Organización de Comunidades Negras en el Pacífico Colombiano [The organizational process of Black Communities in the Colombian Pacific]." In S. Alvarez, ed., *Culture of Politics, Politics of Culture: Revisioning Latin American Social Movements,* 196-217. Boulder: Westview Press.

Human Rights Watch. 2001. *The Sixth Division: Military-Paramilitary Ties and U.S. Policy in Colombia.* New York: Human Rights Watch.

Ismi, Asad. 2000. *Profiting from Repression: Canadian Investment in and Trade with Colombia: Americas Update Report,* November.

Klare, Michael. 2001. "The New Geography of Conflict: June 2001." *The Dark Side of Natural Resources.* http://www.globalpolicy.org/security/natres/generaldebate/2001/0601klar.htm (accessed 4 January 2002).

Leech, Gary M. 2002. "Colombia Court Deems Rehabilitation Zones Unconstitutional." In *Colombia Report,* 9 December. Information Network of the Americas (INOTA). http://www.colombiareport.org/.

Maldonado, Adolfo. 2001. *Está Libro Esta Dedicado a Todos los Que han Sufrido por la Presencia de Ocidental en su Territorio* [This book is dedicated to all who have suffered the presence of the West in their territory]. Quito, Bogotá, and Lima: Oilwatch.

Molano, Alfredo. 1987. *Selva Adentro: Una historia oral de la colonización del Guaviare* [Deep in the Jungle: An oral history of the colonization of Guaviare]. Bogotá: El Ancora Editores.

Mondragon, Hector. 2001. "Plan Colombia y Petroleo. La hegemonía de las Cuatro Hermanas [Plan Colombia and oil: The hegemony of the Four Sisters]." In CENSAT Agua Viva, ed., *Ruiria, el Grito del Petroleo* [Ruiria: The Scream of Petroleum], 1-13. Bogotá: CENSAT AV.

Muggah, Robert. 2000. "Through the Developmentalist's Looking Glass: Conflict-Induced Displacement and Involuntary Resettlement." *Journal of Refugee Studies* 13 (2): 133-64.

Mutis, Aura Maria Puyana. 1999. "Cultivos ilicitos, fumigacion y desplazamiento en la Amazonia y la Orinoquia [Illicit cultivations, fumigation and displacement in Amazonia and Orinoquia]." In Fernando Cubides and Camilo Domínguez, eds., *Desplazados, Migraciones Internas y Reestructuraciones Territoriales* [The displaced, internal migrations and territorial restructuring], 240-73. Bogotá: CES.

Ospina, William. 1999. *Las Auroras de Sangre* [The auroras of blood]. Bogotá: Ministerio de Cultura.

Pardo, Mauricio, ed. 2001. *Acción Colectiva, Estado y Etnicidad en el Pacífico Colombiano* [Collective action, state and ethnicity in the Colombian Pacific]. Bogotá: Colciencias.

PCN (Proceso de Comunidades Negras). 2000. Communique to International Opinion, May.

Restrepo, Eduardo. 2001. "Imaginando comunidad negra: Etnografía de la etnización de las poblaciones negras en el Pacífico Sur Colombiano [Imagining Black community: Ethnography of the ethno-ization of the Black populations in the Colombian South Pacific]." In Mauricio Pardo, ed., *Acción Colectiva, Estado y Etnicidad en el Pacífico Colombiano,* 41-70. Bogotá: Colciencias.

Reuters. 2000. "Colombian Paramilitary Chief Admits Getting Backing from Businessmen." 26 September. http://archives.cnn.com/2000/WORLD/americas/09/06/colombia.paramilitary.reut/.

Romero-Medina, Amanda. 2001. "Colombia: Internal Displacement and Humanitarian Crisis." Michael Baptista Lecture, Senate Chamber, York University, 23 May.

Rossiasco, Paula Andrea. Colombia Journal Online. "Forced Displacement and Women as Heads of Displaced Households in Colombia" June 2003. http://www.colombiajournal.org/displacement.htm.

Sánchez, Gonzalo. 1991. *Guerra y Política en la Sociedad Colombiana* [War and politics in Colombian society]. Bogotá: Ancora Editores.

Schwarz, Daniel, and Ashibindu Singh. 2000. *Environmental Conditions, Resources and Conflicts: An Introductory Overview and Data Collection.* Nairobi: UNEP.

"Special Economic Export Zones." N.d. http://www.coltrade.org/doingbusiness/seez.asp (accessed February 2006).

UNHCR. 2003. "Colombia." In Global Appeal 2003. Geneva: UNHCR. http://www.unhcr.org/cgi-bin/texis/vtx/publ/opendoc.pdf?id=3ddceb6d7&tbl=PUBL (accessed 17 May 2006).

US Department of State. 2001a. "Country Reports on Human Rights Practices: Colombia 2001." http://www.state.gov/g/drl/rls/hrrpt/2001/wha/8326.htm (accessed March 2002).

–. 2001b. "U.S. Policy toward the Andean Region." Fact Sheet 16 May. http://www.state.gov/p/wha/rls/fs/2001/2985.

Valderrama, Mario, and Hector Mondragón, eds. 1998. *Desarrollo y Equidad con Campesino* [Development and equity with the small-scale farmer]. Bogotá: IICH-Mision Rural.
Vargas, Ricardo. 1999. *Fumigación y Conflicto: Políticas Antidrogas y Deslegitimación del Estado en Colombia* [Fumigation and conflict: Anti-drug politics and the delegitimization of the state in Colombia]. Bogotá: Tercer Mundo.
Vargas, Ricardo, and J. Barragan. 1996. *Drugs-Linked Crops and Rural Development in Colombia: An Alternative Action Plan.* London: Catholic Institute for International Relations.

7
Dams, Development, and Displacement: The Narmada Valley Development Projects

Pablo S. Bose

Development-induced displacement (DID) is, as the other contributions to this volume demonstrate, a pervasive and wide-ranging phenomenon. The cases collected here do much to stretch traditional notions of displacement. Focusing on the eviction of populations at the behest of specific projects is not enough. Instead, the examples presented here make a persuasive case that the analysis of DID needs to address macro- as well as micro-level issues, that is, displacement resulting from broad-based policies as well as from individual projects. It is for this reason that other chapters show displacement in such a diverse array of shapes and forms – from private-sector mining operations to conservation schemes, from land reform initiatives to economic liberalization strategies, from forestry management to oil development.

And yet, the more familiar forms of DID must also be acknowledged by any inquiry into contemporary processes of development and displacement. After all, the continuing impact of infrastructure projects such as airports, highways, and dams is considerable, with close to ten million people a year displaced, according to some critics (Cernea and McDowell 2000). The last of these archetypal examples – dams – has received the most attention in the study of displacement. Dams of all sizes dot the face of the planet, altering ecosystems and settlement patterns alike, producing the power base and infrastructure capacity for both rural and urban regions. They are integral components of sustainable growth and development strategies, seen as sources of clean, renewable, and safe energy. Critics, however, view dams as fraught with potentially devastating social and ecological costs and have called into question the safety and longevity of existing hydroelectric projects (Rajendran 2000).

Dams are, of course, an ancient technology; however, in terms of scale and style, many modern hydroelectric megaprojects – the so-called big dams – bear little resemblance to their forerunners. Many are massive structures, altering the flow of large rivers and creating vast new artificial lakes and reservoirs. They are, in a sense, monuments to the vision of industrialized development of recent centuries, symbolic manifestations of the struggle to "subdue" nature and turn its energy towards human purposes. The iconic power of dams in such developmental visions is demonstrated by their popularity as tourist destinations, as thousands each year flock to sites such as the Hoover and Aswan Dams to gaze upon these engineering "marvels."

Dams are, therefore, an excellent lens through which to study displacement, both in terms of the specific impacts of individual projects and the broader context of developmental policy within which such projects are situated. In particular, this chapter focuses on a prominent recent example, the Narmada Valley Development Projects (NVDP) in northwestern India. This is a case in which plans to build a series of massive interlocking dams over a region encompassing sections of three states have been mired in controversy for the better part of fifty years. The story of the Narmada Valley is well known within and outside of India, in terms of both the scale and ambitious nature of the project and the vigorous and sustained opposition that it has engendered locally and internationally. The case has received considerable attention from academics, policy makers, and community activists, including various international institutions and non-governmental organizations (NGOs), and, in India, continues to be an important locus of battles over the meaning and objectives of development.

The events that have unfolded over the past fifty years in the Narmada Valley therefore hold many lessons for those interested in the relationship between development and displacement. This chapter presents a two-part examination of the Narmada case. The first is a project-focused analysis of the history of the NVDP: the locally specific justifications for the proposed dams, the benefits they are meant to bring, the social, environmental, and financial costs they will place on the region's inhabitants and others, and the growth of local, national, and international opposition to the scheme – particularly in terms of the critiques and alternatives that its opponents offer. The second part of the chapter looks at how the Narmada dams typify a part of displacement as it is understood on a much grander scale, in terms of national and, indeed, international development policies. In particular, this section considers the place of mega-dams in India's major competing developmental visions: Gandhian small-scale, Nehruvian state-socialist, and the more recently embraced neoliberal globalization model. The chapter also discusses recent trends in the Narmada Valley, including the move towards the privatization of public infrastructure projects and the increasing involvement of transnational diasporic communities in the funding of development projects. Such trends suggest that development and displacement need to be examined not only in terms of the nation-state and its relationship with its citizens but, more broadly, in terms of the intersection between state power, private capital, and religious, ethnic, and place-based identities.

Displacement in Narmada: A Project-Oriented Analysis

The Narmada is the fifth-largest river in India; flowing for over thirteen hundred kilometres through several districts in Madhya Pradesh, Maharashtra, and Gujarat, it empties into the Arabian Sea some three hundred kilometres north of Bombay. Its catchment area of over 100,000 square kilometres includes 32 percent forest cover – a significant amount, given India's dearth of woodland. A substantial population, including a large number of indigenous people, lives in the Narmada Valley and relies on the river and over forty tributaries for its mainly agricultural and fishing-based livelihoods. The Narmada is also considered one of the holiest rivers in India and its banks are dotted with numerous religious shrines and temples. Before 1947, no major attempts to harness the power of the river had been made, but following independence, engineers began to draw up plans to rectify this overnight in the light of the new vision and demands of industrializing independence, common throughout the third world, and in the image of rapid industrial development as characterized by Soviet communism.

Massive hydroelectric projects were an integral part of the post-colonial vision of a secular and modernized India that was embraced by many of the nation's early political leaders, a vision examined more closely in the latter half of this chapter. One of the architects of that developmental dream, the first prime minister of India, Jawaharlal Nehru, famously hailed high dams as "the temples of modern India" (Nehru 1958). Nehru himself laid the foundation stones in the 1961 Sardar Sarovar project, the most important or "terminal" dam in the Narmada Valley development scheme. But no amount of nationalistic fervour could simplify the planning process for either this dam or the rest of the plan. By the mid-1960s, three riparian states were involved in squabbles over costs, benefits, and responsibilities related to the project. In 1969, the central government stepped in and formed the Narmada Water Disputes Tribunal (NWDT) in order to resolve the disputes.

After ten years of assessment and planning, the tribunal published its award in December 1978, which designated Gujarat as the major beneficiary of the project. As part of its settlement, the NWDT created the NVDP. The full scale of the hydroelectric megaproject in the Narmada Valley, as envisioned by the NVDP encompasses, 30 major dams, 135 medium dams, over 3,000 minor or check-dams, and 30,000 micro water-harvesting (or conservation) schemes (Pathak 1991). Of the thirty major dams, ten are to be built on the Narmada River itself, and the rest on its tributaries. Some of the latter have already been built, including the Tawa, Barna, Sukhta, and Bargi dams.

Project Benefits and Justifications

Developing the Narmada Valley with this complicated and controversial series of large dams is meant to provide three concrete benefits: hydroelectric power (primarily for industries and cities), water for irrigation, and drinking water for drought-stricken regions (interview with Y.K. Alagh, 27 March 2000). Gujarat, as the main beneficiary of the planned dams, is intended to see the irrigation of over 1.8 million hectares of land, the provision of drinking water to 135 urban centres and 8,215 villages, the generation of over 200 megawatts (MW) of hydroelectric energy, and flood protection for 210 villages as well as for the major city of Bharuch. The remaining energy production from the project will be divided between the states of Madhya Pradesh (800 MW) and Maharashtra (400 MW). Additionally, the perennially drought-stricken state of Rajasthan potentially stands to gain from the irrigation of over 75,000 hectares of desert land. These benefits, as noted by the NWDT, accrue primarily to the state of Gujarat, and it has subsequently been the central proponent of these projects. From the very initial planning stages, generating hydroelectric power was viewed as the key benefit of constructing these dams. It was only much later, after technical, social, and ecological concerns had been raised regarding the plans, that the rationale for the dams shifted away from developing a stable energy supply for industry and towards an emotional appeal of "quenching the thirst" of the drought-stricken regions of northern Gujarat, such as Kutch and Saurashtra.

Project Costs: Social and Financial

The displacement effects of the Narmada Valley dams are considerable. The full storage reservoir for the terminal dam alone – the Sardar Sarovar Project (SSP) – is planned to reach a height of 138 metres, resulting in the submersion of 37,000 hectares of land in Gujarat, Maharashtra, and Madhya Pradesh. Estimates are that 200,000 people in 245 villages will be forced to relocate. Of these villages, the vast majority – 191 of them – are in Maharashtra, with an additional 35 in Madhya Pradesh and 19 in Gujarat. Over 60 percent of the affected peoples are *adivasis* (indigenous or so-called tribal peoples), and most of the "Project Affected Persons" (PAP) live in Madhya Pradesh. In addition, over 140,000 farmers will have their lands submerged for the planned irrigation and canal works (Fisher 1995: 13).

These figures do not include thousands of people living downstream from the project, whose lives will inevitably be affected. Compensation packages are available only to those whose lands will be submerged. Nothing is offered to downstream families, such as those of the Hilsa fisheries, whose livelihood will probably be destroyed by reduced water flow. Landless labourers and herders, for example, are excluded from the official tally of affected people. Rehabilitation packages are based on property ownership, yet many of the "oustees" are landless peasants or hill adivasis who do not hold title to their homes but are considered to be "encroachers" on public fields and forests. Those who will be displaced to make room for animal preserves, such as the Shoolpaneshwar Bear Sanctuary, are also excluded from the official count. So are those who will be displaced in order to implement compensatory afforestation – replanting trees to make up for those drowned by the reservoir (Judge 1997). The PAP figures also do not include those who will be affected by what is called "secondary displacement," the forcible removal of one set of persons due to the influx into their region of another group that has itself been displaced. If one counts the groups not included in the official statistics of the project-affected, close to a million people may be affected by this project (Baviskar 1995: 200).

Beyond such sacrifice is the financial burden that the project places on the people whom it is meant to benefit (primarily the citizens of Gujarat). At present, the full cost of the dam is estimated 200 billion rupees (roughly US$4.6 billion) and its completion date is anticipated as some time in 2040 (Alagh, Pathak, and Buch 1995: 35). On 20 January 2003, the Sardar Sarovar Narmada Nigam (SSNNL, the corporation created to undertake the dam construction) informed senior politicians in Gujarat that it would require the infusion of an additional 16.5 billion rupees in order to complete the project (Ahmedabad.com 2003). Gujarat's ability to support this contentious project – economically, as well as socially or ecologically – is therefore highly in doubt. The SSP alone currently consumes 80 percent of Gujarat's irrigation and water budget. The state coffers stand near empty, with the SSNNL leading the list of government agencies leaving contractors' invoices unpaid (Comptroller and Auditor General of India 2003: 17).

Project Costs: Environmental

The ecological consequences of building massive dams in the Narmada Valley are as significant as the social (Alvares and Billorey 1988; Unni 1996). A large area will be flooded and dense forests will be lost in a country that can ill afford further deforestation. Wildlife, including rare and endangered species such as the wild ass and the marsh crocodile, will be killed since there is no adjoining forest for them to escape to when the waters begin to rise and no plan to remove them to safe lands. Fertile fields will be lost and other areas will be in danger of siltation, loss of topsoil, waterlogging, and increased salinity.

In addition, some geologists fear an increased risk of earthquakes since the Narmada Valley is situated in a tectonically sensitive region. Critics also point to a possible increase in waterborne diseases such as malaria due to waterlogged land and stagnant pools created by the reservoir. The ecological costs listed here are only those contained within the valley itself and do not include other losses to be borne by downstream communities, such as the Narmada Hilsa fishery which, as mentioned above, will be wiped out by the project.

Project Proponents' Response to Project Costs

The dam builders' response to such environmental and social concerns has been less than satisfactory. NVDP planners have often simply dismissed "environmental apprehensions" out of hand or engaged in wholesale denial of possible effects (Alagh, Pathak, and Buch 1995: 14). The assurances of pro-dam supporters are often long on rhetoric and woefully short on specifics. In fact, the dam builders' assessment of the environmental impact of their project is so poor that the independent review of the project, commissioned by the World Bank, declared, "The history of the environmental aspects of Sardar Sarovar [is] a history of non-compliance" (Morse and Berger 1992: ii). Indeed, the Indian Ministry of Environment and Forests (MoEF) originally opposed the construction of the SSP on the grounds that an adequate environmental impact assessment (EIA) had not been undertaken. To circumvent this barrier, in the early 1980s, the political leaders of various state governments involved in the project approached the office of then prime minister Rajiv Gandhi to intercede on the dam builders' behalf and, over the objections of the MoEF, a decision was made to carry out the assessments concurrently with the construction of the dam (Turaga 2000). Even this most grudging of clearances has never been officially completed to the satisfaction of the MoEF. To date, the most comprehensive and detailed analyses of the ecological impacts of the SSP and other dams within the NVDP have come not from the planners and architects of the "grand vision" but, rather, from studies commissioned by dam opponents and independent environmental groups in India. Although it is true that prevention and rehabilitation measures have been developed by dam planners, especially in recent years, the political will and capacity to implement such safeguards is often lacking.

In terms of the social costs, for example, project proponents have assured critics that displaced people will be adequately compensated according to the terms of the NWDT award. Governments have promised to provide monetary compensation, suitable replacement land for farmers, and hills and forests in other parts of the country for adivasis to inhabit. In addition, the project planners say they have built adequate new homes for the displaced in resettlement sites. However, the land provided is often unusable or already inhabited. Aside from those in a few model towns that are displayed as showpieces to foreign dignitaries, the new homes for the displaced often consist of little more than a metre-square concrete plinth covered by a tin roof (T. Berger, personal communication, 2 October 1999). Many of the resettlement sites consist of poor-quality land that is not irrigable and is sometimes less than two square hectares in size (Whitehead 2000). Additionally, as former chief minister of Madhya Pradesh Digvijay Singh often argued, in many cases, land is simply not available for resettlement. Cash compensation does little good for these inhabitants, who are forced to migrate to the slums of big cities; this is particularly true for migrants who are familiar with a rural or village and barter-based (rather than monetary) economy.

Further complicating the matter is the fact that, as noted earlier, a majority of those affected by the project are adivasis. The Indian Constitution specifically guarantees under Article 29 the right of displaced indigenous peoples to be transported – if they are to be moved at all – as an entire community rather than as individuals. The idea is to maintain the social fabric and cohesion of the villages being destroyed by transplanting their occupants into a new environment (Sharma 1995). This goal is a difficult one even in principle, as proven by the social stigma attached to "reservoir oustees" in their resettled villages (Baboo 1992: 117). It is made all the more trying when one considers the scarcity of land and resources for resettling individuals, let alone entire communities.

There are additional difficulties in resolving issues of family partitions and of the status of women, especially widowed and unmarried women for whom property rights in some of the states implicated revert to the control of the eldest male in the family (Singh et al. 1992: 28). Given the fact that there is no federal law governing displacement or rehabilitation, and only the Land Acquisition Act Amendment (1984) to offer monetary and not land-based compensation, these complex factors of gender and class make designing adequate rehabilitation and resettlement (R and R) packages extremely difficult.

Opposition to the Project

Given these considerable social, financial, and environmental costs, it is unsurprising that there has been long and sustained opposition to the dam projects within the Narmada Valley. At the very outset of the project in 1960, the land of six villages was seized for the building of the Kevadia colony to house the dam builders and officials. The oustees from these villages were never adequately compensated, and their plight, partly informed the first protests against the SSP (Singh et al. 1992: 31). Since those early days, different groups have rallied against the project. Farmer and merchant groups, labour organizations, social workers, and even the occasional mainstream politician have all, at various times, join the protests (Baviskar 1995). However, the most vigorous and effective opposition has been mounted over just the past decade and a half.

Opponents of the NVDP have criticized the plans on multiple grounds. To begin with, they have decried the lack of transparency in all stages of the project design, from planning to implementation to mitigation. They have critiqued, in particular, the lack of public participation in all of these processes. While state governments, engineers, and technical experts quarrelled among themselves during the 1960s and 1970s, the villagers and farmers whose lands were to be submerged were kept mainly in the dark. By 1985, as rumours ran rampant about their fate, inhabitants of the valley began to organize in order to demand greater access to information and negotiate more equitable compensation packages with the various state governments. Several of these groups coalesced in 1987 into the Narmada Bachao Andolan (Save Narmada Movement, or NBA), an umbrella organization that brought together villagers, labourers, farmers, social and environmental activists, writers, scientists, academics, and a host of others to protest the project.

The NBA helped to raise other questions and concerns regarding the NVDP. It highlighted the fact that many of the anticipated gains from the dams are based upon inaccurate or exaggerated data. For example, the amount of power that the dams will generate may have been overestimated by as much as 25 percent, on the basis of faulty water flow data. Proposed irrigation efficiency is similarly compromised by the siphoning off of water by other and newer dams. Even the emotionally charged objective of delivering drinking water to drought-stricken regions has been called into question by the NBA, which points out that even if it were financially feasible and cost-effective to pump Narmada water four hundred kilometres northwest to alleviate the crisis, the infrastructure required to do so does not exist (Narmada Bachao Andolan 2001).

The effect of this opposition has been to move the issue beyond the local context and to challenge the project at national and even international levels. The NBA, through mass public protests and a series of strategic alliances with international NGOs, forced the World Bank (one of the major financial backers of the project as of 1985) to launch an independent review of the SSP. The men appointed to head that review, Bradford Morse and Thomas Berger (1992: xii), completed their work by denouncing the projects as a whole, declaring unequivocally, "We think the Sardar Sarovar Projects as they stand are flawed. Resettlement and rehabilitation of all those displaced by the Projects is not possible under prevailing circumstances, and the environmental impacts of the Projects have not been properly considered or adequately addressed."

The state governments and dam builders, perhaps unsurprisingly, did not concur with the Morse Report, as the independent review came to be known. Even the World Bank was reluctant to accept this stinging critique of one of its projects. The bank tried to ignore and misrepresent the findings of the report, and only after substantial pressure from concerned individuals, NGOs, and even Berger and Morse themselves would the bank reluctantly agree to suspend funding for the project, pending further investigation (Caulfield 1996: 25-28). By mid-1993, the bank had determined that the project as it stood would be unable to meet the conditions outlined in World Bank agreements guaranteeing social and ecological protections, but the state governments were offered the option of declining World Bank assistance (T. Berger, personal communication, 9 March 2000). Despite the departure of the World Bank and the Morse Report's vindication of the NBA's critique, the government of Gujarat indicated its willingness to continue to fund the project on its own.

The struggle continued. With the World Bank out of the picture, the NBA refocused on action within India itself. It continued to wage a campaign against the completion of the SSP and managed to force the cessation of construction in 1994 after an Indian Supreme Court injunction that halted the dam height at 80.3 metres. This victory – though significant – was short-lived. In February 1999, an interim decision by the Indian Supreme Court allowed construction to resume, raising the height of the dam to 85 metres. On 22 July 1999, the court ratified its February decision and allowed the dam to be further raised to a height of 88.5 metres. On 18 October 2000, in a controversial split decision, the Supreme Court of India approved further construction of the Sardar Sarovar Dam on the Narmada River in Gujarat. On 17 May 2001, the Narmada Control Authority, the body overseeing the project, provided clearance to raise the height of the Sardar Sarovar Dam from 90 to 95 metres despite the fact that over 3,500 families at the current dam height of 90 metres had not yet been rehabilitated as per the provisions of the NWDT award.

As construction of the dam slowly resumed – halted by continued court challenges and political wrangling – the government of Gujarat worked throughout 2000 and 2001 to fulfill its promises to "quench the thirst" of Saurashtra and Kutch with water from the Narmada. With much fanfare, it announced the extension of a pipeline to bring water to the drought-stricken regions. Throughout the following months, however, it became apparent that the cost of actually pumping this water through the pipeline was prohibitive. Moreover, as critics had already warned, there was little infrastructure in place to distribute the water safely or effectively. Despite such concerns, a year later, the central government of India reaffirmed its commitment to the NVDP and the designs of Gujarat and the other partner states. In November 2002, the Indian water resources minister Arjun Charan Sethi proclaimed the SSP to be a "national project," one that the National Democratic Alliance government would support fully. More recently, the Indian home minister, L.K. Advani, and the prime minister of India, A.B. Vajpayee, both offered assurances that the project would be completed on schedule (Narmada Bachao Andolan 2002).

Displacement in Narmada: A Development Policy-Oriented Analysis

The preceding section considered the specific details of the NVDP in terms of project costs and benefits. But how do dams fit into India's post-colonial development strategies more broadly? Examining such a question requires a brief review of the struggle between such visions in the growth of the new country.

India's Competing Visions of Development

At the time of India's independence in 1948, two particular developmental visions were in competition – the Gandhian notion of decentralized development and village-based rule (a loosely communitarian conception of confederation and self-reliance) and a Nehruvian state-socialist model of development with a focus on heavy industrialization, extensive economic planning, and strong state controls on a mixed economy substantially integrated into the world capitalist economy. In the end it was Nehru's vision that won the day, achieving a relatively broad-based consensus among industrialists, socialists, farmers, and intellectuals alike. The choosing of such a path was in no small part due to the need felt by nationalist leaders such as Nehru for India to establish its political autonomy. They felt that full independence could be achieved only by resisting the domination of metropolitan capital and the unwelcome attention of predatory nations such as the European powers who had flourished in the nineteenth century (Ghosh 1997: 166).

The developmental goal articulated by Nehru therefore became to modernize the country in order to prevent it from being dominated by its more technologically advantaged neighbours in the anarchic world system of nation-states. The sense of not falling behind rival states meant that the debate over development was not whether or not to adopt an industrial model, but rather, how quickly such a model could be achieved. Nehru himself declared, "[we] are trying to catch up, as far as we can, with the Industrial Revolution that occurred long ago in Western countries" (Nehru, quoted in Chatterjee 1997: 85). The prominence that developmental visions were to play over the next fifty years in India – as part of both political rhetoric and practice – is important to underscore. Partha Chatterjee (1997: 86) suggests that "A developmental ideology was a constituent part of the self-definition of the post-colonial state. The state was connected to the people-nation not simply through the procedural forms of representative government, it also acquired its representativeness by directing a programme of economic development on behalf of the nation."

In a similar fashion, Niraja Jayal (1999: 194-95) comments that "[the] Indian state has been interventionist by design, and it is arguable that the primary impetus of interventionism, indeed its inspiring and guiding force, has been development. The state's claims to legitimacy have appealed to its commitment to developmental tasks, which have therefore come to acquire the rather exalted status of 'reasons of state.'"

India therefore embarked upon a program of intensive economic planning, directing the economy through a series of five-year economic plans that attempted to create a national heavy industry base to produce and process raw materials and a "cottage industry" to produce consumer goods for domestic consumption. These plans also called for strong capital controls and an active, interventionist central state, as befitted a state emerging in an era dominated by Keynesian economic models. And though the political and social rhetoric of the following decades proclaimed the objectives of a socialist project, as Terrence Byres (1997: 42) argues, what was created in India after 1947 was not state socialism in anything other than name: "The invoking of 'socialism' by the Indian state we take to be no more than empty political rhetoric – increasingly empty as we move forward from the 1950s. Our concern is with a state intent upon dissolving economic backwardness via capitalism."

This developmental trajectory meant that the Indian state did not, for example, confront vested landowning interests through land reform following independence. Instead, earlier intermediary classes were actually able to consolidate their power to become a rich middle and upper peasantry. Pranab Bardhan (1985) argues that such decisions not to directly confront the hierarchical nature of the Indian polity in both rural and urban settings has led to a situation whereby a plurality of classes dominates the economy, generating conflicting pressures for patronage and subsidies. In particular, he describes a heterogeneous and fluid set of alliances between the three dominant proprietary classes in India: the industrial capitalist class (essentially under the leadership of top business families), rich farmers, and professionals (white-collar workers including the elites of the military and the civil service, and the intelligentsia).

Bardhan further points out that conflicts within the dominant coalition between these three proprietary classes (as well as amidst the classes themselves) had, in the 1970s and 1980s, squandered funds that were originally targeted for public investment (and, ideally, directed towards democratic development). In order to smooth over the conflicts and assuage the different parties, public funds were funnelled not into infrastructure investment or economic growth, but into subsidies and patronage to soothe various interest groups. This also meant tremendous outlay for resources to police the unruly masses that were left out of this tidy arrangement – to which expanded police and paramilitary forces can attest. Also, due to the difficult and democratic nature of the Indian polity, an entire industry grew up around the distribution of the subsidies, and ever more groups have become politicized and have attempted to gain for themselves a slice of this pie. Bardhan (1985: 67) argues that this has created a volatile dynamic in which political and social stability is threatened by those who are left out on the margins and are increasingly expressing their displeasure.

Compounding these pressures is the fact that the economic strategy on which India's post-colonial political autonomy and economic prosperity was founded had, by the early 1970s, proven to be a rather dismal failure. Even a decade earlier – scarcely into the first few economic plans – India had begun to run massive balance of payment (BoP) deficits. By 1967, the Indian rupee had been devalued by 20 percent, but the BoP deficits continued. The collapse of the Bretton Woods economic system in 1971 created a further crisis and resulted in the spiralling devaluation of the rupee. In June 1972, the rupee was pegged to the pound sterling and its exchange rate was floated. The Indian economy stayed solvent for the next twenty years, in part through unsustainable deficit spending and by staunching some of its bleeding by drawing on resources of successful Indian émigrés, through remittances and foreign currency deposit holdings (Nayyar 1994).

But the building economic crisis finally reached meltdown status in 1991. Inflationary pressures, coupled with overvalued exchange rates and rising fiscal deficits, had severely staggered the Indian economy. It could not, however, recover from the body blow dealt by a series of external shocks, the most severe of which was the 1991 Gulf War. Not only was the Indian state responsible (at considerable expense) for repatriating hundreds of thousands of workers threatened by war but also the flow of foreign exchange from the Gulf dried up and the sudden spike in oil prices further crippled the economy. In the international loan market, India's credit rating plummeted, as commercial lenders shied away. Furthermore, the second part of the diasporic capital equation – foreign currency deposits – abruptly abandoned ship. Nearly one billion US dollars in deposits made by non-resident Indians exited the country. Capital flight in general was precipitous, severe exchange restrictions often cited as the motivation, and refelcted the general trend of unease regarding the Indian economy.

By the end of June 1991, foreign currency reserves were down to US$975 million (barely enough to cover two weeks of imports). India was forced to pledge part of its gold reserves as collateral in order to access the international overnight market and avoid a loan default. Export and industrial growth were both negative, and inflation was soaring above 16 percent. India's GDP for 1992 was projected at less than 1 percent. Accordingly, the rupee was devalued by 20 percent in July 1991, with a promise of partial convertibility by March 1992 and full convertibility by March 1993 (Seshadri 1993).

In the face of such an overwhelming crisis, India was forced to turn to the IMF and the World Bank, who insisted on a series of economic reforms as part of the condition for receiving assistance. On 13 April 1992, India accepted the Multilateral Investment Guarantee Agency Protocol. Among the package of liberalization reforms that the Indian government was forced to adopt was the loosening of state controls on foreign ownership and investment, in addition to the devaluation of the rupee.

It is worth noting here that this move towards neoliberalism – with its emphasis on a minimalist state and market-driven relations – should not necessarily be viewed as a break or complete paradigm shift in India's post-colonial development policies. Indeed, as Baldev Raj Nayar and others have argued (see Das 1993; Nayar 1992, 2001; Nayyar 1996), the move towards trade liberalization began in halting steps as early as the mid-1970s. In such a context, it is perhaps more accurate to view neoliberalism in developmental terms, as an evolution rather than a change from earlier strategies.

As with other nations that have adopted World Bank/IMF structural adjustment policies, India's move towards trade liberalization has been a mixed blessing. Its economic health, measured in terms of industrial production and export earnings, has seen a marked improvement. The redistribution of positive net economic gains within the country is, however, another story. There are serious questions to be asked about the impact of neoliberal economic policies on poverty alleviation. Moreover, IMF-imposed austerity and modernization measures have increased the marginalization and impoverishment of India's traditionally less-empowered groups, such as women and indigenous communities (Purushothaman 1998: 198).

Dams and India's Developmental Visions

The place of the mega-dams and their displacement effects in these various plans for developing India seems straightforward. Massive hydroelectric projects would be of little use in Gandhi's dream of decentralized development, the "oceanic circle" of village-based rule. Indeed, such grand schemes would seem to run counter to the very nature and purpose of Gandhian development. The sacrifices that Gandhi called for were of a primarily individual nature, giving up on industrializing dreams and aspirations for power and focusing, rather, on "people-centred" capacity building. But Gandhi's plan was not adopted by the emerging Indian state, many of whose leaders felt it would be impractical in an anarchic world system of often predatory nation-states. Gail Omvedt (1993: 30) goes so far as to suggest that by the time of independence, "Gandhi, the only major figure of India's independence struggle who offered a substantially different vision of development, was marginalized." Instead, it was Nehru who emerged, following the deaths or disengagement of his chief political rivals – such as the conservative strongman Sardar Patel, the radical socialist S.C. Bose, and the Gandhian socialist Jayaprakash Narayan – as the premier figure in Indian post-colonial politics. It was therefore his developmental vision – not Gandhi's – that became the dominant one.

Though Gandhi's dream was not chosen by the Indian state, it continues to hold a great deal of rhetorical and ideological appeal for many within the Indian polity. The majority of dam opponents in the Narmada Valley, for example, explicitly declare their belief in a "people-centred" form of development, one that respects both social and ecological balance. They suggest that the Gandhian models of self-reliance and small-scale community confederation are keys to such development. The specific strategies proposed by those in the valley who ascribe to Gandhian ideals therefore are comprised mainly of locally oriented, ecologically and economically sustainable projects. These include small "check" dams and gravity wells, micro harvesting schemes such as rainwater conservation, and very small-scale electricity generation, such as from "cycle-and-sewing" machines (Narmada Bachao Andolan 2000). Proponents of such alternatives – groups like the NBA – do not simply argue for a romanticized version of the status quo: indeed, many social justice organizations within the valley recognize all too well the inequities of class, gender, ethnicity, religion, and caste in the region. But many community activists ask why improving the lot of the relatively powerless in the valley can be done only by destroying their lands and livelihoods – in effect by marginalizing them further.

But relying on such alternatives, though they might sustain a local community and be appropriate for a Gandhian developmental agenda, could not possibly support an industrializing, modernizing vision. And, indeed, in Nehru's version of development, dams figure rather more prominently. Omvedt (1993: 30) describes this model as "a broad consensus around what was in fact a modified version of a state-socialist model of development: a focus on heavy industrialization, planning, and a public sector 'commanding the heights' of a mixed economy substantially integrated into the world capitalist economy." The NVDP stands as a particular exemplar of the importance of dams to the political and economic goals of this developmental vision. From the involvement of Nehru in laying the material as well as ideological foundations of the project to his exhortation to villagers in the submergence zones to leave their homes in service of "Mother India" and to the very naming of the terminal dam – Sardar Sarovar, after Sardar Patel, the Gujarat-born first Indian home minister and, with Nehru, one of the chief architects of the industrial development model – the echoes of modernization rhetoric are to be felt throughout the project's history.

If large dams were an integral part of the goal of building a strong, centralized, and interventionist state during the Nehruvian era, they are no less significant a component of the contemporary context of development in India. As noted earlier, the adoption of a neoliberal economic framework by the Indian state can be viewed less as a break and more as an evolution of earlier trends; thus, it is hardly surprising that mega-dams today have not been abandoned by development planners. The notion that dams are an integral part of "modernizing" the economies and societies of the region continues to be a persistent one.

Yet, in the neoliberal development framework, the state is not meant to play the central role that it held in previous periods. Its place is rather to retreat to the background and both enable and support the wishes of private capital and individual citizens. And, indeed, when we look at the current situation in the Narmada Valley, we see the confluence of Nehruvian and neoliberal development agendas. On the one hand, the justifications for building the Narmada dams have maintained a remarkably consistent devotion to a core belief in industrial development. Recent local state elections continue to see both ruling and opposition parties promising to complete the project as part of their regional development strategies. But, on the other hand, the embracing of neoliberal globalization models – particularly the integration into worldwide labour, commodity, and manufacturing markets – has meant that dam proponents can no longer rely either ideologically or practically on the outlay of massive public resources to fund the project.

Local authorities have therefore looked towards two relatively untapped resources in order to sustain the project: private corporate partners and the wealthy expatriate Gujarati community. Privatization and deregulation are, of course, key components in the neoliberal restructuring agenda. Development, in the Nehruvian nation-building sense, generally involves national and local governments or multilateral agencies such as the World Bank. Private firms and corporations are, of course, often employed as contractors to carry out the actual work; however, accountability and responsibility lie primarily with state actors and agencies. The entrance of private corporations as principals in large-scale public infrastructure projects – not only in their construction but also in their operation – raises serious concerns regarding protection of the public interest. In the Narmada Valley, the shift to a new model of dam building and maintenance – one that fits well with an evolving neoliberal developmental paradigm – can be best seen with the planned Maheshwar dam (Schücking 1999).

One of the thirty major dams planned by the NWDT award in 1978 was the Shree Maheshwar Hydel Project in Madhya Pradesh, originally under the jurisdiction of the Narmada Control Authority. In 1989, administration of the project was transferred to the Madhya Pradesh Electricity Board. Four years later, on the heels of the nationally adopted economic liberalization policy, the Maheshwar project became the first planned hydroelectric dam in India to be privately financed and operated. A controlling share of the concession was granted to the textile manufacturer S. Kumars, and the remaining portion of the ownership stake was to be sought from a foreign investor.

The late 1990s saw a dizzying array of potential partners – all of them foreign-owned utility companies – enter and leave the Maheshwar project. This procession began in 1998 with the US-based Pacificorp, which withdrew from the project on the grounds of social impacts and local opposition. The following year, Pacificorp's replacement, the German utilities Bayernwerk and Vereinigte Elektrizitatswerke Westfalen (VEW) followed suit, citing similar concerns about the planned dam. In 1999, the US-based Ogden Corporation – yet another energy company – tried its hand at a partnership with S. Kumars. A little over a year later, Ogden also pulled out as a result of vigorous local opposition and a growing realization of the project's true social and ecological impacts (*Ecologist* 2001). At present, plans for the dam are stalled as the builders search for adequate sources of funding.

Yet private investment in the Narmada Valley does not end with multinational utility companies. In fact, in the wake of the Enron debacle and the consequent meltdown of other players in the energy sector, the rapid expansion of foreign utilities into South Asia may have been permanently slowed. Perhaps the more intriguing trend is the continued involvement of diasporic communities in processes of development within the valley.

The twentieth century, in particular, saw an increase in flows between diasporic networks and their putative homelands, especially in the postcolonial period, as cores and peripheries saw increasing transfers in populations. Estimates are that the Indian diaspora numbers somewhere between twenty-five and forty million (Singhvi et al. 2001: v-vi). Of particular interest to the Narmada case is the fact that though the Gujarati diaspora makes up less than 0.01 percent of the population of the United States, it controls over 5 percent of US wealth (ibid: 169-73). Given such statistics, it is perhaps unsurprising to have seen over the past few years a steady stream of Gujarati politicians make their way to the US as supplicants to these wealthy expatriates, seeking funds for a variety of causes.

The Narmada project is one such cause. The former chairman of the SSNNL, Sanat Mehta, has on several occasions visited the US to raise support among the so-called non-resident Indians (NRI) for project-related bond issues. In the mid-1990s, following the withdrawal of the World Bank from involvement with the SSP, Mehta exhorted a group of NRI investors in the US to buy dam bonds by stating that "we have reached a stage when the survival of Gujarat depends on the completion of the dam and we will succeed even without the World Bank's support."

Such strategies continue. Jayanarayan Vyas, the Gujarat minister for major irrigation and Narmada, for example, declared the importance of NRIs in the completion of the SSP (Raghu 2000): "Traditionally investment in the bond market is done after looking at the security, liquidity, safety and returns. We will add Emotional Property to tap funds from NRIs. We would appeal to their emotions and ask them to lend for development in the motherland. We hope to raise as much as RS 1500 Crore from NRIs."

Such efforts by Gujarat and other regional governments in India have been remarkably successful. We see here again the fusing of the Nehruvian and neoliberal visions of development: in one, the state plays the primary role, in the other, private capital. But in both models, the centrality of identities – national, local, regional, transnational – is key to mobilizing resources in support of a developmental goal. Despite increasing globalization and economic, cultural, and political integration across the world, locality, place, and "the nation" all still clearly matter. Preliminary studies of investment by NRIs indicate that "emotional ties with India" ranks as the single highest motivating factor spurring these diasporic capital flows (Krishnamurty 1994). Diasporic communities demonstrate a strong desire to participate in the material as well as ideological restructuring of their places of origin. In effect, this is what diasporic communities who are sending their funds to help sustain the NVDP are showing.

Conclusion

The situation in the Narmada Valley is today an unsatisfactory one. There is a war of attrition of sorts going on between dam builders and their opponents. Each year, the dam inches up, a glacial five metres at a time, subject to environmental and social review. Each monsoon season, a few more houses and villages are submerged, a few more fields are flooded, and a few more crops are ruined. Each year, the public coffers empty a bit more and the imagined benefits remain out of reach. There is a battle in the Narmada Valley between competing visions of development and competing convictions about what costs – social, ecological, and financial – the inhabitants of the region and their neighbours should bear.

On one hand, we have the Gandhian model adopted by social justice organizations and community activists who oppose the dams. To them, the only solution lies in scaling back the dreams themselves and concentrating on the people in the valley as the focus for developmental efforts. Schools, better healthcare, land reforms, legal rights (including land tenure) for women, small-scale rural electrification, respect for indigenous rights – these are the types of goals sought by believers in Gandhian development.

On the other hand, linked visions of development – the Nehruvian and the neoliberal – have very different objectives. Industrialization and modernization, the creation of a state, whether strong or small, a focus on accumulation: all of these visions demand schemes such as the NVDP. The question yet to be played out in the Narmada Valley is which sacrifice is the one to be ultimately made: that of industrial dreams or that of local communities and livelihoods?

References

Ahmedabad.com. 2003. "Coffers Empty, but SSP Needs Rs. 16,500 cr!" http://www.ahmedabad.com/news/2k3/jan/20ssp.htm (accessed 6 February 2003).
Alagh, Y.K., M. Pathåk, and D.T. Buch. 1995. *Narmada and Environment: An Assessment*. New Delhi: Narmada Planning Group and Har-Anand Publications.
Alvares, C., and R. Billorey. 1988. *Damming the Narmada*. Penang, Malaysia: Third World Network.
Baboo, B. 1992. *Technology and Social Transformation*. New Delhi: Concept Publishing.
Bardhan, P.K. 1985. *The Political Economy of Development in India*. Delhi: Oxford University Press.
Baviskar, A. 1995. *In the Belly of the River: Tribal Conflicts over Development in the Narmada Valley*. Delhi: Oxford University Press.
Byres, T.J. 1997. "Development Planning and the Interventionist State versus Liberalization and the Neo-Liberal State: India 1989-1996." In T.J. Byres, ed., *The State, Development Planning and Liberalization in India*, 1-35. Delhi: Oxford University Press.
Caulfield, C. 1996. *Masters of Illusion: The World Bank and the Poverty of Nations*. New York: Henry Holt.
Cernea, Michael, and Christopher McDowell, eds. 2000. *Risks and Reconstruction: Experiences of Resettlers and Refugees*. Washington, DC: World Bank.
Chatterjee, P. 1997. "Development Planning and the Indian State." In T.J. Byres, ed., *The State, Development Planning and Liberalization in India*, 82-103. Delhi: Oxford University Press.
Comptroller and Auditor General of India. 2003. *Audit Report (Civil) Gujarat for the Year 2002-2003*. New Delhi: Government of India.
Das, D.K., ed. 1993. *Structural Adjustment in the Indian Economy*. New Delhi: Deep and Deep Publications.
Ecologist. 2001. "Update: Ogden Withdraws from Maheshwar Dam," February. http://www.findarticles.com/p/articles/mi_m2465/is_1_31/ai_70910912.
Fisher, W.F. 1995. "Development and Resistance in Narmada Valley." In W.F. Fisher, ed. *Toward Sustainable Development: Struggling over India's Narmada River*, 3-46. London: M.E. Sharpe.
Ghosh, J. 1997. "Development Strategy in India: A Political Economy Perspective." In S. Bose and A. Jalal, eds., *Nationalism, Democracy and Development: State and Politics in India*, 165-83. Delhi: Oxford University Press.
Jayal, N.G. 1999. *Democracy and the State: Welfare, Secularism and Development in Contemporary India*. Delhi: Oxford University Press.
Judge, P. 1997. "Response to Dams and Displacement in Two Asian States." *Asian Survey* 37 (9): 840-52.
Krishnamurty, V. 1994. *Study of Investment Preferences of Expatriates from India*. New Delhi: National Council of Applied Economic Research.
Morse, B., and T. Berger. 1992. *Sardar Sarovar: Report of the Independent Review*. Ottawa: Resource Futures International.
Narmada Bachao Andolan. 2000. "Domkhedi Hamlet Self-Sufficient in Electricity." Narmada Bachao Andolan press release, 16 August.
–. 2001. *Who Pays? Who Profits? A Short Guide to the Sardar Sarovar Project*. Flyer prepared by Narmada Bachao Andolan.
–. 2002. "Rehabilitation Status of Sardar Sarovar Project as of February 2002." Briefing notes prepared by Narmada Bachao Andolan.
Nayar, B.R. 1992. "The Politics of Economic Restructuring in India: The Paradox of State Strength and Policy Weakness." *Journal of Commonwealth and Comparative Politics* 30 (2): 145-71.
–. 2001. *Globalization and Nationalism: The Changing Balance in India's Economic Policy 1950-2000*. New Delhi: Sage Publications.
Nayyar, D. 1994. *Migration, Remittances, and Capital Flows: The Indian Experience*. Delhi and New York: Oxford University Press.

–. 1996. *Economic Liberalization in India: Analytics, Experience and Lessons.* Calcutta: Centre for Studies in Social Sciences.

Nehru, J. 1958. *Jawaharlal Nehru's Speeches, March 1953-August 1957*. Vol. 3, 2-3. Calcutta: Publications Division, Ministry of Information and Broadcasting, Government of India.

Omvedt, G. 1993. *Reinventing Revolution: New Social Movements and the Socialist Tradition in India*. Armonk, NY: M.E. Sharpe.

Pathak, M., ed. 1991. *Sardar Sarovar Project: A Promise for Plenty.* Gandhinagar: Narmada Planning Group, SSNNL.

Purushothaman, S. 1998. *The Empowerment of Women in India: Grassroots Women's Networks and the State.* Thousand Oaks, CA: Sage.

Raghu, Sunil. 2000. "Gujarat Plans to Raise Rs 5,000 cr viz Bonds" *Economic Times (India).* 6 December 2000. http://www.narmada.org/archive/et/061200.06fina08.htm.

Rajendran, S. 2000. "State Concerned over Cracks in Koyna Dam." *Hindu,* 8 October. http://www.hinduonnet.com/2000/10/08/stories/0408210c.htm.

Schücking, H. 1999. *The Maheshwar Dam in India: A Report.* Sassenberg: Urgewald.

Seshadri, R.K. 1993. *From Crisis to Convertibility: The External Value of the Rupee.* Bombay: Orient Longman.

Sharma, B.D. 1995. *Globalization: The Tribal Encounter.* New Delhi: Har-Anand Publications.

Singh, M. et al. 1992. *Displacement by Sardar Sarovar and Tehri: A Comparative Study of Two Dams.* Delhi: Multiple Action Research Group.

Singhvi et al. 2001. *Report of the High Level Committee on Indian Diaspora.* New Delhi: Government of India, Ministry of External Affairs.

Turaga, U. 2000. "Damming Waters and Wisdom: Protest in the Narmada River Valley." *Technology in Society* 22 (2): 237-53.

Unni, K.S. 1996. *The Ecology of River Narmada.* New Delhi: A.P.H. Publishing.

Whitehead, J. 2000. "Monitoring of Sardar Sarovar Resettlees: A Further Critique." *Economic and Political Weekly* 35 (45): 3969-76.

Part 3
Conservation and Displacement

Part 3
Conservation and Displacement

8

Upon Whose Terms? The Displacement of Afro-Descendent Communities in the Creation of Costa Rica's National Parks

Colette Murray

Conservation and Displacement

[illegible]

8

Upon Whose Terms? The Displacement of Afro-Descendent Communities in the Creation of Costa Rica's National Parks

Colette Murray

"What we want is that we can remain on our properties, and those who want to sell will sell to the state. We don't want the people to sell either to anybody else. This [national park] law is to protect us from something that we cannot see yet, that is coming up ahead of all of us." Thus declared Alpheus Buchanan in 1975, an Afro–Costa Rican owner of a plot of land in what was to become Cahuita National Park (quoted in Palmer 1993: 236). For Buchanan, the relationship between the state and individuals is predicated on the notion that a state works to protect the best interests of its citizens. Yet, when a state perceives resident groups as non-citizens, due to their racial, religious, or ethnic identities and therefore does not represent their best interests in its decision-making practices, one must ask who is actually shouldering the sacrifices made for the well-being of all.

Costa Rica is a case in point. Members of its Afro-descendent population, most of whom have traditionally lived in the Caribbean province of Limón, were generally considered outsiders residing on national soil, particularly between the late 1800s and the mid- to late 1900s. Perceived as the responsibility of the foreign multinational companies for which they worked rather than as citizens, Afro–Costa Ricans have, over the years, been subject to multiple forms of displacement carried out by the state. Although all these have had significant impacts on their lives, and at various points have informed their general attitude towards the state and their position within it, this chapter focuses primarily on displacement due to the creation of two national parks. It highlights the roles that racialized identities, cultural representations, and values have played in both constructing ideas of loss and understanding the unfolding of events within the process of displacement.

Looking at the circumstances of people of African descent living in Limón Province over a thirty-year period, I seek to more fully understand the changing representations and consequences of displacement. I adopt this approach because, within the present volume, we wish to highlight processes within development-induced displacement. For instance, conceptualizations of displacement's consequences, such as landlessness, joblessness, and food insecurity, are depicted as visible and quantifiable because they are framed in terms of the number of lots or jobs lost, the end of relative self-sufficiency, and the dismantling of "community"[1] structures or local associations. Yet, such consequences rarely entail the immediate, straightforward loss of access to one's livelihood (see Cernea 1999). Understanding the processes by which displaced populations become impoverished is an important issue. An equally important component of this process lies in some appreciation of how, over time, residents of the affected areas have interpreted their displacement and expressed their concerns. If the concerns they raise do not always fall neatly into the categories commonly used to define the repercussions of displacement, it is precisely because residents' attitudes regarding displacement change over spaces and times due to resistance, misunderstandings, uncertainties, and the creation of alliances.

In this chapter, the removal of individuals from their land following the establishment of two national parks in 1970 and 1975 provides the starting point for an analysis of displacement and its repercussions. In terms of the national parks, it is shown that each case of displacement or its prospect is directly linked to state-sanctioned development projects, often involving conflict over access to resources and changing definitions of territory. In 1970, Cahuita was designated a protected area, but was later upgraded to the status of a national park, which by 1978 comprised 1,106 hectares. Generally speaking, the establishment of a national park is accompanied by strict regulations governing the management and use of the area. Whereas no human activity that could potentially destroy the biodiversity of the area is allowed in national parks, the designation of protected areas allows for the continuation of traditional subsistance-farming methods (Weitzner and Fonseca Borrás 1999). Between 1973 and 1975, a much larger national park was established in Tortuguero, a remote village on Costa Rica's northeastern Atlantic coast, in the Province of Limón. Tortuguero National Park comprises 29,068 square hectares. Both national parks had additional maritime zones set aside to protect the local marine environment.

In the creation of these sites, I argue, values played an important role in defining the manner in which the national parks were represented. To understand the importance of representation and how the attitudes of the people living in the affected areas have changed over time, it is essential to comprehend how the Afro-descendent population has attributed value to its way of life since the parks' establishment. In this light, and in light of the usual normative and operational criteria used in assessing the costs and benefits of development-induced displacement, we need to examine some key questions: To what extent have affected individuals been engaged in consultative processes wherein their conceptions of harm,[2] benefits, and livelihoods are respected and enforced? Has their conception of harm been considered in decision-making processes? How have affected people viewed and responded to the consequences of their displacement?

In 2000, I undertook fieldwork for the EDID project in the Costa Rican villages of Tortuguero and Cahuita, both of which are located on the coast of Limón Province, at the northern edges of the parks that bear their names. At the time of the national parks' creation, the population of both villages was predominantly Afro-descendant. Using a snowball sampling technique, I interviewed thirty individuals (fourteen women and sixteen men) from the two villages, state agencies, the University of Costa Rica, international organizations, and non-governmental organizations (NGOs). In addition, I conducted research at the National Archives in San José and in government libraries, including that of the Ministry of Environment and Energy (MINAE), and have used it to supplement my interviews regarding displacement from the national parks.

Through this qualitative approach to understanding the implications of displacement, I explore the manner in which the Afro-descendent population was displaced, along with the consequences of that removal. The chapter is divided into four principal sections. First, I provide a context for understanding the displacement of Afro-descendent populations in Limón Province. Second, I examine the involvement of various stakeholders in displacement-related decisions. Third, I analyze residents' understanding of displacement and its consequences. I turn finally to a concluding discussion of the moral obligations that underpin representations of development-induced displacement in Costa Rica.

Limón Province: Displacement of Its Afro-Descendent Population

Limón is home to only 7.5 percent of Costa Rica's population but is the country's largest province, encompassing 18 percent of its territory and its entire Caribbean coastline. Tortuguero, accessible only by air or water, is a northern coastal village of roughly eight hundred residents located close to the province's border with Nicaragua. Cahuita, also on the Caribbean coast, is approximately forty-three kilometres south of Puerto Limón, the provincial capital; it has a population of 5,331 (Instituto Nacional de Estadística y Censos 2001). Both Tortuguero and Cahuita are home to many people of African descent who, like their counterparts elsewhere in the province, can trace their origins to neighbouring Caribbean islands.

Edward,[3] an interview participant, summarized one of the reasons for the African Caribbean migration to Limón Province, beginning in the late 1800s:

> People came here hoping to make some money to go back home. But they never went back because what they made was very little. My grandfather said to me that when he was coming to the country from Jamaica they told

> him that he was coming to the rich coast. So he thought that maybe a lot of money was given away here or that there were a lot of jobs. He said to me that when the ship came up to the shore, the few houses he could see the house tops were rusty. But he could not go back. (Edward, interview by author, Cahuita, July 2000)

Prior to the mid-1900s, Limón Province was of little interest to most Costa Ricans, who viewed it as excessively hot and disease-ridden (Academic C, interview by author, San Jose, June 2000). Due to this belief, few Spanish-descent Costa Ricans were willing to relocate to the country's Caribbean lowlands in spite of the surplus of jobs in the United Fruit Company's banana plantations there. Instead, Afro-descendent people arriving from English-speaking Caribbean islands, such as Jamaica and Barbados, largely filled these positions. Prior to 1949,[4] this population was of non-citizen status; as a result, what contact it had with the national government came principally through the United Fruit Company and the Northern Railway Company, which also brought in Afro-descendent labour to build the San José–Limón railway (Stewart 1999: 11; Academic B, interview by author, San José, June 2000).

Although state authorities showed scant interest in Limón Province during the first half of the twentieth century, lobbying by conservation groups prompted them to take a growing interest in the region in the 1960s and 1970s. Responding to this pressure, the state, invoking eminent domain, established Tortuguero National Park between 1973 and 1975 as a means of protecting the endangered green turtle (Academic A, interview by author, San José, June 2000). Cahuita National Park, established in 1970, was intended to protect the region's tropical wetlands, wildlife, and the coral reef at Cahuita Point. According to one interview participant, the creation of the two parks was undertaken without regard for existing patterns of property ownership, resulting in the expropriation of local people's land (ibid.).

In the initial stages of park establishment, Tortuguero and Cahuita residents assumed that the state worked for the good of all. In Tortuguero, for instance, state planning for the national park was accompanied by the building of a canal system that permitted residents of the village to travel to Puerto Limón in one rather than two to three days, weather permitting. Given the changes occurring alongside the park's creation, it is not surprising that many individuals tended to believe that the laws associated with the park would function in their long-term interest. In this way, residents assured themselves that their land would remain in their hands, or that, should they no longer desire to work their lands, only then would the state assume control of them.

Both Cahuita and Tortuguero residents initially thought they could continue to work on their lands located inside park boundaries. However, the state, some scientists including Archie Carr, N. Cortés, and M. Risk,[5] as well as several international environmental organizations, such as Caribbean Conservation Corporation (CCC) characterized the villagers as unable to effectively conserve the natural environment. Furthermore, media accounts of Tortuguero and Cahuita depicted them as areas "devoid of progress" characterized by "poor lifestyles" and "backward conservation and development ideas" (*La Nación,* 11 July 1974b; *La Prensa Libre* 1992). Subscribing to these attitudes regarding the two communities, the state portrayed the establishment of the national parks as socially and financially beneficial to all concerned (MINAE 1999). Yet, in the case of Cahuita and Tortuguero, residents lacked prior knowledge of what plans the state, influenced by environmental organizations' lobbying, held in store for them.

In the 1970s, when the state informed the people of Tortuguero and Cahuita that their land would be expropriated, no one was willing to sell, with one individual reportedly telling the newspaper *La Prensa Libre* (1972: 14), "I will not sell for anything." Content with their existing lifestyles, a number of people initially refused to accept money for their land, even though Tortuguero's economy, in particular, which was based on lumbering and the sale of turtle eggs, had been subject to market fluctuations and the closing of mills. During these times of economic uncertainty, residents resorted to subsistence farming and hunting. According to Susan Place (1991: 192-93), they were able to survive with little to no cash income because of their ability to access land and wildlife. The national park, which surrounded the entire village, restricted their access to these resources. Pressured to leave their land, some Tortuguero villagers whose land title could be verified did eventually accept the state's compensation package. Interview participants, however, claimed that those who accepted the state's offer received very little compensation. One elderly woman, Claudia, maintained, "Now they are old and have very little money" (Claudia, interview by author, Tortuguero, July 2000). Moreover, residents who opted to remain in the area experienced a loss of food security and income because fishing, farming, and hunting were now prohibited.

Following the establishment of the parks and subsequent loss of access to their land, many Afro-descendent residents moved to the cities, where their lack of marketable urban skills resulted in high levels of unemployment (Government official A, interview by author, San José, June 2000; Government official B, interview by author, Puerto Limón, August 2000). Meanwhile, others relocated to the United States or went to work for the banana companies that established plantations in the region (NGO representative A, interview by author, San José, June 2000). Those who chose to remain in their villages, ill-prepared for the growing tourism-based economy, found that their lives were becoming increasingly circumscribed by outsiders who opened businesses in the area (*Esta Semana* 1996).

In the initial stages of displacement, villagers assumed that the state represented their interests, largely on account of the improvements made to the infrastructure of the area. That optimism soon faded as it became clear that individuals would lose access to their land and, following upon this, their livelihoods. With this process of displacement came changing attitudes regarding the state and their lifestyles. In the following section, the role of participation and the extent to which the residents were party to the decision to displace them are considered in light of their changing attitudes towards the state.

The Question of Participation

Differential power is central to understanding the nature of participation. In general, access to state officials, lobby groups, and international NGOs, not to mention the media, determines a group's capacity to participate in development processes and therefore what can be negotiated. Participation in and of itself, however, is not always equitable because the stakeholders selected and the inequitable access to sites of influence set limits to what is open to discussion. Moreover, participation in development initiatives often increasingly operates to legitimize the boundaries of and, by extension, the establishment of control over territories and people (see DuPuis and Vandergeest 1996). In the current context of Costa Rica and the establishment of the national parks, the question of whether affected residents were able to access sites of negotiation and make their concerns known is crucial, both in terms of defining state control and for determining accountability in the decision-making processes.

Perhaps the two most defining features of the Costa Rican decision-making process are the roles played by the state and the lobby groups. Through the enactment of regulations and laws, the state sets down what is permissible or liable for sanction. Through lobbying, which I understand to be the non-violent attempts of social actors to influence state actions and policies, NGOs have worked on behalf of a particular outcome or agenda. With regard to the establishment of the national parks, the conflict in Tortuguero began with the Caribbean Conservation Corporation's (CCC) intervention to protect green turtle nesting sites from egg gatherers and hunters. The CCC, a non-profit organization based in Gainesville, Florida, used environmental issues to profile and act upon its concerns and influence Costa Rican state policy decisions (Academic A, interview by author, San José, June 2000). The CCC adopted a variety of lobbying strategies to influence policy making at the national level, among them, coalition building and use of the media to convey its messages. In terms of coalition building, it gained the support of José Miguel Corrales Bolaños, an influential politician. Corrales Bolaños spearheaded efforts within the government in support of the establishment of Tortuguero National Park (*La República* 1975). The CCC also had several newspaper reports published in the 1960s and 1970s regarding the need for the park, both in terms of projected benefits for local inhabitants as well as for the country's biodiversity (*La Nación* 1974a, 1974b, 1974c; *La Prensa Libre* 1972).

By all accounts, Archie Carr, the dynamic, personable scientific director of the CCC between 1959 and 1987, was intent on protecting the green turtle. During the course of his work with the CCC, he argued against the commercial hunting of sea turtles, the sale of turtle products, and any attempt to remove sea turtle species from the World Conservation Union's (IUCN) endangered or threatened lists. Under his direction, not only was the CCC able to successfully lobby the government and environmental communities but also, in 1971, in order to protect the nesting population in Tortuguero, the CCC hired local people to tag turtles rather than hunt them. His competence, ability to inspire trust, and personal integrity were all key features in the success of the CCC's lobbying endeavours. Following in his footsteps, the CCC instituted a certificate training program in the 1990s to gain local support for its activities. Tortuguero residents who successfully pass the course are issued a state certificate authorizing them to work as turtle-watching guides. According to other sources, the CCC has also provided the Tortuguero park rangers with uniforms, gear, and training, both in Costa Rica and the United States (NGO representative C, interview by author, San José, August 2000). Thus, prior to 1970, the conservation of nature emerged not as a local concern but, rather, through the lobbying efforts of international environmental organizations.

On a more local level, Tortuguero residents did attempt a unified stand against the national park, once the state's intention to evict them from their land became clear. However, their unity fractured after one person accepted employment as a park ranger. This ranger is alleged to have provided the state with a map showing land ownership within the park, in order to establish who would be compensated for their loss. Even so, several residents claim that their title to land has not been recognized (Carlos, interview by author, Tortuguero, July 2000). As a result of this supposed betrayal of their interests, the individual was ostracized by other villagers. Meanwhile, others decided to cooperate with the park authorities because they needed to support their children, even though they too were subsequently ostracized. For example, Claudia stated that her decision to work for the park led people to approach her and say, "How could you go work for them?" (Claudia, interview by author, Tortuguero, July 2000). However, at the time of the displacement, no ready means of employment was available to local residents, so Claudia felt that there was "nothing to do ... I had children in college. I had to find a way to support them. This is why I went to work for the national park" (ibid.).

In Cahuita, the process of displacement differed somewhat from that in Tortuguero. Donald R. Wallace (1992: 40) states that, in the early 1970s, residents claimed that they received contradictory messages from national park officials, who would first ask them to clear vegetation growing under the coconut trees, only to reverse their instructions and say that the land should not be cleared. Furthermore, people complained about the state's failure to inform them of the legislation that permitted the expropriation of their lands. By the mid-1970s, as a result of the conflict between Cahuita and the state, the village issued a petition. Although one resident, Henry, stated that it was difficult to obtain the support of everyone living in Cahuita and the surrounding area, the petition did lead to a meeting in Cahuita with the national Legislative Assembly deputy from Puerto Limón (Henry, interview by author, Cahuita, August 2000; see Wallace 1992: 40). However, the meeting was conducted in Spanish, despite the fact that the village residents were predominantly English speaking. Alvaro Ugalde, a government official, states that he was among the few who did communicate in English. He maintains, "I told them that in spite of the Park Service's mistakes and serious difficulties in communication between them and the young bureaucrats from San José, our attention was to continue the protection that they and their ancestors had bestowed on those beautiful forests and reefs. I asked them to give us time, and to work with us to solve many problems" (quoted in Wallace 1992: 41).

According to a resident who also took part in the meeting, the people who attended sat silently without saying what they thought. "The officials talk so much that it is only when they [have returned to] Limón that people realize that they [themselves] have not said anything" (Alfred, interview by author, Hone Creek, August 2000).

Although their participation in the decisions to establish the park was limited, most Cahuita residents defended what they saw as their natural right to the land and the resources contained within it, and continued to do so throughout the process of their displacement. However, their economic hardships were associated not only with the loss of their land but also with their growing dependence on one economic resource – tourism. Further displacement through the disruption of the tourist economy became a possibility in 1994, when the state attempted to raise admission fees for foreigners entering the national park (from 200 colones to 2,400 colones, or approximately US$1.60 to US$15.00). Fearing that foreign tourists would go elsewhere because of the price increase, people in Cahuita again saw their livelihoods being threatened by the state. One local leader, pointing out the direct link between tourism and the village, remarked that, if the visitors did not have easy access to the park beach, "we will die of hunger" (quoted in Weitzner and Fonseca Borrás 1999: 138). Although residents had initially trusted the state at the time of the park's creation, they now placed less faith in its intent. So, to ensure that local concerns were heard, they established the Committee of Struggle (Comité de Lucha), which staged a peaceful takeover of the park.

Responding in a more conciliatory fashion than it had in the 1970s, the state agreed on this occasion to negotiate with Cahuita's Committee of Struggle. In 1997, it reached an agreement with the committee: for the park's Playa Blanca, the beach just south of Cahuita, entrance fees would not be levied on those visitors who remained within the area between Kelly Creek and Río Suárez. More significantly, it was on the basis of this action that collaborative management of the park was instituted on 20 May 1998 by executive decree. Although Viviane Weitzner and Marvin Fonseca Borrás (1999: 139) caution that executive decrees do not have the status of national laws and may be modified following a change in government, they nevertheless do have the appearance of some legitimacy and moral force, which accounts for why these authors and the IUCN (2000) cite Cahuita as a model of collaborative management. What remains hidden, however, is that before it was protected by current legislation, the model was not assured of permanency, as well as the fact that this concession was won only after much struggle on the residents' part.

What ought to be emphasized is that the Committee of Struggle opened up a space for contestation in the face of potential displacement. The partitioning of areas into protected (nature) and unprotected (livelihoods) was partially eroded through the success of the committee because, for the first time since the park's creation, local knowledge was brought into the equation (see Goldman 2003). This undermined the hierarchies in participation, as the residents of Cahuita centred themselves within the decision-making process and then redefined the terms of negotiation. It should be noted, however, that though it does contribute to the creation of alternative development practices, the Committee of Struggle has yet to have a woman sit among its members, but Emily did remark during an interview that she had been asked but had turned down the position because she was already involved in other local organizations.

Although the Committee of Struggle has successfully shaped state policy through its act of struggle, villagers in Tortuguero lack any significant role in the decisions that affect them (Academic A, interview by author, San José, June 2000). Tortuguero National Park lacks any participatory mechanism for soliciting feedback. At best, views are sought from the surrounding tourist lodges and the CCC (lodge representative, interview by author, Tortuguero, July 2000), with one hotel representative stating that the lodge's proprietor was in frequent contact with national park authorities. The local residents, on the other hand, have no access to decision makers and are generally patronized as incapable of making appropriate choices, so much so that Tortuga Lodge owner Michael Kaye could ask, "Do the 'humble' people of [Tortuguero] decide what happens in the Park? What if they want to kill turtles, or cut down trees? Do we let them do that as well?" (*Tico Times* 1999).

Since the 1970s, Cahuita's residents have become increasingly effective in ensuring that the state hears their interests and that they are part of negotiations that involve the village's future. In contrast, Tortuguero has not fared as well, with the residents fractured along lines of traitors and non-traitors, and original inhabitants and newcomers. Needless to say, the multiple interests within the village make it difficult to achieve a common stance, with daily survival, the welfare of children and the elderly, business interests, and understandings of state actions all informing the positions adopted. Despite differences in opinion regarding how to react to development-induced displacement, the residents of both Cahuita and Tortuguero have held in common a growing sense of disillusion with the state's ability or desire to meet their needs, and victory has come at a price, even in cases where local struggles have been successful, as in the conflict over park entrance fees in Cahuita. Informing this disillusion are ideas concerning place and identity, and it is to these topics that I now turn.

Local Knowledge

This section examines the manner in which the affected residents have understood their circumstances prior to and following their removal, how they have interpreted sustainable development, and what they have learnt through their displacement. Central to this discussion is the question of culture, which, according to Veronica Strang (1997: 5), is essentially what makes individuals care for or value one thing over another. Yet, culture is notoriously difficult to pin down as an explanatory variable, however central it is in explaining people's understanding of and responses to development and its displacing effects. I understand culture and certain values not as pre-given traits but rather as formed over time and space through the acquisition of knowledge. As such, values attributed to actions and beliefs rest upon both knowledge of an event or thing and the act of comprehending associated ideas and outcomes. In the context of development-induced displacement, then, knowledge accumulated by those who are harmed or forced to relocate through the application of development policies is central to understanding the meeting point between sustainable development and displacement.

One of the key issues in displacement is a state's attempt to sever local residents' ties with their surrounding environment. Strang (1997: 5) remarks that landscapes can physically illustrate how values are accorded socially, culturally, historically, and ecologically. For individuals, therefore, certain places may hold more value than others because they mark, for example, a significant event or the act of religious worship. The physical distinctiveness of the site is not as important to the residents as the relationships and social processes that produce the attachment to it. This sense of attachment, however, is not easily quantifiable, as it draws upon memories, desires, and experiences, becoming as much a social as a personal product. As repositories of information (Strang 1997: 200), these sites, whether a coconut walk in Cahuita or families' farmland in Tortuguero, embody memories that persist in informing the inhabitants' representation of places, despite attempts to subvert the relationship that they may have with the particular locale. However, I argue that though these memories persist, the manner in which they are articulated changes over time.

It is partially due to the multiple interpretations of place that conflicts have arisen in the displacement process. When their impending displacement became clear, the affected residents realized they were being asked to give up a part of their life that defined them. For instance, older village members still recount stories of hunting for food in order to survive, or of women collectively gathering coconuts from the grove they had created. It is not surprising, then, that reaction to their loss was expressed, in some cases, in a physical manner, particularly when all other means of dissent appeared to be closed. In these instances, identity, land, and livelihood are all interconnected. The case of one Tortuguero resident clearly demonstrates the intersection of these issues. This man refused to accept the state-imposed restrictions on activities in the park, deciding instead that he would go back to work on his farm, which was located within park boundaries. When forest rangers arrested him, he evocatively informed them that he had poured his blood into this land and therefore the state could never take it away from him.

This monitoring of movement within the park as a strategy to deter farming and hunting produced agitation among the villagers, who were dissatisfied with their exclusion from decisions that affected them. As a result, they were left with a feeling of injustice concerning the state's activities in the area. The state, moreover, did not address the fact that the villagers' perspectives regarding place differed from those of the environmental organizations. The latter cast the locals' economic activities as a threat to the sustainable future of Costa Rica's natural environment. These conflicting perceptions, in which the expropriated land is presented either as something to be protected from human interference or as a viable source of livelihood, define the bounded means of seeing activities within this displacement process in Tortuguero and Cahuita. The local residents whom I interviewed perceived development as the means of surviving in the mode of life that they had chosen rather than as a preoccupation with physical boundaries that labelled areas as falling inside or outside of a park or an idea, or with the concept of nature as finite (see Sonnino 2004). Moreover, because the story of the Tortuguero man who had defied park regulations to farm his land was repeated over time, the villagers' attachment to the confiscated land was reinforced and perpetuated. Given that people have such close ties to place, it becomes clear that displacement represents a dismissal of their emotional connection with a particular locale.[6]

Over time, state officials' attitudes have changed. According to a Costa Rican NGO representative, some officials are now willing to admit that the conflict over displacement occurred at least in part because the expropriation process did not take into account the value of the land to the affected communities. Furthermore, state officials tended to assume that no one owned the territory within the proposed park boundaries (NGO representative A, interview by author, San José, June 2000). Nonetheless, villagers continued to criticize the state for failing to address other challenges facing them, such as the outbreak of monilia, a disease affecting the cocoa plant, which occurred while land expropriation in Cahuita was under way. One resident, Samuel, stated that prior to the arrival of monilia, people in the area were wealthy (Samuel, interview by author, Cahuita, July 2000). However, the disease outbreak led some of those with land title to borrow money from the state; others allowed their land to remain fallow; but increasingly, many sold it in order to pay their debts. During what residents refer to as the Monilia Crisis, the state was seen as paying limited attention to the interests and livelihoods of local people, focusing instead on establishing the park and reintroducing banana plantations in the areas. According to Edward,

> The central government did not give any technical assistance, nothing whatsoever. The disease damaged all the [cocoa] plantations. Many [people] stayed because that is the only thing they knew about, working on the farm ... [They relied] on subsistence farming. Then the government decided to bring in a new project of developing bananas again in the zone, so they almost forced them to abandon their farms, and so the banana plantation took over the farms. You have no choice because if you have ten to twenty acres of land and the main product you have is under disease, and someone comes to you and offers three to four million colones, you will take it. (Edward, interview by author, Cahuita, July 2000)

The state's handling of the Monilia Crisis, its concurrent plans to expropriate Cahuita residents' lands, and the lack of consultation on both issues left the villagers distrusting of the government. This expressed itself through accusations of systemic racism, which local people argued was manifest in the state's long-standing refusal to grant Costa Rican citizenship to Afro-descendent individuals, the use of racial stereotyping to justify belief in the racial and ethnic superiority of particular groups, the exclusion from public life of those considered "inferior," and the negation of Afro–Costa Rican culture and identity (Campbell Barr 1998: 13). San José–based NGOs that work with the Afro-descendent communities maintain that "racism exists in all areas of our society, economy, and culture. Racism is a political struggle; it is a struggle because we are invisible within the educational system, because we have little access to political avenues, because we continue to be discriminated [against] at work and in attempts to access work" (NGO representative C, interview by author, San Jose, August 2000). The discourse of displacement shifted from the immediate physical threat to local livelihoods to one linked with issues that have affected Afro-descendent people since their arrival in Costa Rica. These issues include access to resources and rights to full citizenship.

Since the 1970s, Afro–Costa Ricans have moved out of Limón Province in search of employment. One Afro–Costa Rican participant, an NGO representative, noted that until that time, his forebears attempted to stake out a living in whatever manner they could. "Back then we had access to land so they were producers in the agricultural field mainly in cocoa production and things like that. Gradually different motives depossessed us from the land so we became workers, ordinary workers on our land with nothing. So we became poorer and poorer" (NGO representative C, interview by author, San José, August 2000).

Today, the discourse used by Afro–Costa Ricans to define their place and identity has incorporated the language of sustainable development. Yet, within this terminology is the underlying issue of displacement. Rather than being simply an acceptance of the dominant discourse for development in Costa Rica, the adoption of the sustainable development argument illustrates a transformation in the method of agitation for recognition of their communities' traditional practices and conceptions of the environment. In the words of one participant, Roberto:

> We are part of the environment, you understand. It is not just the trees and the animals: it is the trees, the animals, and us. We are part of this too. In the 1970s, the national government said, okay, that is the national park, everybody get out. Today, they still have not paid for the land as yet. They have paid a pretty good number of people, but they have not paid everybody as yet. We have learnt to live with it. We never forget that that land belongs to us and we are the ones that take care of the national park now. (Roberto, interview by author, Cahuita, August 2000)

Here the memory of events, the lack of compensation, and the physical removal of people from their land all coexist with an acceptance of their loss, which is rationalized through positioning themselves as the park's guardians.

Moreover, rather than casting what had become a national park as devoid of human occupants, Roberto considered himself to be an integral part of it. He constructed his role as one in which conservation was maintained through the establishment of a pattern of caring for nature. However, deviating from the dominant conceptions of sustainable development, Roberto believed in the value of all life, including human life, as essential in conserving the park's biodiversity.

For Afro-descendent Costa Ricans, the park is more than a tangible expression of displacement and accommodation. Other interview participants also emphasized their historical roots in the region through their attachment to place. As one participant, Humphery, put it, "we have been protecting [the natural environment here] for the last two hundred years" (Humphery, interview by author, Cahuita, August 2000). Consequently, any displacement of the population is seen not only as an economic and ecological issue but also as a challenge to its culture. "In our case, being Afro-Caribbean, we live on the coast; our culture is very strong between us, but it is easy to break. We are trying to preserve what our people have given us from five hundred to six hundred years ago when they came to this part of the world as slaves. We are not slaves any more, and we want to say how we want to live. And we want to live just as we are right now. We don't want to change this" (ibid.).

The struggle of Afro-descendent people to retain their cultural knowledge has extended over time and space, but it is a struggle in which this participant at least would rather not have to engage. He had no desire to change his current lifestyle, a stance those planning and implementing development in local communities usually do not consider. The juxtapositioning of ideas of alienation due to racism and the act of displacement was more explicit in discussions with younger individuals than with those who were displaced from their land. Furthermore, Humphery's understanding of the concept of displacement entailed a process that had plagued people of African descent, one that stemmed from their movement as slaves across the Atlantic to work on plantations or in mines throughout the Americas.

Representations of place have developed over many years in Tortuguero and Cahuita, and remain fundamental parts of residents' lives, including the shift from an immediate relationship with the land to more abstract concepts of dispossession. In their multiple relations within their villages, with the state, and with international organizations, local people's understanding of their displacement is in part expressed through the defence of territory, attachment to place, and potential loss of knowledge that they once held in common. However, the symbolic position held by the parks in Afro–Costa Rican people's imaginations is not informed only through memories of the past. As will be seen in the following section, the displacement of these populations also had profoundly significant economic and social consequences.

Other Consequences of Displacement

The changes that have occurred due to displacement have not only influenced how individuals perceive places or the nature of the state but have also had economic and social consequences that inform their memories of events. Therefore, I will look specifically at the material results arising from loss of access to the land on which they once farmed and hunted.

Since their displacement, not only have the Afro-descendent people of Cahuita and Tortuguero experienced difficulty in securing employment in San José, Costa Rica's capital, but even in the villages themselves. In the words of Alfonso, a Tortuguero resident, "the park hasn't done anything for the community. Only three local people have been hired to work for the park" (Alfonso, interview by author and assistant, Tortuguero, July 2000). At the same time, the establishment of the parks resulted in the replacement of much of the pre-existing local economy with one that depended upon tourism. However, the new economic order did not always benefit village residents. For example, Tortuguero residents asserted that local tourist lodges preferred to hire Nicaraguan staff because they would accept lower wages than would local people. They added that, in many cases, lodge owners told their guests that the village was dangerous so as to discourage them from spending their money there. Alfonso believed that life in the village was much better in 1948. Back then, he claimed, everyone at least was able to work, and the income earned circulated within the "community" (ibid.). In contrast, in 2000, almost all tourist spending was channelled to the region's eight lodges, with little finding its way to the Afro-descendent people. Nor was this trend a new one: in 1988, an Institute of Iberio-American Cooperation report stated that only 8 percent of the total income earned in Tortuguero remained within the region (Instituto de Cooperación Ibero-América 1988).

Furthermore, Tortuguero residents maintained that the tourist lodges tended to receive preferential treatment from the government. In the view of one elderly resident, Arthur, "What I think is that everyone has rights. You have rights and I have rights, and what I really don't like is the way the government lets the hotels cut down trees and do what they want in the park, but when people from Tortuguero do the same thing, they get thrown in jail. They may be rich and I may be poor, but we both have the same rights" (Arthur, interview by author, Tortuguero, July 2000).

Lodge representatives have acknowledged they have had flora removed from the park in order to landscape their grounds. They also admit to the removal of recently fallen trees to ensure that tour boats can easily navigate the canals within the park. By contrast, one resident stated that since the

1990s, officials had refused to let any local inhabitants take anything from the park (Carlos, interview by author, Tortuguero, July 2000). He claimed that in 1990, unaware of the change in regulation, he cut down two trees to repair his home and was therefore forced to pay a 75,000 colones fine. However, no local resident with whom I spoke was aware of any cases in which the lodges had been reprimanded for their activities. Given that the park is supposed to be left in its natural state and that nothing is to be extracted from it, local people resented the selective manner in which punishment was meted out for contravening park policy. Actions such as these in Tortuguero, along with the understanding of systemic racism held by residents in Cahuita, led one Cahuita resident, Roberto, to remark that the Costa Rican state was corrupt and that it "discriminates against Limón Province. They don't like black or indigenous people" (Roberto, interview by author, Cahuita, August 2000). Another resident, Grant, provided his analysis of the situation: "They [the state] don't care. They just want to get a few people rich. The poor people are only going to get poorer" (Grant, interview by author, Cahuita, August 2000).

Although some Cahuita locals do own and operate a number of successful hotels, restaurants, and tour facilities, it is important to note that, in large part, the challenges they face arise from the long-standing presentation of Limón Province as an undesirable and dangerous tourist destination. Interview participants remarked that the media constructed stories of uncleanliness, backwardness, and rampant crime in the province in general and Cahuita in particular (Tony, interview by author, Cahuita, August 2000; Víctor, interview by author, Puerto Viejo, August 2000). They also criticized the state with reference to its treatment of Cahuita: specifically, they claimed that government tourism officials in San José failed to promote Cahuita as a tourist destination, emphasizing instead Costa Rica's Pacific coast. The inconsistency between inclusion in the collaborative management of the park and exclusion from the popular discourse of what is ideal places the Afro-descendent residents in a difficult situation. Their support for the park is tempered by the long-term negative consequences of its creation, which include male prostitution in Cahuita and the lack of access to resources experienced by other villages bordering the park (Roberto, interview by author, Cahuita, August 2000; Emily, interview by author, Cahuita, August 2000). Moreover, the communities' ill-preparedness for the consequences of displacement stemming from park creation has reportedly led to a number of cases of homelessness and alcoholism (Roberto, interview by author, Cahuita, August 2000).

In 2000, though residents in Cahuita and Tortuguero did see the conservation of natural resources as an important issue, they noted that, in many cases, the financial compensation promised them more than thirty years ago still had not been received. One Tortuguero resident, Alberto, wished that the state would compensate him, if not for the land itself then at least for the labour his family had put into it. However, he added that he did not know what he could do to obtain the money promised to him (Alberto, interview by author and assistant, Tortuguero, July 2000). In another case, a participant, Alfred, claimed that though he made several trips to Puerto Limón in order to speak with a senior MINAE official regarding compensation owed to an elderly friend, the official did nothing more than promise that the matter would be looked into (Alfred, interview by author, Hone Creek, August 2000). Overall, residents remained skeptical of the state's commitment to addressing their concerns. This sentiment was captured in the words of one Tortuguero man, Frank, who commented that "What the government write with their hand today, tomorrow they rub it out with their elbow" (Frank, interview by author, Tortuguero, July 2000).

Moral Obligations?

Displacement in the name of conservation reveals a delicate balance between, on one hand, the desire to preserve biodiversity for future generations and, on the other, the wish to encourage the economic management of the natural environment (Kuehls 1996: 128). With regard to these Costa Rican parks, however, the latter is often depicted as existing principally at the local level and is characterized as environmentally destructive actions carried out by those with scant interest in biodiversity. Local communities' interests in the protected areas are said to rest solely on their immediate economic concerns rather than on a consideration of the future consequences of their actions. Yet, the government has selectively used the notions of economic management and biodiversity in an interchangeable manner, promoting ecotourism while simultaneously expressing its intent to preserve biodiversity. For both economic management and conservation, the definitions of sustainable management have tended to reflect the interests of the state and influential environmental organizations to the neglect of citizen input.

In the conflict between conservation and residents' livelihoods, the questions of harm, and the potential for harm, become particularly salient. According to Herrera Ibañez (1994: 257), if harm can be repaired, it ought to be kept to the minimum, and if what is harmed cannot be repaired, it ought not be harmed in the first place. However, what minimum level of harm can be deemed acceptable? Who should be responsible for defining such levels? For both the state and the international environmental organizations, it is the welfare of the green turtle, the coral reef, and the wetlands that has dominated the discourses of what ought to be. Local communities, such as the Afro-descendent populations of Tortuguero and Cahuita, already marginalized by the dominant national discourses of citizenship, emerged once again as a secondary interest in the decisions taken in the creation of the parks in the 1970s. Cast as outsiders, Afro-descendent people developed their own economies and preserved their own traditions, both of which were harmed by the displacement process, with little or no measures provided to mediate the effects. Moreover, since their displacement, Afro-descendent people continue to experience high levels of underemployment, have limited educational opportunities, and suffer racism in many aspects of their lives.

If the nominal conditions of a good life consist of nourishment, health, shelter, emotional contact with others, communication, education, autonomy, and individuality (Krebs 1999: 12), then development-induced displacement in Tortuguero and Cahuita has not come close to achieving this minimum. Clearly the impact has been negative, characterized by loss of land, loss of livelihoods, disintegration of families, and an antipathy towards the government. With the growing recognition among academics, including Johnathon Crush (1995), of the negative impacts of development, more attention at an institutional level has been devoted to ameliorating the process. For instance, in establishing the grounds for the possibility of living a good life, the World Commission on Dams Report (N.d.) maintains that, should development-induced displacement occur, it ought to take into consideration issues such as human rights, participation, accountability, governance, and self-determination, along with an analysis of options, strategies, policies, and legal regulations. In the institutional decision-making process, it is imperative "to have moral concern or respect for others ... to place intrinsic value on their good life, to further their happiness for its own sake and not solely for the sake of your own happiness" (Krebs 1999: 16).

Over time, the Afro-descendent people's removal from their land became central to the formation of their values and attitudes regarding displacement and the state. Initially, they accepted the decision to establish the national parks, and some residents assumed that the government was working on their behalf; eventually, however, due to contradictory orders from officials in charge, limited or no compensation, and the loss of livelihoods, attitudes changed from acceptance to dissatisfaction. In the long run, displacement entails more than boardroom policy making. It provides a link between subjectivities, socio-economic well-being, and moral responsibilities. In the case of Costa Rica's national parks, the decision makers' responsibility then lies not just in securing biodiversity but also in considering those who are seen to fall outside "civilizational" boundaries (Campbell and Shapiro 1999: ix). This consideration ought not simply to be a paper statement but, instead, ought to include their interests and secure their *continuous* and full participation in all decisions that have a direct bearing upon their future well-being.

Notes

1 Because differences exist regarding questions of leadership, gender, and ethnicity, "community" is an essentially contested notion. Within the literature on displacement and environmental conservation, however, there has been limited problematization of the concept. See Michael J. Watts (2000).

2 I define "harm" as forcing individuals to participate in actions or events that are not in their interest, or going beyond the amount of risk these individuals are willing to accept.

3 The participants' names have been changed in order to protect their identities.

4 The mobility rights of Afro-descendent peoples were restricted until 1949. In that year, a law forbidding them to move outside Limón Province was rescinded and they were granted full Costa Rican citizenship (Hernández Cruz 1999).

5 See Cortés and Risk (1985) for the claim that the community was indirectly involved in the Cahuita Point reef's degradation. For a critique of findings that attribute the destruction to forest clearance alone, see M.R. Hands, J.R. French, and A.O. O'Neill (1993).

6 In 2000, when I conducted my interviews, few people in Tortuguero and Cahuita appeared to connect the 1970s' displacement with the current shape of their lives. This, I believe, was largely due to the fact that so many years had elapsed since the time of the displacement. Although the feelings of loss remained, the specific conditions and perceptions of displacement had faded, becoming instead a discontent rooted in memories passed on from generation to generation.

References

Campbell, David, and Michael J. Shapiro. 1999. *Moral Spaces: Rethinking Ethics and World Politics*. Minneapolis: University of Minnesota Press.

Campbell Barr, Epsy. 1998. "Democracia, justicia e igualidad desde la diversidad." In *Justicia y Discriminación en Costa Rica,* 11-18. San José: CONAMAJ.

Cernea, Michael. 1999. "Development's Painful Social Costs: Introductory Study." In *The Development Dilemma: Displacement in India,* by S. Parasuraman, 1-31. The Hague: Institute of Social Studies.

Cortés, N., and M. Risk. 1985. "A Reef under Siltation Stress: Cahuita, Costa Rica." *Bulletin of Marine Science* 36 (2): 339-56.

DuPuis, Melanie E., and Peter Vandergeest, eds. 1996. *Creating the Countryside: The Politics of Rural and Environmental Discourse*. Philadelphia: Temple University Press.

Esta Semana. 1996. "¿Qué pasará se el turismo se va de Cahuita?" 19 June, 12.

Goldman, Mara. 2003. "Partitioned Nature, Privileged Knowledge: Community-Based Conservation in Tanzania." *Development and Change* 34 (5): 833-62.

Hands, M.R., J.R. French, and A.O. O'Neill. 1993. "Reef Stress at Cahuita Point, Costa Rica: Anthropogenically Enhanced Sediment Influx or Natural Geomorphic Change?" *Journal of Coastal Research* 9 (1): 11-25.

Hernández Cruz, Omar. 1999. "De inmigrantes a cuidadanos: Hacia un espacio político afrocostarricense (1949-1998)." *Revista de Historia* 39: 207-45.

Herrera Ibañez, Alejandro, and José Alfredo Torres. 1994. *Falacias*. Mexico: torres Asociados.

Instituto de Cooperación Ibero-América. 1988. *Servicios de Parques Nacionales. Perfil Socio-Económico de los Comunidades Aledañas al Parque Nacional Tortuguero.* San José, Costa Rica: Instituto de Cooperación Ibero-América.

Instituto Nacional de Estadística y Censos. 2001. *IX Censo Nacional de Población y V de Vivienda de 2000: Resultados Generales*. San José, Costa Rica: INEC 35.

IUCN. 2000. *Comunidades y Gestión en Bosques en Mesoamérica: Perfil regional del grupo de trabajo sobre participación conmunitaria en el manejo de los bosques*. San José, Costa Rica: Impresión Comercial La Nación S.A.

Krebs, Angelika. 1999. *Ethics of Nature: A Map*. Berlin and New York: W. de Gruyter.

Kuehls, Thom. 1996. *Beyond Sovereign Territory.* Minneapolis: University of Minnesota Press.

La Nación. 1974a. "Un parque nacional para salar a Tortuguero." 11 July, 4C.

–. 1974b. "Synopsis de un pueblo: Tortuguero." 11 July, 14C.

–. 1974c. "Tortuguero tesoro del Atlántico." 11 July, 1C.

La Prensa Libre. 1972. "Tortuguero: Belleza con abandono." 8 July, 14.
–. 1992. "Conservación sin sustento jurídico." 1 April, 6.
La República. 1975. "Creación del Parque Tortuguero." 13 March.
Palmer, Paula. 1993. *"What Happen": A Folk-History of Costa Rica's Talamanca Coast*. San Jose, Costa Rica: Publications in English, SA.
Place, Susan. 1991. "Nature Tourism and Rural Development in Tortuguero." *Annals of Tourism Research* 18: 186-201.
Sonnino, Roberta. 2004. "'For a Piece of Bread'? Interpreting Sustainable Development through Agritourism in Southern Tuscany." *Sociologia Ruralis* 44 (4): 285-300.
Stewart, Rigoberto. 1999. *Limón Real*. San José, Costa Rica: Litografía e Imprenta LIL, SA.
Strang, Veronica. 1997. *Uncommon Ground: Cultural Landscapes and Environmental Values*. New York: Berg.
Tico Times. 1999. "Government Gets Tough on Turtle Poachers." 9 July. http://www.ticotimes.net/archive//08_09_99_4.htm (accessed 18 June 2003).
Wallace, Donald R. 1992. *Quetzal and the Macaw: The Story of Costa Rica's National Parks*. San Francisco: Sierra Club.
Watts, Michael J. 2000. "Contested Communities, Malignant Markets, and Gilded Governance: Justice, Resource Extraction, and Conservation in the Tropics." In Charles Zerner, ed., *People, Plants, and Justice: The Politics of Nature Conservation*, 21-51. New York: Colombia University Press.
Weitzner, Viviane, and Marvin Fonseca Borrás 1999. "Cahuita, Limón, Costa Rica: From Conflict to Collaboration." In D. Buckles, ed., *Cultivating Peace: Conflict and Collaboration in Natural Resource Management*, 129-50. Ottawa: IDRC.
World Commission on Dams Report. N.d. http://www.damsreport.org/docs/kbase/thematic/drafts/tr13_draft.pdf 2002 (accessed 18 June 2003).

9

Entanglements: *Campesino* and Indigenous Tenure Insecurities on the Honduran North Coast

Sharlene Mollett

> Expropriation of land removes the main foundation upon which people's productive systems, commercial activities and livelihoods are constructed. This is the principal form of decapitalization and pauperization of displaced people, as they lose both natural and man-made capital.
>
> – Michael Cernea (2000: 23)

Honduras is among the poorest countries in the western hemisphere. This small Central American country of almost seven million people has an average gross national income per capita of USD$920 (2002), and roughly 64 percent of the population lives in poverty while another 45 percent lives in extreme poverty. In the nation's rural areas, over 62 percent of the population is afflicted by extreme poverty – manifest in low literacy rates, a lack of arable land, a lack of potable water sources, and chronic malnutrition among children (IDBR 2006). Among the rural poor of southern and southwestern Honduras, there are over 300,000 landless *ladino campesinos* (El Tiempo 2004),[1] who, over the past twenty years, have faced growing land scarcity and sought refuge in the forests of the country's north coast. However inadvertently, these "new arrivals" have chosen forest areas that are already claimed by other groups, namely indigenous people with a long social history and attachment to the forest and its resources. As a result, indigenous natural resource access has become entangled with campesino attempts to cope with their own landlessness. Such is the case in Capiro-Calentura National Park.

Capiro-Calentura National Park is located on the northeastern shore above the small city of Trujillo in the department of Colón. This national park was established by legal decree in 1992. Protected inside the park are Mounts Capiro and Calentura. This park counts among the country's one-hundred-plus protected areas and measures almost five thousand hectares. It is co-managed by FUCAGUA (Fundación para la conservación del Parque Nacional Capiro-Calentura y el Refugio de Vida Silvestre Laguna de Guaimoreto), a non-governmental organization (NGO), and the State Forestry Administration (AFE-COHDEFOR). In 2000, natural resource management in the park was funded by the United States Agency for International Development (USAID).

The park is divided into two zones: a buffer zone and a nucleus zone. The nucleus, or core, zone is the primary area under protection and, in this particular case, is free from human settlement. The buffer zone is designed to provide an extra layer of protection around the core zone. Unlike in the core zone, however, local communities live and draw livelihoods in the buffer zone. In Capiro-Calentura, the buffer zone is considered part of the protected area, as buffer zone forests and natural resources fall under the authority of park officials and national conservation policies.

Interestingly, the growth of protected-area enactment in Honduras parallels the growth of rural landlessness: within those rural areas not set aside for protection, a burgeoning class of landless campesinos grows. Although most of these farmers migrate to the cities of Tegucigalpa and San Pedro Sula, many others opt to move to the sparsely populated north coast. The National Agrarian Institute (INA) had previously designed a Reform Sector to provide land in the form of cooperatives to organized landless campesinos. However, the lands were never legally transferred and most cooperatives have since dissolved. As a result, in an effort to secure land, campesinos invade north coast forests, which are not only enclosed within protected area boundaries but are also claimed by indigenous peoples as their homelands.

This chapter examines natural resource struggles between the Pech farmers and ladino campesinos in Capiro-Calentura National Park. This examination builds upon three months of ethnographic field research conducted in 2000 inside the buffer zone of Capiro-Calentura. The Pech are an Amerindian group with only a few thousand remaining members, who are spread across three departments, namely, Colón, Olancho, and Gracias a Dios. In the park, Pech residents live in the village of Silin, a small farming village consisting of both indigenous and ladino residents. Ladinos in Silin have, since the early 1990s, arrived from a number of departments at an increasing rate, and they participate as wage labourers in local economies.[2] Roughly four kilometers up the foothills of Capiro-Calentura is the village of Tesorito. Tesorito is a campesino community populated by displaced[3] farmers who have come from disparate locations around the country in search of land.

Drawing upon insights from the field of political ecology, I examine Pech-ladino struggles, both material and discursive, to highlight tensions regarding land and natural resources in the buffer zone of Capiro-Calentura

National Park. To begin, I trace some of the factors shaping campesino landlessness, particularly neoliberal reforms to state land policy for campesino and indigenous groups alike. Next, I explore the institutional constructions of campesino and indigenous identities in the communities of Silin, home to the Pech farmers and ladino wage labourers, and Tesorito, home to roughly six hundred ladino farmers. Through examining of Pech and ladino land histories, and by contrasting the roles ethnicity and gender play in natural resource access, I highlight how the state, NGOs, and indigenous people have allied to delegitimize and criminalize campesinos as "migrants" using "predatory" land use practices in Capiro-Calentura National Park. Pech and ladino land contests inside protected areas reveal how indigenous and campesino interests forcibly overlap. Moreover, indigenous natural resource access is increasingly entangled in the tenure security of non-indigenous small farmers.

Power and inequality permeate the struggle for rural land in Honduras: therefore, this work builds upon the insights of political ecology, a popular research approach that aims to link political economy and ecological processes through a plurality of avenues. Within the political ecology framework are three assumptions: first, politics and the environment are thoroughly connected; second, material struggles concerning the environment are also discursive struggles; and third, unequal power relations inform the distribution, control of, and access to natural resources (Blaikie and Brookfield 1987; Bryant 1998; Eriksson 2000; Peet and Watts 1996; Rocheleau, Thomas-Slayter, and Wangari 1996; Stonich 1993). Political ecology acknowledges that global and national political economic processes interconnect with the local politics of natural resource access. In addition, the state has often been a major player in natural resource struggles (Peluso 1992; Vandergeest 1996). Studies in political ecology often illustrate the tendency of the state, with the aid of foreign capital and national elites, to adopt policies that threaten the integrity of natural resources and impoverish rural people (Stonich 1993; Jansen 1998), particularly indigenous people and women (Bryant 1998).

In this case, state agrarian policies, in part, fuel campesino landlessness while conservation enclosures (through the enclosure of protected areas) further reduce the availability of arable land. Since indigenous territories are overwhelmingly enclosed inside protected areas in Honduras, and displaced farmers are not deterred by these boundaries, campesino settlement inside indigenous domains sparks a discourse among campesinos, indigenous populations and protected-area officials, from which emerge various justifications for property rights and natural resource access.

Campesino Landlessness and Displacement

In Honduras, most small farmers possess no formal land titles to their holdings. Nonetheless, prior to the 1970s, campesinos experienced little difficulty accessing farmland (Booth and Walker 1989; Jansen 1998; Stonich 1993). Even the expansion of American commercial banana production in the early twentieth century failed to severely disrupt small farmers and their tenancy relationships with *terratenientes* (wealthy landowners). However, with the cotton and cattle booms of the 1950s and 1960s, spurred by the opening of US markets to the region, new agrarian landscapes were shaped as campesino access to land in the southern agricultural region decreased (Booth and Walker 1989; Stonich 1993). Marginalized from their lands, these campesinos came to characterize a growing rural population. By the 1970s, almost 50 percent of Honduran farmers held less than five square hectares of land each, an area commonly found insufficient to provide sustenance for the average Honduran family (Baumeister and Wattel 1996). Resource access dwindled further as smallholders and sharecroppers lost usufruct rights to commons and *ejidos*.[4] Furthermore, terratenientes perceived that, if lands were made available to campesinos, the small holdings would impede their own potential profits from export. For terratenientes, the military became an instrument employed to evict peasants from their plots (Jansen 1998; Stonich 1993). Making matters worse, large-scale conversions of cropland, both private and communal, to cattle production could not sufficiently absorb the former smallholders' burgeoning demands for work (Stonich 1993). In the southwest, the conversion of village commons and cropland to cattle-ranching pasture, combined with spiralling unemployment, resulted in vast migratory flows to the northern regions of the country, particularly to the departments of Olancho and Colon (Humphries 1998; Jansen 1998). Despite some land redistribution in 1974, agrarian reform, landlessness, and displacement ensued (Booth and Walker 1989).

In an attempt to modernize the Honduran countryside, the United States Agency for International Development (USAID), under the auspices of the National Agrarian Institute (INA), introduced the Honduran Land Titling Project for small producers, Proyecto de Titulación de Tierra para los Pequeños Productores (PTT). In 1982, INA first initiated the PTT in the western departments of Comayagua, Copán, Cortés, El Paraíso, La Paz, Santa Barbara, and Yoro. Grounded in neoliberal ideology, INA officials offered land titles to campesinos as a critical step towards the modernization and augmentation of Honduran agricultural production (INA 1995). The rationale behind the PTT was to increase the value of land as a commercial asset and, simultaneously, to improve rural tenure security by granting land titles of *dominio pleno*[5] to small producers who already held property (ibid.).[6]

However, the PTT accomplished little to increase tenure security for small farmers. INA titles under the PTT became the only legitimate form of property title. Since farmers were expected to pay a portion of the value of the land in order to receive formal ownership, campesinos were unable to retain access to the lands they occupied due to a lack of savings. Instead, terratenientes were frequently able to appropriate land from poorer farmers by paying the fees on campesino land and subsequently registering the property in their own names. Aggressive fee collection by INA officials negated socio-historical relationships with the land and sanctioned ownership to those who could pay first (Jansen 1998). Small-producer vulnerabilities also grew as INA's eligibility requirements directly linked landownership to commercialized choices in land use (INA 1995). For instance, the PTT denied titles to farmers with properties under five square hectares unless the farmers used the land for coffee production. As 50 percent of the rural population held less than five square hectares (Baumeister and Wattel 1996), many of these small-scale subsistence producers were ineligible for dominio pleno. Similarly, farmers with lands that measured between five to seventeen square hectares were eligible only for *dominio útil,* granting them official rights to use but prohibiting the sale of lands that they already occupied. Moreover, INA disallowed sharecropping and land leasing in these departments, which consequently decreased livelihood opportunities and land availability, specifically for landless and land-poor farmers (INA 1995). With little protection from INA, small farmers continued to be displaced.

Despite Honduras' most recent agrarian reform policy, campesinos face further obstacles to natural resource access. The 1992 Law of Modernization for the Agricultural Sector further exacerbated the problems of campesino land tenure. As an International Monetary Fund (IMF) structural adjustment requirement, this Law of Modernization reform contains three overlapping policies that limit livelihood possibilities for land-poor producers (Jansen 1998; República de Honduras 1992). First, the Law prohibits land invasions unless a producer can prove, with the testimony of witnesses, that he/she has farmed a particular property for a minimum of three years without contest. Before the law's 1992 creation, farmers who cleared areas of forest in national territories became de facto owners of the land (INA, personal communication 1999; Humphries 1998). Land invasions typically disregarded a prior policy stipulating that a farmer must prove that he has had possession of the land for over ten years in order to be eligible for ownership (República de Honduras 1975). Second, after three years, a producer is eligible to title lands in dominio pleno. Third, the law stipulates that farmers may be required to relinquish *minifundios,* any area less than one square hectare, to agrarian agencies for redistribution to farmers who demonstrate "high levels of agricultural productivity" (Republica de Honduras 1992). In other words, campesinos can expect further land appropriation in favour of terratenientes. Said differently, the explicit promises of ownership under the three-year rule encourage displaced farmers to migrate to the sparsely populated and heavily forested northern region that to date has held less government interest than has the southwest export production region. Land tensions accompany this influx, as displaced campesinos invade the spaces of indigenous production and ancestral heritage; ultimately, these groups are compelled to compete for the rights to natural resources in the context of declining access.

As campesinos struggle to attain land, north coast indigenous populations work to retain natural resource access in the face of further reforms proposed by the state. The Honduran National Congress, the main lawmaking body, recently amended Article 107, a constitutional gurantee aimed to protect coastal and border lands from foreign ownership. In 1998, the Honduran Congress proposed to amend the article to allow foreign ownership, under the condition that such owners build tourist infrastructure on coastal properties (ODECO 1999).[7] Congress members, insisting that much of the north coast region was "uninhabited" and "in need of modernization," denied indigenous claims because the area's forests were classified as "national territory" (Marín 1998). North coast indigenous groups, roughly 200,000 people, feared losing ancestral territories through the increased land speculation that may be precipitated if the Article 107 reform were to become law. According to indigenous leaders, fear of territorial loss is real – for the potential sale of coastal land to foreigners is only the latest of a long history of violations and of disregard for indigenous land rights by the Honduran government (ODECO 1999).

Indigenous groups are demanding that the government implement territorial guarantees promised in state law. Articles 173 and 346 of the Honduran Constitution commit the state to the protection and legalization of indigenous communal lands (República de Honduras 1982). However, the state ignores these rights through outright negation of legalization, the refusal to extend communal holdings to accommodate population growth within indigenous communities, and unwillingness to title indigenous territories that are enclosed within protected-area boundaries. According to the World Bank Resident Mission in 2003, almost 70 percent of indigenous territories lies within protected areas (Martínez 2003). Additionally, in 1995, Honduras became a signatory of the International Labour Organization's Convention 169. Under Articles 13 and 14 of this convention, Honduras is committed to the protection of indigenous residential territories and must sanction indigenous rights to functional habitats where fishing, gathering, hunting, and farming may take place. This would include fallow areas, regardless of their distance from primary residences (ILO 1989). Although many north coast indigenous people fare better than do those in the interior – some interior groups, such as the Chorti, are completely landless – north coast tenure anxieties remain high.

Silin and Tesorito in Capiro-Calentura National Park

Much of the department of Colón, in which Capiro-Calentura National Park lies, appears sparsely populated. Therefore, many nationals often refer to Colón as "frontier country" (INA representative, personal communication 2000). Since the completion of the coastal highway in the 1970s, reaching Colon from other parts of the country has become relatively easy; as a result, this sparsely populated department quickly became a refuge for the displaced – landless and land-poor farmers from the west.

The small city of Trujillo (population fifty thousand) is the department's primary commercial port and tourism centre, boasting pristine beaches, clear blue waters, first-class hotels, and two protected areas for nature tourists. The two villages of Silin (population five hundred) and Tesorito (population 650) are located six and fourteen kilometres, respectively, outside Trujillo. Lying within the park's buffer zone, they are joined by four kilometres of hilly dirt road frequented by villagers when travelling to sell their produce in Trujillo or the larger markets in Tocao and La Ceiba. Few people in either village own motorized vehicles; a local bus service makes six trips daily between Silin and Trujillo.

Silin is comprised of two main ethnic groups, namely, Pech farmers and ladino wage earners. Pech families make their homes in two distinct clusters close to the centre of the village. The Pech are descendents of South American rainforest tribes who migrated from the communities of Santa María de Carbón and Culmi to work for a major hacienda in the early twentieth century. Silin's Pech community numbers roughly 350 people. Silin is also home to approximately 150 ladinos, who migrated to the village in the past ten to twenty years; most of the men are wage labourers. They claim that they were farmers before coming to Colón but now prefer to work for someone else rather than endure the "suffering" of campesino life in the country. Ladino residences are located along the Río Silin, away from Pech houses.

Tesorito, founded in the early 1980s, is home to a seemingly homogeneous ladino membership that consists of "officially" landless campesinos from a variety of departments. Many insist that they are displaced farmers who relocated to Tesorito due to landlessness in their areas of origin (see Table 9.2). Farmers spoke openly of their experiences on co-operatives and of working for terratenientes but claimed that their goal was to "own" land. Tesorito campesinos cultivate mainly corn and beans, but many also raise pigs and cows. Residences line the road through the village, and campesino fields are located deep within the forests and along the mountain slopes. At first glance, Tesorito and Silin residents seem to enjoy a peaceful coexistence, a harmony marked by their insistence that "everyone gets along" (field notes 2000). However, ladino land use is a focal point for both Pech discontent and institutional discourses that blame "the campesino" for degradation.

Institutional Naming, Migrants, and *Agricultura Migratoria*

FUCAGUA and AFE-COHDEFOR are responsible for protected-area natural resource management inside the park. Officially, conservation authorities exclude people from living and farming in the core areas of the park; they also regulate human activity in its buffer zone. Buffer zone residents are not permitted to light fires in either core or buffer zone and cannot graze animals or hunt in the nucleus of the protected area. Because all wood products are to be gathered from the ground, cutting trees is prohibited, even within the buffer zone (FUCAGUA n.d.).

Formally, the primary concern of FUCAGUA and AFE-COHDEFOR officials is to protect the flora and fauna in core areas. However, their management of natural resource use in the park often mirrors common assumptions embedded in environmental policies that work to reinforce a causal link between degradation and people's neglect for nature (Richards 1998). Both institutions contend that the greatest challenge to managing park resources is the influx of migrant farmers and their concomitant "unsustainable" land use practices (FUCAGUA n.d.; COHDEFOR, personal communication 2000). Officials claim that despite restrictions, deforestation in core area forests has grown due to resource scarcity in the buffer zone (FUCAGUA, personal communication 2000). FUCAGUA directly links Capiro-Calentura deforestation and land degradation to *agricultura migratoria* (migratory agriculture) (FUCAGUA n.d.; FUCAGUA, personal communication 2000). Agricultura migratoria refers to the swidden (slash and burn) agriculture that is common among small farmers throughout rural Central America (Jansen 1998; Sundberg 1998). Conservation regulations, however, prohibit agricultura migratoria. Forestry officials insist that farmers are "careless" when burning and that, undoubtedly, they are largely responsible for fire-induced forest loss. Thus, the use of fire strengthens official resistance to campesino land use (Griffin 2000). Moreover, some forestry engineers assert that forest clearance for agriculture owes much to an "agricultural mentality" in which "Hondurans are more interested in growing crops or cows, not trees" (Aceituno 1994). When soil fertility declines, it is alleged, campesinos move elsewhere (ibid.). This institutional labelling of campesinos as "migrants" implies their instability and lack of commitment to sustaining the park's natural resources.

However, park managers differentiate between resource users in the buffer zone. An agronomist at FUCAGUA insisted that strict monitoring of campesino activities in the nation's protected areas would help protect the environment for the benefit of the country's indigenous communities. This official emphasized the importance of adhering to the ILO's Convention 169, highlighting the priority of safeguarding biodiversity and protecting the very ecosystems upon which indigenous people depend (personal communication 2000).

In the context of natural resource management in Capiro-Calentura, public opinion also overwhelmingly discredits campesinos as migrants, challenging their claims of displacement and criminalizing their land use practices (field notes 2000). Local people speak fondly of the Pech and other indigenous people "who have learnt about sustainable agricultural practices from FUCAGUA and [thus] assist institutions in protecting biodiversity within the park" (hardware store owner, personal communication 2000). At the same time, they are critical of campesino agriculture: Reynaldo, an elementary school teacher in Tesorito, remarked that village campesinos were not interested in learning other forms of agriculture, for "agricultura migratoria is part of their culture" (personal communication 2000). Even non-Hondurans residing in Trujillo blame small producers for deforestation. For example, when I asked a group of long-term visitors whether they had ever witnessed harmful land use activities by campesinos, a business owner replied, "No, but everyone knows they [campesinos] degrade the environment" (personal communication 2000).

Still others believe that it is too simple to blame only the campesinos for deforestation. Nilo Zeta, a former executive director of PROLANSATE, an environmental NGO similar to FUCAGUA, emphasizes that blaming migrants for protected-area deforestation is erroneous. He stresses that the act of restricting natural resource access without providing a livelihood alternative is what in fact threatens the well-being of biodiversity and people within protected areas. In addition, he insists that some farmers are landless because they purchased or inherited infertile land. For others, landlessness is the result of displacement or eviction from land holdings. He adds that, because there is little money to enforce conservation regulations, many officials attack the morals of those so-called destroyers of the environment and criminalize their livelihood activities. However, while officials concentrate on discrediting the campesino presence, deforestation continues (PROLANSATE, personal communication 1999).

Pech Land Histories

For the Pech, the decline in natural resource access is directly linked to campesino land use. In the early twentieth century, a small group of Pech migrated to the Silin area to work as sharecroppers for a large hacienda owned by the Francisco family. According to village elders, for many decades the Silin area possessed flourishing forests and fertile lands (FUCAGUA n.d.; personal communication 2000). As subsistence agriculturalists, the Pech grew a diverse variety of crops within the forested mountain range: yucca, corn, sugar cane, plantains, bananas, rice, beans, and small amounts of coffee for household consumption. The Río Silin provided ample amounts of fish, river shrimp, and crab. Forests yielded a multitude of resources such as avocados, oranges, lemons, cocoa, grapefruit, guava, various oils, and many medicinal plants commonly used by the Pech. Forests were also a source of timber for house and tool construction, and for fuel. Forest fauna proved vital to the Pech, as birds, iguanas and other reptiles, coyotes, monkeys, and jaguars were also hunted for household consumption (IHAH-PNUD 1995; Pech farmer, personal communication 2000). Natural resource access has always been important to Pech families. Fernando Ruiz and his wife, Pech farmers, recall how promising Silin's vegetation proved after their arrival in the early 1960s: "When my family and I arrived here ... roughly forty years ago, before the highway was built, there was [cohune palm] everywhere. The mountains were covered in trees and we could always find fruit, wild berries, and forest animals. At the beginning, when our harvests were small, while we were learning about our new land, the forest fruit helped fill our stomachs ... we also worked for the [Francisco hacienda]" (personal communication 2000).

Pech residents hold a communal title in dominio pleno 1,500 *manzanas* (1,000 square hectares) of forest and agricultural land located adjacent to the Capiro-Calentura buffer zone. Property titles for this Pech zone and Pech residences in Silin village predate the 1992 establishment of the park (field notes 2000). Although the Pech zone is communally owned, each family farms separate plots. This zone and the resources therein are available only to Pech residents, with restrictions on the sale of land to non-Pech people. Outsiders, particularly ladinos, must gain permission from the Pech community council, the *patronato,* in order to enter the Pech zone, but patronato members note that permission is rarely solicited as "they [ladinos] regularly sneak into the [Pech] zone" (Maota, Pech farmer, personal communication 2000). To provide increased security, the village of Moradel was established at the entrance to the Pech zone. Moradel is home to six Pech families who monitor the influx of trespassers. According to residents, trespassers are commonly ladinos hoping to "steal" highly valued Spanish cedar, mahogany, and various other forest products; some gain council permission to enter, only to embark on illegal iguana hunting (Manuel, village healer, personal communication 2000).

The Pech overwhelmingly blame their ladino neighbours, both wage labourers and campesinos, for deforestation and over-exploitation in their territory (field notes 2000). Pech villagers claim they have great respect for the environment and insist that their land use is for "need" only. Instances of forest degradation and crop sabotage are attributed to ladino "immorality" and lack of respect for the Pech environment (field notes 2000). Pech residents claim to have witnessed ladinos at the forest edge selling endangered iguana and prohibited timber to the local elite. Pech access to natural resources is further impeded because they fear to travel "too deep" into the protected area, where an enormous amount of illegal timber extraction occurs. Accidentally interrupting contraband production in the forest has

Table 9.1

Pech perspectives on natural resource decline in buffer zone, Silin

- Increased fencing around cattle ranches blocks access to established fishing locations
- Illegal logging/sale by ladinos of mahogany and Spanish cedar taken from Pech zone and Capiro-Calentura generally
- Water decline in Rio Silin, decreased numbers of shrimp and crab, water pollution due to waste disposal
- Disappearance of cohune palm (used for oil and food) due to ladino migration
- Declining number of water sources (current water project under way to secure village water supply)
- Restricted access to hunting and decline in forest animals in buffer zone
- Increased soil erosion on hillsides
- Restricted use of swidden agriculture for Pech
- Loss of forests due to slash and burn by ladino campesinos
- Air pollution from untreated garbage and sewage

reportedly left some villagers wounded (Martín, Pech teacher, personal communication 2000). Finally, the contamination of the Rio Silin is also blamed on the "careless" location of ladino residences along the riverbank. Today, the river is over-exploited and polluted with "all kinds of waste" (Pech shop owner, personal communication 2000). Pech families clearly resent the ladino collective for its natural resource depletion in the Pech buffer zone. Still, many feel that Silin's ladino wage labourers are the worst violators because they do not depend as much as others on the park's natural resources, "and don't care about those who do" (Pech farmer, personal communication 2000).

Campesino Land Histories

Campesinos opine that their presence in the park is justified. With assertions of state neglect, campesinos claim they are abandoned (*abandonados*). Farmers in Tesorito are openly critical of the "favouritism" accorded to the Pech and other indigenous groups on the coast. At Tesorito, the residency of many farmers also predates the establishment of the park; they believe they are in greater need of land than are their Pech neighbours. Alfredo Gomez, a farmer and twenty-year resident of Tesorito who came originally from the southern department of Choluteca, insists that the small Pech population in Silin does not warrant 1,500 manzanas. Due to the "primitive" crop choices of the Pech and their "simple" production of yucca and beans, valuable land is misused. He believes that he and his fellow campesinos could be much more productive with small-scale coffee, cocoa, or cattle production, cash crops that most Pech farm in small quantities only (personal communication 2000). Likewise, noting the amount of uncleared land in the Pech zone, Tesorito farmers lament that the Pech allow "good fertile land to sit idle" (field notes 2000). Lorenzo, another Tesorito farmer, agrees. He worries that "no one seems to care that campesinos need to feed their families" (personal communication 2000).

With land scarcity as a primary concern, Tesorito residents are adamant about obtaining land titles. Farmers insist that individual titles to property will provide collateral for credit and enable them to invest more in their farms, in higher quantities of seed, better animals, and fertilizers. Yet, INA land officials insist that villagers are ineligible for titles to lands inside Capiro-Calentura, a protected area, since they are essentially "squatting" on state lands. Similarly, NGO officials dismiss campesino land claims due to their continual practice of destructive agricultura migratoria (FUCAGUA, n.d.). Farmers, aware that they are being blamed for park deforestation, suspect that FUCAGUA and AFE-COHDEFOR are blocking their land claims to induce them to leave (Barón, farmer from Santa Bárbara, personal communication 2000). In fact, Carlos, a Tesorito farmer, believes that campesinos are the targets of institutional "discrimination." "It is a difficult situation: our fields are within the park, so they cannot be titled; we don't have *persona jurídica*[8] because we cannot pay for it and we cannot afford titles ... the Pech have all that land just for themselves and they own the land. We want our own private titles to our fields. COHDEFOR blames campesinos for the problems in the park [agricultura migratoria], but they lie, and so does FUCAGUA; we are forgotten here, we survive the best we can" (personal communication 2000).

Campesinos admit to grazing animals within core areas, clear-cutting, and burning tree trunks and dense shrubs. Although they acknowledge that these actions are prohibited, they respond to institutional criticisms with criticisms of their own. Campesinos highlight the immorality of park officials in their attempts to displace them from their livelihoods. They also contend that these so-called destructive practices are part of a long-standing tradition that allows farmers to maximize yields without overworking the land. Many campesinos are adamant that slash-and-burn agriculture is necessary and not solely responsible for degradation in the park: "We know how to burn without burning the forest. They tell us not to burn, we do; they tell us not to cut, we do: do they not realize we need to live? They can say that we are bad, that we only want the land for a short time and then we'll leave – how long do we have to live here, how much do we have to take to prove we want to live here so that our children will have land in the future?" (Tesorito farmer, personal communication 2000).

In fact, campesinos insist that, far from being criminals, they are the victims of state-sanctioned intimidation and threats of displacement:

> There has been two occasions when Honduran soldiers entered the village [Tesorito] and told us to leave. They arrived in large trucks and many had guns. They told us we had twenty-four hours to leave the village. The next day, they returned. They warned us that the land of our village belonged to the military and they wanted to use the area for training ... they told us to move. The next time the soldiers told us we were trespassing on municipal land. They gave us two days to leave, but never returned ... A few years after, a group of men in trucks came to tell us that we were on state land, and the government was establishing a park. These men returned and took much of our land. (Co-founder of Tesorito, personal communication 2000)

"Tesorito" is Spanish for "little treasure." Fittingly, village lands are such a highly valued resource that farmers refuse to be "bullied" by institutions into leaving. Although they regret the land they relinquished when the park was established, and their demands for landownership remain unanswered, families insist that living with tenure insecurity in Tesorito is preferable to living in their places of origin (field notes 2000). Multiple histories of landlessness and land poverty permeate the personal accounts of Tesorito residents. Overwhelmingly, they claim landlessness as their primary reason for migrating from former departments (field notes 2000; see Table 9.2). Don Rigo, a farmer and village leader who arrived in Tesorito in 1985, insists that many campesinos are accustomed to the threat of displacement at the hands of the military. He asked, "If they [the military] wanted to take the village, why would they warn us? They know we have no power; we are nothing to them; they just wanted to scare us ... they did scare us" (personal communication 2000).

Interestingly, ladinos in Silin, despite similar stories of landlessness, appear less concerned with landownership than are their counterparts in Tesorito. For these villagers, wage labour has proved more "reliable" than farming. Most ladino men in Silin work for wages at local shipping yards, beer factories, cattle ranches, and construction companies. These residents use land surrounding their homes to plant crops and supplement incomes from wage labour. Don Fredo, originally from Lempira, is one of the wealthier villagers. He owns a *pulpería* (small grocery store) with a freezer and a generator. He also grows bananas, basil, tomatoes, and papaya around his home. Don Fredo maintains that he rarely thinks about legalizing his land. Instead, he puts his trust in his "good relations" with the hacienda patron, Don Francisco, who recently sold him property adjacent to the buffer zone. Although he admits that the environment in Silin has been

Table 9.2

Profiles of ladino displacement and sources of family livelihood

Department of origin	Causes of initial displacement	Work and Migration stops before arrival at Silin/Tesorito	Year of arrival to Silin/Tesorito	Types of farming and wage labour opportunities in buffer zone
Choluteca	Landlessness: sold land to cover debt incurred due to low yields	2: Coffee co-operative, cattle ranch wage labourer	1985	Maize, beans, corn, chickens, 2 cows (M)*
Choluteca	Landlessness: forcibly evicted by military	3: Palm plantation, cattle ranch, beer factory	1990	Maize, 4 pigs, 2 cows (M)
Choluteca	Landlessness: loss of communal area, previously landless	2: Co-operatives, construction crew	1994	Maize, chickens, 4 pigs (M)
Choluteca	Landlessness: evicted by municipality, no title	1: Banana plantation	1991	Maize, rice, chickens (M)
El Paraíso	Landlessness	2: Co-operatives	1980	Maize, beans, rice, tomatoes, bananas, chickens, 4 pigs (M)
Santa Bárbara	Landlessness: poor land, debt	1: Lived with relatives in Atlantida	1987	Wage labourer (M); General store, Silin (W)
Santa Bárbara	Landlessness	2: Palm plantation, coffee co-operative	1985	Maize, rice, chickens (M)
Santa Bárbara	Landlessness: sold land to cover debt	4: Banana co-operatives	1990	Chickens, 4 dairy cows (M)
Olancho	Landlessness: low yield, no employment; sold land to cattle rancher	None: Family in Tesorito	1985	Maize, rice, beans, chickens, 1 milk cow (M)

Olancho	Landlessness. No work available in Olancho	None: Came directly to Silin to work in shipyard	1995	Wage labourer, shipyard (M)
Olancho	Evicted by brother from family farm	1: Worked on hacienda in Olancho	1985	Owns Silin general store, grows bananas, tomatoes, corn (M/W) (wife helps in store)
Francisco Morazán	Landlessness: forcibly evicted by military	2: Co-operatives	1989	Maize, beans, rice, chickens (M)
Yoro	Landlessness: land stolen by neighbour due to lack of title	2: Co-operatives	1982	Works for hacienda, Silin (M)
La Paz	Landlessness: insufficient land access, low yields; sold land to cover debt	3: Co-operatives	1988	Works for hacienda, grows tomatoes, basil, and corn in yard (M)
Valle	Landlessness	2: Co-operatives	1997	Beer factory (M)
La Paz	Landlessness: evicted for no title by municipality	3: Co-operatives, Chiquita	1984	Maize, rice, 3 dairy cows, 3 pigs (M)
Lempira	Landlessness: no titles, evicted by military	1: Co-operative	1986	Maize, rice, 6 pigs (M)
Intibuca	Landlessness: small yields. Loss of wage labour opportunity used to supplement farm income.	2: Co-operatives	1987	Works for hacienda, grows corn in family yard, Silin (M)
Copán	Landlessness: lost family land due to gambling debt	2: Co-operatives	1986	Works for hacienda and beer factory, Silin (M)
Atlantida	Landlessness: land conflict, no titles	1: Palm plantation	1991	Rice, beans, chickens, 2 cows (M)

* M = Men; W = Women

degraded, particularly along the Río Silin, he maintains that "people need to adjust to changing times" (personal communication 2000). In 2000, Don Fredo was seeking credit from a local bank to assist him with his upcoming cocoa production. He was not alone: farmers in Tesorito also expressed a desire to incorporate this cash crop into their cultivation. During the time of my fieldwork, two other farmers were actively clearing forest for cocoa (field notes 2000). Unlike the campesinos in Tesorito, Don Fredo could rely on his store as collateral and his "good relations" with Don Francisco to receive both formal and informal credit for cocoa production.

Gender, Labour, and Natural Resources Access

Women experience differentiated access to natural resources in the buffer zone. Ethnicity and gender interweave to provide a unique insight into the availability of resources for women at the level of the household and the community. Although Pech women speak quite proudly of their domestic employment as "laundry women" in nearby Trujillo, they self-identify first as farmers. Pech women insist that they participate in both economic and domestic household decisions (Ana, Pech resident, personal communication 2000). Farming tasks are organized along gender lines: men clear and plough land, women plant and weed plots. Decisions about what and where to plant are often made by men, but women are more likely to travel to Trujillo to sell any surplus for much-needed money to purchase items such as salt, lard, batteries, school supplies, and matches. The entire family, children included, works in the field at harvest time (Lisa, Pech farmer, personal communication 2000).

Emphatically, natural resource access for the Pech relies greatly on ethnic identities. Customarily, in Honduras, individual lands are titled in the husband's name. In fact, it is only since 1992 that single women have had the right to title lands in their own names (República de Honduras 1992). For Pech women, communal titles allow exclusive rights to forest resources. That this provides significant protection for Pech women, as compared to non-indigenous women farmers, is suggested by Doña Austenia's story. Doña Austenia has lived in Silin since ladino ranchers recruited her and her husband to work on the Francisco family hacienda. Shortly after their arrival in 1930, Austenia and her husband began to work a parcel of forested land in Silin. They supported themselves with wage work on the hacienda and by farming and hunting in the forest. Sadly for Austenia, after a few "good" years, her husband took another woman into their home and Austenia and her children were forced to leave. Although Austenia remembers this as a difficult time, she maintains that she never worried about feeding her children: because she was a Pech, her community provided her with access to the forest (personal communication 2000).

Austenia's tenure security contrasts with that of many ladino women in the buffer zone. Ladino women in both Silin and Tesorito are commonly responsible for small gathering activities, and some manage home gardens (field notes 2000). Women insist that they "would like to work but [they] have too many children to care for" (mother in Tesorito, personal communication 2000). Yet studies show that Pech and ladino residents in the buffer zone have approximately the same numbers of children per family (FUCAGUA n.d.). Another resident complains that Tesorito is too far from potential work; but even if it were closer, there would be no one to watch her children while she was away (young woman in Tesorito, personal communication 2000). This lack of social/familial networks (social capital) is understandable, as many residents have come from various places. Unlike ladino women in Tesorito, Pech women can rely upon social networks and enlist grandmothers and older children to care for young children while they work in Trujillo.

Household and community activities of ladino women are largely shaped by the attitudes of their husbands. Farmers in Tesorito insist that working in the fields is inappropriate for women; in fact, they believe themselves superior to Pech men who "allow" their women to work in agriculture and outside the home (David, Tesorito farmer, personal communication 2000). Fernando, a ladino, jokes, "My wife knows little about farming; men work in the field ... we are farmers" (personal communication 2000). Income generation, especially from wage labour and the sale of livestock, is a male task among rural ladino men. Even in the wage labour families of Silin, women are primarily responsible for domestic duties in the home (Marie, homemaker, personal communication 2000). Of course, there are exceptions. Lela, the owner of the second-largest home-store in Silin, explains:

> The reason I have this store is that my husband will not let me work outside our home. When we met I was working; I have worked my whole life it seems. I came to Silin to work in the restaurant at the Columbus Hotel [largest hotel in Trujillo]. I lived with my uncle and made my own money. But then I married and my husband wanted me home. But then we realized we needed more money for our new child, so I opened this store. They do not pay my husband enough at the hacienda; I am happy that we have the store. (personal communication 2000)

Even though Lela has paid work, her husband controls her choice of livelihood. Most ladino women have little say in family decisions, apart from those concerning the care of their children (field notes 2000).

Gender, ethnicity, and resource access also interweave to differentiate Pech and ladino men. Available employment is often "informal" or "seasonal" at the nearby beer factory, shipyards, and surrounding haciendas (field notes 2000). However, most job opportunities fail to accommodate the numerous demands for work made by Silin's male population. According to the Catholic Church mission, ladino male unemployment is roughly 60 percent (church administrator, personal communication 2000). Although, officially, Pech unemployment rates are about the same, ethnic affiliation diminishes labour demands because Pech men and some women work during harvests for relatives in the nearby department of Olancho. For their work, they receive cash payments as well as payment in kind in the form of beans, coffee, corn, fruit, rice, and medicinal plants (Lucy, Pech farmer, personal communication 2000). In contrast, male ladino wage labourers in Silin report that when household income is low due to unemployment, they hunt iguana or cut mahogany for sale to the local elite, since both command a high price and "there is an abundance in the park" (construction worker, personal communication 2000).

Coping with Displacement

Narratives in Tesorito disclose how landlessness is gendered in the buffer zone. Although Tesorito men have managed to maintain extended access to land, Tesorito women are indeed landless. Gender roles dictate women's exclusion from farming activities, paid work, and household decision making. Although most couples, both Pech and ladino, are not legally married, the consequences of separation for women differ by ethnicity. Nevertheless, this affects each community differently. In Tesorito, a woman who separates from her husband would have little means to generate an income because "[women] are wives and mothers, not farmers" (mother in Tesirito, personal communication 2000). Honduran women with no claim to land generally have little influence in household economic decisions and are completely dependent on their spouses (Deere and Leon 2001). Despite recent agrarian reforms that grant individual women the right to own land, it seems unlikely that most women will benefit since men often control family farms and have traditionally been the beneficiaries of titling programs (ibid.; República de Honduras 1992). However, because Pech women are legally granted resource access by virtue of their ethnic identity, they enjoy more autonomy in household decision making. Such distinctions between indigenous and ladino women are common throughout the Central American countryside (Smith 1996).

Entanglements

At first glance, Pech communal tenure arrangements appear more secure than do individual holdings of Tesorito's farmers. Nevertheless, I have shown how campesino insecurities can undermine the integrity of indigenous resource access, despite its legalization, due to the manner in which campesinos cope with their own marginalization, displacement, and landlessness. I do not blame displaced campesinos for the tenure insecurities of indigenous people in Honduras. Rather, my objective has been to highlight how policies shaping natural resource access combine with stereotypes of small farmers and indigenous people to place campesinos and indigenous groups at odds over natural resources. Class bias in agrarian policy is in part responsible for campesino displacement. In addition, stereotypes of peasants as "destroyers" and indigenous people as "stewards" of the environment, which are rooted in institutional imaginations, leave campesinos and, hence, indigenous people vulnerable to further displacement.

In Honduras, negative labels associated with "migrant" populations are reproduced by the increasing phenomenon of small farmers who transform forest into cropland, convert it to pasture a few years later, sell it to wealthier farmers in the growing north coast dairy industry, and move on (Humphries 1998). Indeed, this forest-to-cropland-to-pasture conversion has become an attractive livelihood choice for some peasants in Latin America. Once fertility declines (usually after five years in rainforest regions) and employment opportunities remain scarce, converting cropland to pasture provides important capital to small producers (ibid.). However, Tesorito does not conform to this pattern. Many of its residents have lived in the village for over a decade, others for more than twenty years. Most significantly, their continued resistance to multiple threats of displacement clearly defies the campesino stereotypes of perpetual migrancy. Indeed, the case of Tesorito speaks to the heterogeneity of both the peasants themselves and their strategies for coping with the "double squeeze" of landlessness and unemployment (Loker 1996).

The criminalization of migrants in Capiro-Calentura is contingent not only upon their presence and land use in the buffer zone but also upon mutually essentialized notions regarding campesinos and indigenous people. Both are described as subsistence farmers, but there the similarities end. The Pech are commonly perceived as conducting their subsistence production with enormous respect for the environment, maintaining minimal ties to the market, and living in tranquil communities in which gift giving and reciprocity are norms (FUCAGUA n.d.). This image blends well with conservation agendas for sustainable land use. On the other hand, the label "migrant," employed in reference to Tesorito campesinos, implies instability; their subsistence practices, unlike those of the Pech, are called upon to define them as "unproductive" or "bad" farmers (FUCAGUA, personal communication 2000). Officials ignore the fact that subsistence production in Tesorito does not arise from a culture or way of life that is disinterested in economic productivity or profit. Indeed, Tesorito farmers are explicit that the market value of cattle and cocoa production is higher than that of corn and beans (Tesorito farmer, personal communication 2000). However, subsistence in

Tesorito, and in many similar rural villages in Honduras, is in part the result of marginalization from a market in which governments expect campesinos to regularly produce high-value products yet exclude them from the means of competition. This exclusion is evident in many of the following processes:

- the denial of land titles to campesinos with fewer than five hectares,
- the ineligibility of farmers for land titles if their lands fall within a protected area,
- the dissolution of sharecropping and land-leasing opportunities,
- the prohibition of land invasions,
- the eradication of minifundios, affecting 50 percent of the rural population,
- the state appropriation of land for the establishment of over one hundred protected areas in the last twenty years (Richards 1998),
- and the ineligibility for credit without land titles.

Subsistence farming holds little value for national governments, as "subsistence conjures up images of a ... universal level of livelihood which is an impediment to economic development" (Nietschmann 1973). At the national level, campesino subsistence is used to assign campesinos to "residual categories" (Loker 1996). Such a perspective is continually reproduced in policy that "implies that marginality is an elected way of life" (Li 2001: 161). This class bias, both explicitly and implicitly, shapes resource access for small producers. I refer to this bias as *campesino racialization,* building upon the insights of G. Dei (1996). Campesino racialization embeds itself within agrarian policy through an emphasis on export and capitalist bias in agricultural development. Campesinos become racialized because they are differentiated from indigenous people on the basis of characteristics constructed by NGO and state officials. When all campesinos are stereotyped as "migrants," this negative image informs a discourse that assumes all campesinos belong to a culture of instability and destruction. Such perceived cultural characteristics fuel Tesorito campesino illegitimacy in the park.

Another source of campesino racialization extends from state and NGO discourse concerning slash and burn, or swidden, farming techniques. There is little consensus regarding the harmful effects of "swidden agriculture" (COHDEFOR, personal communication 2000; FUCAGUA, personal communication 2000; Jansen 1998; Sundberg 1998). In fact, agricultura migratoria has long been considered an appropriate farming strategy in tropical environments (Sundberg 1998). Most of the opposition to swidden agriculture emerges from middle- and upper-class urbanites and non-farmers, as most intellectuals equate burning with deforestation and erosion; as a result, those who burn are considered "ignorant," "traditional," and "opposite" to all that is modern (Jansen 1998: 113). Consequently, conservation officials seek to "educate" farmers against burning. Perhaps they have succeeded. After continuous anti-burning campaigns in which swidden agriculturalists were painted as "primitive," the Pech differentiate themselves from campesinos in terms of the use of fire. Whether Pech farmers actually continue to burn their fields is unclear.[9] What is significant is how indigenous appropriation of NGO and state rhetoric and the adoption of labels have allowed Pech villagers to accommodate classifications as environmental "custodians" and "stewards" while simultaneously conservation discourse condemns agricultura migratoria and campesinos.

Seemingly, the essentialization of the Pech, based on qualities of "indigenousness," has enabled them to achieve better tenure security and garner an image of legitimacy not accorded to campesinos. That indigenous and tribal communities perhaps benefit from the internationalization of indigenous rights and from the widespread "migrants as destroyers of the environment" discourses is increasingly recognized (Neumann 1997). Indigenous people may evade migrant labels because their land claims as *originarios* [first peoples] and the law of first possession provide them with a political tool that other groups such as the campesinos, though perhaps equally marginalized, poor, and deserving, do not possess (Li 1996).

Yet, despite these apparent advantages, indigenous people's access to resources remains uncertain. Although they have achieved relative success in acquiring title to their ancestral lands, little enforcement exists to stop the influx of migrants from other parts of the country. Notwithstanding that the relationship between indigenous groups and the Honduran government is a contentious one at best, based on a history of neglect and persecution, ignoring the impoverishment and displacement of campesinos in their areas of origin is troubling. Equally troubling is the fact that indigenous people are given little support to protect their lands from this encroachment. Even when indigenous groups possess formal village land titles, these titles do little to deter campesinos from appropriating or destroying resources within these territories. I emphasize that researchers, advocates, and planners who are concerned with protecting indigenous territories cannot separate indigenous interests from those of the displaced campesinos who also demand a sustainable resource base and cultural survival. Campesino land access potentially affects the tenure security of indigenous people because these heterogeneous collectives compete for the very few resources not yet acquired by the state and the national elite. Until campesino tenure is secured, indigenous resource tenure remains in peril.

Final Thoughts

Increased tensions regarding land on the north coast are so severe that even terratenientes are forced to be cautious. Between 1995 and 2000, the ranches surrounding the buffer zone communities were completely fenced to deter squatters from expropriating lands in the future. Indeed, the entanglement of agrarian and conservation policies has created dire circumstances for campesino and indigenous tenure arrangements. Class bias is inherent in Honduran agrarian policy; conservation discourse in the buffer zone stereotypes communities, creating campesino and Pech dichotomies. Furthermore, processes of campesino racialization are facilitated through discourses that malign campesinos and praise indigenous people, despite their similar class positions. Although ethnicity shapes land tenure perceptions, both Pech and ladino land tenure histories exhibit vulnerabilities. Significantly, I am struck by what remains unsaid in discursive land struggles on the Honduran coast: as campesinos and indigenous people cope with land insecurities and deforestation within Capiro-Calentura National Park, the large cattle ranches that line its borders continue to expand.

Notes

1 In Honduras, the term *ladino* is used synonymously with *mestizos* and refers to those individuals who share a dual ancestry of indigenous and European origins. However individuals who identify as ladino see themselves as non-indigenous, Spanish speaking citizens. *Campesino* is Spanish for small farmer, small producer, and peasant. In this chapter, all campesinos are ethnically ladino.

2 In fact, in 2000, over 5,000 campesinos, spurred by promises of land that were made by the National Agrarian Institute, invaded the north coast and settled within a mile of Capiro-Calentura over a period of two weeks (field notes 2000).

3 In this discussion, "displacement," when applied to campesinos, refers specifically to their declining access to land and thereby livelihoods, though displacement occurs in numerous ways. Campesino displacement (landlessness) is directly linked to state policies and institutional representations that marginalize campesinos in rural areas.

4 *Ejidos* are municipal lands that are given to residents of a municipality for use only, not for sale.

5 *Dominio pleno* is an ownership right that includes the right to sell land. *Dominio útil* confers only the right to use a resource.

6 Many rural people have customarily occupied lands to which they have no formal title.

7 This amendment has been passed but not made into law. It has resulted in much controversy, as well as protests by indigenous people, and has essentially been shelved.

8 *Persona jurídica* refers to the incorporation of a group, community, and/or organization sanctioned by the state. It is required before a community may legally title community lands.

9 Initially, many Pech to whom I spoke denied that they burned; eventually, however, most did admit to the practice, though adding "not like ladinos."

References

Aceituno, A. 1994. "Honduran Law Faces Obstacles: New Law in Honduras Designed to Slow Deforestation, Must Overcome Corruption and Tradition." Tropical Conservation Newsbureau. http://www.native-net.org/archive/nl/9407/0109.html.

Baumeister, E., and Cor J. Wattel. 1996. "Una reinterpretación de la estructura agraria y agropecuaria de Honduras." In E. Baumeister, Cor J. Wattel, R. Salgado, M. Posas, D. Kaimowitz, and L. Clercx, eds., *El agro hondureño y su futuro,* 15-53. Tegucigalpa: Editorial Guaymuras y el Centro de estudios para el desarrollo rural.

Blaikie, P., and Harold Brookfield. 1987. *Land Degradation and Society.* London: Routledge.

Booth J., and T. Walker. 1989. *Understanding Central America*. Boulder: Westview Press.

Bryant, R. 1998. "Power, Knowledge and Political Ecology in the Third World: A Review." *Progress in Physical Geography* 22 (1): 79-94.

Cernea, M. 2000. "Risks, Safeguards, and Reconstruction: A Model for Population Displacement and Resettlement." In M. Cernea and C. McDowell, eds., *Risks and Reconstruction: Experiences of Resettlers and Refugees*, 11-55. Washington, DC: World Bank.

Deere, C.D., and M. Leon. 2001. "Who Owns the Land? Gender and Land Titling Programmes in Latin America." *Journal of Agrarian Change* 1 (3): 440-67.

Dei, G. 1996. *Theory and Practice: Anti-Racism Education*. Halifax: Fernwood Publishing.

El Tiempo. 2004. "Las mesas agrícolas quedaron en papel mojado: COCOCH." 17 April, 4.

Eriksson, P. 2000. "Territorial Conflicts in the Northern Atlantic Coast of Nicaragua: Indigenous Peoples' Struggles over Resources and Representations." *Fennia* 178 (2): 215-25.

FUCAGUA. N.d. "Capiro/Calentura. Diagnóstico de la Comunidades – Silin y Tesorito." Trujillo.

Griffin, W. 2000. "North Coast Parks Threatened by Fires, Logging." *Honduras This Week*. http://www.marrder.com/htw/special /environment/76.htm.

Humphries, Sally. 1998. "Milk Cows, Migrants, and Land Markets: Unraveling the Complexities of Forest-to-Pasture Conversion in Northern Honduras." *Economic Development and Cultural Change* 47 (1): 95-124.

IHAH-PNUD. 1995. "Diagnóstico de las comunidades Pech de Honduras. Programa integral de protección ecológica y rescate de la herencia cultural HON/92/024/A/12/92."

INA (Instituto Nacional Agraria). 1995. *Manual del proceso de titulación de tierras*. Tegucigalpa: Programa de Titulación de Tierras.

International Bank for Development and Reconstruction (IBDR). 2006. "Honduras Country Brief." http://www.worldbank.org/hn (accessed 10 February 2006).

International Labor Organization (INA). 1989. "Convention Concerning Indigenous and Tribal Peoples in Independent Countries (ILO, no.169)." http://www1.umn.edu/humanrts/instree/r1citp.html (accessed 8 January 2006).

Jansen K. 1998. *Political Ecology, Mountain Agriculture, and Knowledge in Honduras*. Amsterdam: Thela Publishers.

Li, T.M. 1996. "Images of Community: Discourse and Strategy in Property Relations." *Development and Change* 27: 501-27.

–. 2001. "Boundary Work: Community, Market and State Reconsidered." In Arun Agrawal and Clark Gibson, eds., *Communities and the Environment: Ethnicity, Gender and the State in Community-Based Conservation*, 157-80. Piscataway: Rutgers University Press.

Loker, W. 1996. "'Campesinos' and the Crisis of Modernization in Latin America." *Journal of Political Ecology* 3: 69-88.

Marín, R. 1998. "El artículo 107." *La Prensa*, 9 October, 10a.

Martinez, M. 2003. "Reporte Preliminar: Análisis de las oportunidades y limitaciones de las comunidades indígenas y organizaciones comunitarias en la gestión de comanejo de las áreas protegidas en Honduras." Tegucigalpa: World Bank.

Neumann, R. 1997. "Primitive Ideas: Protected Area Buffer Zones and the Politics of Land in Africa." *Development and Change* 28: 559-82.

Nietschmann, B. 1973. *Between Land and Water: The Subsistence Ecology of the Miskito Indians, Eastern Nicaragua*. New York: Seminar Press.

ODECO (Organización de desarrollo Étnico Comunitario). 1999. "12 de Abril día de la etnia negra de Honduras." *El Tiempo*, 12 April, 56.

Organización Internacional del Trabajo (OIT). 1989. *Convenio No. 169 sobre pueblos indígenas y tribales, 1989*. 4th ed. San Jose: OIT.

Peet, R., and M. Watts. 1996. *Liberation Ecologies: Environment, Development, Social Movement*. London: Routledge.

Peluso, N. 1992. *Rich Forests, Poor People: Resource Control and Resistance in Java*. Berkeley: University of California Press.

República de Honduras. 1975. *Ley de reforma agraria*. Decreto-Ley No. 170, 1974. La Gaceta nr.21482, 08-01-1975, Tegucigalpa: MDC.

–. 1992. *Ley para la modernización y el desarrollo del sector agrícola*. Tegucigalpa: MDC.

Richards, M. 1998. *Protected Areas, People and Incentives: The Search for Sustainable Forest Conservation in Honduras*. London: Overseas Development Institute. http://members.tripod.com/d_parent/michaelr.html.

Rocheleau, D., B. Thomas-Slayter, and E. Wangari. 1996. "Gender and Environment: A Feminist Political Ecology Perspective." In D. Rocheleau, B. Thomas-Slayter, and E. Wangari, eds., *Feminist Political Ecology: Global Issues and Local Experiences*, 3-23. London: Routledge.

Smith, C. 1996. "Race/Class/Gender Ideology in Guatemala, Modern and Anti-Modern Forms." In Brackette Williams, ed., *Women Out of Place: The Gender of Agency and the Race of Nationality*. London: Routledge.

Stonich, S. 1993. *"I Am Destroying the Land!" The Political Ecology of Poverty and Environmental Destruction in Honduras*. Boulder: Westview Press.

Sundberg, J. 1998. "NGO Landscapes in the Maya Biosphere Reserve, Guatemala." *Geographical Review* 88 (3): 388-412.

Vandergeest, P. 1996. "Mapping Nature: Territorialization of Forest Rights in Thailand." *Society and Natural Resources* 9 (4): 159-75.

Conclusion

Peter Vandergeest, Pablo Idahosa, and Pablo S. Bose

> Development has always been an ambiguous idea, on the one hand being virtually synonymous with "progress" and on the other referring to intentional efforts to ameliorate the disordered faults of progress.
>
> – Cowen and Shenton (1996: 7)

> If one aims at overcoming modernity, it becomes necessary to deny the denial of the myth of modernity from an ethics of responsibility.
>
> – Dussel (2000: 473)

Within the diverse sites represented in this book, contemporary development remains open to numerous contestations concerning its practices and its norms. As we noted in the Introduction, development can be viewed as a historically inscribed program of progressive intent with both destructive and constructive ends. In some measure, the EDID project was undertaken to portray the complex nature of one facet of this destruction and attempted renewal – various policies responsible for population displacement carried out in the name of development. As evidenced throughout this book, DID seems ubiquitous: it is enacted by national development institutions and multilateral, regional, and bilateral institutions, as well as by private corporations, and against the backdrop of neoliberal economic policies. In the case illustrations assembled here, across differing cultural circumstances and within various political environments, displacement, whether intended or unintended, direct or indirect, has emerged as a significant component of contemporary development practice. Not surprisingly, there is an overlap between the language and practice of development as such, the justifications for and alleviation of displacement sought in DID resettlement programs, and the criticisms of both found in this book and elsewhere. Yet, equally apparent here is a thread of ambivalence and uncertainty regarding development's displacements, about whether displacement is, or, in fact, need be, inherent to development.

A recent practical policy instance of the compounded elisions between development and DID, and one addressed throughout the book, is the resurfacing of attention to poverty, risk, and vulnerability in both social policy and development circles. The refocus on poverty and vulnerability has occurred, in part, because of challenges to the perceived impact of policies and the role that multilateral institutions have played in the furtherance of an impoverishing globalization. Demands for greater protection from the forces of the market, concerns about growing poverty, social exclusion, inequality, and especially violence visited upon the subjects of development, and questions regarding the prerogative of global governance to restructure relationships between citizens and the state, are all part of a wider shift in development theory and practice (see Norton 2000; Kanbur 2001; Mandle 2003). Many contributions to this volume have made it clear that to the extent DID appears as symptomatic of globalization, it has also been challenged by various constituencies, from development activists to the subjects in whose name development is often invoked but who have borne the bulk of its costs. DID has, perforce, been caught up in the shifting personality of development theory and practice, but it is also part of development's own recent ambiguous reflection and critical self-image.

Much of that criticism, of course, has been levelled at the World Bank. Primarily responsible for the institutional policy shift (see World Bank 2001), the bank also envisaged and supported the idea of displacee resettlement as "a development program"; here, mitigation would be the minimal threshold through which to determine whether acceptable development had taken place. Despite subsequent refinements to the resettlement model, what remains crucial in assessing the efficacy of this "development" is whether there are, to use Michael Cernea's words, "sufficient opportunities to assist resettlers in their efforts to improve their former living standards and capacity *or at least to restore them*" (Cernea 1993: 19-20, emphasis added). Models of development-induced displacement and resettlement (DIDR), such as Cernea's RRMRDP (Risks and Reconstruction Model for Resettling Displaced Populations), seek to *mitigate* displacement through resettlement and have become templates for, as it were, the governance of good inducement. As Dolores Koenig (2002: 13) notes, however, "the most important gap in the literature is lack of explicit consideration of the meaning of development in the context of DIDR." Even when bank guidelines continue to stipulate that DID programs should be approved and executed as "development projects," they fail to provide criteria by which a project might be understood as development.

To somewhat abridge a discussion we cannot elaborate on here, DID's development ambiguities reflect the uncertainty of what development itself stands for, but with which, in a circular way, DID itself has increasingly been identified. In sum, development is what *developers* say they do (see Thomas 2001; Harrison 2004), whether they are governments, NGOs, corporations, or various agencies. This is all consonant, within development's current vocabulary, with the various proposals that seek to mitigate the effects of projects of development intent. When accompanied by some tangible Sen-like[1] improvement in people's lives, much of "official" development has become everything from "pro-growth" adjustment programs to poverty reduction and sustainable livelihoods. However, for many who are dissatisfied with the growth, minimalist, or palliative views of development, there have been attempts to see development as being inclusive of *rights to* development. We have suggested that the latter is more or less the evaluative default position of many of the contributors here, and we shall return to this below.

Much of the research in this book has led to questioning not only whether "all displacement-inducing activities [are] necessarily 'development'" (Koenig 2002: 13) but also to whether even good inducements are development at all. Both of these questions are linked to another key absence in the overlap between development and DID: the lack of a politics that could take account of inducement, coercion, and violence. We would, thus, also claim that a requirement for understanding DID lies in centring discussions of *power* and the *political*. As Koenig says (2002: 3), "the first step in 'doing resettlement as development' is to define development to take into account the distribution of power as well as resources. Existing approaches tend to concentrate on economic and social aspects of resettlement, overlooking the distribution of societal power and ignoring crucial conflicts of interest among different stakeholders."[2]

The EDID project's diversity of findings is tied to the importance of micro politics. The case studies show that local states and local politics, as well as their embedded socio-cultural practices, do matter. First, and obviously, DID's assorted outcomes are achieved through the local conditions under which displacement occurs. They contain the historical, legal, and culturally layered conduits upon and through which identities are reconstituted, resources are expropriated, accumulation is extended, *and* the policies mobilized to further them are often resisted. In Chapter 3's comparative study of Malaysia and Thailand, for example, Keith Barney demonstrates not just that these reconfigurations take place through a global, hegemonic reach of long commodity chains for lumber but also that they require the particularities of local and national states to permit different levels of responses, even dissent, from local displacees, however constrained they might be. However, his narrative thread, one consistent with any storyline of development, particularly in an age of globalization, reoccurs throughout this book. It is that these locales cease to be local when their rearranged social relations, institutions, and resources are penetrated and imposed upon by regional and global demands.[3] By definition, development's intent and outreach have always been about being beyond the local (though they always work through it); increasingly, however, global forces have moved the loci of determination further away. Like development in general, they also are often disruptive of the local, and frequently indifferent to its consequences. That said, the indifference, as Chapters 5 and 7 show, though in differing ways, has more do with local state power than with a distant globalizing development's lack of concern or commitment. Conversely, as others have demonstrated, it also has to do with the capacity and willingness of those who resist. States and agents matter; displacement need not be necessary.

Yet, the burden of resisting displacement imperatives has proven difficult, especially in particular regulatory environments, or where strategic considerations are crucial. Does the pervasive policy environment of neoliberalism account for the range of displacements found within these pages? And do these case studies provide direct evidence of uniformly hegemonic causative consequences in displacement? Are these effects even more removed when the impact of indirect displacement is initiated by states that enact neoliberal reforms, as in the Central American case studies? Does this also hold true where a broader, less directly visible relationship exists between neoliberalism and the development project in question, as is the case in some chapters that show private capital playing a significant role?

Like any programmatic policy, neoliberalism provokes and effects unintended, even contradictory, outcomes. At every level of scale, it opens up political spaces hitherto preserved for the powerful and upon which they mapped themselves and their interests in the name of economic growth or the national or public interest. Some of this opening up has, at times, allowed for a remapping of political landscapes that have had to reluctantly acknowledge, even tolerate, less powerful but more emboldened representations that seek to have their voices heard and their sense of interests as entitlement acted upon. Another side of globalization and its neoliberal personification encompasses, after all, the universal, though often opaque and compromised, demands for transparency, good and efficacious governance, and forms of participation in development (Harrison 2004).

These emergent developmental norms, coupled with the turn to the local and increasing emphasis upon validating and utilizing the resources of local cultures and institutions, have supported a claiming of entitlements to which both activists and subjects of development have drawn attention, not just at the national but also at the global and institutional levels. In principle, these development values and programmatic criteria have often forced those making development policies to respond more accountably to the needs of those whom reforms are meant to benefit. This is in evidence whether these policies are assigned towards, for example, privatization or individualized land titling, indigenous resource use, or the environmentally and ecologically sensitive and protected areas of national parks. These are norms that have sometimes also allowed for less top-down development stakeholding, have appeared to increase the participatory dispositions of local states, and have somewhat allowed for degrees of transparency of process that would not otherwise have existed and that can hold states accountable to the people being displaced.

The backdrop and reconfiguring of neoliberalism, nonetheless, looms large in nearly all of these studies. Its prescriptive and institutional presence, and the scope of its financial authority,[4] provides much of the incidence of the displacements studied, and it makes a context of development that provides, albeit sometimes indirectly, for many of the justifications for DID, direct or indirect. Conservation and the need for national parks are not so much ends in themselves as links to deregulated policy environments joined to various forms of privatization and the need to establish newer niches in globally more competitive sustainable development tourism markets. If there is extensive variation across the different kinds of displacement, even in the case of the indirect forms, there is also evidence that, in neoliberal environments and in a world of *realpolitik,* a convergence of accommodations takes place. As established in Chapters 1 and 3, accountability, for example, can be narrowly accommodated in politico-legal cul-de-sacs, or, as is shown in Chapter 5, local forms of moral-legal codes can be reshaped by liberal reforms. Here, the residential beneficiaries are often the powerful local, national, transnational, and multilateral coalitions whose interests can thwart displacees' aspirations and grievances. Likewise, Chapter 7 reveals that powerful politico-economic alliances can retain the ultimate displacing sanction, despite indefatigable activist and displacee efforts to seek redress through all stages of judicial and political review and notwithstanding the fact that the plight of the displacees has been brought to global attention.

In different ways, this global reach and strategic attention (or inattention) can also reinforce the power and importance of particular resources or locales, as is shown in the Chapters 2 and 6 case studies of Sudan and Colombia. In the former, the struggles and achievements of marginalized, displaced communities have given rise to alternative forms of gender empowerment; in the latter, they have produced alternative conceptions of development. In both instances, these attainments have occurred under conditions of tremendous duress. Politically constrained and violently purged from their livelihoods, these communities have little recourse to the resources that political liberalization is supposed to open up. Rather, their cases are situated at the extreme end of an uneven and unequal process in which people in displacee communities confront forms of extractive power linked to global-strategic considerations. Invoking an ideological tenacity *not* to relinquish resources in Sudan, while appealing to national integrity against the indifference or failure of the international community, or, in the case of Colombia, citing security and strategic necessity under the watchful eye of a global power, can allow "development's" self-serving spokespersons to claim that displacement is for the greater good. To all of those similarly displaced, even where new forms of politics have been generated, transparency, accountability, and political openings, or opportunities to create alternative development vistas, will probably seem small consolation, given the violence they have endured and/or the losses they have suffered.

Although they focus on diverse locales and forms of direct and indirect displacement, these chapters, as well as Chapters 8 and 9, show that DID doesn't just remove people from their livelihoods: it removes them from their sense of place and from their identity and, in some instances, from their sense of worth. It is equally clear that the status of the displacees has a great deal to do not just with local power but with their identity: historically, all the communities in these case studies consist of marginalized and vulnerable minorities – "tribals," indigenous groups, Afro-descendants, minority women, and so on. In reconfiguring relationships of power and resources within communities, displacement does not always work to the detriment of those with less power, such as women and youth. Obviously, caution is required when homogenizing communities or when invoking simple notions of consensus around the retention of existing cultural norms and practices. Although focusing on very different locales, both El Jack's discussion of Nuer women in refugee camps and Murray's analysis of Afro-descendants displaced from Costa Rican parks point to the uneven benefits for gender and intergenerational displacement respectively. There is a need to acknowledge the multiple forms of differentiation within (and across) communities, especially where gender and age are concerned. One can certainly conceive of circumstances in DID in which changes in the social relations between men and women, and between older men and younger members of communities, result in gains in greater autonomy that generate more opportunities for many outside the traditional locus of decision-making power. Nevertheless, this often occurs by happenstance and default, not by design.

Irrespective of scale, then, all of the contributions point to the inherency of unequal political processes in DID, to the ways in which development constituencies, actors, and institutions contest and seek to shape development intentions and outcomes, and to how those outcomes are likely to be extremely unequal. DIDR is a practical normative template of good inducement in the face of criticism about DID. Like all current models of development, it has to defend the norms that guide and inform its practices. To a degree, it has to be legitimated to those in whose name development is said to occur, and to those who might criticize development practice on their behalf – activists, practitioners, and academics. Where DIDR is often found wanting is in its inability to sufficiently address the many dimensions of politics and power that constrain the likelihood of alternatives, or in its failure to satisfactorily confront areas such as violence and gender that should be central to any normative appraisal of power and any understanding of how DID works or claims to work. This may be seen in the work of Michael Cernea (1993, 1996, 2000): his understanding of social disarticulation does acknowledge the uneven consequences of power over resources; nonetheless, when mitigation is to be provided through compensation, as he advocates, the fact that resettlement programs focus on economic aspects of resettlement to the detriment of the political augurs poorly for their eventual outcome.

The relatively recent emergence of development ethics and the growing interest in human rights conventions have forced onto the development agenda questions about the meaning we give to the norms and ends of development – of human well-being, of social "improvement," and the quality of life. Increasingly, these critiques also raise questions that acknowledge the importance and the specificity of culture, which, while valorizing the local, also query and deconstruct its significance (see Gasper 2000: 231; Goulet 2000). Ultimately, all the contributors to this book show at work various examples of a world of *realdevelopmentpolitik* and might be more or less agnostic about displacement as such. In appraising the content of development politically, most contributors appear to support, whether broadly or tacitly, some variation of the right to development (RTD), even though Chapter 1 is equally critical of some aspects of individualizing neoliberalism. A core ingredient of RTD is now "asking people to take their own decisions rather than being the passive object of choices made on their behalf" (Department for International Development, quoted in Piron 2002: 38). Such agencies now characterize "development not solely in terms of economic growth, but as a comprehensive and multi-faceted process, with social, cultural, political as well as economic elements" (Piron 2002: 10), together with protocols against gender discrimination in which "the right of women to participate, and the duty of the state to ensure their participation, is emphasized" (ibid.).

Open to numerous interpretations, RTD is not without its own ambiguities. Used for very different ends by different development agencies and agents, such as NGOS, it has been employed as an enabling programmatic tool for children's access to primary goods, conditionality around participation and the diminution of social exclusion, and as a rhetorical device depoliticizing and minimizing rights talk in development by linking it to tradable economic "rights" (see Piron 2002; Cornwall and Nyamu-Musembi

2004). We are aware that "a rights-based approach would mean little if it has no potential to achieve a positive transformation of power relations among development actors" (Cornwall and Nyamu-Musembi 2004: 1432). We also recognize that, except in a rhetorical sense, RTD may have little salience in circumstances of extreme violence and dispossession, such as in the cases of Sudan and Columbia, where displacement is violently direct (or directly violent). Similarly, as Chapter 7's poignant case of Narmada demonstrates, RTD appears ineffective when, confronted by independent power, the hope of mitigation evaporates. As we have also seen, little leverage can be placed upon a powerful local state which, aided by dominant local classes and a financially supportive diaspora, has resources to avoid obligations of genuinely compensatory mitigation and is able to restrict levels of participation that would give displacees an authentic voice in decision making.

Nevertheless, like the models of DIDR, it can be used as a guide for assessing projects of development. As we suggested, RTD's utility lies in its focus upon power and social relations; and, through recognizing that development is also a *political* enterprise, RTD makes the politics of appraising DID more explicit. It also normatively sharpens the central critique about the absence or undeveloped nature of politics in DID and DIDR. In general, so evident is the powerlessness of displacees in circumstances of involuntary displacement that even by the minimum standards of RTD, true mitigation is unlikely. Not only are they unequally located to take advantage of any development opportunities arising from displacement but the severing of ties between the historical locations and local forms of power and control over resources always tends to result in a rapid diminishing of their capacity to control "the reproduction of their own institutions. Involuntary resettlement by its very nature disrupts control" (Koenig 2002: 14) and, by definition, community.

What other meaning could be given to mitigation? Is it possible that there can *never* be mitigation? What would constitute a successful mitigation or, to put it differently and paradoxically, has DID in fact occurred if it is mitigated? With respect to the latter question, one cannot have it both ways: either displacement in the sense of a physical relocation has taken place, or it hasn't. There can be an analytical elision here between the physical sense of displacement and the psychically normative dimensions of removal and loss of location. Both forms can also appear in ordinary voluntary "push and pull" migration, where, however constrained, choices define whether people are voluntary migrants or displacees. If, according to the displacees, satisfactory mitigation takes place, that might appear sufficient. Here too, however, there could be problems. Even under circumstances of voluntary resettlement with "willing" participants, and even where successful mitigation appears to have taken place, other questions still need to be addressed. We cannot rehearse all of them in detail here,[5] but one important set of issues concerns how the choices made under varying conditions of power, powerlessness, and duress are therefore ethically constrained and compromised. For example, Chapter 1 shows clearly that liberal legal regimes have an entrenched historical architecture of policy prescriptions that trade upon local people's ignorance of the legislative directives and legal procedures that are supposed to benefit them. More fundamentally, these regimes recognize individual and corporate rights only. And, as regards the practice of appointing exogenous experts as representatives, one can hardly talk about organic intellectuals who speak to and for the interests of the displaced. Thus, certain questions need constantly to be reviewed to determine the conditions in which the voluntary decisions were made: Were deceit and fear of victimization absent? Were there adequate awareness and the ability for all to reject *and* renegotiate the terms of compensation (see Gasper 2000: 1065-66)? On the evidence of most of the essays presented here, even in those instances where some participation and consultation did take place, many of these conditions did not exist.

Thus, although the analytical distinction between voluntariness and involuntariness needs to be maintained, there are surely conceptual slippages between the two that could preclude an analysis of the background conditions for choice. In sum, the issue here is not one of simple voluntary versus involuntary movement. What needs to be understood is the *context* for choice, which can be restrictive. RTD offers a means of understanding how choices or decisions can be made under an accumulated regime of power and law. Further, what kind of representation and participation in decision making would be sufficient to claim that mitigation had taken place? As it is unclear in some instances *who* gets to define and measure mitigation in many communities where DID occurs, and in light of the issue of difference and conflict within communities, we need to know who gets to participate, which members of the community get to decide what is legitimate decision making around the success and failure of projects.

Such queries are tied to other, perhaps even more fundamentally ethical questions – of the need to interrogate the nature of the incentives (or inducements) that encourage "voluntary" displacees to move. Incentives run the gamut of forms of interests and power. They may compel, bribe, or seduce, but all are set along a spectrum of ways through which people can be brought to do as one wishes. An incentive is, as Ruth W. Grant (2002: 138-39) has so persuasively suggested, a "relation that, along with persuasion and coercion in their various forms, [is] a member of the set of ways in which power and influence are exercised – that is, as a form of control, rather than simply as an alternative to it."

These questions may appear to constitute an ethical highground from which to judge DID, but they are the necessary, and minimal, tools through which to measure the claims of those who would speak on behalf of persons whom they allege will benefit from DID. Before one talks of mitigation, then, one must show greater transparency concerning the circumstances in which voluntary decisions to migrate were induced. Indeed, in posing matters in this way, we can see that the language of DID as inducement could be euphemistic pragmatism masking where a structure of power resides and determines an unclear practical ethics that elides complex questions about the nature of choice.

Some might agree with Cernea's (2000) assertion that risks come with all development. One could also recognize that mitigation could take place and acknowledge the possibility of genuine future benefits if all DIDR criteria were in place. There are some who see DIDR, with its continual targeting of best practices, as nonetheless consonant with the interests of the powerful. For others, no criterion is enough: for them, the problems lie deep in the structure of modernity and development itself, where development represents pathological forms of power that are, in effect, impossible to mitigate. A deeply historical phenomenon, DID is also a modern one. More abstract than development, modernity is nevertheless nearby in the everydayness of development's consequences to displacees; modernity is rendered real and concrete through its connection to the ideologies and institutional practices of development. At this end of the critical spectrum is the view that the overdetermining structures of development are built upon reorganizing societies and cultures for expropriation and through violence (Kothari and Harcourt 2004). This is not simply a matter of a social contract breaking down around development values because of conflict and violence (Murshed 2002). Rather, development and violence go together. In this rendering (Escobar 2004), DID is a symptom of modernity; it is essentially about development within the sites of local communities in the name of a capitalist development to which national, global, and nakedly imperial interests are increasingly tied, and to which development agencies, corporations, and, in some instances, NGOs, are parties. Mitigation appears irrelevant, since what is destroyed cannot be replaced or compensated.

Of the contributors, only Gruner, understandably influenced by Arturo Escobar, holds to such a view of DID. Envisioning alternatives may appear a fruitless venture in light of such violent displacing. Yet, notwithstanding the apparent constriction of local initiatives under these conditions, such critical accounts of displacement nevertheless suggest the need for a genuinely constructive moral commitment to acknowledging local initiatives. Such populist initiatives are examples of constantly resistive and reconfiguring attempts at projecting different understandings of modernity, and therefore alternative development possibilities, even under conditions of globally supported local violence. Within the distinction between *modernism* as a particular local stance towards history, a stance that is not without desire to modernize and bring things up to date, and *modernity,* the wider cultural and political discussion in which modernists play a role, a space opens up for local actor initiatives to specify development paths that are to be taken.[6] Such compromise with the violence of development certainly envisages a discussion *of* development. One such understanding is *the right to say no* to projects instigated by people who invoke the utilitarian modernist heritage of the state's development projects.

Concluding Remarks

Until recently, DID was taken for granted and executed in the name of a development improvement. Seeking to move people towards the justificatory utilitarian horizons of development improvement is, however, no longer a sufficiently acceptable ethical calculus. Actions can no longer be considered right just because they tend to promote modernity or the "national" interest, or because they promote growth alone. It is not only that the horizons of developmental well-being appear to many of their intended beneficiaries to be no closer: it is also that the site and scale of development practice have changed so much from the national to the local. Therefore, the utilitarian use of the language of development can often be conceptually, morally, and practically counterproductive, since development has also become identified not only with displacement but also with fragmentation and the destruction of livelihoods, ways of life, and senses of place. This book reflects not a negative skepticism towards DID but a critical engagement with it, and not only with DID but also with development and who defines it.

Nonetheless, within several of its chapters, we find consistent misgivings concerning the outcomes of DID and, particularly, with how DID as development redistributed resources and therefore power. DIDR's unequal distributional outcomes of power and resources are often characterized as from unacceptable to *unnecessary* disruptions of the lives and livelihoods of many of those who find themselves displaced. Development need not involve displacements. A second and related tension lies in finding a practical-normative standpoint from which to evaluate DID while, simultaneously, remaining aware that this broader standpoint might generate problems that demand further enquiry. We can, however, identify one line of normative expectation and questioning that at least sheds light on many of the unstated moral claims involved in forestalling DID or its amelioration. The thrust of many contributors in this collection, like that of many NGO activists, transnational movements, and academic commentators, is that many of the displaced no longer wish to be accounted for by the voices of development's advocates. Instead, they suggest listening to alternative voices of authority rather than accepting as a given the necessity of displacement. They do so not to avoid complex questions about hard choices or realizable alternatives to the outcomes promoted by proponents of DID and DIDR. Nor do they ignore many other contradictory outcomes that characterize DID. Rather, they wish to bring attention to the voices that so much of the history of DID has silenced, but for whom a responsible ethics and a set of adequate practices have yet to be achieved. As it stands, however, this collection is a statement regarding the unfulfilled promises and gaps in the practices of mitigation, because DID, like development and modernity and the criteria by which we assess them, will remain a contested notion and practice.

Notes

1 Some confusion also arises from the compounding of means, or instruments, with ends (see Goulet 2000). An example is Amartya Sen's (1999: 38-40) influential account in which development projects per se are perceived as increasing the capabilities and freedom of individuals to achieve various lifestyles, and in which development as a whole is presented as the freedom to further human progress.

2 When depicting the relative equivalencies of claims, the language of stakeholding euphemizes development power. Although Koenig does recognize power differentials, stakeholder analysis does not appear to be an especially useful tool if it cannot address those pathological forms of displacement that are explicitly tied to political violence.

3 As many of the case studies make clear, it is not that the historical utilization and/or expropriation of "local" resources were without regional reach. Rather, as per "national" development and globalization, the many ways in which resources are now expropriated are also claimed to benefit those in whose name they occur.

4 As should be clear from the case studies and the tenor of our Introduction, we believe that the principal agents and structures in displacement are states, multilateral and regional agencies, corporations, and powerful local classes. By dint of their power and financial ubiquity, they dwarf other actors. Increasingly, however, the issue is how other actors become key players in, and indeed even legitimators of, institutional development practices. In many instances, NGOs no longer play a neutral role; and sometimes the line between advocacy and self-interest is thin, where all manner of groups try to entrench themselves as interested stakeholders (see Idahosa 2002).

5 One question concerns how the point at which mitigation occurs is to be determined and how much time may be permitted to elapse before it does. What timeframes are to be used in assessing whether the disarticulations of DID have been eliminated? Although there is no easy answer to this, it is clear that different constituencies and their advocates have competing senses of what is an appropriate length of time: states and agencies focus on the medium term; activists stress both the short and the long term because the impoverishing effects of displacement will probably be immediate and because there is a need for certainty regarding appropriate resource and environmental use in the locations where displacement and development occur (see Kanbur 2001: 9-10).

6 As Marshall Berman (1982: 15-16, emphasis added) put it, "To be modern ... is to experience personal and social life in a maelstrom, to find one's world in perpetual disintegration and renewal, trouble and anguish, ambiguity and contradiction: to be part of a universe in which all that is solid melts in air. To be a modernist is to make oneself somehow at home in the maelstrom, to make its rhythms one's own, to move within its currents in search of the forms of reality, of beauty, of freedom, of justice ... *to be a modernist is to grasp and confront the world that modernization makes, and strive to make it our own.*"

References

Berman, Marshall. 1982. *All That Is Solid Melts into Air: The Experience of Modernity.* New York: Penguin Books.

Cernea, M. 1993. "Anthropological and Sociological Research for Policy Development on Population Resettlement." In Michael M. Cernea and Scott Guggenheim, eds., *Anthropological Approaches to Resettlement: Policy, Practice, and Theory,* 14-38. Boulder: Westview Press.

–. 1996. "Understanding and Preventing Impoverishment from Displacement: Reflections on the State of Knowledge." In Christopher McDowell, ed., *Understanding Impoverishment: The Consequences of Development Induced Displacement,* 13-32. Oxford: Berghahn Books.

–. 2000. "Risks, Safeguards, and Reconstruction: A Model for Population Displacement and Resettlement." In M. Cernea and C. McDowell, eds., *Risks and Reconstruction: The Experiences of Resettlers and Refugees,* 11-55. Washington, DC: World Bank Publication.

Cornwall, Andrea, and Celestine Nyamu-Musembi. 2004. "Putting the 'Rights-Based Approach' to Development into Perspective." *Third World Quarterly* 25 (8): 1415-37.

Cowen, Michael, and Robert Shenton. 1996. *Doctrines of Development.* London and New York: Routledge.

Dussel, Enrique. 2000. "Europe, Modernity, and Eurocentrism." *Nepantla: Views from South* 1 (3): 465-78.

Escobar, Arturo. 2004. "Development Violence and the New Imperial Order." *Development* 41 (1): 15-21.

Gasper, Des. 2000. "Anecdotes, Situations, Histories: Varieties and Uses of Cases in Thinking about Ethics and Development Practice." *Development and Change* 31 (1): 1055-83.

Goulet, Dennis. 2000. "Ethical Analysis in Development Economics." In Amitva K. Dutt and Kenneth P. Jameson, eds., *Crossing the Mainstream: Ethical and Methodological Issues in Economics,* 29-51. Notre Dame: University of Indiana Press.

Grant, Ruth W. 2002. "The Ethics of Incentives: Historical Origins and Contemporary Understandings." *Economics and Philosophy* 18 (2): 111-39.

Harrison, Graham. 2004. "Introduction: Globalisation, Governance and Development." *New Political Economy* 9 (2): 155-62.

Idahosa, P.L.E. 2002. "The New Legitimacy of Development: The Case of NGOs." In George Kieh, Jr., ed., *Africa and the New Globalization,* 154-83. Aldershot, Hampshire, and Brookfield, VT: Ashgate Press.

Kanbur, Ravi. 2001. "Economic Policy, Distribution and Poverty: The Nature of Disagreements." Stockholm: Globkom. http://www.globkom.net/rapporter/disagreements.pdf.

Koenig, Dolores. 2002. *Toward Local Development and Mitigating Impoverishment in Development-Induced Displacement and Resettlement.* RSC Working Paper No. 8. Oxford: Queen Elizabeth House, International Development Centre, Oxford University.

Kothari, Smitu, and Wendy Harcourt. 2004. "Introduction: The Violence of Development." *Development* 41 (1): 3-7.

Mandle, Jay R. 2003. *Globalization and the Poor.* Cambridge: Cambridge University Press.

Murshed, S. Manson. 2002. "Conflict, Civil War and Underdevelopment: An Introduction." *Journal of Peace Research* 39 (4): 387-93.

Norton, Andrew. 2000. *Can There Be a Global Standard for Social Policy? The "Social Policy Principles" as a Test Case.* ODI Briefing Paper. London: Overseas Development Institute.

Piron, Laure-Hélène. 2002. *The Right to Development: A Review of the Current State of the Debate for the Department for International Development.* London: Overseas Development Institute (DFID).

Sen, Amartya. 1999. *Development as Freedom.* Oxford: Oxford University Press.

Thomas, Alan. 2001. "Development as Practice in a Liberal Capitalist World." *Journal of International Development* 12 (4): 773-87.

World Bank. 2001. *World Development Report: 2000/2001: Attacking Poverty.* Washington, DC.

Contributors

Keith Barney is a PhD candidate in the Department of Geography at York University in Toronto. He is currently completing his dissertation field research on the political ecology and political economy of commercial tree plantation development in Laos, funded in part by the International Development Research Centre and Canada's Social Sciences and Humanities Research Council. In recent years, Keith has also worked as a consultant for research projects by the Centre for International Forestry Research and Forest Trends/Rights and Resources Initiative on "Transforming China's Forest Impacts in Southeast Asia."

Pablo S. Bose is a Henderson and SSHRC Postdoctoral Fellow at the University of Vermont and a Research Associate with the Centre for Refugee Studies at York University. His research focuses on development and diasporic communities and, in particular, on transnational cultural, economic, and political practices. His current work looks at Indian Bengali communities based in North America and their involvement in contemporary urban transformations of the metropolis of Kolkata, India.

Sheila Gruner has been working with ethno-territorial, labour, and gender-based social movements in Colombia and Canada for over ten years and has been actively involved in research and coalition-building with community-based organizations. Co-founder of Pueblos En Camino, she also holds a Master's degree in Environmental Studies from York University and is working towards a PhD at the Ontario Institute for Studies in Education, University of Toronto.

Pablo Idahosa is an Associate Professor in the Division of Social Science at York University, where he also coordinates the African Studies Program. He has lived, worked, and taught in West and North Africa. He has written on development ethics, African political thought, the politics of ethnicity, and globalization and development. He is currently researching the relationship between ethnicity and displacement in Nigeria and co-writing a book on African modernities.

Amani El Jack is a feminist, activist, and PhD candidate in Women's Studies at York University, Toronto, Canada. She has been engaged in the field of gender and development in Africa for fifteen years, specializing in research on gender and armed conflict, post-conflict reconstruction, human security, and forced migration. Currently, she is a Research Associate with a SSHRC-funded project on the Globalization of Homelessness in Long-Term Refugee Camps at York University. She has written on gender and armed conflict as well as on gender perspectives on the management of small arms and light weapons in the Sudan.

Michelle Kooy is a PhD candidate in the Department of Geography at the University of British Columbia in Vancouver. She is completing her dissertation on the (post)colonial production of urban water supply in Jakarta, while managing an IDRC funded Urban Poverty and Environment research project that investigates the access of the urban poor to basic services in Jakarta. The equity of access to urban and rural water supply has been a focus of her professional and academic work in Palestine, Thailand, and Indonesia.

Sharlene Mollett is a critical human geographer who focuses on the entanglement of race and property rights in Honduras. Building on insights from political ecology and critical racial studies, her current research examines the case of the Honduran Miskito Indians in the Rio Platano Biosphere Reserve. With an emphasis on ethnography and discourse, her work critiques state-led conservation and the ways in which indigenous representations from the past are reproduced in contemporary natural resource policies. She is a past recipient of the International Development Research Centre's (IDRC) Doctoral Awards Program, the Ontario Graduate Student Awards Program, and the Social Science and Humanities Research Council of Canada's (SSHRC) Doctoral Fellowship Program. She is an Assistant Professor in the Department of Geography at Dartmouth College.

Colette Murray is a PhD Candidate in Geography Department at York University, Toronto. She is currently completing her dissertation on post-conflict societies and identity politics, focusing specifically on the Garifuna in Guatemala. Her work on Guatemala has been complemented by her experience with the Latin American desk for the Department of Foreign Affairs and the United Nations Commission on Human Settlements in San Jose, Costa Rica, the Central American regional office. Her written work has appeared in a variety of media, including refereed publications, general interest magazines, and technical reports.

David Szablowski is an Assistant Professor in Law and Society at York University in Toronto. He has been conducting research on the transnational governance of development disputes. His book, *Transnational Law and Local Struggles: Mining, Communities and the World Bank,* will be published in 2006 by Hart Publishing.

Peter Vandergeest is an Associate Professor of Sociology at York University, and Director of the York Centre for Asian Research. He has been conducting research in Southeast Asia on social aspects of forestry, resource tenure, agrarian change, and agro-food systems for the past twenty years. His current research focuses on governmentality and regulation in agro-food transitions in Southeast Asia; state power as expressed through professional forestry in Indonesia, Malaysia, and Thailand; and the social justice implications of emerging environmental certification regimes for shrimp and salmon.

Index

Printed and bound in Canada by Friesens
Set in Stone by Artegraphica Design Co. Ltd.
Copy editor: Deborah Kerr
Proofreader and indexer: Dianne Tiefensee